TECH TRENDING

AMY ZUCKERMAN

TECH TRENDING

THE TECHNOLOGY SURVIVAL GUIDE FOR VISIONARY MANAGERS

FOREWORD BY STEWART CHEIFET

CAPSTONE

First published 2001 by
Capstone Publishing Limited (A Wiley Company)
8 Newtec Place
Magdalen Road
Oxford OX4 1RE
United Kingdom
http://www.capstoneideas.com

CIP catalogue records for this book are available from the British Library and the US Library of Congress

ISBN 1-84112-137-1

Typeset in 10/14 pt Palatino by
Sparks Computer Solutions Ltd, Oxford, UK
http://www.sparks.co.uk
Printed and bound by
TJ International Ltd, Padstow, Cornwall

This book is printed on acid-free paper

To my husband and political advisor Don Moon and daughter Julia Beth "Bela" Biederman, for sustaining me with love and laughs through my own struggle to become a tech trender.

(And no, Julia, this word of thanks does not mean you are free to play with the icons on Mommy's desktop.)

How to Use This Book

Tech Trending offers a unique multi-layered experience. The explanatory portions of the book, as well as the examples, are presented in a variety of different layouts and boxed designs for easy identification. In most cases these offer additional information that you can read at your leisure. On other occasions, they amplify and expound on the main body of text. The different elements you'll find throughout the book are:

SOUND BYTES provide real-life, concrete examples.

PLATFORMS provide meticulously researched background information.

APPLICATIONS provide information on how to apply technology to your organization to achieve results.

SOLUTIONS reveal ways to approach technology, management or training concerns.

TECH VISIONS provide visionary sketches of how technology may be applied in the future.

UNPLUGGING TECHNOSTRESS looks at the humorous side of technology.

TECH STATS are statistics pertaining to the technology world.

TECH CHARTS are charts designed to illustrate text.

How to Stay Tech Aware

The message of Tech Trending is that staying tech aware and tech savvy is an ongoing process. We would like to keep you posted on the latest in technology trends and tips for staying ahead of the competition.

E-mail us at info@wiley-capstone.co.uk to join our list of tech trenders who want to be kept updated with frequent news and information on a regular basis.

Contents

Foreword

Stewart Cheifet

Host and Managing Editor, *Computer Chronicles* (PBS)

It's a little disconcerting to realize that everything you learned in school is wrong. That all the assumptions you have used all your life in business have to be thrown out. But that is the reality of the tech revolution. We are redefining everything – value, ownership, business relationships, power. It is as if, at the beginning of the 21st century, humanity is again coming out of the trees and has to create an economic system, a set of rules to guide how we do business, how we decide what economic value is, and how we create wealth.

The hard part is that tech trending is not about technology. It is about everything you do, every dollar you spend, every business decision you make, every business relationship you have.

Let's start with the fundamentals. Nothing is as it used to be. And that is not surprising. Why should the business world be any different from the world of science. Even in so-called hard science, we have learned that, with new technology, we must rewrite the most fundamental rules, throw out the most basic assumptions.

We all grew up with comfortable, reliable Newtonian physics and Euclidian geometry. If we know the rate of speed and the distance, we can figure out where an object will end up. Not true anymore in the subatomic world of quantum physics, where the old rules break down.

We learned in geometry that we could measure a line and "know" how long it was. Not true anymore in the relativistic world of cosmology. We have learned that the old rules apply only in the comfortable middle; that at the extremes of bigness, and smallness, the rules all change. Welcome to the digital world. Welcome to the Internet, at once the smallest and biggest business universe we have ever known. The new global Web is the smallest economic entity imaginable – you, or your customer – one person. Yet it is at the same time the largest economic entity we have ever known, a virtually infinite economic circle that potentially includes every human being in the world. The rules have changed. You will lose the game if you're still playing by the old rules.

In the old analog world of "things," we assumed simple truths like – resources are depleted with use. Not so in the digital world. Digital resources often increase in quantity with use as collaboration leads to more data than existed before. Remember, the critical resources today are not machines or raw materials but ideas, data, and the intelligent mining of that data.

In the old world we believed that originals had more value than copies. Not true anymore in the digital world. Digital copies, depending on where they reside, and how they behave, may be more valuable than originals.

In the last century, we assumed that people were always better than machines at exercising judgment and problem solving. We sent astronauts into space, not robots, because only humans could learn to adapt to a changing and unpredictable environment. Not true anymore. We now routinely use, and often prefer, machines to do many tasks that once were assumed to be the sole province of people.

In school you no doubt learned that the shortest distance between two points is a straight line. Not true anymore. Because distance doesn't matter. It is irrelevant in the global, digital, networked world. The "shortest distance" between two points may be a trip up to a satellite and down again, if that distance is "shorter" in terms of time or cost or convenience.

The moral of the story is, there are new rules and you'd better learn them. The survival of your business, your career, your sanity, may depend on it.

These new rules are fundamental and very real. This is not some invention of the media. This is not pop management stuff that is a fad now and will pass in a year or two. We are talking about a new economic force as fundamental as gravity. You learn very quickly that if you jump off a roof, you land very hard and probably don't survive. You then learn that a parachute, or a plane, will also get you there. And you will survive.

It is a dangerous mistake to attempt to solve future problems with outmoded or inappropriate technologies. For decades, inventors tried to develop flying machines by using an old, inappropriate model. They looked at birds and decided to build flapping machines, emulating the technology of the past. They all failed. Until the Wright brothers realized that men are not birds. And a different technology is required. It was stupid to look backwards at how old things flew. So the Wright brothers invented the airfoil and the propeller and changed travel, the transportation of goods, and business relationships, forever.

In this book, Amy Zuckerman helps you think forward, not backward, about applying technology to your business and to your career. She helps explain that today's and tomorrow's technology trends and changes are fundamental and transformative and essential. They will redefine your business, your way of communicating, and your relationships with employees, customers, suppliers, and shareholders. These changes in technology require you to change too.

The question is – change to what? How do you change attitudes mid-stream? How do you develop a new perspective? How do you muster up the courage to throw out everything you always assumed was true? About business fundamentals such as staffing, inventory, supply chain, recruitment, pricing, markets.

Tech Trending explains *how* to do this, but more importantly, it explains *why*. Because you have no choice. When your eyes start to change and you can't read the fine print anymore, you'd better get a pair of glasses or you won't be able to see what's in front of you. And others will.

Tech trending is in front of you. If you walk down the street and see what you think, based on what you learned years ago, is a cute puppy dog, you might get hurt. If that dog has been transformed into a fierce pit bull, you will get bitten. And you may never fully recover. Better to learn now the difference between puppies and dogs.

This is not necessarily obvious stuff. The tech revolution is changing so much that it is easy to slip up and miss some of it. And in today's fast-paced, competitive world, one slip is all it takes to lose your lead or lose the opportunity to get the lead.

If you look at an airplane propeller spinning around at a couple of thousand RPM, you can't see it – all you see is some vague, fuzzy, gray disturbance of the air. In fact, it seems that you can see right through these pieces of steel. But there sure heck is something there. And if you don't adjust, don't teach your senses to "see" that object, you'll get killed. That is just as true right now when it comes to seeing and understanding the consequences of new technology.

I have a friend who knows classical music very well. One lovely summer day we were walking down the street and we could hear the sounds of Beethoven's *Fifth Symphony* being played on someone's stereo in an apartment up above us. I was very proud to have recognized that it was Beethoven's *Fifth*. But he turned to me and said, "Yes, it's Von Karajan and the Chicago Symphony." I thought to myself – I want to be able to recognize business and technology trends the way he can recognize orchestras and conductors.

Amy Zuckerman writes in this book that "tech trending is survival." She is right. Survival is the number-one instinct because, without it, there is no you. But the truth is that tech trending is about more than survival. You don't just want to survive, you want to win. And increasingly, in today's global, consolidated hyper-business climate, there is very little room for losers. You'd better be number one or number two, or you may not be at all.

Understanding tech trending is important but, frankly, it is not easy. You need a teacher and you need a text. Yes, it's school all over again. It is not easy because it is about change. And change can be a pain. You have to do things differently, throw out bad habits, alter, learn, edit, streamline, and tame this technology beast. Change is like a wild stallion. Ignore it and it can kick you in the butt. Learn to ride it, and it can take where you want to go.

The fundamental notion in understanding tech trending is to understand that the tech revolution is not about technology. It is about relationships, changing relationships.

Tech trending means learning how to use technology to change relationships in the direction that benefits you. It means learning how to morph your organization into a virtual organization. It means understanding the new value of digital property. It means understanding that, in fact, tech trending is a competitive differentiator.

Already, there are piles of business case studies showing that companies who are number one in their markets are there because they use technology better. It couldn't be simpler than that. Your products may be similar, your services may be similar, but if you have access to better data, if you know more about your customers, if you can better manage and integrate all the aspects of your business, if you harness technology, you will win. Understanding technology trends is absolutely the difference today between being number one and number two, between winning and losing, between success and failure, between survival and demise.

Finally, the history of technology and business have in fact always been intertwined. They evolve together. And those who succeed in business are the ones who are the first to see the new technology trends and who then figure out to use that technology to get an edge on their competition.

Perhaps the best example of all is the little-known story of Galileo and the invention of the telescope. About four hundred years ago, Galileo was working on this great new piece of technology. Take two curved pieces of glass, connect them with a tube, look in one end, and the objects at the other end appear larger. Much larger. What Galileo wanted to do was look at the moon, look at the planets and the stars, and figure out the formula for the clockwork mechanism of the solar system. But that wasn't much of a business. He had trouble getting venture capital from the VCs in Padua. So he had a brainstorm. He saw a tech trend that he thought could revolutionize business. He called in some of the merchants and traders from Venice and told them he had invented a new piece of technology that would give them a competitive advantage.

In the early 1600s, the big business in Venice was importing commodities from other countries and bringing them into the Italian market by ship. Trouble was there were no communications between the ships and the merchants waiting on the docks. Galileo said to his would-be investors, "Imagine this, even while the ship is several miles out at sea, with my 'telescope,' you will be able to read the labels on the packing crates. If you see that boxes of cocoa and sugar are coming, you'll know there will be more supply than demand, that the price will go down, and you should sell. On the other hand, if the market is expecting coffee, tea and spices and you see that none of the crates on deck contain coffee, tea, or spices, the supply will be less than the demand, the price will go up, and you should buy."

Galileo raised the money, his investors won out over their competitors, and everyone lived happily ever after. And, oh by the way, we figured out that the earth rotated around the sun, not the other way around.

Business advantage is all about seeing the future better than the other guy and seeing it first. The tech revolution is still in its early stages – act one, scene one, of a three-act play. Wouldn't you like to know how the play ends before the other guy does?

Tech trending is a look into the future – but, unfortunately, you have to understand it in the present. It's easy to be a Monday morning quarterback. What *Tech Trending* teaches you is how to be a Sunday morning quarterback … while there's still time to win the game.

Acknowledgments

Tech Trending is truly a team effort. More than 50 people played an active role in producing this visionary guide. Editors downloaded whole publications for rewrite and citation. Researchers conducted surveys with analysts and other IT experts. And many, many individuals in the IT and standards arena donated their time, their thoughts and advice to help managers of all sorts become tech trenders.

There are a few people who stand out as deserving extra special praise and thanks: to Stewart Cheifet, first, for such a rousing and important foreword to this book. Stewart produces a number of IT shows for PBS and other networks – including "Internet Cafe" and "Computer Chronicles" – and is constantly criss-crossing the world promoting the tech-trending message. Thanks for the honor of your imprint on *Tech Trending*.

More than anyone interviewed for *Tech Trending*, David Washburn, principal consultant at Amherst Information Architects, Inc. – an Amherst, MA-based IT consultant – deserves heaps of thanks and praise for the long hours he put into this project. Thanks David for training me to be a tech trender, for your explanation of the intricacies of networking and for outlining how tech trenders can make sensible technology selections. David combines an unparalleled knowledge of IT with a sense of human-management foibles. His thoughts and wisdom can be found throughout this book.

Jim Harrington, chief executive officer, Systemcorp, Quebec, Canada, and former consulting principal for quality at Ernst & Young spent quite a few hours downloading his considerable knowledge of management issues and the burgeoning dot.com world. As noted in the Introduction, Jim is the quintessential tech trender. He's gone through many career changes, from IBM engineer to a leading quality guru, and now in what might be his retirement years he's embraced technology. His wisdom permeates *Tech Trending*.

Randy Bernard, the Amherst-based editor and project manager for the Pax World Funds quarterly newsletter and a freelance writer/editor for Clean Yield Publications and others, saved me in the early hours of *Tech Trending* by agreeing to act as project manager. His steady support – not to mention his willingness to sort through voluminous e-mails – helped keep this project on track. Randy also backed up researchers on the analyst front and provided many of the tools that tech trenders will use to stay profitable. No amount of thanks would be sufficient.

Eddy Goldberg, an Amherst, MA-based technology writer, downloaded both his own superb work on the evolving Web-based world for citation, as well as spent many hours interviewing CIOs, analysts and other IT professionals to gather their thoughts on what it takes to be a tech trender. His thoroughness shows, and has helped make *Tech Trending* as useful as it is visionary.

Many editors pitched in with locating content that could be useful. Four went beyond the call of duty and downloaded both major amounts of content and their brains to help the cause. Thanks to Bob Rosenbaum, who's now publisher of *Supply Chain Technology News*, for his superb insights into the burgeoning networked, B2B world plus massive content infusions. To Kevin Fitzgerald, former editor of *Purchasing Magazine* and now editor of *Supply Strategy*, for his insights into managing and operating a Web-based company or institution. To Perry Trunick, editor of *Transportation & Distribution* for content and support. And to Mark Vigoroso, executive producer of NewMediary.com for downloading his white papers on e-procurement that provide so much of the backbone of Chapters 2 and 6.

A number of editors have helped me stretch my technology awareness and encouraged me to write in a way that a general audience can comprehend. Thanks to Pat Lyons, Vivian Marino and John O'Neill of the *New York Times*; to Jeff Davis of *Business 2.0*; to Tom Strah of *Transport Topics* and Kevin Borras of *Traffic Technology International* for the many hours of reworking and editing material that helped influence *Tech Trending*.

There are many individuals who worked to provide me an overview of the evolving networked, B2B arena. Thanks to Charles Mann, correspondent for Inside.com and *The Atlantic Monthly*, and a contributing editor to *Science*, for his insights on peer-to-peer. Scott Bradner, Vice President for Standards at the Internet Society (ISOC) and co-director of the Transport Area for the Internet Engineering Task Force (IETF), not only provided a good deal of information on Internet trends, but set me straight on the importance of networking as the backbone of the supply network. Rikki Lee, editor of *Wireless Week*, and Gerald Peterson, senior manager at Lucent Technologies, helped me sort out global cell phone trends and Jim Turner, Chief Democratic Counsel for the US House of Represenatatives Science Committee, provided material on evolving electronic formats for industry.

Seth Rothberg, principal of /home/industries, Amherst, MA, has provided ongoing information on the evolving technology world. Many of the definitions in *Tech Trending* are his, along with training tips and insights into developing Web sites. Mike Cunningham, author of both *Smart Things To Know About E-Commerce* (Capstone) and *B2B* (Perseus Publishing) also played a dual role. Cunningham, who is president and CEO of Harvard Computing Group, Inc., Westford, MA, provided interview time, charts and other materials on the ever-growing B2B world. He also deserves thanks for his cogent training tips for the non-IT manager. And Peter Schwartz, chairman and chief executive officer of Descartes Systems, Waterloo, Ontario, was extremely helpful in providing information on the developing world of online services.

Many analysts offered their time and thoughts to *Tech Trending.* Special thanks to Karen Peterson, research director, the Gartner Group, for both her time and materials on assessing vendors and selecting technology that will help tech trenders develop a collaborative trading vision. Other analysts of note who helped out were Laurence Smith, a specialist in e-commerce management, Boston, MA; Merv Adrian, VP and research manager, Giga Information Group, Cambridge, MA; and David Yokelson, the META Group, Stamford, CT. Thanks to all of you.

CIOs, CEOs and institution directors also provided their thoughts and advice on everything from building a networked organization, to selecting technology and bridging into the Web-based world. Thanks to Krimo Salem, CEO of If & Then Inc., San Jose, CA; Jeanmarie Gelinas, vice president and CIO of Rodale, Inc., Emmaus, PA; Eric Fliegel, CIO, eTour, Inc., Atlanta, GA; and Pam Kleier, CEO of constructionzone.com, Louisville, KY. And Irene Starr, director of the Foreign Language Resource Center at the University of Massachusetts, Amherst, MA provided tips on how institutions can purchase technology.

Tracking technology change is a specialized field and those who know it best are standards experts. *Tech Trending* was blessed to have Sergio Mazza, former president of the American National Standards Institute (ANSI) and now a Greenwich, CT-based advisor to charitable organizations, to offer advice on how to play the standards game. Thanks, as well, to both Bob Feghali, vice president of business development and chief information officer at ANSI. Bob gave valuable interview time both describing ANSI online services and offering insight into how technology has affected this membership organization. And Stacy Leistner, director of communications and public relations, ANSI, deserves praise for the detailed chart in Chapter 1 that connects standards organizations with various technology sectors.

Tech trenders can't ignore human skills – gathering, sorting, storing and disseminating information, not to mention analysis. Special thanks to Hal Buell director of photo services, PR Newswire, former assistant general manager for the Associated Press News Photos, and a former member of the AP Senior

Management Group, for presenting a model for both organizing tech-trending companies and institutions, and advising tech trenders on benefiting from the information that technology makes available to them. Hal also had some important things to say about handling images on the Web.

The dot.com world also contributed heavily to both the visionary and practical aspects of *Tech Trending*. Thanks to Bernie Gwertzman, editor of nytimes.com for his tips on how to apply news world judgement and editing skills to corporate or institutional Web sites. Colin Mulcahy, ScreamingMedia director of technical implementation and support, and founder of the New York City-based content aggregator, was helpful describing resources tech trenders need in the dot.com world, as well as tips for setting up a Web presence. Phil Cole, European Marketing Virtual Prototype Inc., Quebec, Canada, was particularly helpful assessing training needs for the Web world. Thanks, also, to Jay Venkatesan co-founder of BioSupplies.com and CEO of Varro Technologies, Philadelphia, PA, for his thoughts on the resources required to make a dot.com startup profitable.

Being able to manage change is a critical aspect of becoming a tech trender. Alan Hurwitz, principal of Alan Hurwitz Associates, Amherst, MA, is a world-renowned organizational change specialist who spent many hours describing ways technology alters an organization. He also provided tips and exercises to help tech trenders manage change. B. Michael Zuckerman, executive director of the Mid-Atlantic Center for the Arts in Cape May, NJ, provided thoughts on the ways technology affects a non-profit arts organization. Izzy Gesell, principal of the Northampton, MA-based Wide Angle Humor provided both interview time and materials on managing technology change with humor. Izzy is also co-author of the many Unplugging Technostress boxes that should ease your reading experience. Thanks, also, to Andrea Pedolsky, a principal at Altair Literary Agency in New York City, for her thorough editing of the original text – *When Bad Computer Things Happen To Good People* – from which the Unplugging Technostress boxes were adapted.

Training is another major concern for tech trenders, and many IT consultants and trainers offered thoughts, tips and advice to provide you a pathway to becoming a tech trender. Particular thanks to the following for their interview time and insights: Don Lesser, president, Pioneer Training, Inc., Holyoke, MA, had a lot of solid training advice for managers of all levels; Harold Wolfe, president of Helios Custom Training, Inc., Northampton, MA, provided information on combating the IT/Knowledge Gap, and Mark LaPolt, an IT consultant based in New Haven, CT, also had good tips and advice for those who want to become techno-literate.

Additional thanks to others who provided information on ways to train to be tech aware and tech savvy, including Janet Wikler, president, Wikler and Company, Inc., New York City, who had lots of insights for would-be tech trenders culled from the worlds of the media and academia; Dana Sohr vice president for the Enterprise Systems Group, RWD Technologies, Columbia, MD, and Felicity Wright team leader, RWD Technologies, Inc., both brought their years of training experience to *Tech Trending* with warnings to be compassionate and patient with tech-trenders-in-training. And finally thanks to Andrea Goodman, swamp drainer, who is also a part-time member of the Assumption College Computer Science Department, Worcester, MA, for excerpts of her technology course for liberal arts majors.

Tech Trending wouldn't exist without the help from top-notch researchers and writers like Rosalind McLymont, a principal in McLymont & Kunda Co., who handled interviews with industry sector chiefs at the International Electrotechnical Commission (IEC). Lydia Long, operations director for Verité, Amherst, MA, conducted a number of interviews with corporations on their communication training and knowledge management efforts. And thanks, also, to Dale Miscynzski, former head of standards at Motorola and now president of the Isoagile Group, Austin, Texas, for his information on telecomm switches.

This project would be missing many of those special Sound Byte boxes without the help of my husband, Don Moon, a professor of government at Wesleyan University and political advisor to my company, A–Z International Associates. Thanks for all those *Economist* and *New York Times* clips, your thoughtful advice, support and thorough read of the final version. You are a gem of a husband, political advisor and editor.

And big thanks to my agent, John Willig, who has stuck by me and helped guide my work. No one knows the New Economy the way John does and *Tech Trending* owes him a tremendous amount for his support and insight. Finally, this book wouldn't exist without the tremendous backing of my publisher and editor, Mark Allin. Mark coined the term "tech trending" during our first spin session and has been there to provide that extra edge of tech awareness that should make this book so important to all who aspire to be tech trenders.

Introduction

The pathway to becoming a tech trender

To thrive in today's hyper-paced economy every manager from the most senior on down must become a tech trender.

Tech trenders are not merely informed about technological change, but know how to apply technology to their business and institutional goals.

Tech trenders are innovators and strategic decision-makers, risk-takers and shrewd pragmatists who recognize that technology is not a trend, but the major force defining the global economy.

Tech trenders know intrinsically that technology presents innumerable opportunities for those smart enough to harness its power. Technology is the path to future economic growth, to profits and the good life. Conversely, they realize that those who don't evolve with technology will be left in the dust.

Tech trenders embrace technology. They know that to do so means joining the "haves" of the world. To ignore technology means being one of the future "have-nots."

Tech trending equals survival

If you have any doubts about technology's influence on the global economy or whether you need to join the tech-trending club, consider these points:

> "IT is all pervasive: it can boost efficiency in almost everything a firm does, from design to marketing to accounting, and in every sector of the economy ... This could be the first technology revolution to boost productivity in services, from health care and education to finance and government. That would be no small matter: services account for nearly three-fifths of America's GDP (gross domestic product)."[1]

Companies and institutions that refuse to evolve with technological change do so at the risk of their survival. Xerox, a major high-tech pioneer, has been flirting with bankruptcy because it stuck with its laser-based copier business rather than restructure itself to take advantage of Web technology. Other companies like Charles Schwab have been able to successfully harness the Internet – in this case creating an online securities brokerage – without disrupting their core business.[2]

Some major organizations are considering making techno-literacy a condition of employment. If you can't work on a computer, don't know what a basic operating system is, or can't even use a basic word-processing program, you may find yourself out of work. Those of you who embrace technology as a part of your daily work life still need to protect yourself in a world where the consumer is often the "beta tester," meaning the place where software manufacturers work out the bugs in their products. The ability to function in this environment presupposes that you are tech aware and tech savvy enough to communicate with tech support about the glitches in your system.

This is a world where many technologies are converging and new technologies are being developed daily. At the same time vendors are bombarding managers with hype about their products. Cutting through that hype is a time-consuming, sometimes maddening process, but it's something all managers must be able to do to avoid the quagmire of poor purchases and major financial losses. You want to be able to select hardware and software that supports business and institutional goals, that is flexible and able to evolve with new technologies. To do so requires some basic technology knowledge.

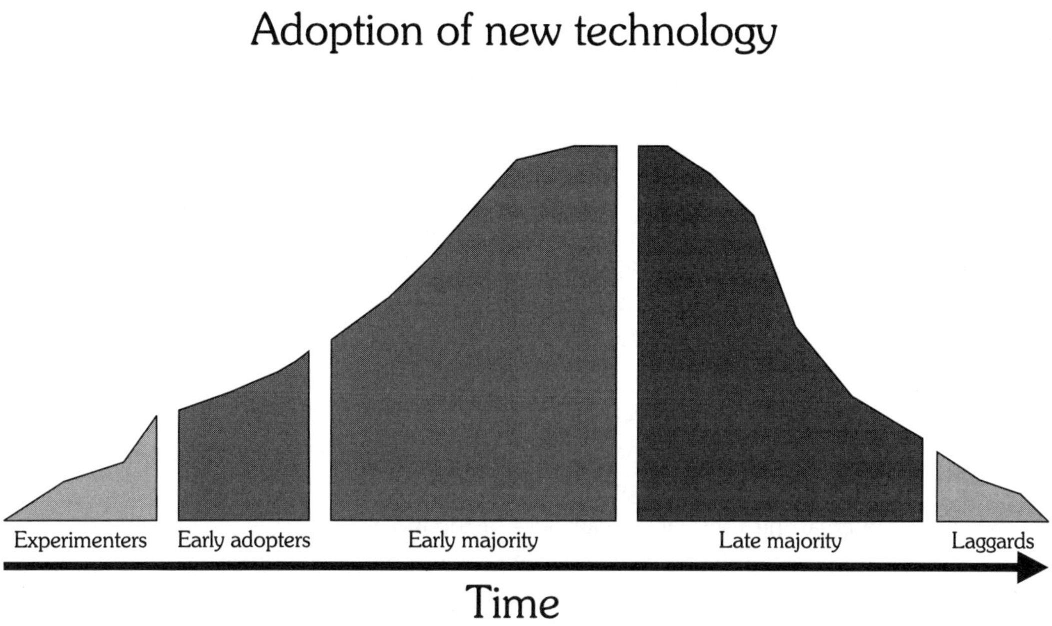

There are people who are always ahead of the curve and risk takers – early adopters – versus those who want to see technology up and running, long-standing before using it; the so-called early and late majority. The chart generally illustrates that the bulk of the population fit into the early to late majority category, which has major implications for technology manufacturers and service providers. This chart also has implications for how people select technology and organize their operations around it.
© David Washburn, principal consultant, Amherst Information Architects, Inc., Amherst, MA. Concept from Geoffrey Moore's book, *Crossing the Chasm* (1999, HarperBusiness, New York).

Tech trending as a way of life

Becoming a tech trender for many will involve not only a change in mindset, but alteration of daily work habits. In essence, tech trending is a way of life; a life-long learning process. Tech-trending managers track technology change as avidly as they study the stock market or other economic indices. They build technology awareness and learning into their regular work schedule, whether that be learning about new emerging technologies, mastering a new word-processing program, or gaining hands-on knowledge of networking.

Jim Harrington is your quintessential tech trender. Now in his mid-60s, Harrington is CEO of two dot.com startups. A former consulting principal for quality at Ernst & Young with over 20 books to his credit, not to mention software products, Harrington could easily retire and spend his days fishing and golfing. But instead, he's chosen to immerse himself in the cyberspace world.

The transition from an earlier career path to online product sales hasn't been without its costs and headaches. Harrington has had to learn a great deal – and in a hurry. But he finds his new life in the ever-changing technology arena to be "invigorating" and "life-giving."[3]

For many managers and strategic decision-makers, becoming a tech trender will mean starting from ground zero. There is growing evidence that many managers struggle with the IT/Knowledge Gap, meaning they lack awareness of the most basic technologies that are employed in workplaces on a daily basis. Prevalent throughout the global business and institutional worlds, the IT/Knowledge Gap affects all levels of manager and strategic decision-makers.

In fact, there are many IT experts who believe that the male CEO over the age of 50 is possibly the most techno-illiterate species on earth. These are men, often afflicted by what IT trainers call the "pride factor," who don't even use computers because typing is beneath them. Yet they are the same people being asked to sign off on their corporation's technology direction with enormous financial implications to their business, as well as to society and the global economy.

Of all the issues addressed in this book, the IT/Knowledge Gap is possibly the most serious.

When a CEO hasn't a clue about the basic workings of a PC or the most common computer programs, and a low-level manager is thrust into making decisions about software solutions way beyond her knowledge base, there's a serious crisis a-brewing. Many of the so-called failings of enterprise resource software (ERP) solutions could be blamed as much on lack of human knowledge as the software, itself. Techno-illiteracy, which is a contributing factor to the IT/Knowledge Gap, threatens to upturn technology's progress and even the huge spurt in global productivity that technology has spawned. It also threatens future economic growth that properly harnessed technology could promote for a number of years to come.

As Harrington will attest, there is no snap-your-fingers or wave-a-wand approach to becoming a tech trender. There is no technology product you can buy and plug in that will provide you with instant technology awareness. To become a tech trender many of you will have to devote a good deal of your time to boning up on technology basics and altering your work life to accommodate the need to continue technology learning. But that doesn't mean that the route to becoming a tech trender has to be arduous or tiresome.

The pathway to becoming a tech trender

Tech Trending is your visionary guide to the profits and opportunities that await any and all who have the patience to become tech trenders. This book is your pathway. You will learn how to:

- recognize what technology trends are here to stay,
- track technology change like the analysts and technology experts,
- organize your company and institution to stay nimble and flexible as technology continues to evolve, and
- recognize what human skills and training will be required to stay on top of new technologies.

Tech Trending puts you in the driver seat and lets you control your technology future, rather than letting technology control you.

Moreover, *Tech Trending* is geared to any and all of you facing technology choices. That's whether you're a mid-manager in a government agency or the CEO of a major corporation, an entrepreneur running a small company, the president of a university, or the director of a research center or museum. Anyone caught on the hot seat of determining what technologies best suit business or institutional goals, will find solid advice, case studies and tips to aid you through the dizzy, hyper-paced world of technology change.

What the flashy high-tech mags and hordes of e-commerce books don't tell you is that many companies and institutions don't have the foggiest idea of how to move into the e-commerce world. Talk to consultants, analysts and IT trainers and they're still helping their clients integrate back-end functions like invoicing and sales figures. *Tech Trending* illuminates the concerns of average managers and business owners, providing solid information on how to transition from the world of the supply chain to business-to-business (B2B) e-commerce. With a focus on practicality, *Tech Trending* provides a great deal of emphasis on integration and networking that is often missing from products that focus solely on the glamour of new technologies.

Tech Trending is divided into three parts.

- Part I – *Tracking Change: Today's Trends are Tomorrow's Technology* offers fairly in-depth information on those trends that are here to stay, plus the tools to track technology change.
- Part II – *How to Manage and Organize Your Company or Institution to Reap Technology's Benefits* provides solid advice on managing technology change, setting up your organization to take advantage of technology, and tips on selecting technology that will grow with you.
- Part III – *Training to Meet Tomorrow's Technology Challenges* provides detailed information on the human skills required to work in a networked, B2B environment, plus numerous training tips for the non-IT professional.

These three divisions of the book are further broken down into topics presented in such a way as to ease you into the world of tech trending. Let's take a more detailed look at these topics.

Part I – Tracking Change: Today's Trends are Tomorrow's Technology

The first step to controlling technology is to be able to track the trends with an eye to what is here to stay. Without this knowledge you can't make cost-effective technology decisions, organize your company or institution to roll with technology change, or train yourself and your employees in the skills they'll need to survive in the New Economy. You can't become a tech trender.

Experts worldwide agree that we are evolving into a networked, B2B e-commerce world where information will flow instantaneously throughout an organization, to outside training partners, vendors and collaborative trading groups. Some visionaries are talking about peer-to-peer (P2P) where millions of computers will be networked on the Web for data mining and information sharing without the need of Web browsers or filters. Information will be communicated anywhere in the world, and using Web-enabled cell phones you will be able to access whatever data or information you need to operate a company or institution while on the fly.

The media, and even technology experts, tend to focus on new technology developments as if they are emerging in a vacuum. You hear about Palm Pilots, new cell phones, and super chips, but very rarely does anyone connect the dots to explain how various technologies are being integrated to create the networked, B2B world of the near future. Shipping is almost entirely ignored even though it's one of the main underpinnings of e-commerce. You're told you will conduct all purchasing in cyberspace, but no one talks about delivery of tangible products.

The first three chapters of *Tech Trending* connect those dots for you so you can view technology change as it affects the entire organization and attendant supply network, which includes customers, vendors, suppliers, trading partners, shippers and transport companies. You will see the transition from paper-based organizations that operate within a supply chain to fully networked organizations that function within a supply network. Chapter 4 provides you with the tools the experts use to track technology change.

Technology Trends: Communication in a Networked, B2B World (Chapter 1)

Communication technology is the life-blood of today's world, touching every aspect of your company or institution. Whether you are an entrepreneur, or a manager in a corporation, non-profit institution or service sector, you need to be able to communicate in real-time within your organization and to all suppliers, trading partners and customers to function in today's hyper-speed world. For manufacturers there has to be seamless communication from your back office to the loading docks, manufacturing sites to that ocean carrier shipping your goods, or that service center providing online information. For institutions like hospitals or universities it is crucial to promote improved internal communication, online purchasing and online customer service.

The communication world is practically seething with new wireless communication developments that aim to free tech trenders from offices, and even continents, while promoting customer relationships rather than merely improving customer services. Cell phones are so ubiquitous it's almost impossible not to literally bump into people in airports too engrossed with that device tucked under their chin to pay attention to where they're going. Wireless pagers are all the rage worldwide, both in offices and on the home front. And the big talk is no longer the latest generation in cell or mobile phones, but equipment that will make the wireless Internet a reality.

Chapter 1 outlines the major forces that are driving communication developments, both within organizations and in cyberspace. Tech trenders learn about everything from the evolution of telecomm switches to the emerging Web technologies.

Technology Trends: Moving from the Supply Chain to Supply Network (Chapter 2)

Many of you are still at the stage of automating individual business functions and need to understand how the next stage – integration of business functions – leads to developing an internal network. Take that network and plug it into the Web and you have moved from a supply chain to a supply network. You will learn about the evolution of e-commerce from merely being able to source information, goods and services on the Web, to the not-too-distant future when computers talk to computers and make direct purchases without humans acting as intermediaries (B2B).

Chapter 2 traces the technology trends relevant to the evolution from a paper-based to networked, Web-based economy. It's important to understand the principles of moving information electronically within an organization – and those technologies available today to do so – before looking at the more futuristic approaches to developing a supply network. Tech trenders will learn what trends to focus on today to transition to that networked, B2B world of the near future.

Technology Trends: Transportation and Logistics Empower the New Economy (Chapter 3)

No matter how much of your back-office work is eventually transferred to cyberspace, tech trending companies still have to be able to ship, store and deliver raw materials and products in the three-dimensional world. The very technology that is helping you manage your business so much more cost-effectively is also driving customer expectations for goods to be delivered just-in-time and on a global basis.

Because transportation and logistics are so crucial to maintaining material goods and product flow in this New Economy, these industries are using technology in enormously creative ways. Basic computing, satellite, radio frequency, bar codes, cellular,

X-ray and now the Internet – just about every technology imaginable – is being combined to literally and figuratively drive the supply network. It would not be possible to source goods, track shipments, inventory goods or send freight bills on a real-time basis – let alone on a global basis – without advanced technology.

Chapter 3 alerts tech trenders to transport/logistics trends that matter, and shows you the pathway to utilizing advanced technologies to move from a supply chain to a supply network.

Tracking Change: Tools the Experts Use to Monitor and Affect Technology Trends (Chapter 4)

Tech trenders want to be able to track technology change like the experts. If you want to beat the analysts you need to know about the tools they use. A number of prominent analysts offer insights into the tricks of their trade and reveal the tools they use to assess technology trends. These include technology user groups, conferences and the journals and publications the experts cite as the best source of technology news and information.

The real insiders know how to play in the world of standards where technology is developed and harmonized for global use. You will learn about the organization of both the international standards arena and the world of high-tech consortia. Key working groups and committees are provided so you can contact those players who are directly at the forefront of technological change.

Part II – How to Manage and Organize Your Company or Institution to Reap Technology's Benefits

Tech trenders now know what trends appear to be long-lasting and pertinent. The next stage is knowing how to manage your organization under the stress of near-constant change, how to apply advanced technologies to your companies or institutions, and learning how to make technology choices that will be flexible and allow your organization to grow as the New Economy evolves.

Managing Your Organization in a Networked/B2B World (Chapter 5)

Technology will make change. That's the most important factor tech-trending managers and strategic decision-makers, professionals and entrepreneurs have to know and accept to stay competitive while designing networked/B2B-oriented organizations. Change is confusing, difficult and often painful. But, as all of you know, there's no way to avoid technology change. Accepting the change technology brings rather than resisting it will help ease you into a world in which technology serves you and your organization, rather than you serving it.

This chapter provides the tools you need to manage the "yin-yang" of technology change, meaning the fact that change provides both pain and opportunities. How technology affects organizations is explored in full so you can better grasp the changes it will produce. You will learn the emotional stages both you and your employees will experience so that you will be better equipped to promote change within your company and institution. Practical tips are provided to help you better orient technology to your business and institutional goals, and humor is offered as a key management tool. New Economy management positions like chief information officers (CIOs) and chief technology officers (CTO) are explored to provide insights for hiring and promotion of better management practices.

Setting Up a New Economy Organization (Chapter 6)

Many companies and institutions are still light years away from the networked, B2B organization of the future. Most likely you are still grappling with issues like networking all departments, controlling e-mail, determining whether or not to implant an

ERP system and whether to buy or create software packages to automate various business functions. You may be considering outsourcing back-office functions and many of you are in the throes of designing Web sites. Practicing mobile commerce when you can barely communicate electronically from department-to-department is hardly high on the lists of some companies and institutions, even if they aspire to be tech trenders.

This chapter will offer you an organizational pathway and advice on set-up that will allow you to move to the networked, B2B world of the near future. Right now, tech trenders have to function in two worlds: the three-dimensional and the virtual universe that cyberspace creates. Until technology develops enough to allow for image and voice on the Web there won't be integration of the three-dimensional world of your office and the water cooler, and the cyberspace world where your transactions are taking place. As humans, we have to bridge the gap between the so-called real world and virtual world of the Web. And that means that our real-world functions have to be in tip-top shape to match the speed and performance demands of the Web.

A good deal of this chapter will look at ensuring that you are preparing your companies and institutions to work in a high-speed B2B environment. As always, business strategy should be top on the list when dictating a technology course. Management issues are also key. You will want to explore how information flows in your company, and the sorts of skills your employees have – or lack – to handle the tasks of working in a networked, Web-based fashion. Ensuring that employee schedules are flexible to meet the demands of this new world is also crucial.

Making Practical, Cost-Effective Technology Choices (Chapter 7)

Ah, the crux of the matter ... How do tech trenders know what technology to select today that will be worth anything in say, six months' time? How to build towards the B2B world without bankrupting your company or institution?

This chapter will provide you with the tools you need to make those practical, flexible and cost-effective technology decisions that will help you transition to a networked, B2B world. No, you won't necessarily be prepped to choose between an SAP or Oracle ERP software solution, or decide how many servers your organization requires. It's impossible to address individual technology questions in this context. But you will be able to work more effectively with your IT department, vendors, consultants and online technology service providers. For a good percentage of what will help tech trenders take charge of technology choices is mindset – a willingness to take the time to learn enough about technology options to pose intelligent questions to technology experts, coupled with a willingness to make change.

There are other factors, many of which you can control, that will help you make informed technology choices. Tying your technology decisions directly to your business goals is a key way of making technology serve your tech-trending organization rather than you serving it. But learning to articulate business goals in the context of selecting technology isn't as easy as it sounds. This is particularly true in large organizations where communication between departments – particularly technology and general business departments – is either non-existent or strained. So learning to bridge the technology/culture gap will also be an important factor in successfully selecting and using technology. You also have to ensure that your employees or staff have the skills and wherewithal to handle new technologies. And you will want to be able to respond to internal and external demands for technology improvement.

Part III – Training to Meet Tomorrow's Technology Challenges

Tech trenders can have all the knowledge in the world, but if you and your employees lack the skills required to apply technology awareness – if you lack technology savvy – all that learning and all the expense of technology implants will be wasted. The first and most basic concern is to make sure that you and your employees have the "human skills" such as reading, writing and analysis required to process the information, and even knowledge, that advanced technologies can provide your organization. And you may all require training of various sorts to be able to make smart technology choices, and apply technology strategically to business or institutional goals.

Human Skills to Improve Technology Use (Chapter 8)

Downloading information into databases is a fairly worthless task if you don't have the resources to analyze information and utilize it for strategic purposes – what's called practicing knowledge management. Technology provides the tools to sort and disseminate information, and some software programs can even prod the thinking process. But in the end it's the human brain that is the tool you need to hone for maximum utilization of data, information and even knowledge.

Being able to manage vast amounts of data and information accurately, let alone relay that information throughout a global supply network or post it on a B2B site, requires an entirely different set of skills than implementing a software solution. Establishing a Web site and then maintaining it on an ongoing basis is an editorial job, not something one practices in computer engineering. Making sure that the information you transmit to trading partners, or what you promote in your e-catalog is accurate, is an editing task that has nothing to do with comprehending the technology that underlies the electronic aspect of this process.

To best manage a supply network, set up a B2B operation, begin to practice knowledge management, or simply get the greatest bang from your technology investments, tech-trending organizations must set up information/communication chains to match workflow. Employees need to be able to gather, sort, store, analyze and disseminate data and information. This chapter turns to the news world as a model for the communication flow and training you will need to move into the networked, B2B world and practice knowledge management.

Training to be a Tech Trender (Chapter 9)

To become tech trenders means learning technology basics and keeping up with the trends. To become tech aware and tech savvy you're going to have to devote a good deal of your time to the learning process, and may have to alter your work habits to accommodate the need to continue technology learning. Once again, IT trainers suggest that technology learning be considered life-long learning. As they point out, the technology innovators and movers and shakers aren't going to sit on their heels and stop developing new technologies because Joe Tire Manufacturer in Akron, Ohio has finally mastered networking basics.

It will help if you organize technology awareness and technology understanding programs in your company or institution. But IT experts – trainers, consultants, analysts, CIOs and CTOs – encounter few organizations that do so on a routine basis. What they do find is that information on technology is gathered in an *ad hoc* fashion and distributed in a fragmented way. As a result, the IT department usually drives business goals based on what they believe them to be rather than based on concrete, affirmed knowledge. And there's often no one at the top, or in the middle, who's knowledgeable enough to stop them.

A number of consultants, trainers and tech-trending managers have been asked what they think managers at all levels need to know about technology, as well as the depth of knowledge that's appropriate for various management positions. They all agree that conquering the IT/Knowledge Gap isn't merely about knowing a server from a browser or an intranet from the Internet. Becoming a techno-literate tech trender means making changes in work habits and boning up on the human skills outlined in Chapter 8. This chapter focuses what level of technology learning managers need to become tech trenders, provides actual training approaches and tips for altering work styles and habits, and looks at ways you can train for the demands of the Web world and B2B.

Applying humor to the tech-trending process

Tech Trending recognizes that many of you approach technology awareness and learning with the enthusiasm of going to the dentist or paying your income tax. The vast bulk of the population dreams of a plug 'n' play world where they don't have to think about technology at all. Or they want to purchase technology the way they buy a car – based on look, feel and drive.

To make the process of becoming a tech trender more fun, humor boxes called Unplugging Technostress are sprinkled throughout the text to offer a lighter look at the world of technology. And humor is promoted as a management tool that will help both you and your employees defuse the mounds of frustration that technology presents to many of you. Hey, if you can't beat it, at least you can laugh at the foibles of constant upgrades, right?

So, as a last thought before you turn the page and start the process of becoming a tech trender, here's the PC Surrender Prayer to offer you some comfort along the way:

> Dear PC/Mac God,
> Give me the strength to accept there is little in Computer Land I can comprehend,
> the courage to upgrade my equipment in a wise and timely fashion, and
> the wisdom to call computer support personnel before I lose my mind.

If you find this prayer lacking, feel free to add:

> … and the patience to wait for a customer representative even though my call may be monitored.[4]

Notes

1 "Elementary, My Dear Watson," *The Economist* Survey of the New Economy, September 23, 2000, p. 8.

2 "Xerox and the Innovator's Dilemma," Ed Robinson, senior writer, *Business 2.0* online edition, November 24, 2000.

3 "At Midcareer; Unlikely Segues into Dot-Commerce," Amy Zuckerman, the *New York Times*, Personal Business, Sunday, June 11, 2000.

4 *When Bad Computer Things Happen To Good People*, a work in progress, Amy Zuckerman and Izzy Gesell, 2000.

Part I

Tracking Change: Today's Trends are Tomorrow's Technology

1 Technology Trends: Communication in a Networked, B2B World

Communication technology is the lifeblood of today's world, touching every aspect of your company or institution. Whether you are an entrepreneur, or a manager in a corporation, non-profit institution or service sector, you need to be able to communicate in real time within your organization and to all suppliers, trading partners and customers to function in today's hyper-speed world. For manufacturers there has to be seamless communication from your back office to the loading docks, manufacturing sites to that ocean carrier shipping your goods, or that service center providing online information. For institutions like hospitals or universities it's crucial to promote improved internal communication, online purchasing and online customer service.

The communication world is practically seething with new wireless communication developments that aim to free tech trenders from offices, and even continents, while promoting customer relationships rather than merely improving customer services. Cell phones are so ubiquitous it's almost impossible not to literally bump into people in airports too engrossed with that device tucked under their chin to pay attention to where they're going. Wireless pagers are all the rage worldwide, both in offices and on the home front. And the big talk is no longer the latest generation in cell or mobile phones, but equipment that will make the wireless Internet a reality.

There are four basic technology developments propelling this explosion in the communication arena:

1 *Networking* an organization means that all members can share information in near real time.
2 *Internet transmission* allows for near instantaneous communication.
3 *Wireless technology* frees communication flow from the restrictions of electrical plug-ins.
4 *The World Wide Web* creates a humungous cyberspace storage tank for data and information, as well as a platform where millions of parties can interact without face-to-face contact.

Combine these forces with the business-to-business communication developments outlined in Chapter 2, and the transportation and logistics trends outlined in Chapter 3, and tech trenders will soon have the ability to run operations while on the fly. When synergy takes hold on all fronts you will be working in a networked, Web-based world of cooperative trading partners that make up a supply network. Add the ability for computers to communicate directly to other computers and conduct transactions over the Web and you will also be living in a business-to-business (B2B) electronic commerce environment. So, for the sake of brevity, we will talk throughout this book of the evolution of a networked, B2B world.

Putting communication trends into perspective

Those tech trenders over the age of 35 remember the days when there were five basic tools for transmitting information – phones, fax, snail mail, telegraphs and carrier pigeons. Since the 1960s, you've experienced the enormous communication change produced by the introduction of wireless technology, fiber optics, electronic data interchange (EDI), and the emergence of the Internet and World Wide Web.

TECH VISIONS

It's a networked, peer-to-peer future

Talk to the technology visionaries and they say it's a networked, peer-to-peer future looming over the next server. Of course, a key ingredient to this mixture is the Web, which will allow for the interoperability of many technologies. But the Web won't be the only factor. For example, the networked home won't necessarily rely on the Web. If you forgot to program the freezer to make ice cubes for a party you will be able to relay a signal while *en route* from the office utilizing any number of communication technologies, but not the Web.

Others point out that networking offices is as much a human function as something based on technology. Networking is a matter of providing clear information flow and being able to store, integrate and share information. That can be accomplished using phones, paper and fax machines. The technology of servers and platforms amounts to a structural matter, not the integral factor. Rigid, hierarchical organizations can implant huge amounts of technology and never achieve a networked operation. The bytes may get through, but they won't be applied to strategic advantage.

But let's not diminish the importance of the technology that underlies networking or the Web. Paper-based, networked organizations will never be able to achieve the cost-savings and extraordinary speed of information flow that allows for just-in-time manufacturing or shipping, let alone collaboration with customers, suppliers and trading partners in real time. Collaborative trading groups couldn't share information in real time without the Internet or Web.[1]

And then there's the looming vision of peer-to-peer (P2P), a new development that would allow millions-plus to communicate on the Web directly to each other without the necessity of a central server. And to be able to communicate all the time in what some experts describe as a "perpetual digital swarm."

"The implications are head-spinning. Today the principle means by which people buy goods and get information is to go to some central location: a store, a library, a Web site. But when people are linked without interruption, they will get more and more of what they want from each other – from the swarm. Like the populace of a tiny 18th-century village, the inhabitants of the swarm will be interdependent, constantly talking to each other as they work and play. The 21st-century village will be just as close and sociable, but it will contain billions of people."[2]

Fiber optics, which first started to appear in the 1980s, proved a major communication breakthrough because fiber optic cables allow far more information to flow on phone lines and at greater speeds. EDI, one of the first forms of electronic transmission, allows organizations to send large amounts of information between trading partners. The creation of mobile phones has made it possible to communicate, and work, outside of offices. And the advent of the Internet and World Wide Web in the 1990s has made for the electronic transfer of information at tremendous speeds and quantities worldwide, prompting the electronic commerce revolution.

PLATFORMS

The evolution of fiber optics

Industry experts who advise international organizations such as the International Electrotechnical Commission (IEC) consider fiber optics one of the most important areas for tech trenders to tag. Not only is the fiber optic market booming, but continued developments and advancements in this arena will serve as the basis for addressing transmission capacity (bandwidth) concerns as the Internet/Web continues to grow.

Moreover, cellular or wireless technology relies on cables that feed into the transmitter, or some other aspect of the cellular network. There are some experts who consider cable technology coupled with fiber optic cables to be preferable to wireless technologies, or find the combination of cable and wireless to be complementary.

Fiber optic capacity has really skyrocketed since the introduction of the technology in the 1980s. The first fiber optic links were installed at 34 megabits per second, meaning 34 megabits on one fiber. The next major advance in fiber optics capacity was from megabit to gigabit. Then there was an increase from one to five gigabits per fiber.

Moving beyond five gigabits to 20 or 40 on a single fiber has proved difficult. Another trend is in allowing several wavelengths to travel over the same fiber each with a "trade" of 1 gigabit. Standards experts are working on ways to harmonize fiber characteristics, new components and filters.[3]

In the new millennium, as tech-trending managers you are constantly confronting explosive technology developments that offer the promise of increased productivity, but also threaten to swamp your organization. Just as you've become adjusted to e-mail, you are being told by analysts, customers, the media and major technology manufacturers that you have to be able to function in a Web-based world. But, in reality, many of you are still dependent on older technologies like the phone and fax. Many of you still utilize EDI, as cumbersome as it can be, albeit some utilize the Internet for transmitting EDI formatted messages. And those of you who venture onto the Web aren't conducting much business out there outside of ordering a shipment from UPS or FedEx. Today, the Web is used mainly for information gathering, sourcing and advertising with the promise of B2B still to be realized.

Preparing your tech-trending organization for a networked, B2B world

But smart tech trenders like you are already preparing to function in a networked world. You know that B2B is no mere trend – it's the way the world will conduct business in the next 10–20 years. Note the timeframe. That means the next decade or so will be devoted to transitioning over to a world of networked, Web-based trading communities and you must help your organization make that transition or face being left out of whatever market you are in.

The key is to make the right changes at the right time – utilizing the changes in technology that will enhance competitive advantage and improve customer satisfaction without disrupting current business practices that are making you successful. Not only must you know when to hold or fold, but in this world of revolutionary communication change you must be able to function for a number of years with a variety of technologies – some old, some new and many that are incompatible.

Thriving during this transition period means being nimble, flexible and prepared to make those technology shifts that will provide a competitive edge, while not jumping at the first hint of a trend. Step number one is being informed about the way communication technology is evolving. This awareness will empower you to make informed decisions and choices for your business. In terms of communication technology, it may help to separate the developments taking place in the way data or information flows from the ways it is made available, which is how this chapter is divided.

1 Transmission tools or pipes: phones, cables, satellite, radio frequency, etc ...
2 Electronic information/content sources: Internet/World Wide Web.

APPLICATIONS

Sorting out cell phones from mobile from wireless

If you are like most everyone else, the evolving world of telecommunications lingo is just as confusing as the changing technology it represents. Here is how the experts differentiate between cell phones, mobile phones and wireless:

- *Cell phones.* A term used in general to describe the "handset" used to receive telephone messages via a radio signal. The term applies to phones with both analogue (AMPS) and digital (TDMA and CDMA) capacities. It's improper to use the label "cell phone" to describe a "cordless phone" or a "fixed wireless" phone, though people will confuse the designations.
- *Wireless.* This term generally describes telephones, and all of their services that are delivered not by wire, but by electromagnetic radio waves.
- *Fixed wireless.* Fixed wireless is a term used to describe a system that remains in one spot (such as a home or office) but operates on a wireless network, such as a wireless local area network, wireless local loop, high-speed wireless broadband Internet services, etc. The fixed wirelesses you find in your homes have very little range as they only connect to one "cell" base station. If one carries the handset too far (as if it were mobile) it will not switch to another cell and just stops working.
- *Cordless wireless.* Fixed wireless is not synonymous with cordless. A cordless phone handset operates on a licensee-free RF link to a base unit that's part of the customer's wired terminal phone equipment.
- *Mobile phones.* This is a cell phone that is "mobile," that is, it isn't fixed – as in fixed wireless – and can pick up signals wherever service permits because the subscriber terminals are in motion. It will operate when moved over a wide geographic area limited only by the service area supported by the service agreement.
- *3G wireless and mobile phones.* The third generation of wireless phones are designed to offer the same type of functionality and speed that fixed networks offer today. The so-called 3G mobile phones are considered a subset of 3G wireless in case some applications are fixed, but mainly the terms are used interchangeably.[4]

The technology for transmitting data and information is undergoing its own revolution. No one knows today what technology, or combination of technologies, will reign as the supreme data/information transmission tool. And no one knows what combination of equipment or hardware will act as receivers. These are the sorts of questions that communication technology developers and service providers are all asking about the future of communication transmission:

- How will Internet/Web information be transmitted in five years – phone lines, wireless, TV cables, other?
- What hardware will be used to access this information – TV sets, phones, mobile phones, desk and laptop computers, personal digital assistants (PDA), and others?
- Where will you be able to access Internet/Web information – home, office, automobiles, airplanes, trains, gas stations, toll booths?
- Will microphotonics provide the enormous speed that its developers predict?
- Will bandwidth be able to keep up with the huge worldwide demand for information flow in cyberspace?

There is a second revolution underway that affects how you access information. Organizations still use paper to float information and content around offices, and between trading partners, customers and suppliers. But the paper-based world is rapidly being supplanted by electronic information flow. More and more information is being transmitted via the Internet, and in that enormous worldwide storage bin we call the Web.

The Internet and Web are growing constantly as are their capabilities. In the not-too-distant future you will see the widespread convergence of video and audio on the Web, which may very well alter how you conduct business. Much of this change is a result of the work taking place in high-tech consortia like the Internet Engineering Task Force (IETF), the International Telecommunication Union (ITU), and World Wide Web Consortium (W3C), which are actively involved in maintaining a functional

Internet/Web infrastructure that will sustain growth, to help standardize practices, provide quality services and data security.

Tech trenders can take some comfort – or discomfort, depending on your bent – from the fact that even the technology experts don't know exactly what communications will look like in the next decade. Standards developers at the International Electrotechnical Commission (IEC), based in Geneva, Switzerland, admit that they're a bit stymied about where to focus standards efforts in the computer information technology (IT), communications arena.

Helping tech trenders sort the real trends from the hype

That means as tech-trending managers and strategic decision-makers you must keep constantly alert to technology change, and must be able to sort out the real trends from the hype.

This chapter focuses solely on the infrastructures evolving around communication and is divided into two sections: Part I explores telecommunication trends, particularly the evolution of microphotonics as well as the mobile world; Part II looks at Internet and Web developments.

As noted in the introduction, Chapter 1 is the first of a trilogy of chapters addressing technology trends. Chapter 2 addresses how the electronic, online revolution is affecting the supply chain and has created e-commerce. And Chapter 3 looks at how technology is affecting both transportation/shipping and international technology trends, which are the backbone of the B2B world. Although it does not address specific technology trends, Chapter 4 is included in this section of the book because it focuses on providing tech trenders with the tools the experts use to track the trends.

PART I: TELECOMMUNICATION TRENDS

Imagine a world where you can conduct all functions affecting your entire business from a mobile phone in any corner of the world, using all media. Much of the technology that will make this scenario a reality is taking place in the transmission front and at lightning speeds. Major changes are taking place in optical switches, those tiny behind-the-scenes devices that are rapidly turning the Web into a multimedia entity. You can expect real alterations in corporate and institutional life, not to mention budgets, when you can conduct a videoconference from a mobile phone anywhere in the world via Web-enabled mobile phones. With the evolution of digital signatures that will allow you to sign documents electronically, you will be able to carry out decisions at the push of a button that will affect finance, manufacturing, distribution and shipping anywhere you happen to be.

Here's a glimpse of major developments the telecomm industry is promoting that will help you cost-effectively and efficiently operate networked, B2B organizations.

TECH VISIONS

A look at the new mobile world

"You're travelling in East Afghanistan trying to forge an international alliance. All of a sudden your phone beeps and you have an Internet message indicating a troubled order taking place in a sales rep's territory. What can you do from Afghanistan?

"In the future, you will be able to access the Web from your cell phone, access the orders, transfer them to your laptop and then print them out to see the nature of the exception. You see this is a simple issue, so through your Internet or Web connection you alert manufacturing and by pushing a button an entire information stream is posted along the supply chain network, validated and documented.

"Once we can send secure transactions through wireless the automation of all systems can go wireless. That's the theory."[5]

1 Telecomm switches (microphotonics, multimedia and remote management of telecomm networks)

There's a hidden world of telecommunications switching that may very well revolutionize the way tech trenders do business. Just as fiber optics has allowed for greater information transmission via phone lines – paving the way for Internet and Web use – microphotonics technology is expected to exponentially increase the amount of data that can be transmitted via telecommunications networks. And microphotonics is expected to resolve the problem of the "electronic bottlejam" that is predicted as multimedia hits the Net in a big way.

Microphotonics is based on an "optical switch," which directly routes information, in the form of photons of light, without the need to convert to electronic signals. Optical switches are infinitely smaller than anything now on the market. And they can outperform existing devices, orchestrating 32 beams of light in less than one-hundredth of a second. Companies from Nortel Networks to Lucent Technologies have been reportedly pouring millions into optical switch research and development, even going as far as to buy startup companies working in this arena.

PLATFORMS

The first generation of photonic switches

"... Network operators are already beginning to install the first generation of these photonic switches, using them much like the mechanical switches in a busy railroad terminal. One immediate advantage is that telecom providers will be able to reconfigure their networks on the fly rather than having to send out technicians to patch a maze of optical fibers. If a backhoe in Des Moines takes out MCI's Denver-to-Chicago line, tiny tilting mirrors may be all it takes to divert billions of data packets around the break. Operators will also be able to offer dedicated circuits linking a client's corporate headquarters to its manufacturing plants and customers."[6]

Besides their speed and capacity, experts consider optical switches an advancement that promises to reshape global communications networks. Some researchers believe optical switches foretell the development of a tiny, but complex optical device that may change how data is transmitted in everything from communication systems to computers. The first application of photonic switches will be to eliminate the costly electronic switching that makes up the fiber optic backbone of today's communication networks that run from city to city. Increased Internet use is stretching today's fiber optic infrastructures.

The Yankee Group, a high-tech market research firm in Boston, estimates that new wireless technologies alone will connect

Organizations worldwide making up the Communications Standards Arena

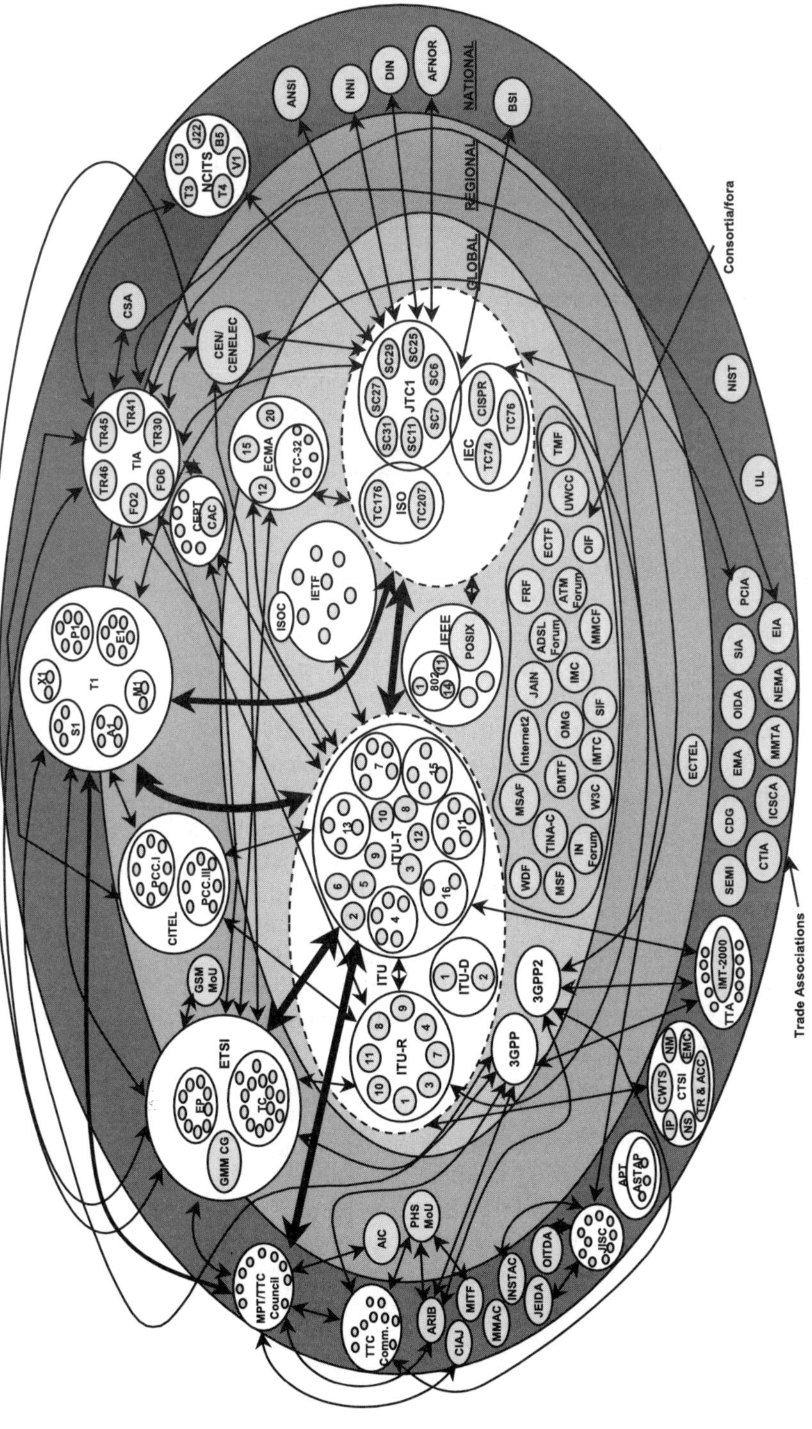

Printed by permission, Lucent Technologies

a billion cell phones, laptops and personal organizers to the Internet worldwide over the next three years. And besides the increase in Internet traffic, the infrastructures must be able to handle the growing demand for multimedia applications – particularly video and music.

APPLICATIONS

Cisco and Nortel push the optical Internet

Both Cisco Systems and Nortel Networks are among top companies, including Lucent Technologies, promoting development and use of new technologies to increase fiber optic capacity for Internet use. For example, Cisco is promoting Dense Wavelength-Division Multiplexing (DWDM), or multi-channel fiber optic technology, as an economical means of expanding existing fiber optic networks.

Reportedly, the Cisco DWDM platform can support up to 128 channels and reach 1.28 terabits per second of transmission capacity. It can be installed as a one-channel system and upgraded incrementally to its full capacity of 128 channels. The system includes an optical protection feature to help assure quality of service and promoters say it has demonstrated its functionality and flexibility with a range of fiber types and channel combinations – critical issues for today's network providers.

Nortel Networks is also promoting technology to produce what they call "an all-optical Internet." It is building systems that will transmit data at speeds as high as 80 gigabits per second. Wider systems will enable 160 channels – or colors of light – to be transmitted on a single fiber no thicker than a human hair. The company claims that Nortel Networks Optical Internet systems can transmit light up to 4000 kilometers without the need for electrical regeneration.

Also in development are management systems that will allow service providers to manage individual channels of light, giving them the ability to quickly allocate new capacity to specific segments of the network or for specific applications on a network. Next generation capabilities from Nortel Networks will provide much greater control and flexibility in manipulating individual channels of light inside (DWDM) networks.

Industry experts believe explosive bandwidth demand will push manufacturers to move into the terabit level, requiring an all-optical core. Today's "opaque" electrical core will be superseded by a "transparent," all-optical or photonic core that will offer massive bandwidth, reliability and performance available only from an all-optical network.[7]

Future generations of photonic switches are expected to become smaller, offer more capacity, be cheaper and "smart" so that they have the capability of reading the messages carried in them. This is particularly important to Internet design where being able to read the messages attached to switching nodes will allow for better quality service, quicker relay and maintenance ease. The new optical switches will actually replace Internet routers.

Transfer these advancements to integrated photonic circuits, and tech trenders will be able to share information from computer to computer, a major concern for the evolving of the supply chain into a supply network, as well as developing B2B to its fullest capacity. Experts also see the use of photons as the key to faster computer chips, which are facing their own version of electronic bottlenecks. The result would be smaller transistors on silicon wafers and greater computing power.[8]

New developments are taking place in the area of remote management along telecommunications networks that aim to allow for increased communication and remote management. When a network was point-to-point, from one desk to another, it was easier to manage. Now with cross referrals it becomes more difficult to track and control. And as networks expand in size, it's no longer possible to conduct repairs on points or elements in person. With thousands of elements in a network, it's crucial to be able to make repairs and adjustments from a central point. For example, one query would be from a manager asking if the network elements are clean and healthy. The element can then respond to the query about its health.

Work is taking place on all aspects of telecomm networks, with special emphasis on protection switching, multi-technology data communications integration, bandwidth management, fault management and security. Industry experts are also interested in developing reference architecture for multi-technology networks, and they are also working hard to define a markup language that will allow for network management on the Web.

APPLICATIONS

The future of phone/video conferencing

Tech trenders hear a lot about the future of conferencing, as in phone and particularly video. But some experts don't see much future for either, at least within organizations. There certainly is a market for conferencing capabilities for organizations that want to cut back on business travel, but many companies that maintain global operations report the need for face-to-face meetings. Telecomm and communication experts advise you to consider these sorts of technologies as adjuncts or help mates. But don't bother restructuring your corporate or institutional network to support videoconferencing.[9]

2 Mobile phones

From African rainforests to Midwestern-American airports, mobile phones are a ubiquitous part of today's world and hold the promise of global communication for tech-trending managers. But getting reliable service worldwide that is available to all users, and on all products, is still on the drawing board. Manufacturers and service providers are slowly moving towards this goal through the development of a family of global standards.

In 2001 it's possible that manufacturers worldwide will be producing mobile phones that are operable anywhere on earth. That's because global standards are becoming available that both improve mobile communication and provide companies with the options to support more and more advanced applications for mobile phones. These are the so-called standards for the third-generation (3G) mobile communications that are

SOUND BYTES

GSM enters the global mobile mix

The European GSM standard – Group Speciale Mobile – has now entered the global mobile mix of specifications that are being considered for use by the 3rd Generation Partnership Project (3GPP). GSM standards are developed by the European Telecommunications Standards Institute's (ETSI) Technical Committee SMG (Special Mobile Group), and form the basis of European mobile phone design.

ETSI officials report they will close their GSM technical committee and transfer most remaining work to the 3GPP – a group based on a cooperative working arrangement among standards development organizations (SDOs) from around the world who are committed to the European approach. GSM has over 330 million users in more than 150 countries.

The work to be transferred to 3GPP concerns the evolving GSM radio technologies, radio-specific operational and maintenance requirements and mobile station testing, and smart card work specific to Universal Mobile Telecommunications System (UMTS) and GSM.[10]

developed by two groups – the Third Generation Partnership Project (3GPP) and 3GPP2. Members of these so-called PPs believe the new specifications offer major implications for the mobile phone market.

The new generation of specs supports global roaming and access to the Internet and other multimedia services at speeds up to two megabits per second (Mbits/sec). This is in addition to voice services already familiar to mobile users. These specifications include new radio access technologies known as Universal Terrestrial Radio Access (UTRA) and CDMA (code division multiple access) 2000. Both of these specifications utilize wideband CDMA technology and are being incorporated into the International Telecommunication Union's (ITU's) IMT-2000 family of 3G Radio Transmission Technologies (RTTs). IMT is short for international mobile telecommunications.

Applied to mobile phone products, standards developers report that the new family of specs offers better voice quality, better built-in security systems, and a much higher bit rate than in generation-two technology. How you use the data is up to the imagination of the application and service provider because there is more than one way to accomplish better voice quality, better data capabilities and all that the futuristic third-generation services offer.

Already, work is taking place worldwide on more advanced 3G specs that are supposed to provide for major improvements, including Internet connection to mobile, or cell phones. Here are some of the new 3G developments in the works:

- Multimedia Subsystem Domain capabilities will be developed. This will allow the creation and introduction of multimedia services.
- The core network for both the second-generation and third-generation mobile phones will, and should be, the same. This is needed to ensure that the same, evolved core network may be used by the operators to provide both more refined second-generation services, and the third-generation services. Actually, there will be a blurred dividing line between evolved second- and third-generation capabilities.
- Another goal is to have a flexible service development and introduction environment. This will allow the operators to introduce services as they see fit, from their vantage point of business goals, and not to be constrained by some monolithic vision of all operators introducing the same services at the same time.
- There will be "positioning-based" service capabilities. These are the services that will take advantage of the knowledge of where you physically are at a given time. You may use these capabilities to do things such as manage a pick-up and delivery schedule for a fleet of trucks; or, say, provide an advertisement on the handset for the store nearest to you at a given point.
- There is growing concern about privacy issues involving this sort of technology that allows people to track your position every minute of the day.[11]

APPLICATIONS

Will the US lose out on 3G?

Whether or not the American market will enjoy the advantages of 3G technology in the near future is a cause of debate. *The Economist* has argued that the Federal Communication Commission (FCC) has been auctioning off "near useless" 3G licenses, as most of the frequencies best suited to the mobile phone market are taken in the United States. The most desirable band – the 700-Megahertz range that allows signals to travel easily through buildings – is already allotted to UHF TV channels, even though only about 100 TV stations in the US transmit in this mode. It's up to the "winners" of 3G licenses to coax TV stations to give up these frequencies, which are generally considered to be quite valuable.[12]

Because the US held onto its own cell phone standards rather than adopting Europe's more widely used GSM (global system for mobile communications), many experts believe the US will lag behind both Japan and Europe in adopting 3G technology. In general, cell phones have caught on more fiercely outside the US, where older people (past 65) tend to ignore them altogether, and baby boomers tend to relegate them to office use or for emergency purposes. Some abandon cellular technology altogether, because they find it frustrating.[13]

Some argue that it won't matter if the US lags in adopting 3G technology because they don't believe 3G will hold to its promise of rolling out an era of "go anywhere, do anything communications." Rather, some technology writers believe that 3G networks will be "as fragmented and incompatible – i.e. as confusing and frustrating for users – as today's cellular networks. In particular, one of the most critical features of wireless communication – roaming, or the ability to use a device outside of one's home network or country – will remain a headache for some time to come." The reason is a lack of national, let alone international, infrastructures to handle the competing hodgepodge that makes up today's wireless world.[14]

US industry takes umbrage at this summation citing, as an example, the recent announcement of a $5 billion contract between Lucent and Verizon to build Verizon's CDMA2000 3G network.

SOLUTIONS

How to improve mobile phone service

Business consumers living or traveling in the United States are wending their way through a minefield of mixed cell phone coverage zones, confusing and sometimes deceptive billing practices and must cope with evolving cell phone technologies, many of which are not compatible. The following are key sources of static and ways you can get the most of US cell phone service:

Static source	What you can do
Consumer ignorance. This is a new industry. You can't simply sign on with a cell phone service provider without bringing some knowledge to the picture.	The more you know about your equipment, and even the technology underlying it, and the more you press a service provider for information on coverage and billing the closer you will come to approximating the service you want. Don't impulse buy. Look at consumer publications and talk to friends and colleagues about their experiences with given equipment and plans.
Coverage. Overloaded networks, dropped calls and holes in coverage are major sources of consumer aggravation.	You want to seek out coverage maps to see when you're in or out of network, but don't rely on that map to be entirely accurate. Make sure you get the newest map possible as coverage is constantly shifting. Know that weather, obstructions like towers and even thick walls can obstruct coverage.
Billing mishaps. Cell phone bills are detailed and hard to understand and the way minutes are billed can be confusing. You get billed for whole minutes even if you didn't use up the full minute. For example, if you spoke for a minute and a half you get billed for two. Often users don't realize that they've set their phones for roaming and are being charged. Know when you're roaming and when you're not (see below).	Don't get lured into buckets of free minutes. They can be consumed far more quickly than you realize. A 30-minute allotment can be used up in half that time. To get a clear sense of how much time you should purchase keep a phone log and time the calls you are making today. OK, that's tiresome, but it will save in the long run. Another thing you can do is thoroughly question service providers about late fees. If you're operating a business see if they will provide a master bill for all employees on the service. That will be important if you are offering employees a discount.
Roaming charges. Unanticipated roaming charges really jack up those bills and are prime sources of consumer confusion, not to mention annoyance. You thought you signed onto a national plan that advertised no roaming charges, but there they are on the bill.	Industry experts say consider roaming to be like a spare tire in your car – only use it in an emergency. Most phones can be set so they won't roam. Inside is a computer that can be set to the network your company owns, and that network only. When you are outside network, inside a building, or need to receive a call you can activate the roaming capacity. That way you'll never get a roaming charge you don't anticipate. Always check on a service provider's network when they advertise "no roaming charges." That may only apply when you're traveling in their network, not when you cross over to a network that's provided by an alliance partner. Look for well established companies with well established networks. Someone who's been in the cellular business for a number of years may be preferable to a newer company. Once again, ask for their most recent coverage maps to find out.

Static source	What you can do
Equipment. You don't have to be a telecommunications engineer to purchase a cell phone, but some knowledge of the underlying technology would help. Yes, the major carriers match their phones to their plan. Even so, users can get off-base and try to use older phones, or mix and match phones with carrier plans. Your coverage will suffer.	Don't buy a phone based on a fashion statement. Know what a phone can do. You can't interchange phones between carriers. The equipment and coverage are inextricably connected. Basically, the phone you buy is a radio that operates on cellular power. The radio and phone are matched, so the phone you hold in your hand and service provider are all one package.
Service quality. You have the newest equipment, a national plan and keep getting those tiresome "no service" messages, or calls cut off mid-sentence.	To check on quality of service talk to neighbors or associates living in the coverage zone. The network may be established, but frequencies can be blocked by antennas and other factors that affect quality of reception. Find out if there are numerous busy signals or dropped calls in that zone. You won't get great service inside buildings with thick walls or in hilly locations like San Francisco where the landscape obstructs signals.
Service contracts. Providers offer a multitude of options and a huge amount of fine print in their contracts. Sprint PCS claims to be the only carrier that allows you to sign on month-to-month without a contract.	As in any contract, take the time to really read the fine print. Apply what you've learned about coverage zones, roaming and billing.

Design by Amy Zuckerman[15]

3 Alternate connections to Internet/Web

Although most of you tech-trending managers are still using phone lines to connect to the Internet/Web, Cable TV is providing an alternative that is becoming more and more viable. Another alternative is dedicated service lines (DSL) that are being offered by regional telecomm providers. Although speedier than regular phone access, both cable and DSL can be costlier. Yet a third option is the new asymmetric digital subscriber line (ADSL), which represents the largest growth in high-speed lines in the US.

It's hard to get a take on what is really happening in the high-speed arena, at least in the US. During the summer of 2000, National Public Radio reported only two percent of the American public was using DSL. Part of the issue was cost, but the other had to do with the lack of service for DSL, in particular, outside of urban areas – an issue that could affect your business as well as individual homeowners. These issues, NPR says, must be addressed for high-speed Internet access to be accomplished.

On the other hand, the online edition of *Business 2.0* in November 2000 was reporting high-speed Internet connectivity in the US having increased from 2.8 million subscribers in the second half of 1999 to 4.3 million in the first half of 2000. That's a 57 percent rise. High-speed service is now available in all 50 states, as well as the District of Columbia and Puerto Rico.[17]

Whichever report rings true, there's no doubt that high-speed access is the way for trenders to go. Files that would take hours to download on conventional phone hook-ups flash on screen in a matter of seconds. As more and more information, graphics, voice and video are being transmitted to you as a matter of course, you will need the speed to keep on top of your daily work. Tech trenders can't afford to be shut down by slow Internet access.

SOUND BYTES

FCC studying Cable/Internet access

The chairman of the Federal Communications commission is proposing formal proceedings on the issue of whether regulation is needed to ensure that multiple Internet service providers have access to a cable system operator's platform. He has expressed his preference for an open cable platform to be achieved through market forces.

Experts believe the standards used for interconnecting cable television systems with Internet service providers will play a major role in implementing any policy developed by the FCC. To assist the FCC with standards policy issues, the Center for Regulatory Effectiveness has drafted a white paper – "Market-Driven Consortia: Implications for the FCC's Cable Access Proceeding," which discusses issues concerning the development and use of non-consensus standards.

Concerned tech trenders can locate this paper on the CRE Web site at www.thecre.com.[16]

4 Web-enabled phones and Web service

Right now it's possible to buy Web-enabled cell phones that allow you to check e-mail and make travel arrangements while on the fly. Many users of Web-enabled phones are inveterate business travelers, who are starting to rely on the Web when flights are canceled. Some report they can beat the airlines in the US by tapping directly into the Federal Aviation Administration's (FAA) flight schedule.[18]

Being able to surf the Web at ease via a cell phone, let alone run a business or institution, is still several years away. Users find service erratic, handsets clumsy and Web searches via wireless to be slow. Then there's the issue of size. With an aging baby-boom generation worldwide, there's concern that the screens on the phones are just too small for an older population to read. Others say that the screen is just too small to provide a real context for work. For now, the best bet is downloading information from the phone to a laptop. And that means that the much touted mobile commerce (m-commerce) still has a way to go. In fact, there are whole contingents of experts pooh-poohing the much-hyped Web phone concept and just as many touting it.[19]

The main debate among technology developers is whether Web phones should be based on development of a standard called Wireless Application Protocol (WAP). WAP is supposed to provide the capabilities for cell phones to wirelessly surf specially formatted Web sites. These capabilities already exist in Europe, though in very limited way. The *Wall Street Journal* has reported that only 1.3 percent of subscribers to Deutsche Telekom's T-Mobile unit are utilizing the WAP service. Part of the reason WAP is lagging is that manufacturers like Nokia, Ericsson and Motorola reportedly aren't delivering the hardware as rapidly as promised. They aren't certain the new models will work on existing networks. And WAP phone users say the features are unwieldy and the service inconsistent.

PLATFORMS

More about the WAP Forum

Chapter 4 will be devoted to information on standards bodies and consortia that are handling a lot of technology development that concerns your companies. One of these organizations is the WAP Forum.

With over 200 members, the forum has developed the *de facto* world standard for wireless information and telephony services on digital mobile phones and other wireless terminals. Its primary stated goal is to bring together companies from all segments of the wireless industry value chain "to ensure product interoperability and growth of wireless market."

WAP Forum members represent over 90 percent of the global handset market, carriers with more than 100 million subscribers, leading infrastructure providers, software developers and other organizations providing solutions to the wireless industry. These include SBC Communications, Phone.com, Ericsson, INOVATEL, IBM, Matsushita Communication, Alcatel, DDI Corp., Telstra Corp., Nokia, Motorola, Sprint and many others.[20]

Those backing the WAP approach believe technology and market difficulties can be overcome in the near future. They point out that WAP can be used on all major different types of telecommunication technology, which means global interoperability is feasible. Industry analysts believe that 70 percent of wireless devices will be WAP-enabled by the end of this year. And the Boston-based Yankee Group is predicting five million WAP-enabled handsets will be in use by 2004. Only time will tell about this trend.[21]

Some experts consider WAP very much out of date and a dead end because it restricts the ability to put up new applications, and consider WAP a needless gateway that gets in the way and is not a requirement for Internet service. They point to the combination of wireless and the Internet as a gateway for translation and a means of controlling the applications you can run on a Web phone.[23]

Others believe WAP will be just one "brand" of Web phone on the market. They point to the Japanese iMode cell phone variant of 3G, that offers "killer applications" like packet switches, faster and speedier voice, data and transaction capabilities – anytime, anywhere – and a one-monthly bill for line usage, content choice and Web purchases. NTT DoCOMo, the Japanese producer of iMode, is hooking up with AOL for content and is supposed to develop a European partnership by 2003 and bring the technology to the US in 2005.[24]

To bring the advantages of m-commerce to tech trenders, software manufacturers are already developing what they call business portal software to spare businesspeople, particularly, from having to learn new applications written for wireless devices. The marketers believe the key is to ensure that business portals can be transferred from a fixed setting to mobile devices. They are calling these sort of mobile portals "untethered" por-

SOUND BYTES

Two-way wireless developments

Track-One.net, an alliance of four European third-party logistics providers, has implemented a two-way wireless feature that enables all actionable parties to respond to and resolve transport problems through any Wireless Application Protocol (WAP) device.

The feature comes as an update to the Web-based supply-chain collaboration system, IQuator, from Qiva, a San Francisco-based provider of supply-chain execution solutions. For now, the two-way wireless feature in the supply-chain execution software field is considered "modest," although it is expanding. The catch is that most supply-chain execution solutions have the capability to notify users of a problem through a WAP device, but they don't have the capability to resolve the problem that way.[22]

tals. Surveys show there is a growing demand for this sort of product. Over 50 percent of companies surveyed by the Boston-based Delphi Group indicated interest in using their business portal to deliver corporate information to a growing workforce of mobile professionals.[25]

TECH VISIONS

Reducing the static around m-commerce

To actually make money on m-commerce, the experts say the following has to happen:

- design new and different interactive content for the wireless Internet,
- form fixed-wireless alliances among telecomm and content providers,
- turn mobile phones into miniature information appliances,
- target mobile phone sales to the twenty-somethings (Gen Y), on up to the forty-somethings (baby boomers),
- build brand communities as product-based experiences for users worldwide, and
- market "anywhere" voice and data communication based on values and lifestyles.[26]

APPLICATIONS

Surfing the Web on rotary phones?

All the emphasis in communications has been moving away from use of the handy, old fixed telephone. But there is a movement to provide the ability to surf the Web via voice using the telephones sitting on your desks. Voice portals like Tellme, BeVocal and Quack.com have been springing up to allow you to conduct Web searches by voice. Even old rotary phones will work, if you have any still around. Not all parts of the Web are accessible and some describe wandering through these voice portals more like wading than surfing, but this may be an option for making the Web accessible to computer-phobic employees.[27]

5 Global telecomm trends

Within the next five years, telecomm standards experts expect to see 10 billion subscribers to fixed lines and mobile lines worldwide. As phone-use skyrockets, officials at the International Telecommunication Union (ITU) in Geneva, Switzerland are working hard to promote global interoperability and mobility of phone service.

ITU officials don't view fixed lines as competing with the mobile phone arena, and are promoting integration of technologies as much as possible. Like many telecomm manufacturers they see the developing countries gravitating to mobile phones because of infrastructure issues. But generally, their aim is to provide both individual and business consumers like you with different choices or packages that all function worldwide. For example, you should be able to "roam" and communicate anywhere worldwide on a mobile phone, and at reasonable cost.

ITU officials agree that with IT, telecomm and broadcasting technologies all converging, the solution for companies and individuals, alike, will lie in producing standards for compatible software systems. Nowadays, you can telephone from any country worldwide because that tradition has been assured by the operators. But that isn't the case for software where different solutions exist everywhere. Standards allow for the development of different packages and solutions that are compatible. If multiple standards are developed that will allow for competition, it will cost users more because they will have to sort through more solutions.

Having the same terminals, the same level of service worldwide and portability of telephone numbers all fall under global mobility. Basically, ITU officials would like to see the sort of interoperable system that Europe enjoys be replicated worldwide, though not necessarily utilizing the same technology or types of service. There is current debate within the ITU – a United Nations agency – over how to structure future work on global mobility. Support within the ITU for creating a separate study group on mobility is mixed, and unanimity is required. Some resolution of this issue is expected within the next year or so.[29]

TECH VISIONS

The ITU's view of the telecomm future

"All technologies are both competing and integrating. Each service provider will offer a package of service. Each person will choose what's best for them. The way they offer the service depends on the infrastructure. There are vast choices. A user may choose to have cable, have a given capacity with a given quality with a price. The limitations embedded with the quality are linked with cost."[28]

PART II: KEEPING TECH TRENDERS ABREAST OF INTERNET AND WEB TRENDS

There can't be too many of you tech trenders who don't suffer the joys that the Internet has brought to your offices. Who could live without those e-mail jokes and being able to surf the Web for discount airline tickets when you should be putting together the annual budget? Actually, there are very few of you who could survive for long today without Internet access, and in the next few years the same will be said about conducting business on the Web. Not only is the speed of communication unbeatable, but there just won't be any choice. Companies like IBM are already making all major purchases on the Web. If "Big Blue" is going B2B, you can be sure that the rest of the world is sure to follow.

The Internet/Web world doesn't come without a price, as any of you fielding 80, mostly useless, e-mail exchanges a day know, not to mention the headache of viruses, figuring out the best and speediest way to gain Internet access, or the inability to read half of your e-mail attachments. Knowing how to manage change with humor is one key to controlling your technology future, particularly in the burgeoning Web-based world (see Unplugging Technostress below, and Chapters 5 and 8).

But a little knowledge about Internet design and the ability to track changes in Internet technology are also key tools for tech trenders. This section will also provide information on technology developments you should be tracking in the Web arena, an outline of the infrastructure of the Internet economy, policy issues – particularly concerns about Internet/Web security – Web accessibility and the evolution of Web languages.

UNPLUGGING TECHNOSTRESS

Failed attachments

This is an era of failed attachments both in the human world and in the e-mail world, which of course affects the human world. The statisticians tell us that one out of two marriages will fail. The rate of failure to open e-mail attachments is far higher, which means just more loss of intimacy and connection, not to mention the inability to access that raunchy picture your colleague has been circulating throughout the office.

"Attachments," in the lingo of the Web world, are those funny little boxes that appear on the screen next to your e-mail transmission. They mean that someone out there wants to send information that is either too lengthy to write – let alone cut and paste – into an e-mail message. As you know, what people send as attachments is as varied as the human imagination. Work documents, journals, manuals of all sorts can be transmitted this way, along with just about anything else that is fit or unfit to print. But some computer users out there with really fancy equipment – and here's where the technohipsters really excel – will send graphics, cards and even multimedia experiences this way.

When e-mail attachments are accessible they provide an extraordinary means of communicating, especially for shy individuals who would not necessarily share sexy cards, lewd jokes or suggestive photographs with utter strangers, let alone friends and lovers. But in the quiet, evanescent space the Internet provides, many intimacy-shy people feel free to come out and play. They can share their thoughts and fantasies. And they can pour out their hearts to loved ones who exist somewhere on the other side of the quiet void between modem connections. As *Newsweek* has noted, we have become a population of Cyrano de Bergeracs and Roxannes.

But when attachments fail, that experience can be terribly disheartening, and possibly lead to loss of human attachments. One participant in this project reports actually missing out on dates because he could not open attached pictures of potential relationship candidates. (It is not certain any of the women whose attached pictures he could not recover would have appealed to him, anyway, but that's not our problem. However, we are eagerly seeking out such examples.)

What we do know is that failed attachments are a widespread problem, and one fraught with tension and annoyance for a variety of reasons, depending on whether the party is the sender or receiver. Senders are obviously frustrated if their messages and/or material can't be accessed, but receivers report their own set of annoyances with failed attachments. Both parties can feel as if they are in a parallel universe, or the bizarro world of "Superman" comics fame …

There are two main reasons that attachments fail:

- equipment incompatibility, and
- lack of human desire and/or communication issues.

Often both reasons are not mutually exclusive. Let's look first at the equipment side of the equation because incompatibility can rear its ugly head in many formats. There may be incompatible software, incompatible hardware or a more rare form of incompatibility that takes place when the sender's modem port is an Aries and the receiver's is a Capricorn. Regular checks of one's cyberscope will help weed out those sorts of incompatibilities right from the start.

One tech person wondered where equipment comes into this picture and we had to explain to him that it's important to differentiate between the two. Even experts like us, on the human misery side of technology, know that insufficient memory means not being able to carry more advanced types of software. So, you see, there is an equipment issue here that could eventually lead to a human issue surrounding upgrading. And we all know how traumatic upgrades are to the technozombie crowd.

The fact that so many e-mail attachments come encoded is a serious problem that has even the most ardent technonerd – not to mention the CIA – absolutely stymied. There are some products that purport to help, but even those have their floppy moments. Computer users should not despair at the sight of an encoded attachment. Feel safe in the knowledge that most of the world simply dumps them and then do the same.[30]

1 Internet design

The Internet is built around packets – strings of data that find their destination by hopping between local and regional "nodes" where the mesh of transmission lines that form the Internet intersect. There are thousands of packets that travel separately from node to node, each carrying with it an Internet protocol (IP). This is the infamous IP that telecomm engineers are always speaking about, and that allows an address to be read by electronic switches – routers – at each node. The IP address tells the routers where the packet is going, and then the routers – which must contemplate each packet – forward them on to the appropriate node.

This process is repeated until the individual packets that make up a message have arrived at their destination and are reassembled. Experts say it's this forwarding arrangement that makes the Internet resilient. If a node goes down or is temporarily swamped, neighboring routers simply divert the flow of packets around it. There is a concern that the size of the routing table – the table of Internet destinations – is growing too fast and is changing too frequently. There is much discussion taking place right now about how to address this issue, but no immediate solution is in sight. This is something that should concern you, and an issue you should certainly tag. Always remember that the Internet is now an integral part of your business; one you can't afford to lose.[31]

PLATFORMS

The Internet's simple goal

The Internet was originally created with a simple goal in mind: linking up the large, costly mainframe computers prevalent in the 1960s. Imagine having to fly around the country to view graphics for computing operations rather than being able to transmit them to a colleague's computer. The whole purpose of the Net was to deliver the mail and send those packets of data, no matter what.

"And deliver the mail the Internet does. E-mail is an obvious example, but so are instant messaging, buying goods through e-commerce, upgrading software with downloads, accessing Web pages, and the whole panoply of activities performed today on the Internet. Although these phenomena seem quite different to typical Web surfers, all of them involve one computer sending or receiving a discrete package of zeroes and ones (a letter, so to speak) to another computer via a middleman computer called a 'server' (a kind of digital post office, which takes in messages and fires them to their recipients)."[32]

2 Internet technology developments

There are many organizations like Descartes Systems – an Internet logistics service provider based in Waterloo, Ontario – now exploring placing all their services on the Web. Tech-trending organizations like these are banking on the Internet functioning properly. Performance, capacity and bandwidth are all important, not to mention reliability when it comes to offering foolproof customer service. So far, horror stories about bandwidth crunches haven't come true, and customer fears about security haven't materialized, but those are fears that tech-trending managers say are quite real.[33]

As the numbers of Web-based operations escalate, these sorts of concerns will grow, as well. The good news is that a great deal of work is taking place in standards organizations to improve Internet capacity and assure quality service as usage spirals upwards. Equally good news for tech-trending managers, eager to see B2B become a daily reality, are developments in Web mark-up language that will provide the capabilities required to place catalogs on the Web and hook buyers to sellers on the global scale.

For example, Internet maintenance committees at the Internet Engineering Task Force (IETF) are working hard to assure quality Internet service. IETF is a volunteer-run consortia and a subset of the Internet Society (ISOC) based in Reston, Virginia. Keeping the Internet working in the midst of rapid growth is a major concern of standards developers at IETF, who are working on everything from telephony to Internet security and development of e-mail standards. The following is an overview of the sort of work IETF volunteers are performing to keep the Web running smoothly for your tech-trending organizations.

- *Telephony.* The IETF has a protocol for carrying telephone calls that's seen in the marketplace as competing with a protocol of the International Telecommunication Union (ITU). The ITU protocol is called H.323 and the IETF protocol is called SIP (Session Initiation Protocol). H.323 is being used in NetMeeting®, for example, while SIP is being used in some cable modems and some of the new intelligent phones. There is work taking place that will allow you to gateway between the two protocols, but in the long run experts say in this case the market will have to decide which protocol to pick.
- *Quality of service.* IETF is concerned that the user is able to define the quality of service they want, and that level of quality should be manageable and controllable for Internet Service Providers (ISPs). This isn't a question of whether the Internet can function, but being able to control the quality the user is getting. The controls have to be there so the ISP can provide any level of service they want – from the worst, to the equivalent of a private wire.
- *Internet security.* The IETF has defined technology for encryption and key management, but the commercial infrastructure isn't yet defined. This issue isn't about standards, which are designed, but what sort of certification authority will be set up to operate programs for secure mail or electronic data interchange (EDI) message-set transmissions that will promote business-to-business selling. Various certification authorities have been established, but they aren't linked and certificates aren't yet available for individuals.
- *E-mail standards.* IETF is maintaining an ongoing project to define new and fancier e-mail functions. This would include more fluid EDI transmissions, voice transmissions and new multimedia applications and other similar functions. A standard has been recently designed to cover voicemail trans-

mission and new multimedia standards are emerging almost weekly.[34]

APPLICATIONS

Internet suffixes and country code domains

It used to be that .net versus .com meant something on the Internet exchange. Although the experts say those distinctions no longer count, here's a look at the common suffixes you encounter in your daily e-mail:

- .com
- .net
- .org

These are all "generic top level domains" (gTLDs) with no restrictions on who can register subdomains in them. The following suffixes have restricted uses:

- .edu for four-year educational institutions
- .gov for US government sites
- .mil for US military
- .arpa for Internet infrastructure data
- .int for international treaty organizations (e.g. the UN and the ITU)

In addition to these suffixes, there are 260 two-letter country codes such as .fr for France, or .jp for Japan. The rules for inclusion are local. Total registrations in country-specific domains has risen from just under one million in early 1998 to over five million in mid-2000.[35]

3 The infrastructure of the Internet economy

Tech trenders must know not only what technology is driving Internet development, but also how the Internet fits into the economy. According to Small Business Administration (SBA) accounts, the Internet infrastructure consists of computers, software, Internet service providers (ISPs) or Internet access, Internet-enabled businesses, high-speed Internet connections, and the high-tech innovators that make electronic connectivity possible. Fixed-line communications, cable television, cellular mobile networks, satellites, broadcasting networks, and electricity distribution networks are all technologies that relate to the ongoing evolution of the Web and the Internet.

The Internet economy indicator, which was created and issued by the Center for Research in Electronic Commerce at the University of Texas, consists of the following four layers: Internet infrastructure, application infrastructure, an intermediary layer, and the Internet commerce layer. Here's some more detail on that break-out.

- The Internet infrastructure layer is made up of companies that provide products and services to create Internet provider (IP) network infrastructure, for example, Internet backbone providers, Internet service providers, security vendors, fiber optic makers, line acceleration hardware manufacturers, and telecommunications companies.
- The Internet application layer, made possible through the Internet infrastructure layer, in turn enables business activities to be performed online. This layer provides software production and services to facilitate Web transactions. Involved in this layer are Internet consultants, inter-commerce applications, multimedia applications, Web development software, search engine software, Web databases, and online training.
- The Internet intermediary layer increases the efficiency of electronic markets by facilitating the meeting and interaction of buyers and sellers over the Internet. Firms in this category act as a mechanism through which transactions are processed through the previous two layers and changed into business transactions. Categories in this layer include online travel agents, such as TravelWeb.com; brokerages, such as E*Trade; creators of online advertising; and Internet ad brokers and portal/content providers, such as Yahoo! and Excite.
- The Internet commerce layer deals with the sales of products and services over the Internet to consumers or businesses.

This includes, for example, "e-tailers," manufacturers selling online, subscription-based companies, online entertainment and professional services firms, and airlines selling tickets online.

The Internet economy generated an estimated $301 billion in revenue and added more than 1 million jobs in 1998. The Internet infrastructure layer contributed the most in revenues during the first quarter of 1999, while the Internet commerce layer added the most jobs to the economy over the period. In addition, more than one-third of the total real economic growth between 1995 and 1998 came from a variety of information technology-producing industries.

A study titled *The New High-Tech Entrepreneurs* divided the computer industry into three horizontal layers: hardware, software, and services. Hardware consists of computers, servers, routers, disk drives, and scanners. Software deals with packaging, operating systems, word processors, spreadsheets, and database management. Services involve designing, installing, consulting, Internet hosting, and accessing. To date, the small business contributions to each layer have not been measured.[36]

The Internet Economy Indicator was created by the University of Texas. See http://www.internetindicators.com/indicators.html for more information.

4 Internet policy issues

There are a number of unresolved policy issues circling around the Internet/Web that are just as important to tech-trending organizations as the underlying technology. Maintaining an open, functional Internet, protecting consumer rights and data security top the list of policy concerns currently being debated in international organizations. Chapter 4 will provide information on a multitude of agencies and organizations – from the United Nations to government agencies worldwide – focusing on ways of protecting consumers in an evolving B2B world.

Of foremost concern to many is data security. E-commerce and B2B can't develop without the assurance that data can be protected and individual, corporate or institutional privacy is being maintained. This issue becomes even trickier as competitors team up to develop collaborative trading communities. Moreover, data security has to be examined and policy set up on a global basis as the Internet/Web is a global tool.

For example, IETF members are concerned about data security regulations being proposed in countries like Germany that Americans consider technically impossible. Germans have been studying imposing rules that make Internet Service Providers liable for anything transmitted over the Internet, which is impossible to technically control. No one will want to provide an Internet connection because no one could cover the liability.

And many in the US high-tech industry are also concerned about European efforts to try to dictate the Internet's future through control of Internet standards development, particularly standards used for Internet protocol. Over the last five years the Europeans have tried to hold meetings on controlling the standards process, all of which the US government has vetoed. (See Applications section below for information on data privacy standards and certification programs emerging to address these sorts of concerns.[37])

APPLICATIONS

Data privacy standards, certification programs and biometrics

In this world of electronic commerce, the issue of data privacy has to be of concern to all of us. Regional economic blocs such as the European Union (EU) have put data privacy top on their list of government concerns. The EU has been attempting to mandate data protection for European market entry, an issue that has been a matter of heavy negotiation between US and European government officials over the last year or so.

Now international organizations are getting into the data privacy act. Several new international e-commerce standards for security privacy and service have been released. There is at least one for B2B transactions and another for business-to-consumer transactions, both produced originally by the Customer Service Institute of Australia (CSIA).

How do you provide customers, or even government regulators, with the assurance that your company's electronic data is protected? The British Standards Institution (BSI) is promoting an information security management standard called BS 7799 to help companies manage and protect all information assets "by ensuring that the confidentiality, integrity and availability of data and information is maintained," say BSI officials.

BS 7799 certification involves a risk assessment to identify the most appropriate control objectives, as well as controls to be implemented, to secure electronic data. The risk assessment reportedly identifies all the major information assets within an organization and the associated threats and vulnerabilities. Containing over 100 controls, the standard contains 10 sections and objectives that provide management direction and support for information security.

Wright Publications, a British producer of technical publications, is one of the first companies to earn certification to the new BS 7799 standard. In some cases, customers have demanded proof of an information security system as a condition of doing business with them.

According to a company spokesman, "It was surprising the speed with which we had to react, to establish controls for this new (electronic) environment which were not addressed in our paper-based systems."

And if standards and certification programs don't match up to the task, the field of biometrics is maturing. This is the use of bodily characteristics like fingerprints or eyes to provide foolproof identification in electronic signatures. Proponents of biometrics envision a world where tech trenders can sign on to your office computer using a fingerprint scanner, or take money from a cash machine that scans your eyes to ensure you are the account holder. Biometrics is still in its infancy, facing difficult technological challenges, but in a few years it could be only a fingertip away.[38]

5 Small business policy issues

Those tech trenders who own or operate small businesses will face a number of practical challenges as they enter the world of e-commerce. For example, those who focus primarily on providing Internet access and ISP services for a fee are likely to face challenges, as ISP and Internet access become available gratis. Most small firms, aware of this trend, have started making gradual changes in their business structures to adjust to the market.

The SBA reports small firms involved in the use, design and production of Internet-related goods and services are becoming important stakeholders in issues that will determine how the Internet develops and how these developments will affect business growth, both domestically and internationally. Significant debate has already begun on issues such as the taxation of goods and services sold, privacy, fraud, patent reform, copyright and trademark protection, abusive domain name registration, digital signatures and electronic contracting, encryption and a slew of others.

Tech trenders interested in these issues should be aware that many of them are already under consideration in the Congress, regulatory agencies, and state legislatures, and that other issues will emerge as technology expands. SBA officials advise small businesses to become involved in both the legislative and regulatory processes to ensure that Internet-based markets and technology remain open and accessible to them and that their rights are protected. The Internet is a new worldwide frontier and presents new challenges in need of imaginative solutions.[39]

6 Web accessibility

As the World Wide Web Consortia (W3C) defines it, the Web is a universe of information accessible through networked computers. As all of you who surf the Web know, moving from Web site to Web site along the Internet has its own sets of intricacies, as does developing the ability to carry on transactions from Web site to Web site – what amounts to the crucial underpinning of your future B2B efforts.

W3C's mission is to lead the evolution of the Web and boasts its inventors as its acting chairman and president. Active work is taking place in Web accessibility, XML activity (see below), operating systems, multimedia collaboration systems for education and programming languages, television and the Web, user interface, technology and social activities. The organization's stated goals are as follows.

1 *Universal Access.* To make the Web accessible to all by promoting technologies that take into account the vast differences in culture, education, ability, material resources, and physical limitations of users on all continents. This effort also includes making sure the Web page is compatible with available bandwidths. Any of you developing Web pages know the difficulties of transmitting to customers with low bandwidths, who can't read your graphics.
2 *Semantic Web.* To develop a software environment that permits each user to make the best use of the resources available on the Web.
3 *Web of Trust.* To guide the Web's development with careful consideration for the novel legal, commercial, and social issues raised by this technology.

7 Web languages

Using the Web as a B2B tool means overcoming a multitude of interoperability issues that could swamp e-commerce in its infancy. Experts realize there needs to be wide acceptance for various sets of coding, technical, and process specifications for e-procurement to become a day-to-day business tool.

Extensible markup language, commonly known as XML, is the much-touted innovation that's supposed to revolutionize e-commerce by giving companies an inexpensive pathway to electronic integration with their customers. Imagine creating an interactive shopping catalog on the Web and that's where the need for Web markup languages comes in. HTML, the earlier

Web language, emphasizes formatting and information delivery via Web browsers while XML focuses on describing the data or the document and doesn't care about the format at all. XML wants to describe the intelligence behind the data.

To work, though, XML messages have to arrive with rules, so-called document type definitions (DTDs) that describe how they were assembled. This advancement allows for standard XML parsers to dismantle messages and direct data to the correct back-office systems, rather than expensive proprietary programs. For the time being, there is no single, agreed-upon library of DTDs. E-commerce won't necessarily die without standardization. However, the costs will be far higher, the data less reliable and not as clean, as it will be forced to pass through multiple translation programs.

SOLUTIONS

IBM and XML

IBM officials view XML as a powerful data standard that promises to help IBM rationalize the mountains of data available on the Web, and to create relationships with suppliers who lack the resources to set up electronic data interchange (EDI) exchanges. In the absence of a comprehensive set of rules for XML – called document type definitions (DTDs) – IBM is creating its own XML definitions for procurement even as it participates in XML standardization activities. And IBM is also deploying an XML translation layer directly outside its enterprise resource planning (ERP) and other legacy purchasing systems.

For future protection, "Big Blue" is watching the standards bodies very closely to ensure IBM's proprietary DTDs share the fundamental properties of standard DTDs in order to minimize migration efforts down the road. While IBM is creating its own XML specifications, the company intends to quickly migrate to standard document definitions – if and when they become available. A spokesman says, "As suppliers and applications in the marketplace adopt XML capabilities – as soon as there's a robust library of XML standards – IBM will be well positioned to transact XML with its trading partners across the entire procurement process."[40]

International standards organizations and consumer groups from 25 countries are starting to address the issues of creating order, and protection, for business and individual consumers on the Web. Technology harmonization is a chief focus as there is concern that even tech trenders like you could lose your shirt purchasing needless equipment and hardware that promises to provide instant B2B. While 10–15 organizations are working on standardizing XML (see Chapter 4), there are counter efforts taking place in industry to develop industry-specific XML approaches. It wouldn't hurt for you to check with your trade associations about these efforts.[41]

8 The push for Web interoperability

As you will see in Chapter 4 there are a number of standards organizations and consortia also working to standardize Web interoperability. Worldwide that figure is estimated to be about 10–15, but this book will explore the most prominent involved in the Web interoperability game.

The analysts believe that one or two standards now in development will shortly emerge as *de facto* standards unless some "killer app" emerges to set the tone for the entire industry. The ideal, some believe, would be universal standards so that back-office applications can manage self-extracting messages without the need for translators. But it's more realistic at this time to assume that multiple specifications will reign, at least for now. In the absence of standardization tech-trending professionals like you will have to rely on translators to move from one XML standard to another.[42]

Notes

1 Scott Bradner, Vice President for Standards at the Internet Society (ISOC).
2 "The Unified Theory," Charles Mann, *Yahoo Internet Life*, November 2000, pp. 146–154.

3 Source is Michel de Vecchis, Chairman, Sector Board 4: Infrastructure of Telecommunications Networks. IEC; Cable and components sector, director for standardization for the telecom products division, ALCATEL. Interview conducted by Rosalind McLymont.

4 Gerald Peterson, Global Telecommunications Standards Director, Lucent Technologies and Rikki Lee, Editor, *Wireless Week*.

5 Bob Rosenbaum, editor, *Supply Chain Technology News.*

6 "The Microphotonics Revolution," *Technology Review: MIT's Magazine of Innovation,* Peter Fairley, June/July 2000.

7 Press releases from both Cisco Systems, San Jose, California, and Nortel Networks, Branpton, Ontario, summer 2000; Greg Mumford, president, Optical Networks (a division of Nortel Networks), and Dale Miscynski, president of The ISOagile Group, Austin, Texas.

8 This material is adapted from "The Microphotonics Revolution, 'Technology Review: MIT's *Magazine of Innovation,* Peter Fairley, June/July 2000. Additional source is Gerald Peterson, Global Telecommunications Standards Director, Lucent Technologies.

9 Scott Bradner, Vice President for Standards at the Internet Society (ISOC).

10 Alliance for Telecommunications Industry Solutions (ATIS), Washington, DC, August 9, 2000.

11 Sources are Asok Chatterjee, Chairman of T1's Technical Subcomittee T1P1, the Alliance for Telecommunications Industry Solutions (ATIS), Washington, DC, and Gerald Peterson, Global Telecommunications Standards Director, Lucent Technologies.

12 "Battle of the Airwaves," *The Economist,* July 29, 2000, p. 57.

13 Adapted from *Conquering the Wireless World: the Age of M-Commerce,* Douglas Lamont, Capstone Publishing Ltd, Oxford, 2001.

14 "Next-Generation Wireless: No Panacea," Robert Poe, *Business 2.0,* October 24, 2000, p. 84.

15 "Those Black Holes in Your Mobile Phone Service," Amy Zuckerman, *New York Times,* December 24, 2000. Sources are Mike Althschul, Vice President and General Counsel of the Washington, DC-based Cellular Telecommunications Industry Association (CTIA); Annabel Dodd, author of *The Essential Guide to Telecommunication* (Prentice-Hall, Englewood Cliffs, NJ, 1999); Owen Stokes, who works in telesales at Cellular One's Boston office, and Chris Pearson, Executive Vice President at the Washington, DC-based Universal Wireless Communication Consortia (UWCC).

16 The American National Standards Institute (ANSI), August 23, 2000.

17 "High-Time for High-Speed Access in the United States," *Business 2.0* online edition. November 8, 2000.

18 Stewart Cheifet, president, Stewart Cheifet Productions (SCP), based in Mountainview, CA.

19 David Washburn, principal consultant at Amherst Information Architects, Amherst, MA.

20 The WAP Forum Web site, www.wapforum.org.

21 "The Long Wait for Web Phones," Jesse Berst, AnchorDesk, ZDNET, July 6, 2000.

22 "2-Way Wireless Executive for 3PLs," Jennifer Scarborough, *Supply Chain Technology News* online edition, August 14, 2000.

23 Scott Bradner, Vice President for Standards at the Internet Society (ISOC).

24 Adapted from *Conquering the Wireless World: the Age of M-Commerce,* Douglas Lamont, Capstone Publishing Ltd, Oxford, 2001.

25 "Business Portals are Vital Link for Mobile Workforce," *Business 2.0* online edition, October 9, 2000.

26 Adapted from *Conquering the Wireless World: the Age of M-Commerce,* Douglas Lamont, Capstone Publishing Ltd, Oxford, 2001.

27 "Web Surfing, at the Sound of Your Own Voice," Circuits, *New York Times*, August 3, 2000, p. 1.

28 Fabio Bigi, Deputy Director of the ITU's Telecommunication Unit; "Standards, Technology and Global Trends," Amy Zuckerman, 2000.

29 Adapted from "Standards, Technology and Global Trends," Amy Zuckerman, 2000.

30 *When Bad Computer Things Happen To Good People*, Amy Zuckerman and Izzy Gesell, (work in progress).

31 Adapted from "The Microphotonics Revolution," Peter Fairley, Technology Review: MIT's *Magazine of Innovation* online edition.

32 "The Unified Theory," Charles C. Mann, *Yahoo Internet Life*, November 2000.

33 Peter Schwartz, Descartes Systems chairman and CEO.

34 Scott Bradner, Vice President for Standards at the Internet Society (ISOC).

35 Scott Bradner, Vice President for Standards at the Internet Society (ISOC); and Network Solutions.

36 "Small Business Expansions in Electronic Commerce," the US Small Business Administration Office of Advocacy.

37 "Internet Standards Issues on the Rise," Amy Zuckerman, *Journal of Commerce*, December 15, 1999, p. 10.

38 Sources are the American National Standards Institute (ANSI), September 19, 2000; "BS 7799: Solution to Telecom Group Security & Privacy Issues," Anthony Vlamis, British Standards, January/February 2000, p. 10; and "The Measure of Man," *The Economist*, September 9, 2000, p. 85.

39 Source is "Small Business Expansions in Electronic Commerce," the US Small Business Administration Office of Advocacy.

40 "The Hunt for Interoperability," Anne Millen Porter, *Purchasing* magazine, June 15, 2000.

41 "The Hunt for Interoperability," Anne Millen Porter, *Purchasing* magazine, June 15, 2000.

42 "The Hunt for Interoperability," Anne Millen Porter, *Purchasing* magazine, June 15, 2000.

2 Technology Trends: Moving from Supply Chain to Supply Network

It only seems a few months ago when all you tech trenders heard about was the supply chain. The supply chain was the "in" concept, king of the management heap. Driven by customer demand for efficient, expedited service and the need to reduce inventory costs, the message was that managing the entire supply chain – from raw materials to delivery of finished product to the consumer – was revolutionizing the way major manufacturers, transporters and logistics companies were doing business. And you heard that message over and over again in magazines, corporate seminars and even on the Web.

Those principles of customer satisfaction, cost containment, inventory management, efficient and accurate information flow and just-in-time shipping still pertain in the world you tech trenders know today, and will matter in a networked, B2B environment. Even if all of your negotiating, purchasing, and business functions take place on the Web, you will still need to produce, inventory and ship products, not to mention manage orders, invoicing and other financial matters. But those on the cutting edge of this new Web world no longer talk about supply chains, but about supply networks, collaborative trading communities and value webs. In other words, the world of the supply chain and e-commerce are merging and creating a whole slew of new business practices.

Consider the Gartner Group's definition of c-commerce: "C-commerce is a form of E-business – the most advanced form. E-business has become synonymous with conducting business over the Internet. It includes a broad set of sales, marketing and service activities that until now have been about connecting an enterprise with existing and new, immediate suppliers and customers. The c-commerce vision includes interenterprise Internet connection, but it goes a step further by enabling multiple enterprises to work interactively online to find ways to save money, make money and solve business problems – often by dynamically restructuring their relationships."

Whether the terms you hear are B2B, c-commerce or value webs, what really matters to you today is starting the transition from supply-chain thinking to evolving a supply network for your organization. A supply network is the backbone of B2B. It presupposes that your own organization is fully networked so that data and information are accessible to all parties. Using the Web as a tool, you then link your networked organization to all your suppliers, trading partners and customers for continuous data and information sharing. If peer-to-peer (P2P) technology evolves, communication may be even more direct. But even without P2P, computers from all organizations will be able to communicate directly and carry out transactions without direct human intervention.

PLATFORMS

The supply chain circa 2000

For those tech trenders who haven't been indoctrinated in supply-chain management theory, the next few paragraphs pretty much sum up the world, circa 2000. In fact, this material was assembled at that time to run in a supply chain Web site and was considered quite *au courant.*

Cutting edge supply-chain management not only examines ways to promote cost containment throughout the supply channel, it must also balance growing customer demand for timely and efficient service and take into account rapid changes in technology. Also, in several industries, there is growing recognition that efficient supply-chain management involves new thinking about inter-company relationships. All of this has made advanced technology a key piece of the puzzle as corporate chief executives battle to remain competitive on a global basis.

One way of cutting costs involves sourcing for the best quality goods possible at the lowest prices. And that may mean sourcing globally, rather than domestically. Another approach to cost cutting involves reducing inventories of everything from finished goods to raw materials, and reducing manufacturing cycle times through the ever-speedier delivery of goods. This effort has spawned a whole new, technology-based approach to purchasing, logistics and transportation with efforts made to ship raw materials "just-in-time" for production, rather than having companies maintain large inventories of materials or components.

If the warehouse is not yet obsolete, it has more and more become a turnaround point for goods. Introducing automation into the warehouse environment – the industry word for the combination of computerization and bar-code-scanning technology – allows for quicker turnaround time in the warehouse and helps reduce the costs of carrying inventory. More and more retailers, for example, electronically transmit information on inventory counts to warehouses; information that manufacturers can use to reduce production cycles. In the process, retailers and wholesalers are increasing the turn cycle, allowing them to cut costs and better meet rapidly changing customer demand.

Quality becomes more important than ever in this new world of supply-chain management. This is not just as a means of improving customer service, but as a means of reducing defects that inflate manufacturing costs. And the use of advanced technologies helps to reduce inventories and makes just-in-time shipping possible. Employing technology wisely for well-directed information flow means that manufacturers can be nimble, producing only what stock is needed to meet service quality demand and then to continually replenish that stock. Speedy, reliable deliveries also help keep inventories at the most cost-effective level. Less inventory, or in many cases more controlled inventory, means less waste and improved profits for manufacturers.

Technology also affects long-range sales forecasting. The ability to access sales information on an almost real-time basis allows for quick adjustment of sales and marketing approaches.

Manufacturers can look at actual sales rather than relying on forecasts made six months to a year earlier. And advanced technologies allow for the tracking and tracing of shipments on a regional and global basis. Keeping better tabs on shipments is a crucial element to just-in-time shipping.

As the use of advanced technologies becomes more widespread, it becomes imperative for companies to practice efficient information management. Companies are trafficking in information, as much as in goods and services. Information on shipment location or condition. Information that arrives virtually in real time, allowing decisions to be made quickly to meet customer demands. Information that allows manufacturers to purchase raw materials when needed and produce goods as close to just-in-time as possible. Combined, efficient supply-chain management enables a company to coordinate the manufacture and flow of products throughout the entire channel, from the supply of raw materials or components to the movement of finished goods into the customers' hands."[1]

APPLICATIONS

How technology transformed MIT and the world

Tech-trending institutions like the Massachusetts Institute of Technology (MIT) have been developing ways to automate their services and systems since the late 1970s. In the now famous Project Athena, the MIT administration explored what would happen if they looked at all university functions from a technology perspective, rather than making technology an add-on to existing functions. Campus-wide electronic communication became a priority and the developmental work that ensued not only revamped the institution, but led to creation of the Internet and helped spur work in networked systems.

Imagine the change e-mail made to something as mundane, but important, as inter-departmental mail. Like most colleges and institutions, MIT once used those brown folders that would be recycled until they fell apart. Not only were huge numbers of folders required, but the system was slow and inconsistent. People received messages at different times, folders were lost or ruined. E-mail revolutionized how people communicated, despite those occasional academic recalcitrants who refuse to use it.

Technology also vastly improved MIT's purchasing and provided huge cost savings when purchasing schedules were automated. Automatic ordering became feasible, which saved time and allowed for additional bulk purchasing. That process affected the activity at the loading docks, inventorying and a slew of other functions, which technology was able to make more efficient and cost-effective.[2]

SOUND BYTES

Purchasing managers embracing e-purchasing

According to a Visa survey presented to the National Association of Purchasing Managers, 83 percent of companies still place orders of less than $5000 by phone, fax and mail; 86 percent use these old methods for orders larger than $5000. Payment, too, remains largely on paper; 73 percent of companies pay by check for orders less than $5000, while 83 percent do so for larger orders.

Even so, the survey shows e-procurement growing quickly. While most companies may still do most of their buying the old way, fewer remain that don't at least dabble in e-commerce. Currently, two-thirds say they do some amount of electronic purchasing and that number is expected to be 85 percent in 2001.

Further, the actual use of the Internet in the purchasing process is understated because surveys tend to focus on actual transactions. W.W. Grainger, the large catalog-based distributor, has discovered that many people use the Internet for research that leads to buying decisions.[3]

Of course, this world doesn't really exist today, but major companies like IBM and the big three auto makers are pushing the envelope on the procurement side, and many companies are heavily investing in software solutions that promote integration of internal functions. Others are exploring the ways to integrate all business functions with their trading partners. The US Small Business Administration reports that e-commerce is the fastest growing technological innovation. And if small businesses are going gangbusters on e-commerce, you know that this is no mere trend.

These are good reasons for the grand push to B2B and a fully Web-based business, and they are very much the same motives that drove the earlier supply-chain management movement: cost containment, increased productivity and customer satisfaction. Although the online volume of buying is still low – only 0.64 percent of the total economy at the beginning of 2000 says the US Commerce Department – those in the field aren't hearing many naysayers.

For sure, the B2B world has suffered plenty of setbacks, particularly with the stock market shakeup of the winter of 2000. Many dot.coms took a tumble and the predictions are that venture capitalists will be keeping a tight lid on startup money through the early part of the decade. Those who are financing dot.coms are demanding conventional business plans and proof of profitability, seasoned management and other indicators that point to long-term growth.

But analysts and those operating successful dot.coms believe that B2B – not to mention an entirely networked, Web-based company – is a known process that will evolve into reality. The argument is how big and fast B2B will come and how fast total integration will come, not whether it will happen as was commonly heard in the late 1990s. Now the issues are, when will companies begin living B2B, and how do you define what "living B2B" means? Is it 50 percent of transactions? Some experts believe this world is 10 years off, some 20 and even 30 years. No one knows the answer to that question, but everyone says that to be a tech trender you have to start working towards this goal now, today, immediately. Learning the B2B trends and assessing what, if any, of the related technologies you need to start implanting in your operation today is the first step to entering the New Economy.[4]

This chapter will focus on the key technology trends you need to track to keep abreast of the ongoing evolution from supply chain to supply network. After a brief introduction to the benefits of the networked, B2B world, Part I looks at the technologies available today that will help tech trenders make the transition to a supply network and B2B. Part II outlines B2B trends that are integral to creating a networked organization. And Part III looks at the trends that are making B2B feasible. Chapter 6 shows you how to organize your companies or institutions to make the leap from a supply chain to supply network that will support a B2B environment.

The following section summarizes the technologies being employed today and those new developments you need to capture to operate a supply network:

Tech chart: How technologies are evolving the supply chain into a supply network (source Amy Zuckerman)

Business function	Supply- chain technology	Supply-network technology
Internal organizational communication	Telephones and faxes.	E-mail and company/institution intranets, and Web-enabled cell phones allow tech trenders to share information and communicate while on the go.
Business process communication	Business data and information flow from department to department via e-mail and enterprise resource planning (ERP) software.	New standards for business-to-business communication will allow the transmission of everything from invoices to reports throughout a supply network. Peer-to-Peer (P2P) software will allow you to network with millions of computers worldwide without the need for a browser.
External communication	Telephones, faxes and electronic data interchange (EDI) are being aided by the Internet as a transmission tool.	New standards will eventually eliminate EDI messaging sets and allow company and institutional computers to communicate directly.
Computing	Mainframe computers dominate to store massive amounts of data.	Networked systems that rely on servers are supplanting mainframe computers. Servers are being connected to Web browsers to allow data and information to flow directly to cyberspace. Peer-to-Peer software (P2P) may make the browser unnecessary, if not obsolete.
Purchasing	Phone, faxes and EDI.	The Web is becoming the place where purchasing managers can source goods electronically. As Web languages evolve, computers will handle purchasing directly.
Inventory management	Computerization aided by EDI, and now the Internet, has allowed information to flow from warehouses to manufacturers and shippers so that all parties have accurate, real-time inventory counts and can manufacture and ship just-in-time.	Advancements in radio frequency and bar-code technologies, and the introduction of remote messaging technologies, allow for instantaneous stock counts with the wave of an RF wand.
Shipping	Phones, faxes and EDI are coupled with computing, as well as satellite, global positioning and cellular technologies to allow for near real-time global tracking and tracing of goods.	The introduction of the Internet as a data transmission tool means that real-time information is now available. Intelligent transportation systems (ITS) coupled with computers are moving goods more quickly along highways, promoting safer transportation and providing pass-through capabilities at border crossings. And transportation and logistics services – including tracking real-time tracking information and software products – are now available on the Web.

What a networked, B2B world promises tech-trending organizations

Transitioning to a networked, B2B world will at times be costly, time-consuming and even maddening. There is no easy, plug or play route that will transform your organization miraculously into a state-of-the-art, networked, B2B operation. But economists and other experts all concur that making this transition is tantamount to survival. Moreover, the networked, B2B world promises tech trenders increased sales and profits, transactional and operational cost savings, timely delivery and increased customer satisfaction and loyalty – all of which add up to additional profits.

> **TECH STATS**
>
> ***Small business e-commerce statistics***
>
> Right now an estimated 61 percent of small businesses are connected online. Small businesses in the US are expected to generate 30 percent of their annual income online right now, according to Cahners In-Stat. B2B sales by small businesses in the US are expected to total $23.5 billion today with that figure growing to $2 trillion by 2003. Moreover, businesses that moved assertively into B2B reported cost savings on materials of up to 15 percent.[5]

If it helps, know that there is no real turning back or relying, entirely, on older technologies. Even the smallest companies are embracing the Internet and other technological changes. (see boxes) And the allure of profits and growth is hard to ignore.

To be sure, B2B won't fulfill its promise without electronic product data that is robust with attributes and descriptions; flexible enough to allow for real-time updates and successful customer searches, and extensible enough to allow for back-office integration and syndication to selling partners. Once you have the ability to create this sort of data, have trained employees and have a viable management structure in place, here's what the experts are predicting B2B will do for your organization.

> **TECH STATS**
>
> ***Some statistics on purchasing professionals and Internet use***
>
> - Nearly eight in ten purchasing professionals expect the Internet to become the primary means of communicating with suppliers of indirect goods and services.
> - Seventy percent of purchasing professionals already use the Internet for communicating with suppliers.
> - Buyers' activities on the Internet (with percentage of polled buyers) include:
>   - requests for information (89 percent);
>   - requests for quotes (86 percent);
>   - shipments tracking or expediting (76 percent); and
>   - ordering (75 percent).[6]

- *Increase sales.* B2B is supposed to build your brand and make it practically ubiquitous. The hope is that this approach should build sales. And it makes sense, at least in theory.

The fact that your entire product line will be available to the end user is supposed to increase sales on its own. Furthermore, the Web means that product data that is current and complete will more readily meet customer demand and will ensure steady sales.

- *Improved profit margins.* B2B should mean you are pocketing much of the money previously spent on offline order processing and support, which should mean a dramatic increase in profit margins. Some of the savings can be passed on to customers.
- *Transactional and operational cost savings.* Ask any sales or customer-service representative what they spend a disproportionate amount of time doing, and they will tell you: product and order support on the phone. Customer questions range from order status, to product clarification, to general catalog inquiries. Following up with customers, whether they be distributors or end-users, on routine issues accounts for countless hours and dollars spent by manufacturers. By offering complete product data online, coupled with order status evident at every stage, the self-service component of sales should rise. There should be a concurrent decrease in employee time spent on customer and order support.
- *Back-office integration.* B2B aims to allow for back-office integration with accounting, materials planning, procurement, and enterprise resource planning (ERP) systems. Since each SKU (stock unit) is treated independently in the database, they can be fully tracked throughout the sales, accounting, fulfillment, and purchasing cycles, thus reducing the manhours spent on cross-checking and reconciliation. Savings should follow.
- *Timely delivery.* This is the cornerstone of the old supply-chain movement, and certainly counts in a Web world. The idea is that by leveraging the speed of the Internet, you will be able to disseminate current and complete product information to all prospective customers in an instant. Transactions can be processed and reconciled with integrated back-office systems in another instant. With offline physical fulfillment pro-

cesses remaining constant, the end-to-end fulfillment cycle is dramatically short-cycled by electronic transactive product data, further shoring up customer satisfaction and loyalty.[7]

TECH VISIONS

B2B means "Net" gains

"B2B e-commerce can cut firms' costs in several ways. First, it reduces procurement costs, both by making it easier to find the cheapest supplier and through efficiency gains. It is much cheaper to place an order online, and there are likely to be fewer errors in ordering and invoicing. That may seem trivial, but Cisco reports that a quarter of its orders used to have to be reworked because of errors in its phone and fax ordering system. When it switched to online ordering, the error rate fell to two percent, saving the company $500 million …

"A second possible saving is from much lower distribution costs for goods and services that can be delivered electronically, such as financial services, software and music. The marginal cost to a bank of a transaction over the Internet is a mere cent, compared with 27 cents via a cash machine, 52 cents by telephone and $1.14 by a bank teller. Online commerce also allows more efficient supply-chain management, cutting out layers of middlemen. And lastly, better information reduces the need for firms to keep large stocks. Dell Computer's build-to-order model completely eliminates inventories, and is being widely copied."[8]

PART I: KNOWING WHICH OF TODAY'S TECHNOLOGIES STILL MATTER

While you tech trenders keep your eye on the B2B prize, it's important to focus attention on those practices that are attainable right now and will help you transition to a networked, Web-based environment. A tremendous amount of progress has taken place in the last ten years in automation of the work place to eliminate paper flow and remove humans from redundant processes that electronic equipment can handle more efficiently and accurately. The grand design is to utilize humans to think, analyze and act strategically rather than as paper shufflers. The even grander design, as outlined in Chapter 1, is total integration of all business functions and the entire supply network that – when coupled with mobile communication – allows you to operate a company from anywhere in the world.

In reality, even the most forward-thinking and progressive tech-trending organizations can only approximate this dream. The business world is still held together with electronic Band-Aids called middleware and a pastiche of transmission tools like electronic data interchange (EDI) that are just starting to utilize the Internet. A huge business-function software industry has emerged to meet all sorts of niche business functions, as well as to attempt to integrate all company business practices. This makes for incompatibility and is cumbersome, at best. The hope is that in the next few years e-commerce will mature enough for you to be able to abandon all but the most effective software tools and truly work out on the Web.

As will be discussed in later chapters, you shouldn't rush onto the Web without doing your homework. Many analysts believe that older processes like EDI and ERP will be with us for quite some time, and may very well offer answers for small and mid-size companies. For the next few years just learning how to use the Internet and Web may stretch your company to the limit, as anyone suffering e-mail overload or trying to manage a company Web site – let alone provide interactive Web functions with the consuming public or suppliers – already knows.

So here's a summary of technologies aimed at electronic transmission and integrating business processes, many of which you can employ today.

EDI still links the business world

Emerging from the telex technology of the 1940s, EDI (electronic data interchange) is one of the pioneer forms of e-commerce. Starting with the rail industry in the early 1960s, and then branching out throughout the transport sectors and into general business by the 1980s, EDI allows for high-speed transfer of standardized electronic data. Over the years coded formats have been designed to cover just about any imaginable information transfer, from ocean bills of lading to basic business purchase orders.

Unlike the Internet and other forms of online communications, EDI is not a seamless technology. Information is transmitted from user to user via a value-added network (VAN). Application software, sometimes called a "translator," is required to translate coded EDI messages for processing in a PC. Despite the fact that EDI has been considered cumbersome, it has managed to eliminate a great number of paper transactions. Users also credit the technology with being superb at transmitting the myriad of forms required in shipping, transport and logistics so that with the help of application software they are readable on a computer screen.

EDI is probably the most mainstream of technologies in place today. At Strategic Technologies Inc. (STI), a transport-related software company based in Iselin, NJ, one manager is "finding that just about every company we've worked with is either EDI capable or very close. And that's not just the Fortune 100. Those that aren't EDI capable are doing a lot to overcome that. They're using third-party [software assist] like what we offer or outsourcing to consultants. We have 500 carriers transmitting through us right now and many aren't in the top 10 percent in terms of market share."

Although there's lots of talk making industry rounds that EDI is obsolete, purchasing managers from companies like Donnelly Corp., IBM, General Motors and Maytag believe that EDI is still a useful supply-chain tool and may live on for many years. Purchasing managers report that it reduces inventory management costs, order management costs, physical distribution and transportation costs. And they say it remains the preferred method of communicating such documents as purchasing orders, invoices, shipping documents and notifications.

You don't necessarily need EDI to transmit data. But those tech-trending companies supplying major, original equipment manufacturers (OEMS) risk being shut out of the market if they don't use EDI. And that's the same for Goodyear as for GM.

APPLICATIONS

EDIFACT gaining acceptance

Although X12 is still the norm for most American manufacturers and transportation companies using electronic data interchange (EDI), the international EDIFACT is gaining in acceptance. And the fact that General Motors has mandated EDIFACT for its 6000 suppliers is already having an impact on how EDI transmissions take place in the US. There are many in the EDI community who believe that companies of all sorts will have to have the capacity to transmit in both X12 and EDIFACT because the GM mandate is causing other manufacturers to rethink X12.

For example, Ford and Chrysler, and heavy equipment manufacturers such as Caterpillar, are talking about migrating to EDIFACT. Moreover, GM will eventually utilize EDIFACT for all transactions, including financial and transportation, though no deadline is set for those moves.

And already, GM customers are responding to the EDIFACT mandate. Steel producers such as LTV Steel in Cleveland have adopted EDIFACT, as are major producers such as US, Bethlehem, National and Rouge Steel.

Although many transportation carriers in the US – including air, ocean, rail and motor – are already working in EDIFACT, many American companies continue to use X12. EDI programs officials at the Auto Industry Action Group (AIAG) in Southfield,

MI, say that the switchover between EDIFACT and X12 is mainly a software issue for any company already employing EDI. However, they warn that EDIFACT is completely different from X12 and has its own rules and syntax.[9]

The EDI/Internet connection

Many business people confuse EDI messaging sets with the mode of transmission, which until the advent of the Internet took place on special lines called value-added networks (VANs). One thing that is keeping EDI very much alive is the switch from VANs to the Internet for transmission. As EDI experts explain it: "It's not EDI versus the Internet. It's a question of whether you want to transmit over the Internet in French versus English. EDI is a commonly understood transaction messaging set and the Internet is a communication pipeline."

The good news for those of you who haven't moved to EDI is that you don't need to have EDI equipment and direct computer link to communicate with major EDI-equipped corporations. Many buy translation software that allows them to communicate with an EDI-equipped company like GM, which requires EDI capabilities of their suppliers. However, some experts believe that companies that opt out of full EDI capability are opting out of performing true electronic commerce, and missing the benefits that direct EDI linkage provides. EDI can eliminate many human data entry functions that create errors.

One supplier to Goodyear, for example, is linked directly into the tire manufacturer's mainframe computer and EDI "mapping" is already laid out between computer systems. This allows the supplier in question to produce automatic commercial invoices, and even transport booking requests between Goodyear and freight lines, without human interaction. This company used to have nine, different, data-entry systems for inputting. Now there is no data entry and they have direct computer implant.

But it seems that adopting some hybrid system that combines EDI messaging sets with Internet transmission is the way most companies are going. At Lufthansa Systems, Division North America, executives believe that both technologies serve a purpose and say they won't dismantle their EDI setup. "We've invested a lot in these programs. I think a lot of big corporations still have big administrative systems they use to link messages. I think the Internet will be a supplement," according to a Lufthansa spokesman. "EDI gives you the logic and structure of the messages you want to exchange. It's not so much a question of whether I do this via Internet or protected line, but having a structure for the computers to understand each other."

TECH VISIONS

Skipping EDI, altogether

Some organizations have never employed electronic data interchange (EDI) and don't intend to start now. Take Memphis Light, Gas and Water in Memphis, TN, for example. "Because we're a municipality – and not privately-owned – we were able to completely avoid it," says a Memphis spokesman. "I believe it was just that the avenues for doing it didn't seem to be efficient for those who were in charge at that time. They just didn't think they could get competitive bids that way." Today, Memphis Light, Gas and Water uses the Internet mainly for information gathering, and for locating different sources for products, but hasn't started using it for e-commerce yet. That's just a light switch away.[10]

Enterprise resource planning

One of the hottest trends of the 1990s centered around integrating business functions such as ordering and invoicing for more efficient, cost-effective management – what are commonly called back-office functions. The process that has evolved to handle these functions electronically is called enterprise resource planning (ERP), which should not be confused with the wide array of ERP software solutions that have grown up around the term. As one ERP expert defines the process, "it's viewing the entire organization as a collective group of resources, and then optimizing those resources to meet customer demand."

Technically, a company could run an ERP system on paper, but few ERP specialists consider this practical or even feasible, because of the large number of people in a company's communication chain who feed into an ERP system, and the huge amount of data generated. Most involved in ERP agree that it's very difficult to discuss this process without talking about the underlying technology or the companies like SAP, Oracle, PeopleSoft, Baan and others promoting it.

Like EDI, ERP is evolving to meet the demands of a world that is reaching more and more to the Internet as a transmission tool and where more and more functions will be handled via the Web. Originally, ERP's focus was on integrating business practices in a single enterprise. And critics said many solutions provided mixed results, at best. Not only did they not integrate all business functions – warehousing was notably absent – but the early packages couldn't act as collaborative tools with trading partners and often meant organizing a business in ways that were anathema to many managers. You may remember the ERP horror stories that abounded in the media featuring many a major companies who sunk millions into ERP systems that promised too much and fulfilled too little.

ERP vendors like German giant SAP promise that all of that is changing. Moving rapidly to adapt their systems to an e-commerce environment, the ERP software crowd are rapidly working on ways of moving ERP outside of the enterprise and positioning their products as supply-network collaboration and integration tools. The trend is to install more powerful networks where power is defined increasingly by the ability to manage applications, devices and software remotely and centrally. As ERP matures, analysts recommend that small and mid-size companies should consider this process as a bridge to the B2B arena.

Moving ERP outside the enterprise

The idea of moving ERP functions outside the enterprise is really still in its infancy. Whether order-taking, data mining or invoicing, companies want to translate the data integration that ERP supplies within an enterprise to their current supply chain and eventually to a supply network. ERP experts say moving ERP into the supply chain is feasible, but not without a lot of customization and even development of proprietary solutions.

"We're still in a jerry-rigged mode where you have to put the pieces together yourself. You can't solve it with one package," says one analyst. "People are doing collaboration products, but most of them are supply chain planning vendors. Most of the work, if not all, involves customized versions of packaged software that's proprietary ... And more and more the focus isn't on ERP, at all, but on handling those same functions through the Web and E-commerce."

As Bridgestone-Firestone, Inc. (BFS) and Strategic Technologies Inc. (STI) have learned, connecting an ERP system to an outside vendor, customer or third-party logistics operation requires plenty of cash, forbearance and creativity. BFS approached STI at the end of 1999 to integrate their third-party vendor payment system with BFS's then-new SAP software system that provides in-house ERP solutions. STI is a third and sometimes fourth-party provider of electronic audit and payment services for clients that outsource their payables to STI. With BFS, STI has been handling their freight payments using its own internal system and process, as well as BFS's legacy system.

The two parties managed the job, but not without a great deal of upfront discussion, planning and organization. As an STI spokesman explained, when STI first started processing vendor invoices for BFS the manufacturer was using a legacy system called MAC (Material Acquisition and Control). STI, whose whole regional Nashville office was in the same building as BFS, was able to establish systems integration through terminals connected directly to BFS through a direct-connect lease line, or open communication link. Because of the proximity of the two offices, an Internet connection was not necessary. With the establishment of an open communication link, STI was able to become a "node" on the BFS communication network.

The technological issues were fairly easily resolved. More challenging, STI learned, was working with a company that was transitioning to an ERP software solution. BFS was then rolling out SAP in stages, at different plant locations. For STI this meant keeping the former payment systems alive simultaneously as both companies migrated to the desired SAP interface. They learned that a company intent on extending ERP processes had to be able to handle disasters, including system meltdowns. Literal insurance and recovery plans had to be in place in case the ERP system broke down. The keys to coping, according to both parties, were advanced planning, training and a strong relationship between the two parties making the interface.[11]

PART II: NETWORKING TRENDS THAT TECH TRENDERS SHOULD TAG

It's one thing for tech trenders to integrate back-office functions and quite another to network an entire organization so data and information are available to all, and on a real-time basis.

Chip manufacturers are making huge strides, which means that your computing memory and power are growing. Java provides a platform for all operating systems and is something tech trenders should know about (see Chapter 9). And your basic server, which holds your database(s), is evolving so that through a Web server and Web browser your operation can be networked with the Web.

Even though there have been constant predictions – Moore's Law – that new, smaller and faster computers would replace mainframes, that hasn't happened. Some jobs just require the computing power a mainframe offers. IBM, for example, still makes a significant profit on its mainframes. Mainframes are mostly used for large transaction processing, so if you're in an industry like financials or insurance you'll continue to need that sort of computer.

In the business or institutional world, when you hear about networks it's not necessarily a bunch of individual PCs that are connected. That's only part of what networking is about. Just as organizations have specialists, so more and more computers are serving specialized needs. These are called special hardware servers that run operating systems like Windows 2000, Linux, and Unix. Fairly small – about the size of a pizza box – these servers aren't connected to monitors or keyboards. Up to 40 hardware servers can fit on one rack. On each hardware server there can be one or more software servers running to provide functions like database management, Web serving and the new emerging business logic server. Business logic stands for data processing rules that implement your business process within the computer.

So, when you hear about networking, what people are describing is a network of dedicated hardware servers. For example, companies like Yahoo! use over 1000 Web servers that are tied into other servers using a database software server called Oracle. The user only sees Yahoo! when you access the site, not the individual servers. What matters is that these numerous servers add flexibility to their site because you can simply add servers as the need arises, which is what the experts call a scaleable solution.

The latest trend is to separate the business logic, from the human interface and the data storage, into distinct layers. Human interface is what you, the tech-trending human operator sees, when you personally activate your Web browser through either your PC or terminal. All of these functions, and more, now connect to your Web browser, which is where your human interface takes place today. In the B2B world that human interface will be supplanted by a second computer and computers will actually talk to each other without human intervention at that point.

Often, people have transformed mainframes into powerful hardware servers because of their huge capacity to process transactions. You can think of a mainframe as just another server, albeit an ultra powerful one. You will see Web servers, firewalls and other specific services hanging off the network. In order for all of these servers to function, they have to operate on a common protocol, or language. That's why standards are critical to successful implementation. Ethernet is the hardware connection that ties most of these computers together. TCP/IP is the communications protocol that allows the computers to talk to each other, and is the basis of the Internet.

But not all organizations have the resources – both financial and human – to purchase and implant the most advanced servers, platforms and networking applications, let alone Web-based variants. More often than not, tech trenders will work, first, on integrating existing technologies before making the grand leap to a fully networked company or institution. Joining a supply network and practicing advanced forms of e-commerce will be your end goal. The following are some of the technologies available today that will help you transition into a networked operation.

Niche tools, middleware and groupware.

There are many products on the market that aim at specific supply-chain functions such as inventory visibility, control and warehouse management that allow companies to optimize and reduce inventory, speed up manufacturing and distribution. Many of you likely use these sorts of tools in tandem with ERP to fill in the missing gaps of an ERP system. In fact, integration of many systems may be the way to go for several years as the Web world matures.

Middleware is the tool for integrating ERP products, legacy systems and other supply-chain-related applications like inventory management to meet tracking, tracing and other functions that play into the supply chain. These technologies offer you the ability to either retain existing systems or choose the best of breed, and then link them together. For now, middleware may be the way to go to link with your suppliers' or customers' computers as it allows applications to interact in very much the way the Internet allows computers to interact.

PLATFORMS

Some basic networking terminology

Unless you relegate all your IT decisions to your IT professionals – which this book does not advise – tech trenders need to know a few technology basics. Included are some basic computing terms that relate to networking and to the Web. This list should help you sort out your bytes from your RAM.

1 *Bytes, kilobytes, megabytes and gigabytes*. The byte is the basic unit of information – and the smallest measurement of storage space – on a computer. Asking what a byte is about as useful as asking what a second is. A kilobyte is 1024 bytes. And a megabyte is 1024 kilobytes. A gigabyte is 1024 megabytes.

2 *Hard disk and RAM*. Because both the hard disk and RAM use the same system of measurement, people often conflate the two. For example, 256 megabytes of RAM is a lot, but these days 256 Megabytes on your hard disk is not. So what's the difference? RAM is a three letter acronym (TLA) that stands for random-access memory. When you load programs and your personal files, the operating system takes them off the hard disk and puts them into RAM.

Think of your hard disk as an airport and your computer's RAM as the sky. In this analogy the word processor on your hard disk is like an airplane. Your files are like the airplane's passengers. Until the plane loads its passengers and takes off, it sits on the runway, or hard disk.

3 *Operating system*. A computer operating system sits between the computer and its peripherals (the hardware) and the programs (word processors, spread sheets, browsers) you run. It is your computer's underwear, but not the lacy kind. The operating system is practical in that it provides services for the programs that run on it. For instance, when you save a file in your word processor the word processor doesn't really do much of the work. Instead it supplies the operating system with information about the file and asks it to save the file. Because the operating system knows where it can put the file on the hard drive, the word processor doesn't have to perform that function.

Operating systems do other complex work in addition to saving files. Modern operating systems can run more than one program at the same time. That's why you can check your e-mail while loading a Web page in your browser. That's called multitasking. For this to happen, the operating system must be more than just your computer's underwear. It becomes something like a traffic cop. When you load your e-mail program the operating system assigns it an area in random-access memory (RAM). The operating system patrols the area, making sure that it remains inside the assigned boundaries. In Windows when you get a message that Program X has performed an illegal operation, that usually means that the program has trespassed it's assigned boundaries and you're seeing the ticket the operating system has given it before it shuts the program down.

Different operating systems are good at different things. Operating systems like Linux and Windows NT or 2000 have reputations as good, secure multitasking operating systems.

When a program performs "an illegal operation" in NT or Linux, the program crashes, not the whole system. Windows 98 or ME are better known for supporting more kinds of hardware and are less good at keeping programs from violating assigned memory boundaries. This often results in system crashes.

4 *Clients and servers*. You will see or hear the paired terms client/server in almost every discussion of computer networks. Client/server computing is a very simple concept. A client is a program that requests services from another program called a server. It's very much the same as when you, the client, ask a waiter, the server, to bring you a meal. In computing, however, clients and servers run, more often than not, on different computers. Many of the programs you use to do things on the Internet are client programs that talk to server programs on the other computers all over the world.

5 *Browser.* Your Web browser is an example of a client program. It asks Web servers anywhere on the Internet to send you the Web pages you request. When you click on one of your bookmarks to go to a Web site, the browser asks the Web server at the address of the site to deliver the Web page.

6 *HTTP.* Hypertext Transfer Protocol is the language that allows Web servers and browsers to communicate.

7 *URL*. The Universal Resource Locator (URL) is the part of the HTTP protocol that allows browsers to locate servers. URLs have become synonymous with Web addresses.[12]

More and more software tools are being developed to provide online analytical processing and improved collaboration throughout the supply chain. There are software processes to facilitate this sort of analytical processing at all levels and for all functions. Another niche area that is producing its own variety of software solutions is customer-relationship management (CRM). Both areas are considered add-ons to ERP systems, as well as collaborative products that are designed to hook up various departments in your company, whether design to sales or sales to manufacturing and finance – the sort of big-picture integration that ERP didn't traditionally address.

Many tech-trending companies are also starting to explore ways of integrating marketing more closely with sales. In just-in-time manufacturing and shipping environments, you can't afford to be caught with increased orders from a marketing/ sales promotion without advanced warning. But in too many companies there is little or no coordination between the marketing and manufacturing divisions. Once again, the means to integrate these sorts of tools with legacy systems is middleware.

The more companies automate the more they need the ability to audit the electronic processes flowing around them. Vendors are producing solutions to meet these needs that they call "visibility alert." These sorts of software suites are designed with an exception mode that kicks in when a transaction isn't running as programmed. The system sends out an alert so the problem can be fixed before it derails the supply chain. There's a big market in visibility alert among computer manufacturers who are on the frontline of implanting technology in their own companies.

And there's a new category of software that's called groupware that allows organizations to share documents such as calendars, conduct online discussion groups and handles basic workflow automation and task assignments. It's possible to purchase, or design, groupware that has a Web-browser base.[13]

SOUND BYTES

Battles in chip land

Most of you don't pay much attention to those handy little chips that provide computing memory, but there are big battles taking place that involve who has to pay whom licensing rights and forfeit big cash in profits. The affect on tech trenders isn't yet known, but could result in higher computer prices down the line.

The main protagonist is Rambus, Inc. of Mountainview, California. Rambus has been fighting in the courts to extract royalties – otherwise called licensing rights – on SDRAM and double data rate (DDR) memory chips from big-name chip manufacturers like Intel Corp., Micron Technology Inc., Hyundai Electronics Industries Co. Ltd. and Infineon Technologies AG.

Silicon Valley insiders and analysts believe that Rambus is trying to gain royalties from the more lucrative memory controller (chips) rather than focusing only on DRAM. Little wonder the company has been taking the heat in court from these companies and others. Tech trenders can expect more of these cases, especially if the market for PCs continues to slow down and manufacturers are scrambling to make their profit margins.[14]

STEP addresses incompatibilities

At the dawn of the new decade, century and millennium the Big Three automakers estimated they were losing $1 billion annually because of lack of interoperable technology, not to mention data errors. Given the fact that in the US the automobile industry affects about one out of 34 companies nationwide, the National Institute of Standards and Technology (NIST) has developed a special focus on improving the automotive supply chain. In the process, NIST and automotive experts have been experimenting with a standardized form of data transmission called STEP (Standard for the Exchange of Product Model Data) which is also an international standard ISO 10303.

What is STEP? A professional staff member of the House of Representatives' Committee on Science describes STEP as a translator that's particularly strong for transmitting standardized, large-scale graphics of the sorts used in any manufacturing design. "It is a neutral data format for the exchange of complete product models including both geometric and non-geometric data. Because of the extensive interoperability testing already done in the automotive and aerospace industries, through STEP more than 95 percent of data can be translated," he explains.

Rather than translating data from one software system into another, STEP reportedly provides a complete computer interoperable product data format. This means that STEP allows users to integrate technical systems and production data and covers all aspects of the production cycle, from design to analysis, from production to product support. As STEP boosters explain, "One can exchange drawings and specifications using STEP. One can exchange production data and all things necessary to go from concept and design to manufacture of a product. The bottom line is that the Big Three can save a billion dollars a year by implementing this system."

In pilot programs with both automotive and aerospace companies like General Motors, Delco Electronics, Boeing, Pratt & Whitney and others, STEP shows promise in solving the data exchange portion of the massive interoperability problem. STEP is performing far more successfully as a means of providing interoperability than its predecessors and has much wider acceptance with the companies as well. NIST and other government officials have been hoping to garner federal funds to move STEP beyond this trial phase and have it adapted to other industries whether for design in manufacturing or product services. For example, shipbuilding, textiles and construction industries have shown interest in the process.

However, STEP is still coming into its own and has a long way to gain wide acceptance outside these industries. Awareness is an issue, but STEP can also be costly to suppliers. For others, STEP may be introduced through software upgrades and there's hope that eventually companies will be able to access STEP technology over the Web.

If STEP lives up to its promise, the original equipment manufacturers (OEMs) and their suppliers will move rapidly towards "true virtual manufacturing." This also represents an opportunity for small companies to grow in high-technology, high-dollar-return areas. Federal funds have been provided to help develop STEP, but it's not clear whether any federal subsidies will emerge for implementation beyond the auto industry pilot program.[15]

SOUND BYTES

Open-source operating systems

At least in the software world there is more and more evidence that the open-source software is taking hold. Open source means the code is open and available to all without intellectual property constraints. Developers share their code in the hope that others will use it and improve it. Sharing is encouraged.

Over a period of 15 years, the open-source movement has produced "a collection of operating systems, applications and tools that is often better than most of the commercial tools out there ... The next generation of Macintosh OS, for instance, is based in large part on open-source operating systems like FreeBSD and NetBSD. Computers based on Gnu software (like Unix, but free), Linux or FreeBSD are used to run more than half of the sites on the Web, and they're found in increasing numbers in offices around the world. Even new appliances like the TiVo digital video recorders are based on Linux."[16]

Integration wizardry

Imagine a world where there is no need for paper, no need for middleware and translators. All systems could communicate with each other both inside and outside your tech-trending company. That's the dream that RosettaNet, the powerhouse high-tech consortium, is promoting (see Chapter 4). Although the consortium is supposed to be releasing about 100 specs to affect business-to-business communication, its work can be broken down into the following three categories:

1 *Partner interface processes* (PIPs). These are paper documents that break business processes into highly defined pieces, providing structures for programmers creating e-business applications. Based on the web language XML, PIPs basically offer standardized electronic routines for conducting the most frequent transactions that occur in a Web-enabled supply network. For example, the PIP defines such things as when a buyer and supplier need to communicate, what types of information they need to convey, etc. The PIP also defines a series of exceptions to alert those running the system that they are in default. Retail giant L.L. Bean has garnered much publicity in recent months for conducting a pilot program utilizing PIPs. If this test is successful, the company has announced it will cease working in a paper-based system.
2 *Framework.* PIPs can't operate without an underlying structure. Using a train analogy, RosettaNet managers liken PIPs to the train and framework to the tracks, the signaling apparatus, the safety measures and all sorts of knowledge required for the PIPs to navigate electronically as a train navigates through tunnels, across bridges, etc.
3 *Technical dictionaries.* In technology terms, e-commerce amounts to huge amounts of data aggregation and electronic searching. RosettaNet is creating specs to develop technical dictionaries (see Chapter 1 on Web integration) that lay out the attributes by which people define different products. These dictionaries are supposed to eliminate the reliance on huge search engines.

The overall effect is to help member companies automate all checkpoints between partners so they can reduce costs, be more flexible, make decisions and be much faster to market so they can focus on core competencies and not on shuffling papers.

Consider the example of promoting new product information. Using RosettaNet's process standards, companies will be able to integrate business operations like promotion with sales and shipping, with all functions bound together in one seamless electronic exchange. Tech trenders like you will not have to rely on faxes or information packets and will only phone sellers and customers when follow-up is required.

SOLUTIONS

RosettaNet faces uphill battle

Despite the obvious need for RosettaNet standards, some experts point out that the consortium faces an uphill battle to gain acceptance in the marketplace. For example, implementing a new standard or replacing a legacy system can cost a large company anywhere from $100,000 to more than $1 million. Cost is not always the issue. There's also the time factor, as getting competitors to agree on specs and what works for the industry takes time.

There are some who believe that RosettaNet is pushing out specs and standards too fast. Last August, the Computing Technology Industry Association – which represents 8000 companies in the computer hardware and software industries – rejected 42 RosettaNet PIPs. CTIA officials cited more than 200 questions and comments it felt the consortium needed to address before it would adopt any of the PIPs.

Even so, RosettaNet plans to keep publishing additional PIPS. And the consortium isn't daunted by the fact that so far only seven companies – Arrow Electronics, CompUSA, Hewlett-Packard, Ingram Micro, Intel, SAP, and 3Com – have adopted PIPS in their operations.

For all its critics, RosettaNet has plenty of supporters. Consortium officials know that developing a common B2B e-commerce language is necessary if companies want to do business electronically or participate in business-to-business online exchanges. What companies are beginning to realize is that B2B is not just about having a slick-looking Web site but about being able to connect on the back end as well.[17]

RosettaNet isn't the only consortium working on ways to integrate business functions that should some day mean you tech trenders will live out there on the Web. The Object Management

Group (OMG) is another major consortium that focuses on standardizing electronic "objects." These are things like computer calendars and editing functions that appear in most computer programs. Standardizing the underlying code – to offer a simple example – means less work for programmers. On a grander scale, OMG has developed specifications for operating systems that are used worldwide. Its Internet protocol IIOP (Internet Inter-ORB Protocol) is being used as the infrastructure for technology companies like Netscape, Oracle, Sun, IBM and hundreds of others. These specifications are used worldwide to develop and deploy distributed applications for vertical markets, including manufacturing, finance, telecomm, e-commerce, real-time systems and health care.

And the National Industrial Information Infrastructure Protocols (NIIIP) Consortium has entered into a cooperative development agreement with the US government to develop open-industry software protocols that will make it possible for manufacturers and their suppliers to effectively interoperate as if they

TECH VISIONS

P2P may reshape computing architectures, provide Web collaboration

One of the early potentials for peer-to-peer (P2P) is the ability to reshape corporate computing architectures and augment existing infrastructures. Others see P2P as an improved file-sharing arrangement. And there are those who are adapting the architecture to business-to-business applications.

For example, New York-based Liquid.Net is developing an institutional trading application that helps identify buyers and sellers of large blocks of securities and then facilitates their deals. P2P is being integrated with the company's client/server order-management system, with most of that software residing on the server. Traders send information from desktop to desktop, but the server manages the transfer.

Consilient and Interbind are also using P2P architecture to address their business-to-business problems. Both companies have products that can tie together supply-chain processes into a collaborative environment allowing people as well as processes to interact. They want to introduce humans back into automated business processes. Couple P2P with tools like Groove – an Internet-based program that allows for close collaboration in small groups – and tech trenders may soon have the ability to really collaborate on the Web.

The question facing IT executives, is whether to build P2P from the ground up or somehow connect P2P with classic client/server networks. Some analysts believe the key is to understand the business need and then embed P2P into the existing workflow. Security is another concern, along with the issue of standardized applications and bandwidth. IT managers have to be reassured that P2P won't affect corporate networks in the same way as its cousin Napster did.[19]

were part of the same enterprise, even though many of these interactions are unscheduled, and occur between both sophisticated and relatively unsophisticated users who utilize a wide range of computer systems, operating environments and business processes.

These protocols are supposed to allow you to conduct collaborative computing in support of highly efficient and globally competitive "virtual enterprises."

A virtual enterprise is a temporary consortium of independent member companies, who come together to quickly exploit fast-changing worldwide product manufacturing opportunities. Virtual enterprises assemble themselves, based on cost effectiveness and product uniqueness, without regard for organization size, geographic location, computing environments, technologies deployed or processes implemented. Virtual-enterprise companies share costs, skills, and core competencies, which collectively enable them to access global markets with world-class solutions that could not be provided individually.[18]

TECH VISIONS

Will the network be the computer?

A team of University of California scientists have been trying to prove that the network could really be the computer and in the process have successfully developed the SETI@home screensaver program. They have over two million subscribers worldwide who run the program on their PCs and office servers, collectively racking up the equivalent of 280,000 years in processing time. The total overhead cost is zero.

It's too soon to say if the concept of sharing computer time will create a new business model for the networked society. Popular Power, a San Francisco-based startup, is offering discounts on ISP billing and other incentives for businesses to donate their idle CPU cycles to be used for a variety of data-crunching projects. Management experts see other uses for this model, including using the network to locate jobs and skills.[20]

PART III: KEEPING AN EYE ON THOSE B2B TRENDS

Despite all the tech buzz, the trend to paperless, fully automated organizations is well underway, and has been for over five years. Moreover, no one is about to abandon using the cheap, ubiquitous Internet as a transmission tool. Tech trenders can be certain that whatever trend really delivers and promotes cost cutting and profit making is here for the long term. And B2B holds the promise of cost savings, increased productivity and more. Purchasing experts are predicting that fully-evolved B2B systems will provide productivity improvement, reallocation of procurement resources, material cost reductions, decreases in the need for invoicing, electronic expense report savings, and cycle time reduction savings.[21]

Remember though, that this is a transitional phase and that the hype around B2B is rife. Much of B2B purchasing today is still in the pencil-and-paperclip stage, as companies sort out issues of trust and fraud on the Internet that were outlined in Chapter 1. Like the first wave of dot.coms, many of the first e-tailers may go under if they can't start making a profit. And most of the 1000 or so online marketplaces have been around less than two years, which means that many of the "claims and promises remain unfulfilled potential."[22]

Given this sort of tumult in the pioneering land of the dot.coms, it's best not to focus on the *"application de jour,"* as a well-known analyst calls it. Tech trenders need to put energy and resources into what will add value to your organization right now. Only the big companies or institutions are putting in place the software solutions that will encompass all kinds of e-procurement. B2B is more evolved on the supply side than the sell side, as IBM procurement's move to online purchasing indicates.

SOUND BYTES

E-comm goes global

Just as the US lags behind the rest of the world in mobile phone use, so also is there less interest in e-commerce and e-finance than in other countries. In a survey of 30,000 Web users, IDC reports that countries like Sweden have more users willing to buy stocks and investments online than US users. The stats are 27 percent of Swedish users versus 24 percent of American users.

This same survey shows Venezuelans to be the most receptive to buying software online, followed by the US, Brazil, the Netherlands, Australia and Japan. Users in Argentina are very willing to purchase information from the Web.

This is good news for any company interested in global product sales. IDC reports many countries willing to conduct cross-border commerce online. These include Chile, Venezuela and Malaysia.[23]

Experts warn that the components, or underpinnings of B2B that are being hyped today by the software vendors won't necessarily be important in a year or two. These will most likely give way to solutions being developed by supply-chain management vendors and collaborative vendors.[24]

SOLUTIONS

The need to build consumer confidence in e-commerce

There has been growing awareness among international consumer organizations and standards developers of a need to build global confidence in the Web, or the whole promise of e-commerce will fall flat. In the spring of 2000, 25 consumer groups worldwide and standards organizations such as the American National Standards Institute (ANSI), and ISO's Committee on Consumer Policy (COPOLCO) agreed to form a global forum to address e-commerce issues and create standardized e-commerce practices for worldwide use.

They cited "mounting evidence that many consumers are reluctant to engage in electronic commerce due to a lack of confidence in the reliability of e-commerce merchants, concerns about privacy and security, and confusion about the reliability of online codes and seals programs which claim to protect and promote the consumer interest," according to an ISO spokesman. And their concerns didn't rest with questions about how to protect purchasers. In subsequent meetings, the e-commerce forum has raised wider questions about whether the Web was evolving in a technologically compatible way to support a global e-commerce structure.

Issues range from what information Web sites need to provide for consumers – both individuals and businesses – about a product, to online warranties, return policies and information on customs and other import/export regulations for foreign purchases. Among the most important concerns was just insisting that Web sites provide online contact information.

The forum also has been addressing the need for standardizing the actual technology used for B2B or e-commerce on the retail level, the issue of data privacy and security, as well as legal issues. For example, which jurisdiction applies, especially when buying state-to-state in the US, or purchasing worldwide? How to settle claims across borders and what dispute settlement process to standardize? How to prevent fraud? And, finally, the forum is also exploring applying third-party marks and labels to provide consumer confidence. These may be things like Federal Drug Administration (FDA) symbol on prescription drugs, or something like the well-known safety marks for electrical equipment.

Members say they know they have assumed an enormous task that's almost beyond their ability to handle. The control of cyberspace fraud may not be entirely possible. But there are controls that you, as tech-trending professionals, can bring to the B2B world by practicing smart purchasing just as you do in the paper-based world. ANSI, which is based both in New York City and Washington, DC, welcomes input on these issues from individuals and companies (see Chapter 4).[25]

PLATFORMS

The alternative view

Some experts believe the entire B2B world – whether you talk about c-communities or value webs – is being overestimated and overplayed. For quite some time they argue you will be where you are today. The real emphasis, they say, will be on improving your information flow within pre-existing sales channels. Online trading communities may increase the number of vendors a purchasing agent can pick from, but until you work with them you don't know. You may discover that your existing vendors are fine. Maybe they charge more, but they provide what you need.

And they don't believe existing processes for promoting information flow or integrating businesses like electronic data interchange (EDI) or enterprise resource planning (ERP) will go by the wayside for another 20–30 years. The argument is that the majors like Wal-Mart and General Motors have spent lots of money on their EDI systems and won't be eager to throw them away. If they didn't abandon these processes during the Y2K scare, why dump them now? The same for ERP, in which many companies have invested heavily.

What will change, they say, will be more opportunity to access EDI through your browser. This will allow for more flexible use of EDI messaging, which is still mostly one-way. This approach spares small companies the $100,000 or so in EDI equipment purchases, not to mention translation and value-added network (VAN) fees. Professionals like psychiatrics, museum directors and others in the service sector will focus more on information flow than purchasing. Some of you may never enter the B2B arena. You may find your handy voicemail suffices.[26]

Technologies tech trenders need to make the B2B jump

Think of your basic networked operation with its servers hosting a variety of databases, and then move the whole shebang onto the Web. The following is the sort of technology tech trenders will need, to make the leap to a Web-based, B2B world.

On the hardware side you're going to need to connect your company or institution's network to a back-end database and a Web server to be able to transmit data – like catalog information, shopping carts and other e-commerce tools. Web servers are servers that contain specialized software geared to the sending and receiving of data; the computer version of a switch.

On the software side you will need a database to drive the system, and that may require application and development tools, authoring and maintenance tools, and network and integration tools. Now that you're out on the Web, data security is a main concern and you'll have to decide whether you want to encrypt your data, post firewalls or work in Secure Electronic Transactions (SET).

You will want to consider implanting a content-management system, that will manage data presentation, enable distributed updating, and quickly post customized changes. Knowledge-management tools will allow you to post something as simple as Frequently Asked Questions (FAQs) on your Web site, or something as complicated as the ability to provide information to a client, in need of online customer support. The more you edge out onto the Web, the more solutions you will both want and need. There are customer relationship systems, systems for ad management, and portal development software. If you're involved in e-tail you may want a taxation software package, and if you go global you'll want software to manage everything from duties and tariffs to exchange rates.[27]

Then there's the question of what you actually want to do out on the Web. It may be as simple as sourcing goods or as complicated as conducting all your business transactions in cyberspace. You will have to decide what sort of Web-based marketplace or exchange to enter. Maybe these concerns are several years out, but there's no doubt that the world is lining up to produce a Web-based environment. Here are the trends and tools the experts say will get tech trenders through the transition to a networked, B2B world.

Value webs

Value webs represent a model for reconfiguring the supply chain into an interactive supply network that simultaneously connects customer needs to component sources, product assembly, rapid delivery, and support services – all woven together in order to drive higher levels of customer satisfaction and profitability. These webs encompass customer choice, value creation, and on-time delivery, basically representing the model for a Web-based future.

Unlike traditional, linear supply chains, which begin with component sourcing and manufacturing capabilities, in a value web everything focuses on the customer – whether a consumer or a business. Each customer selects the product and service characteristics that best match their needs in a self-design process at the value web's front-end. The value web then rapidly creates and delivers the customized solution to the consumer or corporation, or at least that's the theory.

The four major processes of an interlocking value web are customer choice, sourcing, assembly and delivery, all of which are constantly interlocking and interacting. Each element must be designed to enhance accuracy, speed, revenue and productivity in a non-linear process. It's the seamless integration of all four aspects that results in a value web that promotes customer satisfaction and higher profits.

Some value webs, which are most prevalent in the high-tech industry, involve rudimentary e-commerce. But the Internet is not a necessary front-end prerequisite to designing an effective value web. As will be examined more closely in later chapters, technology must always be viewed as a tool, only. Human organization must be considered first, and then the technology implanted on top of a functional human system for any benefits to be felt.[29]

APPLICATIONS

Reinventing your business for the Web

At Valley Books in Amherst, MA, the owner sits behind the counter of his North Pleasant Street store chatting with walk-in customers and answering questions about his two floors, containing approximately 40,000 books. In between, he stays busy filling customer orders online, buying and selling books over the Internet.

Fitness By Day is a Web site that provides online personal fitness training. For $35 a month, members receive the benefits of "professional exercise program design and expert monitoring" by a certified personal trainer in the Boston area, who started the online program to fill downtime. Now his Web site has testimonials from as far away as Santa Monica.

What these two businesses have in common is that they are not merely augmenting their traditional distribution channels: they are using the Internet to reinvent themselves. They are turning to e-commerce to expand their businesses by offering new, value-added services their customers want – services that were not even possible a few years ago.

Consider how travel agencies are reinventing themselves to operate on the Web. Airline ticket buyers are finding it easier to go online and view screen displays than try to jot down times and flight numbers over the phone. The Web also allows customers to play with scenarios at their own pace in their own time, find bargains, and bid on tickets. In 1999, 16 million travel reservations were booked on the Web. Travel agencies must learn to provide new, value-added services or they will perish. Is your business similarly imperiled?

Reinvent yourself!

There is hardly a business in the New Economy that can perform without some Internet connections. This is true whether your company is Internet-based, like eBay or Amazon, or Internet-enabled, meaning it uses the Internet to support the business, but is not 100 percent dependent on it. Either way, success today will hang, to some degree, on how you work the Web.[28]

APPLICATIONS

Nortel Networks Global Logistics goes customer-centric

In recent years, telecomm giant Nortel Networks has gone through a major divestiture of its manufacturing and is now relying on contract manufacturers to take over production. The focus is on handling the requirements of a handful of major clients worldwide, and that may mean everything, from manufacturing to their specifications to installing large-scale telecomm systems.

As a result of this new emphasis, Nortel Networks' global logistics operation, based in Nashville, TN, has been turned inside out and upside down. Nortel Networks Global Logistics has changed from a traditional, in-house distribution process to an organization that relies entirely on alliances with third-party logistics operators and transportation companies. And thanks to sophisticated technology, the Nortel Networks and its logistics operation now function as a supply network, not a supply chain.

Under this new system, logistics "sits in the middle" of the entire Nortel Networks operation. Besides attracting compatible, reliable transportation and logistics partners and schooling them in the Nortel Networks system, the new operation depends on eventual creation of 20 Logistics Operating Centers (LOCs) worldwide. Many are currently under construction and 15–20 centers are expected to be fully operable in 2001.

In the center there's the customer, and then in the second ring out there are all Nortel Network partners, whether in order management, supply and demand or technical operations, etc. And in the outer-most ring are all multiple sources for key parts, which can be assembled by contract manufacturers or original equipment manufacturers (OEMs). "Basically, we've got sources all over the place, but it all starts with the customer in the middle. Then information or data (on orders, manufacturing and shipping) has to move between any layers of the circle," says a Nortel spokesman.

What happens under this system is that an order gets placed against Nortel Networks. The order management people determine the best source of product for that order and may make a commitment to the customer that involves placing an order against multiple sources. The LOC becomes the focal point of order fulfillment for the customer. The object of the LOC is to keep inventory close to the customer. The eventual plan is that each LOC will be totally focused for a customer. For example, when a major telephone service provider comes to them for inventory they want to maintain, then Nortel agrees to give them availability.

But Nortel Networks aims to be more than an inventory manager. The purpose behind the regionalized LOC system is to allow Nortel Networks to "integrate with its customers. We will help them plan inventory for production. Our objective isn't to build excessive inventory worldwide, but to have the right amount of inventory in the right place. We've placed our LOCs at an ideal distance of no more than 100 miles drive time to customers," says a Nortel source. When an electronic order comes in, the LOC determines inventory availability. If it's there on site, there can be delivery within hours.[30]

Some B2B models

As you tech trenders know, B2B is still in its infancy. Most B2B is taking "indirect production supplies" rather than in the purchasing of "direct production supplies." Indirect supplies are those needed to maintain and operate a facility that don't necessarily relate to direct production of a product. What is being purchased today involves items such as lighting or electrical and plumbing supplies that don't affect a supply chain network and don't involve much risk. These are high-volume, low-cost items that every company needs to purchase, and where online purchasing can eliminate waste.

A lot of B2B activity also centers on gathering information for sourcing to obtain lower prices. For companies to move into the direct-purchase side means eliminating the element of risk that offers. Buyers and suppliers will have to gain confidence that B2B produces results, and there will have to be management buy-in. As B2B emerges from the fantasy stage to reality, a number of models are evolving. Of these, the application service provider (ASP) format appears to be really taking off. The Phillips Group predicts 56 percent growth in this model among large companies by 2004. Here's what you can select from now:

1 *Online marketplaces.* Companies like Ariba, SAP, Oracle and Ford have announced online marketplaces that offer a collection of catalogs that allow buyers to source and purchase. The more sophisticated sites have provisions for customer-specific pricing or total site volume pricing. They also offer content to attract users, such as vertical industry news, articles, and even entertainment. And they support some degree of integration so that orders and related documents generated on the site can be automatically downloaded into a user's financial systems. That's one reason that ERP vendors like SAP and Oracle are setting up their own marketplaces.

2 *Trading communities.* In the e-commerce sense, companies use the term "trading community" to describe a group of buyers and sellers that work in the same market space, sharing common needs, information and business partners. For example, companies that buy and sell on the chemical supplies site, Chemdex, would be considered a trading community.

3 *Buy-side procurement systems.* Still pretty limited to Fortune 100 companies with lots of money to invest in end-to-end systems, this model allows a purchasing department to direct their end users to preferred suppliers. Companies like Commerce One, Ariba, Intelisys are providing these sorts of applications. The major drawback is cost, which can range from $250,000 to $5 million.

4 *Service bureaus.* Also known as application service providers or infomediaries, service bureaus basically provide an aggregation of suppliers and distributors of indirect supplies. This allows buyers to access indirect supplies from one location. Service bureaus represent the most common form of B2B sites.

5 *The sell-side model.* This is the least sophisticated form of B2B and usually involves a supplier setting up shop on the Web with his own products or products available for purchase. This model replaces phone sales, but doesn't add

much other value. An example is Staples putting up a Web site and selling its products.

6 *Exchanges*. These host many-to-many buyer-seller relationships for more commodity-type items. A common type of exchange involves transaction fees to the sellers. In other words, someone brings buyers and sellers to a Web site, facilitates one-on-one purchasing and takes a piece of the transaction.
   - Public exchanges: Not long ago public exchanges were all the rave. These are places where all sorts of buyers and sellers can meet. Volume and having the right commodity to sell are crucial to making a public exchange work.
   - Private exchanges: Another growing option is the private exchange. Mainly being embraced by large companies with certified suppliers, private exchanges offer the benefits of added security, anonymity, help maintain business relationships and mean that companies can retain electronic formats like EDI rather than standardizing to XML.

SOUND BYTES

An open Internet exchange for the computer and electronics marketplace

Twelve of the hottest high-tech industry leaders have formed High-Tech Exchange – an open Internet exchange to serve the needs of the high-tech supply-chain community.

Companies involved are AMD, Compaq, Gateway, Hitachi, HP, Infineon, NEC, Quantum, Samsung, SCI Systems, Solectron, and Western Digital. Their aim is to provide services to buyers and sellers involved in computing and electronics-related industries. The exchange is expected to enable these businesses to manage their supply chains more efficiently and effectively, improve delivery of products and services to the marketplace, and increase customer satisfaction.

According to spokesmen, the exchange's end-to-end services will be open and available to all parties in the supply-chain process – consumer and business electronics makers, contract manufacturers, suppliers and distributors. All participants in this electronic marketplace will be able to manage a wide array of their e-procurement purchases and sales through this new exchange.

And founders say the new company will use best-in-class technology to deliver a variety of services to participants, including open sourcing, e-catalogs, auctions and dynamic pricing, supply planning and logistics. It will acquire some of this capability from its founders, who have already developed services for efficient buying and selling over the Internet. The exchange will use this expertise to start delivering immediate value to all members. More details on the exchange, including information for companies interested in becoming founders, are available at www.ehitex.com.[31]

7 *ASP models.* These are software-rental arrangements where the vendor hosts and maintains a piece of software and simply sells the right to access the software. Many see ASP models taking over, and that the days of buying a piece of software for local installation and ongoing upgrades are limited. If and when ASP takes over, it will be much cheaper and more scalable to rely on a service provider for upgrades and maintenance. ASP is also supposed to promote the growth of various types of intermediaries facilitating communications/transactions between buyers and sellers. Product data preparation, maintenance, and dissemination are emerging as basic needs in the marketplace. These solutions are often based on ASP models.

8 *Sell-side auctions.* This is where multiple buyers compete for products and services with upward price pressure.

9 *Buy-side auctions, or reverse auctions.* Buyers of indirect materials and services turn to buy-side auctions or reverse auctions because sell-side doesn't work for them. In this model, you, the buyer, get to auction off your requirements. Sellers get the chance to "bid" on fulfilling your need, and at a predetermined point in time, the bid is "over" and the cheapest supplier is given the chance to earn your business.[33]

TECH VISIONS

Contracts a new focus for exchanges

Survivors of the B2B exchanges are moving away from auctioning commodities to the harder, but more lucrative game of contracts. FreeMarkets, which designs and runs "reverse auctions" – in which the price falls rather rises over time – is a prime example of this new focus. FreeMarkets codifies all the elements of a contract – from the specifications of the product to performance guarantees – so that bidders can compete fairly in an auction.

Other companies like Perfect.com and Commerce One are trying to write software that will help automate bidding across industries. This is a complex, time-consuming prospect and progress has been relatively slow. Working within a single industry is a somewhat easier proposition. GoCargo, an exchange for the container-shipping industry, is having some success expanding from a relatively small spot market to a far larger contract market.[32]

Some additional tech-trending B2B tools

By now you've got a pretty good picture of the business world as evolving in fits, starts and sometimes giant leaps from a relatively slow-paced paper system to the vision of a Web-based business universe. Communication is speeding up and becoming more efficient, the Internet/Web structure is evolving as an information platform and all sorts of work is taking place to integrate the business functions and help companies work collaboratively with all members of their supply networks. While telecomms and the Internet/Web steal the headlines, there are lots of lesser-known – but equally important – activities taking place that are serving as the underpinnings of a networked world.

New technology is pushing bar codes outside of the warehouse and becoming integral to the operation of an efficient supply network that will support B2B. Other developments are taking place in classification coding and standardization of purchasing functions that are the underpinnings of global B2B.

APPLICATIONS

Electronic product catalogs

Electronic product catalogs hold lots of promise for companies that want to advertise their full product line, very little of which is usually carried by distributors. Electronic catalogs allow for instant updating. The idea is to emphasize and strengthen your brand by offering your complete electronic product data on your own corporate Web site. Flexible and extensible product data can also be transmitted like a radio signal to distributors, resellers, e-marketplaces, and procurement vendors with no degradation in quality or currency. This "syndication" process further extends your brand and claims exponentially more "eye-share" among end-users.

Some manufacturers may balk at establishing direct contact with end-users, hesitant to disrupt long-standing relationships with distributors. But the truth is, existing sales channels need not be disrupted by an "e-content" strategy, as you can disseminate complete product information to end-users, but still route all transaction requests to distributors of choice. This way, the product information bottleneck goes away, without alienating important players in the supply network.[34]

Bar codes as tracking/tracing tools. On any given day in any warehouse, airport, truck yard or port, shipments get displaced and supply-chain flow sloshes to a messy trickle, upending manufacturing deadlines and retail sales, alike. It would be helpful if every shipment could carry a detailed history of what it is and where it's been – a history that meshes seamlessly with the enterprise system of whatever organization is in current possession of the goods. That would allow wayward merchandise to be redirected quickly, and prevent other goods from getting lost.

Of course, that system exists. It's what bar codes are all about. But until now, bar codes have had their own limitations. They couldn't hold very much information; they could only be scanned by line-of-sight and while moving at modest speed; their content couldn't easily be changed or checked for quality. Now, traditional bar codes are being combined with other emerging technologies to overcome these physical limitations. As a result, they are emerging from the confines of the warehouse to become a key tool for simultaneously propelling goods and information through a fast-moving supply chain.

Much of the technology exists today that allows for more information to be encoded in bar codes, for the bar codes to be read from a distance and for more accurate reads. For example, every package handled by UPS now contains a two-dimensional bar code that looks like a target surrounded by bit-mapped arrow strikes. Called MaxiCode, it's a public-domain symbology that can pack 100 characters of data per square inch – compared with perhaps 10 characters per linear inch on traditional bar codes, which is only enough to carry a stock-keeping number. The MaxiCode's central target is a focusing device that allows the code to be read at high speeds, while the hexagonal dots around it contain information packed both vertically and horizontally. The data can be read no matter how the code is oriented when scanned. The MaxiCode provides UPS with information on a particular shipment at a glance, so that it can be tracked and traced more efficiently.

SOLUTIONS

Global bar codes will promote trade

The standards world is working on integrating computer hardware into bar code printers that will allow for integration with ERP business functions, and promote many new bar code functions to improve information flow throughout your global supply network. The International Organization for Standardization (ISO) subcommittee 31 on bar codes is working on standardizing two-dimensional (2D) bar codes. The advantage of 2D bar codes, whether they're stacked, matrix or dot technology, is that they take up less space and typically have error-correction built in to enhance the read reliability.

When applied to a warehouse, 2D bar codes make it possible to encode more information on the package itself. Shippers can use 2D as a traveling database. Getting 2D bar code printing capabilities isn't hard. All the major manufacturers offer it. But widespread implementation of these codes has only started in the last year or so on shipping labels to obtain data that would traditionally be on a packing sheet or slip.

Experts agree that the use of radio frequency identification (RFID) and bar codes with smart labels – basically, labels with embedded programmable chips – will grow quickly because this combination allows for long-distance identification and tracking of products. With RF technology you don't have to line up a laser beam to read the codes. And the chips can contain unlimited information that won't take up any more room on a label than traditional bar codes. Further, data contained in the chip can be edited. The use? Let's say an order of commodity parts bound for one customer is re-routed at the last minute to another customer who needs the parts immediately, and will pay premium price to get them.

At the distribution center, the smart labels can be edited not only to reflect the change in destination, but also to reflect the new delivery date and price. Moreover, these smart labels are durable. They can be baked into plastic or frozen. So a chip with RFID capabilities can be embedded on a frozen food container that's planted in a truck body to read information about the temperature and other conditions, allowing for a written history of the product during shipping.[35]

Product classification codes. Anyone who works in accounts payable knows the headaches of aggregating data. The promise of e-procurement is that it should route transactions through a single system, capturing in one place all the relevant data needed for spend analysis. The aim is to be able to rationalize supply bases, negotiate better prices with suppliers, easily quantify your global spending and standardize buys from across far-flung operations.

A new global classification code has been recently developed that should help you tech trenders identify companies and classify products and services so that e-procurement can provide the efficient, cost-saving system of any manager's dreams. It's called the United Nations Standard Product and Services Classification Code (UN/SPSC) – a long name for what some consider one of the most useful coding systems ever devised.

The UN/SPSC is an internationally accepted, eight-digit commodity code standard, that classifies more than 8000 products and services worldwide. The first system, in fact, to classify both products and services for worldwide use, the UN/SPSC has been in operation for a couple of years. It is based on the United Nations' Common Coding System (UNCCS) and Dun & Bradstreet's Standard Product and Services Codes (SPSC).

Sounds pretty dry until one considers how this open standard relates to electronic commerce. According to its creators – a team of analysts and researchers from Dun & Bradstreet and the UNDP's Inter-Agency Procurement Services Organization (IAPSO) – the UN/SPSC enables companies from any region and of any language background to electronically communicate more accurately and efficiently about products and services they're buying or selling.

Developers explain that the UN/SPSC's precise codes are incorporated into the company's electronic and paper-based trade documents such as Web sites, product catalogs, invoices, purchase orders and inventory/sales slips. A company can then automatically and consistently track its entire supply-and-demand-chain activity.

Companies use the code in combination with a universal business identifier, such as the D&B D-U-N-S® number that identifies more than 50 million businesses worldwide. This enables them to track and manage their relationships with suppliers. Firms can also identify their interrelated suppliers and gauge opportunities for consolidating or leveraging suppliers.

When applied to product catalogs, the UN/SPSC will help companies identify suppliers anywhere in the world. It can also be used as an index to cross-reference all products and services with given suppliers. Moreover, its developers say it can be used also with procurement systems such as ERP (enterprise resource planning), as well as legacy and desktop procurement systems. For example, VISA says it is working with Dun & Bradstreet to provide cardholders and other customers with detailed, accurate reporting, based on the UN/SPSC standard.

UN/SPSC developers say that thanks to the new code, purchased goods and services finally have common global definitions, allowing companies to leverage, standardize and obtain high-compliance supplier contracts. As global sources evolve, the code is supposed to allow you to make supplier identification and qualifications from your desktops.

ECCMA – the Electronic Commerce Code Management Association – is the organization that now manages, improves, and promotes the UN/SPSC classification scheme. ECCMA officials explain that UN/SPSC creates a common cyberspace registry of suppliers that is promoting open procurement. However, they suggest you don't scrap your old part numbering systems because UN/SPSC doesn't drill down to the attribute level of parts. For example, it won't tell a person whether a pencil is a No. 2 or No. 3 lead.

For purposes of spend analysis, many experts suggest that few tech-trending companies will go to the expense of mapping their old part numbers to UN/SPSC or other classification schemes. Rather, they'll simply capture the information going forward in time as increasing numbers of suppliers map their catalogs to

UN/SPSC or other codes. Moreover, UN/SPSC is only one of many possible product classification schemes. Different industries are evolving their own ways of classifying products.[36]

APPLICATIONS

UN/SPSC in practice

A number of companies have tried out UN/SPSC, coding their catalogs to the global standard. The feedback from the front is that the standard is emerging, but immature. A Michigan-based electronics company found some product categories to be "not bad," but had difficulty with electronic components. The market, for example, differentiates between electronic and electrical switches, but UN/SPSC does not. The good news is this same manager finds the UN/SPSC process to be ever open and accommodating, and he is actively involved improving the system.

The United Nations Standard Product and Services Classification Code organization has been formed after the code was created to help oversee UN/SPCS. But actual management of the code takes place under the purview of the ECCMA. UN/SPCS is available free of charge by reaching www.unspcs.org, or calling 800–424–9081. At www.dnb.com/UN/SPSC/, companies can get help in assigning the code.[37]

PLATFORMS

Standardizing registration criteria

There is no purchasing without trust, and there is no B2B without that same trust transferred to the Web. Company identifiers, registration and authentication criteria are some of the quiet, hidden ways companies can offer assurance. E-procurement boosters are working on ways to standardize these sorts of practices.

Experts say the idea is to create a universal unique descriptor for any supplier on the Internet worldwide. In the US and Australia, Dun & Bradstreet's DUNS numbers are widely used and recognized. Beyond these two countries, however, they do not have broad acceptance.

Authentication is another serious area of concern because it's difficult, not to say restrictive, for buyers and sellers to procure different user identification and passwords for each marketplace. E-procurement experts are developing schemes to identify entrants and authenticate their rights to access different services.[38]

Notes

1 *Global Tool Kit: Supply Chain,* Amy Zuckerman, A–Z International Associates, Amherst, MA, 1999.
2 Charles Mann, correspondent for Inside.com and *The Atlantic Monthly,* and contributing correspondent to *Science.*
3 "Impact Hard to Measure, But E-procurement Is Gaining", *Supply Chain Technology News,* August 2000.
4 Kevin Fitzgerald, publisher and editor of *Global Supply* magazine.
5 *Small Business Expansions in Electronic Commerce,* the SBA's Office of Advocacy.
6 *Purchasing* magazine, June 2000.
7 "Why Manufacturers Should Take E-Commerce Seriously," Mark Vigoroso, executive producer, NewMediary.com
8 "Elementary, My Dear Watson," *The Economist* New Economy Survey, September 23, 2000, p. 11.
9 Adapted from "Edifact Gaining Acceptance," Amy Zuckerman, *Journal of Commerce,* November 10, 1999.
10 Adapted from "What Ever Happened to EDI?," Bridget McCrea, contributing editor, PurchasingCenter.com, July 17, 2000.
11 "Stretching ERP Beyond the Enterprise," Amy Zuckerman, *Chief Logistics Officer,* March 2000.
12 Seth Rothberg, principal, /home/industries, Amherst, MA.
13 Sources are Bob Rosenbaum, publisher, *Supply Chain Technology News,* and David Washburn, principal consultant at Amherst Information Architects, Amherst, MA.
14 "Rambus Reveals Plans to Collect Royalties from Chipset Makers," Steven Fyffe, *Electronic News* online edition.
15 "STEP Addresses Supply Chain Incompatibilities," Amy Zuckerman, *Journal of Commerce,* October 13, 1999. Source is

Jim Turner, Chief Democratic Counsel for the US House of Represenatatives Science Committee

16 "Whose Intellectual Property Is It, Anyway? The Open Source War," Peter Wayner, *New York Times*, August 24, 2000.

17 "The Paradox of RosettaNet" Hildy Medina, *Line56* online edition, August 24, 2000.

18 Most of this section was culled from *Global Tool Kit: Supply Chain*, Amy Zuckerman, A–Z International Associates, Amherst, MA, 1999. Some of this material appeared on PurchasingCenter.com and was adapted from earlier articles the author wrote for *Journal of Commerce, Transportation and Distribution, Chief Logistics Officer, Supply Chain Technology News*, and *Electronic News*. Material on consortia comes from *The Consortia Boom*, the author's work in progress, and from "The Hunt for Interoperability," Anne Millen Porter, *Purchasing* magazine, June 15, 2000.

19 "P-to-P Intersects with B-to-B," Ed Scannell and Martin Lamonica, Infoworld.com, November 24, 2000. (Sources include Rob Hegarty, an analyst at Tower Group, in Needham, MA, and Simon Yates, an analyst at Forrester Research, in Cambridge, MA); and "Ray's Back in the Groove," Steven Levy, *Newsweek*, November 6, 2000.

20 "The Network is the Brain," Jeffrey Davis, senior features editor, *Business 2.0* online edition, October 25, 2000.

21 "How to Start an e-Procurement Initiative: Three Experts' Advice," Joseph Mazel, Supplier Selection & Management Report, July 1, 2000. Sources include Richard G. Weissman, former Director of Purchasing, PurchasingCenter.com; Kevin J. Williams, purchasing specialist, ESPN, Inc., and Russ Boyd, Supply Contracts Manager, Perot Systems Corporation.

22 "Promises, Promises," Michelle Grappa, *Business 2.0*, October 24, 2000, p. 58.

23 IDC survey sponsored by eTranslate.com posted on eMarketer's eGlobal Report, November 1, 2000.

24 Source is Karen Peterson, Research Director, The Gartner Group.

25 "Filling a Shortage of Standards," Amy Zuckerman, *New York Times* E-Commerce Special, October 25, 2000, p. 30. Sources include the American National Standards Institute (ANSI) and Linda Golodner, President, National Consumers League, Washington, DC.
26 Source is Bob Rosenbaum, Publisher, *Supply Chain Technology News.*
27 *Smart Things To Know About E-Commerce,* Michael Cunningham, Capstone Publishing Ltd, Oxford, 2000, pp. 53–71 (Chapter 3 – "E-Commerce Technologies that Matter"), and Charles Mann, correspondent for Inside.com and *The Atlantic Monthly,* and contributing correspondent to *Science.*
28 "Taking it to the Web," Eddy Goldberg, April 21, 2000, info@entrenetwork.com. Information source is Les Ball, co-director of the Interdisciplinary Center for Electronic Enterprise (ICEE) at the University of Massachusetts Computer Science Department
29 "Value Webs: The Next Business," David Bovet, Mercer Management Consulting, appeared on PurchasingCenter.com, June 2000.
30 "Nortel Networks Global Logisitics: Placing the Customer at the Center of the Global Spoke," Amy Zuckerman, *World Trade,* August 2000, pp. 60–62. John Lebowitz, vice president of Nortel Networks Global Logistics and Delia Caldwell, project leader for Logistics Communications, a subset of Nortel Networks Global Logistics, provided information.
31 Forrester Research, Inc., February 2000.
32 "The Container Case," *The Economist,* October 21, 2000, p. 76.
33 "Navigating the E-Commerce Maze: An E-Commerce Primer," Deborah Wilson, Deborah Wilson Consulting, December 15, 1999; Mark Vigoroso, executive producer, NewMediary.com, and Kevin Fitzgerald, publisher and editor of *Global Supply.*
34 "Why Manufacturers Should Take E-Commerce Seriously," Mark Vigoroso, executive producer, NewMediary.com.

35 "Belly Up to the Barcode," Amy Zuckerman, *Supply Chain Technology News*, September 2000.

36 "UN/SPSC: What is This E-Commerce Phenomena?" Amy Zuckerman (with research help from Rosalind McLymont), PurchasingCenter.com, January 25, 2000; and "The Hunt for Interoperability," Anne Millen Porter, *Purchasing* magazine, June 15, 2000.

37 "The Hunt for Interoperability," Anne Millen Porter, *Purchasing* magazine, June 15, 2000.

38 "The Hunt for Interoperability," Anne Millen Porter, *Purchasing* magazine, June 15, 2000.

3 Technology Trends: Transportation and Logistics Empower the New Economy

No matter how much of your back-office work is eventually transferred to cyberspace, tech-trending companies still have to be able to ship, store and deliver raw materials and products in the three-dimensional world. The very technology that is helping you manage your business so much more cost-effectively is also driving customer expectations for goods to be delivered just-in-time and on a global basis.

Remember the horror stories from Christmas 2000 when so many new e-tailers went online only to find their businesses crash because they couldn't meet deliveries on time? That's a lesson to all of you tech trenders, that you can't forgo sound business principles based on customer satisfaction in the rush to make Web-based fortunes. The old nuts-and-bolts worlds of transportation and logistics matter more than ever in the New Economy.

In large part because of the demands of a highly competitive, global economy, the transportation and logistics industries have been going through massive change in the last decade. Very few tech-trending organizations today maintain their own transportation fleets, or manage their own warehouses and inventories – what's called logistics. More and more of you have turned over your transportation and logistics operations to third-party companies. This makes for smaller, leaner operations, but the dependency on third-party outsourcing also ups the ante tremendously on the communication front.

Because transportation and logistics are so crucial to maintaining material goods and product flow in this new economy, these industries are using technology in enormously creative ways. Basic computing, satellite, radio frequency, bar codes, cellular, x-ray and now the Internet – just about every technology imaginable – are being combined to literally and figuratively drive the supply network. It would not be possible to source goods, track shipments, inventory goods or send freight bills on a real-time basis – let alone on a global basis – without advanced technology.

Moreover, the Internet and Web are having an enormous impact on the transportation and logistics industries. For example, the rush to shopping in cyberspace has created a bonanza for expedited overnight carriers like FedEx, UPS and others. These same carriers have been at the forefront of moving many of their business functions to the Web. And there's been a huge push to develop Web-based transportation and logistics dot.coms where all business transactions take place on the Web. However, only a handful of the pioneering transportation and logistics dot.coms are expected to survive into maturity.

Transportation and logistics visionaries see the Web being used more and more to better manage real-time operations. For truck fleets, the sort of optimization software that is already allowing the big companies to better manage truck capacity and ensure that all space is utilized each delivery, will be available via the Web to smaller companies. In the logistics world there will be creation of more and more collaborative trading groups so that members can "grab" inventory from member warehouses in real-time rather than maintaining private stock. This development could eventually turn warehouses into collaborative trading retail operations.

This chapter will provide an overview of some of the different ways that technology is helping you operate the transportation and logistics side of your business or institution in real-time to become more efficient and competitive. Consider this example of how technologies are improving supply chain flow: with one transponder connecting to a roadside reader and a networked system in the cab, the truck drivers of the future will be able to pass through any toll booth in the country, plus gain pre-clearance for safety checks *en route,* access online navigation advice and even order food without having to pay cash. All that will happen with the combination of intelligent transportation systems (ITS), in-vehicle networking and computing (see ITS section below).[1]

PLATFORMS

Using satellites for tracking, tracing, safety, the works ...

In the business of global tracking it's becoming imperative to provide real-time information on where containers are located at any given time. Since the early 1990s, satellite technology has become the technology of choice for some transport modes. Although satellite technology is also permeating the rail and ocean markets, it's still most prevalent in the trucking industry. There's general agreement that airlines haven't yet found much use for satellite technology in the area freight tracking.

Cost is one reason that companies hold off on implementing satellite technology. Units reportedly can range as high as $5000 (per truck) including installation. Communication charges can be as high as $80 to $90 per unit per month. Most involved in the satellite or cellular markets are convinced the costs will come down as the technology improves. And they are convinced that all sorts of industries, even pipeline manufacturers, will want to take advantage of satellite technology.

Here's some of the ways that companies are using satellite technology:

- *Tracking.* Whether the issue is locating a railcar, a truck or a container onboard a steamship, satellite technology can be used to both locate the equipment in question and then transmit information on that location in almost real-time.
- *Tracing.* Satellites can provide constant positioning reports, producing historical data that allows transport companies and shippers to be able to trace the course of a shipment and determine what went right and what went wrong.

- *Monitoring for command and control.* Satellites can monitor all kinds of details that affect a shipment, including temperature and pressure changes that are crucial to refrigerated items or chemicals, and/or can indicate possible equipment malfunctions. Information can be relayed in almost real-time to dispatchers and drivers, for example, and adjustments made while a shipment is *en route*. Technology is being developed to allow some adjustments to be made remotely.
- *Inventory management and reduction.* Roberts Express has found that being able to access information in close to real time helps with inventory reduction. Information that satellites provide allows Roberts Express to be "integrated at both ends of the shipment," according to a Roberts spokesman.
- *Fleet control, productivity and maintenance.* Whether it's a truck company, steamship line or railroad, satellite technology can pinpoint the location of equipment, determine whether it's moving according to the designated path and take corrective action if there's a problem – all essential components of fleet management.
- *Payroll.* Telecommunication companies are reportedly utilizing satellite communication to gain payroll information from their drivers and then integrate that data with general payroll records, according to an American Mobile Satellite spokesman. For example, the number of hours logged on the road can be transmitted directly from the cab to the payroll department.
- *Security.* The same close-to-real-time messaging capabilities can be applied to security measures. Satellite allows carriers to tell where trucks are at all times. In more dramatic circumstances, satellite technology allowed Skyway Freight officials to intervene in a hijacking.[2]

The immigration to a networked, B2B transport/logistics world

Either be an e-business, or go out of business is the sort of message tech-trending transportation and logistics companies are hearing at conferences, work shops and magazines.

Whether you are a transport/logistics professional, or are managing a company or institution that depends on shipping goods and products, you must feel the bombardment of this message and feel overwhelmed by it. And you will be experiencing resistance from employees.

Resistance or no, tech trenders best start organizing to meet the demands of a networked, B2B world right now. The B2B-based economy is already placing heavy demand on tech-trending transport/logistics operations. Analysts predict there will be over a million workers involved in fulfilling e-commerce orders by 2003.

The good news from software vendors and experts in your field, alike, is that conversion doesn't have to happen all at once. In the transport/logistics scene making the transition will involve many changes along what is now the supply chain – from warehousing practices to distribution sites, transportation and overall management of what will become the supply network.

The eventual goal, just about everyone agrees, is to create seamless communication throughout the supply network. And as tech-trending organizations, you know your transport/ logistics operations – whether in-house or outsourced – sit squarely in the middle of that network. In fact, companies like Nortel Networks have reorganized to place their global logistics operation in the middle of concentric business operations (see Chapter 2) while still promoting core competencies that keep them competitive.

SOLUTIONS

Nortel promotes core competencies

As noted in Chapter 2 (boxed section, p. 99), Nortel Networks Global Logistics has evolved a customer-centered logistics operation. But even with all the focus on organization and networked communication, Nortel managers believe that tech trenders like you can't forget an emphasis on what they call core business competencies that must function to keep the system afloat.

These competencies involve everything from building trust throughout the network to developing a comprehension global payables system, adherence to international standards and regulation, having the right technology in place, and the promotion of key management skills such as communication. Here are some details on how Nortel Networks handles everything from payables to transportation alliances:

- *Global logistics payables.* Nortel Networks is currently developing a program to allow global bill payment anywhere worldwide. They have a centralized system that now covers all of North and South America and Asia, and are in the process of implementing Europe. The real objective is to tear down geographic barriers and extend our process throughout the world.
- *Global transportation programs.* Transportation is no longer regionally bound. The Nortel Logistics International Alliances Program has been set up for this purpose and now involves 10 partners who cover the globe for Nortel Networks.
- *Compliance strategies.* The company has a very active global compliance strategy in place to make sure we're in regulatory assurance with all major trading countries. They have organizations, systems and processes supporting these processes.
- *Technology and human communication.* Nortel Networks utilizes a wide variety of technology from the Internet to EDI, but managers are aware that human information flow is important too. They recognize that communication is key to a smooth-flowing supply chain, especially a global supply chain which involves so many internal and external players.
- *Management.* Flawless execution in a system based on third-party providers means locating the best-skilled people globally to manage relationships between all network parties. It also means constant work on integrating alliance partners. To this end there are about 200 staff who just focus on resolving global management issues.[3]

Talking about seamless communication is one thing and accomplishing this goal is quite another – and the meat of later sections of this book. Basically, to develop a networked/B2B, transport/logistics operation means adopting new business models that will integrate a number of players. In effect, brand owners, knowledge brokers, program managers, global distribution operators, capital providers, sourcing agencies, and innovation houses will be integrated with internal supply-chain management operations. An integrated view of planning, execution, and support processes is essential.

Some experts define the new business model as having the sense and ability to respond to the opportunities and requirements of the marketplace while allowing tech trenders to stay focused on what makes sense for your operation and for your customers. Sharing information and collaborating with trading partners, customers and even competitors, is one of those major shifts in values that must take place for smooth-running transport/logistics operations to contribute to efficient supply networks. Besides learning to share information, tech trenders have to develop modular, changeable business processes that may very well upturn the hierarchical aspects of your businesses and organizations (see Chapter 5).

Developing an attractive Web site matters, but getting your human operation in order matters more. You must make sure all functions, from picking to replenishment, are functioning in top-notch fashion without technological intervention. And get rid of extra inventory. If you don't know what you have in stock in a three-dimensional world, you certainly won't know how to translate that stock to a virtual world.

On the management side, the experts are saying that more and more you have to align your logistics operations with the rest of your organization. It's essential to integrate logistics in corporate planning, rather than see it as an afterthought. And there must be accountability throughout the organization for logistics, starting with the CEO and CFO.

Start thinking in terms of what it means to function in a networked, B2B world. And start taking into consideration the issues that working online creates. This is a virtual world where you have very little idea of who is seeing offerings you place over the Internet. There is no history to rely upon – or demand patterns – which makes forecasting so difficult. Once again, it's time to go to the drawing board to address ways of forecasting in this sort of environment.

APPLICATIONS

Information sharing key to inventory management

In the not-too-distant past, when a retailer like Macy's sold a brand-name shirt, the buyers might not put in for a reorder until store inventories had become visibly low. Imagine that this one type of men's white shirt becomes a hot seller, not just in one Macy's, but in stores across the world. But the manufacturer has no idea that this one shirt is selling so well. He hasn't geared up to make this item and when reorders come in he has trouble meeting demand.

With the introduction of technology it's now possible to vastly fine-tune the inventory management process. Inventory counts can be made electronically right at the Macy's checkout counter. This means that the manufacturer can keep tabs on sales daily, if there's a need. Those involved in promoting these sorts of inventory control processes know that the continuous flow of information and information sharing are key to success. That's particularly crucial with the manufacturer, warehouse and retailer now tied in electronically and information flows so quickly.

It's great for manufacturers to be able to start producing hot items in real-time rather than twiddling their thumbs for weeks and weeks. But they'd rather not be producing the wrong item.[4]

Transport companies are already reorganizing and adopting new business strategies to meet the demands of the growing B2B economy. Some are contemplating creating private, dedicated fleets to handle the demand of large customers. On the logistics side, the transition to a networked, B2B world is raising havoc in many warehouses. There is less storage, more orders, value-added services, more consumer-specific SKUs, smaller order sizes, and more customization. Given that small warehouses tend to be more efficient than large ones, one way around this transitional dilemma is to carve your large warehouse into smaller sections.[5]

The fledgling transport/logistics dot.com world

In recent months there's been a surge of venture capital that's gone into creating somewhere between 40 and 100 transport/ logistics dot.com businesses. These are services that aim to bring together potential buyers and sellers of just about everything from logistics to cargo services. Given that this world is in its infancy, no business model has yet emerged that can be taken as the standard. Besides lack of startup capital, questions abound on the legal side involving the potential for software patent infringement, and who has to pay software-licensing fees.

The software issue is particularly problematic because a number of the new services are actually emerging from software companies. They are no longer selling just software, but Web-based services. These include public and private marketplaces, software provided on an application service provider (ASP) basis, and even news content and services designed to make customers behave like a business "community" online. Other companies that started as online marketplaces are being swallowed up into a software service universe where online load-matching and rate negotiation are among the offerings.[7]

Only the strongest of the transport/logistics dot.coms are expected to survive the fallout of the market drop in the spring of 2000. Although all signs are that the venture capital party is over for this sector, that isn't to say that money has dried up entirely

SOUND BYTES

Is the venture capital party over for transport/logistics dot.coms?

The analysts are mixed on how many dot.coms will survive the market drop of spring 2000. Some say only the biggies – three to four – will be offering dot.com services in the next few years, while others hazard that niche players still have a chance of making a go of luring customers onto their sites. Investment analysts say there's plenty of money still available for strong niche players, with five or so surviving in the various niches that range from trucking exchanges to tariff and customs management. Firms are still investing in mid-to-later-stage rounds of financing in firms they believe to be winners.

The reason is that there are many different facets of transportation and logistics addressed by these new Internet companies, and the jury is still very much out as to whether we will have a few companies providing all types of services related to supply-chain management, or whether there will be a larger number of best-in-class companies providing niche services. However, there's general accord that it would be difficult to start an e-transport or e-logistics company from scratch today and expect pure venture capital package. That's because they say there are so many models in existence and venture capitalists are trying to decide which model they like and will back.[6]

for those companies that are fairly well established. Analysts agree that for several years to come money will be near scarce for anyone in the proposal or even early startup phases. Expect to see lots of consolidation among general and niche players, alike. Where the experts disagree is how the estimated 100 or so players currently active in the market will fare.

SOLUTIONS

How transport/logistics dot.coms can become effective

More and more carriers and shippers are providing Web-based services including rates and ordering, but getting customers to use their Web sites is still problematic. Industry analysts believe a big part of the problem is the fact that the majority of shippers don't know how transportation exchanges actually work. You'll still hear the refrain, "We have good relationships with our core carriers, so why bother with an online exchange?"

The experts say what these shippers are missing is that exchanges offer them the ability to communicate with your trading partners via the Web. The bidding is secondary. Exchanges allow shippers and their customers to tender loads electronically, track loads, pay carriers and reduce auditing.

But customers, in this case the carriers or trucking companies, won't join exchanges unless they have proof it will increase or improve their business. Exchanges like freightquote.com are reportedly gaining in popularity because they show both pricing and transit time. Carriers don't simply want the cheapest deal but the fastest, so freightquote.com is singing their song. The fact that they also handle front-end sales and marketing, customer service and administrative work such as filling out bills of lading for shippers – making them a single point of contact – has increased the appeal of this exchange.[8]

What the analysts do believe is that raising venture capital, amassing corporate backers and targeting the right market are essential to dot.com survival. Companies like Celarix and Logistics.com have raised in excess of $30–60 million in venture capital. An estimated $100 million is considered necessary to take a new business to profitability. Having a strong market focus is also considered key to making it in this hot new field, especially as there isn't much of a track record for how customers will react and whether they'll even go online to do their business.

Some analysts say that to be a winner the dot.coms have to provide full supply-chain services.

In the meantime, the move among the new transport/logistics dot.coms to consolidate is already taking place as they scramble to handle multiple services and multiple transport modes in a hurry to make themselves as strong as possible. There's been a rush to buy up companies that allow access to long-term customers while still functioning in the "spot market."

The dot.com analysts don't expect much change in this general course for the next year or two. As for transportation companies developing their own dot.coms, it's generally believed they don't have a chance of succeeding because transport companies lack the knowledge, the resources or agility to move onto the Web. Most of them will end up partnering with dot.com startups with these sorts of service offerings already in place. Or they may outsource (see below).[9]

APPLICATIONS

To outsource or not outsource

Companies assessing whether to start their own transport/logistics dot.coms are confronted with the choice of building their own infrastructure or outsourcing. The rule of thumb is if you handle less than 1000 orders a day you might consider building your own. But those organizations with 1000-plus orders a day best seek out third-parties with fulfillment expertise. In fact, if fulfillment isn't a core competency – which it isn't for many in the shipping side of the industry – then outsourcing makes the most sense. Many companies are outsourcing the entire back end of their e-commerce sites, from order to delivery.

There are a number of third-party service providers ranging from those who construct physical dot.com infrastructures, to technology providers and integrators. Others handle inventory management, physical management and transportation matters, distribution. Here are a few examples:

Connextions.net handles distribution – from order taking to fulfillment – for a variety of customers. For example, a coffee and tea outfit hired Connextions.net to handle distribution for all locations. When a customer places an order for coffee it goes straight into Connextions.net order entry system through a direct DSL line. It's picked from inventory and then shipped. The coffee and tea outfit has complete visibility of all sales, inventory and any other pertinent information.

Submitorder.com offers a complete business model for e-commerce companies. All they have to have is a Web site and some products. Submitorder.com has distribution centers, customer call centers, and IT integration information services. For example, they reportedly offer automatic inventory stock updates handled through their Web site.[10]

The emerging ITS, networked vehicle world

As tech-trending professionals, imagine a world where a small plastic box fitted to your car or truck ceiling – a piece of equipment called a transponder or "tag" – allows you tech trenders to drive through toll booth plazas without paying. Trucks fixed with transponders can breeze by weigh stations and gain pre-clearance at state crossings. This same tag fitted with "smart card" sort of credit information will allow you to operate in mass transit systems nationwide and can even be used to purchase food at highway stops. Thanks to this same sort of technology you will be able to cross borders without stopping. And tags fixed to containers and packages will be able to be read with a flick of a radio frequency (RF) gun aimed across a warehouse, providing tech trenders instantaneous identification of packages and containers.

Enter the world of intelligent transportation systems (ITS). ITS is the catch-all phrase for an array of operations that are made possible with the combined use of radio-frequency technology, computers and sophisticated bar codes. Already, manufacturers are experimenting with ITS, coupled with cellular and other technologies like GPS for global satellite positioning, so that large amounts of data can be picked up while *en route*, or relayed to various destinations. Combine ITS with telematic platforms in networked vehicles, and it will be possible to download advanced and detailed navigation information at gas stations, toll booths and just about anywhere your vehicle will be traveling.

From more efficient warehousing and tracking of everything from raw materials to containers, faster and more efficient toll collection, improved highway safety, traveler information, and navigation equipment, there seem to be no limits to the way ITS applications can promote supply-chain movement. For these reasons, government officials and business leaders, alike, are pinning high hopes on ITS for promoting trade in a networked world. The reason is speed and ease of tracking and tracing goods – both raw materials and packages – while *en route* to consumers, retailers and manufacturers. There's even hope that ITS will boost international trade as it offers the option – when coupled with x-ray equipment – for pre-cleared crossings at international borders.

Nowadays, ITS is mainly used for toll collection or in warehouses for inventory management. An estimated 40,000 trucks are now equipped with transponders, or small plastic boxes that relay information to roadside readers for functions like electronic toll collection. The federal Department of Transportation (DOT) says that figure could grow to 750,000 for long-haul truckers in the next five to ten years. The estimated market for general transponder use, which includes short-haul trucks and cars, is 40 million over that same timeframe.

A lot of work is also taking place utilizing ITS to better manage traffic flow on highways and bridges. Moving trucks along highways without having to stop for routine safety checks and weighing is a major concern for tech-trending companies and government officials, alike. Everyone wants to speed along shipments in the safest fashion possible. Providing a means for diagnosing maintenance issues before a truck breaks down is another way that ITS will keep your tech-trending company competitive.

TECH VISIONS

ITS expected to boost NAFTA trade

US, Canadian and Mexican officials are experimenting with an array of ITS functions that could one day make crossing NAFTA borders both quicker and safer. For example, American officials are exploring new wireless applications that integrate GPS and ITS and allow relay of information on a vehicle long before arrival at the actual border crossing. The aim is to allow pre-clearance so drivers with clear records won't need to be inspected unless custom agents think an inspection is warranted.

On the Canadian border, the NAFTA Land Transportation Subcommittee is exploring opening up a corridor between New York and Montreal to relieve trade crossings at Detroit, Buffalo and Niagara Falls. ITS will be key to speeding up traffic while giving this effort a definite safety focus. Earlier efforts have been more on relieving congestion than on safety. ITS offers the opportunity to collect a great deal of data on shipments, carriers and drivers.

Much of this work fits the US government's vision of a seamless transportation system throughout the western hemisphere where trucks, and passengers, can travel without stopping at borders for customs, safety checks and any other clearance. Tech trenders will be able to ship goods from Mexico City to Vancouver seamlessly, meaning you don't stop at borders, you don't need to be stopped to be weighed or even inspected. Although much of the work of implanting ITS at border crossings is still in the talk stages, officials from the US, Mexico and Canada predict that these activities will increase with the passage of the 1999 Motor Carrier Safety Improvement Act of 1999.[11]

And many highway pre-clearance operations – including safety checks and weigh-in-motion – are becoming automated thanks to ITS. Officials at the Intermodal Freight at the Office of Freight Management and Operations of the Federal Highway Administration (FHWA) are also exploring setting up advisory boards along major corridors to create interoperable technology use along stretches like I-35 from Mexico to Canada. Part of the purpose is to make it possible for officials to conduct non-invasive vehicle diagnosis along an I-35 or I-95. Sensors planted on an engine will be able to read major vehicle maintenance concerns and read them at high speeds. This will provide the means for real-time diagnosis that can be relayed to a fleet's maintenance facilities.

Researchers at the University of Texas are exploring what they call ITS "checkpoint passes." Employing ITS, carriers get verification when one of their trucks goes past a particular checkpoint. The idea isn't to check on the driver, but gain real-time information on a shipment's progress. Coupling ITS and GPS radar capabilities is just another means being explored for tracking trucks or containers *en route* to their destinations, and providing routine maintenance checks before major problems evolve.

The technology exists today to employ ITS to speed goods along highways and in far safer fashion, while providing all parties to the supply network with instantaneous information on shipment time, condition of the goods and of the vehicle in question. Political, bureaucratic and financial issues have to be resolved before ITS can be utilized to develop truly intelligent highways. Government officials at FHWA are hoping that market pressures from companies like yours will move things along.[12]

APPLICATIONS

Commercial uses for ITS

Drivers no longer have to pay at the pump at Shell stations in American cities like Cincinnati, Ohio and Indianapolis, Shell's new EasyPay program allows for drive-through payment using the same toll tags employed for drive-through toll collection.

At McDonald's franchises in Southern California customers don't have to ante up when they purchase a Big Mac and fries. Utilizing a similar system as EasyPay, McDonald's customers in this region will be able to use their toll tags to make drive-through purchases.

These examples represent some of the first efforts in the US to utilize ITS to promote commercial interests. And this is just the beginning of ways that gasoline and food franchises envision using ITS. From drive-through payment at the pumps, for example, Shell is considering using ITS to create drive-through parking capabilities. Part of the motive is to promote faster sales, but Shell officials mainly view ITS as a means of boosting sales of other products and services.

Three or four years from now, company representatives imagine completely changing the drive-through environment at a service station. They plan to be able to talk to customers over a voice net that will be able to track their preferences and payments and generally make things easier for them. They'll provide you with everything from a car wash to a sandwich and meet all your tech-trending personal needs.

Besides becoming services providers, companies like Shell envision creating electronic commerce alliances to provide transactions right at the pump. The oil giant, in conjunction with Texaco, is developing all sorts of goodies for the high-end car owner, or lease company, once networking of automobiles is complete. These include at-the-pump diagnostics, the ability to download DVD or video games to kids, or even offer auto insurance and tires while robots pump gas.[13]

ITS facing critical technology juncture

Some key technology issues need to be resolved for ITS to really achieve its promise for improving trade and shipping in a networked, Web-based world. In fact, at this writing, ITS technology is at a critical juncture. The US Congress has mandated creation of a national, interoperable ITS system (see Tech visions box below) where one transponder can be utilized for a wide variety of functions and throughout the country. How to make that happen is the cause of a major debate between the government and ITS equipment manufacturers and will affect expenditures for tech-trending companies like yours.

Most ITS experts and some government officials are pushing development of future equipment to a new 5.9 gigahertz (GHz) bandwidth that the Federal Communication Commission (FCC) allotted for ITS in the fall of 1999. According to experts, the new band allows for far greater applications than the lower bandwidth formerly used for ITS functions. For example, the higher frequency would allow one transponder to handle messaging for everything from toll collection to e-mail downloads.

Unfortunately, moving in the 5.9 direction means developing standardized technology that doesn't exist today. For that reason it will be several years, at the very least, before products can be deployed to this new bandwidth. The US DOT has proposed a middle-of-the road approach that allows for interoperability to some functions like toll collection and can serve as a transition to the 5.9 approach. As of this writing, some equipment vendors appear ready to work in this interim fashion.[15]

TECH VISIONS

A national interoperable system?

At this juncture, there are a number of ITS-based toll operations throughout this country and the world, each utilizing different equipment. A trucker traveling from the Northeast to Florida and from Florida to California and then Oregon would have to carry as many as four transponders to participate in electronic toll collection.

Under the so-called "Tea-21" legislation (Transportation Equity Act for the 21st Century), the government is calling for standardization of ITS. The aim, according to officials at the Federal Highway Administration (FHWA), is improved highway safety and efficient toll collection. To this end, about 80 standards relating to intelligent transport are now in the works relating to 30 user services – including those serving traffic management, air, traveler information, incident management, and others.

Utilizing standards developers such as the Society for Automotive Engineers (SAE) and American Society for Testing Materials (ASTM), the DOT is pushing hard to create standards that will be the backbone of a national, interoperable ITS that Congress has mandated. In all, it's expected that 100 standards will come out of the hopper and affect the sort of equipment that both commercial vehicles and travelers use.

The concept behind a national interoperable ITS system is great – one transponder per vehicle, reduced truck stops on the highway, easier toll clearance and improved safety. But the "getting there" has been strewn with battles over technology and manufacturers' market share, not to mention service providers fighting over turf. In fact, the DOT's activities have kicked up firestorms from Florida to Oregon, and even have the Europeans up in arms because the standards the US is promoting do not match theirs (see the section below on international ITS issues). The problem is that the DOT has come into this picture at a time when differing ITS technologies are embedded in various regions of the country, and even the world. That means that DOT is bucking entrenched interest groups intent on protecting their technology investments and markets.

Tech trenders like you are caught in the middle. On the one hand, a truck fleet must purchase a variety of transponders to cover long-haul routes. Moving to a national interoperable system will allow them to use one transponder, but that also means replacing existing equipment. Manufacturers of ITS equipment and toll authorities have even more at stake. Whichever way the government moves on ITS standardization, some manufacturers may find their products are obsolete. Toll authorities may have to rebuild toll plazas to accommodate the change.[14]

Whether one transponder can eventually meet all applications depends, in part, on how electronics will be networked within vehicles. Some experts believe there will be one transponder eventually, but your navigation system will be different from your security system. The key, they say, is creating an interface between ITS and IDB – intelligent transportation systems data bus – technology that's used to network electronic functions in vehicles.

Others believe the technology is there to handle all your tech-trending needs – from inventory management to speedier,

SOUND BYTES

US standards committee pushing easier Internet connectivity

Connecting intelligent transport systems (ITS) to the Internet may be easier in the future, as will be networking cars, but it's questionable that the world will see a global ITS standard any time soon.

That's the word from standards developers emerging from meetings in Santa Barbara, California on January 24 and 25, where the first round of votes from a working group designated to develop a US standard for ITS indicates most support for a pre-existing Internet standard – the IEEE (Institute of Electrical and Electronic Engineers) 802.11a wireless Internet standard.

IEEE 802.11a is the favorite of telematics companies, like Belgium-based Acunia, that are working to network automobiles, as well as provide Internet access to vehicles. Options that are lagging in this first round include harmonizing with the Japanese or working with a Motorola concept called Freespace.

It will be at least four months before the working group makes a final decision on a US standard, according to Lee Armstrong, who is co-chair of the standards working group. A final round will take place "as soon as the group feels they are ready to do so."

He says the ballot results were as follows: 11 votes for the 802.11a proposal, 8 for the Motorola Freespace proposal, and 6 for the Shared Band proposal (harmonize with the Japanese). "The Manufacturer's Consortium all voted for Freespace. By this vote, we will not be harmonizing with the Japanese and will be striking out into new directions for future DSRC, by using either Freespace or 802.11a," according to Armstrong.

Each choice means building to the new 5.9 GHz bandwidth – the bandwidth that the Federal Communications Commission (FCC) allocated for ITS use in the fall of 1999. And each would greatly alter the current design for transponders, which are the devices currently used to transmit short-range messaging from vehicles to toll booths or from truck cabs to highway weigh stations. In fact, experts say this new direction will alter the concept of dedicated short-range communication (DSRC), which is the technology underlying transponder design.

safer shipments – but what are standing in the way are competing business interests and entrenched regional bureaucracies that have already bought into earlier ITS technologies. To really promote ITS properly and create a national interoperable system, this camp argues that transponders should be implanted directly into vehicles upon manufacture. The auto industry is game, but not unless they is a large user population. Commercial entities like gasoline companies and highway food vendors could also drive transponder use, but are also

SOUND BYTES

Cell phone connection not yet a plug in

Despite a lot of talk and enthusiasm centering around moving ITS from toll collection into the Internet age by coupling ITS with cell phone technology, current vendors say they aren't prepared to make that move at this time. Companies like Mark IV and Amtech Systems Division of Intermec – now part of Transcore, Inc – say there's no live interest in coupling ITS with cellular technology to allow for Internet access at toll booths and other places, like highway weigh stations. In fact, much of the discussion of coupling cell phone technology with ITS is coming from telecommunications experts within the general ITS community.[16]

capable of destroying interoperable efforts if they promote their own proprietary technology.[17]

PLATFORMS

International ITS issues

From developing a global transponder to relay information, to vehicle warning and control systems, to map databases, application interfaces map publishing and message sets there's all sorts of work taking place on the ITS front. Here's a quick walkthrough of some of the work taking place to create globally harmonized ITS technology:

1 *New directions for transponders.* Thanks to the emergence of the new 5.9 GHz bandwidth, the potential for developing intelligent transportation system (ITS) products that can function both in the US and the European Union (EU) appears to be on the horizon for the first time. Japan has already been developing standards to this frequency, but American vendors consider the Japanese approach costly.

European ITS officials, who expect to provide new standards for transponder design in 2001, are eager for the US to adopt the 5.9 GHz approach, as that would allow compatibility for many functions. But a decision by the US to adopt the 5.9 GHz direction may not entirely lay to rest US/EU bickering over ITS, much of which is economically and politically motivated.

US standards developers have contended that although serviceable, the European approach to ITS standardization is limited to electronic toll collection. Standards officials like Lee Armstrong, a Boston-based consultant who heads up US ITS standards work in international committees, says the European standards don't meet American needs to develop a national interoperable ITS system. And he and others in the US take umbrage at European efforts to promote their standards in overseas markets at the expense of the US approach.

Europeans, on the other hand, believe their ITS standards function just fine and don't care that the more sophisticated US technology provides more bells and whistles than what the Europeans are producing. They are pleased to see their ITS standards being adopted in countries like Australia, Malaysia and Brazil, which means increased market share for EU vendors.

2 *Providing global navigation standards.* The International Organization for Standardization's (ISO) Technical Committee (TC) 204 is working on a number of standards to promote global ITS interoperability and compatibility. Some of these foundations aren't sexy from a technological viewpoint. Things like data registries won't get your adrenaline flowing but they will help you when you want to work more efficiently in global market.

   TC 204 is focusing a lot of attention on standardizing message sets, so navigation information can be played in any language and displayed on any computer screen in the world. They also want to make navigation systems for vehicles interoperable and provide compatible ways for manufacturers to provide accurate location references. This is far trickier than it might seem as many locations are listed differently from one printed map, or reference location, to another. Being able to update navigation locations while on the fly is another goal, as well as harmonizing approaches for publishers like AAA and Rand-McNally to produce navigation information for all vehicles.[18]

Networked vehicles rolling into reality

The days are not far off when tech-trending drivers will be able to reach for a button or switch on the steering wheel and activate in-cab navigation equipment without reaching halfway across the cab to do so. Stopping for the night, this same driver will be able to turn his cab into a "home" entertainment center with drop-down video screens and music at his or her fingertips.

This sort of plug-and-play capacity is being developed through IDB, which was mentioned in the last section. The "bus" in the title stands for an electronic network, not the vehicle for transporting passengers. IDB technology provides interconnectivity and networking capabilities for better integration of equipment in a vehicle. By 2005, vehicles will be manufactured with navigation and traffic-information systems that have plug-and-play capabilities and with greater functionality than those on the market today.

For example, a car or truck may have a pager in it that will allow drivers to unlock the doors remotely in the event keys have been locked in. The same pager will allow for remote starting in a far easier fashion than today. And IDB technology is supposed to promote development of navigation systems that will tell you the location, read the fuel levels and tell you – based on fuel consumption – how far you can go. They will actually route you right in to a gas station that's closest.

IDB addresses safety concerns, as well, which is one reason the government has been backing IDB technology development. As the call for congressional hearings in the US on cell phone uses in cars and navigation equipment indicate, there is concern to better integrate these devices in vehicles for safety reasons. There's even been talk of banning current products from vehicles, altogether. At 70 mph the last thing any of you want is to be fumbling with a navigation device. The current systems are mounted three feet away and 18 inches from the instrument panel. The reach is difficult and the voice prompts are hard to hear. Current devices aren't integrated into a vehicle.[19]

SOLUTIONS

IDB standards under development

Work on IDB technology has been ongoing since 1996 under the auspices of the Society of Automotive Engines, which has been issued $185,000 in FHWA funds for IDB standards development as part of a larger effort to create a national, interoperable ITS system. SAE is developing a family of standards to create an open architecture to allow electronics to be implemented easily into vehicles. This would mean taking anyone's device and incorporating it into anyone's vehicle. Standards have been rolling out for over a year or so, so it won't be too long before you tech trenders will see networked vehicles on the highway and for your corporate use.[20]

Telematics provide in-vehicle data processing

Navigation devices for vehicles already exist that can pinpoint locations and some services even connect drivers to operators who provide directions. The next-generation navigators don't simply provide Internet connection for quick information download, but the ability to process information so humans are removed from the link.

For example, a driver is lost in Detroit. His new navigation system will provide location and directions without human intervention, and even remote diagnostics in the event of a breakdown.

This sort of technology falls under the category of telematic platforms for vehicles. Cutting-edge telematics manufacturers don't simply want to place Internet connections in vehicles, which they consider old-hat even though most of you tech trenders don't yet have the capability to download e-mail while on the road. The real visionaries want to provide drivers with the ability to process information while *en route* using a relatively new technology called "intelligent agents." This would allow you to get information, coupled with functionality, and massage them into your specific needs.

The telematics market is growing sufficiently to warrant surveys and symposiums. It involves consumer products, services and supporting systems that deliver information, communications and entertainment to vehicles and mobile devices. International Data Corp. (IDC) estimates the telematic markets will grow from $1 billion in 1998 to $42 billion in 2010. Ford Motor Co. has projected that virtually all its cars and trucks will be equipped with some telematics by 2004.

Some companies are exploring combining a pot-pourri of technologies, including cellular for point-to-point connections, long-range broadcasting technology like that employed in digital radios and ITS. These combinations would provide what they call "synergies." For example, you would be able to download a DVD movie for the kids, or download your e-mail while driving through a toll-booth.[22]

APPLICATIONS

Priming vehicles for e-commerce

In the future, tech trenders will get plenty of work done while sitting in gridlock. The visionaries see each automobile or truck, equipped with onboard computers with the screen easily visible and accessible. You will have the same capabilities in your vehicles as a desktop computer in a home or office. Internet capabilities and a fully-networked car will mean having the capabilities to download information and carrying on interactive activities such as e-commerce purchases.

Not surprisingly, with these sorts of capabilities, commercial entities are itching to turn your vehicle into an instant e-commerce purchasing center with at least three marketing segments – driver, passenger and back-seat area, described as the "entertainment center." Each individual, when occupying each segment, has different needs or interests. For example, drivers will be concerned with automobile upkeep and maintenance, and would welcome information at their fingertips about the wear and tear of the vehicle. They would then be primed to purchase items, such as tires or insurance.

Passengers, in the meantime, are considered very different people. Usually the passenger handles navigation. They may want to download a map of the area (while waiting for gas to pump).

And those in the back seat, especially children, may be interested in renting items like tapes or DVDs. Instead of buying a game for an onboard game machine they may want to rent a game for $5 or so. They'll be able to download the game and charge it, or be issued a token that terminates the game by a mileage or time counter.

If you don't drive a Mercedes or Cadillac, don't expect to experience any of these advancements for at least a decade. Apparently, there's little interest or market penetration of information technology to the lower-end economic levels.[21]

APPLICATIONS

Technology is pushing a new business model

E-commerce won't enter your vehicle, or become a competitive tool in transport, without the evolution of new business models. Already, oil companies like Shell are envisioning cooperative arrangements – called electronic coupled affinity – to offer additional services to tech trenders while *en route* to business and other destinations. This translates into creating alliances with service providers and merchandisers of the sort that credit-card companies maintain. You buy my gasoline and I'll subsidize your hamburgers or dry cleaning, for example.

Because all drivers need to gas up on average of once a week, market researchers at companies like Shell believes gas stations are natural locations for the purchase of both information and products. As they describe it, the car becomes a node on an electronic commerce network and the gas pump becomes the dock which provides the time efficiency that drives e-commerce.

Companies driving development of networked cars – like Belgium-based Acunia – are also pushing new business models. Acunia won't sell directly to consumers, but considers itself a "business-to-business company." The aim is to turn interested parties – whether car manufacturers, insurance companies or cell phone operators – into service providers. In the future, insurers may sell pay-as-you-go insurance that can be purchased online right in the vehicle.

Much as cell phone providers make their profits on service contracts not equipment, Acunia managers are finding the major auto companies contemplating the same approach. They will still sell cars, but a certain profit share will come from providing remote auto diagnostics or traveler information. That's because car manufacturers see future profits in becoming the service provider and connecting link for some services.[23]

In-vehicle computing opening tech-trending opportunities

In-vehicle computing, also called mobile device computing when coupled with wireless technologies, allows two radios to send signals back and forth using each other's networks. In some instances – the Blue Tooth technologies, for example – these wireless connections are coupled with technology that allows various devices to interface, self-discover and auto configure much the same way a PC computer automatically reads and installs CD information.

There are different types of in-vehicle computing that work in different ways. When coupled with other transmission technologies like satellite, radio frequency and dedicated short-range communication (DSRC), in-vehicle computing can take place from a variety of distances, and transmission can be triggered in a variety of ways. For example, digital announcement technologies work for transit companies through the combination of in-vehicle computers, a database of announcements and bus-stop locations, as well as the storage medium to store the database, namely PCMCIA cards.

A highly-specialized technology, experts say digital announcement technologies work in the opposite way from what people think. The in-vehicle computer stores all the announcements and all the bus-stop locations on the medium held on the bus through a PCMCIA card. Basically, once you put the card into the computer it has the capability of playing all the announcements. The GPS (global positioning system) equipment for remote positioning then determines the location, and that location is matched with the data in the card.

For instance, school bus companies that deploy their fleet for non-school purposes in the summertime find this sort of technology helpful when they want to change routes or schedules from summer to fall and need to update their databases. Using what's called a "spread spectrum radio" built right into a PCMCIA card, the driver can download new route or schedule information when it arrives at the depot for gas service or oil change.

APPLICATIONS

In-vehicle computing in action

One afternoon the vice president of Hollywood Car Carrier in Los Angeles, was sitting in the office with his drivers when they saw one of their tow trucks zoom off the lot. Using remote programming technology, he was able to keep an eye on the vehicle from his office and tell the police exactly where it was at all times, via his computer screen.

"Within 10 minutes, the thief was in the back seat of a police car, and our truck was returned to us unharmed," he reports, adding that in quieter times he uses the technology to track his fleet from his desk chair.

Remote programming technology can also be used to improve customer service in buses using a process called Automatic Vehicle Location (AVL). A customer already onboard a city bus wants to transfer to a different bus. The driver types information into the terminal about the route switch, the message is sent to a central computer and then messages back to the driver the new route and any other information pertinent to helping the customer make the switch. Simultaneously, the central computer alerts the other bus to stop at a specific location to pick up the customer. It can even alert parties to the time that will lapse.

This same sort of technology can provide automatic passenger counts on transit buses that correlate with fare-payment systems. And it can signal traffic lights – using a process called traffic signal preferential treatment – so a driver can change a traffic light to green as the vehicle approaches.

Another application involves helping truck, bus or road maintenance fleets monitor vehicle parts from remote locations. For example, this technology makes it possible to determine from a central office whether a snow plow blade is up or down, where the plow is located and other information pertinent to managing a far-flung fleet. And in logistics, remote programming technology can help companies connect trailers to warehouses for quicker relay of delivery or pickup information.[24]

Because of the potential for varied applications, the market for in-vehicle computing technology is vertical and highly specialized. A company who makes products for long-haul trucking may not have a product in a different niche. Some companies focus on waste disposal, taxis or secure cargo for South

America. And software developed to make remote programming applications work for one niche can't be applied to another.

For example, satellite communications giant Qualcomm, based in San Diego, CA, concentrates on providing long-haul fleet vehicles with AVL technologies and services. Companies like Linthicun, MD-based Orbital Sciences Corp. build products for fleets within a specific location. And Clever Devices, Ltd. of Syosset, NY, is known for providing GPS-triggered signs and announcements that would go on a bus indicating, for example, the next stop.

Coupling remote programming with Internet technology is already expanding applications, especially for smaller fleets that couldn't afford the $100,000 or more startup costs of traditional systems. Internet-based technology allows smaller fleets of 20–50 vehicles to access remote programming services. Internet technology is not as advanced as working directly with software packages, but it provides the advantage of ease of use and cost.

Companies like Clever Devices and Orbital Sciences are exploring the use of the Web to provide customers with remote-vehicle, data-monitoring services. Clever Devices, for example, is putting transit agencies on the Web so the company and passengers can track performance information. Orbital Science is working on helping carriers track loads and then being able to post that information on customers' personal Web sites. It's possible to view this technology in action – called ViaWeb – on www.wheresmyload.com.

Providing larger amounts of data access is a concern of Qualcomm, which envisions all sorts of uses for remote technology coupled with high-speed, high-capacity wireless technology. Downloading movies while *en route* to a destination or e-mail into a laptop while waiting in an airport would be feasible with this sort of technology combination.[25]

SOLUTIONS

Alternative in-vehicle computing uses

Combine remote programming technology with satellite and cellular and all sorts of applications emerge. Qualcomm, for example, has technology that can be embedded in handsets, laptops, notebooks and other fixed, portable and mobile devices. It can support e-mail, Web browsing, e-commerce, telematics and many other applications. The following are examples of the wide variety of applications for these technology combinations:

Routed delivery
- Armored car service
- Auto parts supply
- Beverage distribution
- Chemicals and allied product
- Consumer products wholesale
- Corrugated and solid fiber boxes
- Florist and wholesale flower supply
- Furniture retail of manufacturer
- General line groceries
- General warehousing
- Medical and hospital equipment
- Petroleum products distribution
- Used merchandise stores
- Wholesale distribution
- Wholesale food/produce

Consumer service
- Auto repair shops
- Carpet and upholstery cleaning
- Electrical repair
- Home healthcare services
- Pest control
- Plumbing heating/air – residential
- Roofing repair
- Security systems
- TV broadcast systems

Commercial service
- Coin operated amusement, laundry, merchandising
- Elevators/moving stair construction and repair

On demand delivery/pick up services
- Air courier service
- Local trucking
- Medical
- Messenger

Construction
- Highway
- Electrical

Equipment/vehicle rental

Utility

Emergency response[26]

Bar codes moving from the warehouse to being key to a supply network

The lowly bar code, most commonly thought of at retail check-out locations or as a warehouse tool for tracking inventory, is becoming key to the functioning of a supply network. Bar codes are now coming in two-dimensional (2D) form – stacked, matrix, or dot technology – that allows for a far larger of amount of information to be implanted so that a product's history can be read at a glance. Couple this new type of bar code with intelligent chips, and that same level of information can be implanted on containers and packages for detailed tracking and tracing of materials.

When applied to a warehouse, 2D bar codes make it possible to encode more information on the package itself. Shippers can use 2D as a travelling database. Getting 2D bar code printing capabilities isn't hard. All the major manufacturers offer it. But widespread implementation of these codes has only started in the last year or so on shipping labels to obtain data that would traditionally be on a packing sheet or slip.

Experts agree that the use of radio frequency identification (RFID) and bar codes with smart labels – basically, labels with embedded programmable chips – will grow quickly because this combination allows for long-distance identification and tracking of products. With RF technology you don't have to line up a laser beam to read the codes. And the chips can contain unlimited information that won't take up any more room on a label than traditional bar codes. Further, data contained in the chip can be edited. The use? Let's say an order of commodity parts bound for one customer is re-routed at the last minute to another customer that needs the parts immediately, and will pay premium price to get them.

At the distribution center, the smart labels can be edited not only to reflect the change in destination, but also to reflect the new delivery date and price. Moreover, these smart labels are durable. They can be baked into plastic or frozen. So a chip with RFID capabilities can be embedded on a frozen-food container that's planted in a truck body to read information about the temperature and other conditions, allowing for a written history of the product during shipping.

TECH VISIONS

Future bar code trends

From new frequencies to composite bar codes and Internet access, there appears to be no end to up-and-coming bar code applications. The International Organization for Standardization (ISO) Subcommittee (SC) 31 of Joint Technical Committee 1 is working with the Universal Code Council and European Article Numbering Association to recommend a specific frequency for RFID as applied to logistics.

Imagine a truck travelling down a road with its own RF tag and containing pallets with their own RF tags and numbers. Standardization committees have to make sure roadside or portable readers can identify each of these tags individually. Standards developers are now discussing applications with users, manufacturers and scientists, trying to decide which are the best frequencies to standardize, an effort being duplicated on national levels.

Composite or combination codes are another area of interest for standardizers. According to experts, combining one-dimensional and two-dimensional bar codes will mean being able to read still more information than is now possible, and allows more information to be implanted. For example, a label on an apple will not just identify breed and state or origin, but date picked.

And the Internet is surfacing as the tool of the future to carry bar code applications for easy transmission of information. Some in industry envision running applications from the Internet – perhaps from a company's Web site – rather than on local computers. Besides speed, this approach can promote accuracy as customers will be able to direct the order process from their own computer systems.[28]

The applications for RFID range from implanting chips into shirt collars for easy identification in a laundry to more far-reaching uses in trucking and shipping. And chips implanted on trucks will allow for tracking of vehicles in truck yards or even *en route* through roadside transponders. The transponder is a separate piece of equipment that activates and reads the chip.

The international standards world is working on integrating computer hardware into bar code printers that will allow for integration with ERP business functions, and promote many new bar code functions to improve information flow throughout your global supply network.[27]

Notes

1 Some of this material is adapted from *Global Tool Kit: Supply Chain,* Amy Zuckerman, A–Z International Associates, Amherst, MA, 1999. Source is Keith Goldsmith, Director of Technology Services, CTI Logistx, Jacksonville, FL.

2 *Global Tool Kit: Supply Chain,* Amy Zuckerman, A–Z International Associates, Amherst, MA, 1999.

3 "Nortel Networks Global Logistics: Placing the Customer at the Center of the Global Spoke," Amy Zuckerman, *World Trade,* August 2000, pp. 60–62. John Lebowitz, vice president of Nortel Networks Global Logistics and Delia Caldwell, project leader for Logistics Communications, a subset of Nortel Networks Global Logistics, provided information.

4 *Global Tool Kit: Supply Chain,* Amy Zuckerman, A–Z International Associates, Amherst, MA, 1999.

5 Much of this section is based on August T & D, pp. 28–38, "Logistics Conquers a Brave New World," Mary Aichlmayr. Additional information source is Peter Schwartz, chairman and chief executive officer of Descartes Systems.

6 "Slow to Download," Amy Zuckerman, *Journal of Commerce,* August 21, 2000, p. 25.

7 "The Ever-Changing Business Model of a Transport Dot.Com," Helen Atkinson, *Journal of Commerce* online edition, June 23, 2000.
8 "Transportation Turns to Technology," Roger Morton, Management Editor, *Transportation & Distribution*, November 2000, pp. 36–40.
9 "Slow to Download," Amy Zuckerman, *Journal of Commerce*, August 21, 2000, p. 25. Sources include Izhar Armony, general partner at Charles River Ventures in Boston; Jeff Pribor, Managing Director for ING Baring's Transportation and Logistics Group; Jim Dowling, Managing Director of Shipping Finance at ING Barings, and Mark Lotke, Managing Director of Acquisition at ICG.
10 Adapted from "From Data to Delivery: Finding Fulfillment in E-Business," Mary Aichlmayr, assistant editor, *Transportation & Distribution*, November, 2000, p. dot.com3–dot.com10.
11 "Seamless Borders Nearing Reality," Amy Zuckerman, January 19, 2000, *Journal of Commerce* online archives. Sources are Dan Brady, Vice President at Transborder and Trade Corridor Systems in San Diego; Norman Schneider, who is Director of the Passenger and Freight Safety Division of the New York State Department of Transportation, and Fenton Carey, Associate Administrator for Innovation, Research and Education at the US Research and Special Programs Administration (RISPA).
12 "Turning Highways Into Warehouses," Amy Zuckerman, *Journal of Commerce* online archives, May 31, 2000.
13 "Personal Services," Amy Zuckerman, *Traffic Technology International*, June/July 2000, pp. 51–56. Sources are Jon Edmondson, head the Marketing Innovation Group, Shell Oil, Houston, Texas, and Joe Marsh, a Spring, Texas consultant to Equiva, the Shell/Texaco/ARAMCO alliance.
14 "Can National ITS Become a Reality?" Amy Zuckerman, *Journal of Commerce* online archives, May 3, 2000.

15 "A Whole New Game with 5.9 Bandwidth," Amy Zuckerman, *Journal of Commerce*, February 23, 2000, p. 10.

16 "ITS Manufacturers Will Go for 5.9 Standard," Amy Zuckerman, *Journal of Commerce* online archives, March 15, 2000.

17 "Intelligent Transport Sector Gears up for 5.9," Amy Zuckerman, *Journal of Commerce* online archives, March 15, 2000. Sources include Lee Armstrong, a Boston-based ITS standards consultant and Paul Najarian, Director of Telecommunications for ITS America.

18 "Can Europe and the U.S. Live in ITS Harmony?" Amy Zuckerman, *Electronic News* online archives, May 29, 2000; and "Global ITS Standards Efforts Pushing The Envelope on Worldwide Interoperability," (working title) Amy Zuckerman, *Traffic Technology International*, Fall 2000.

19 "Plug 'n' Play May Drive Trucks," Amy Zuckerman, *Journal of Commerce* online archives, December 1, 1999. Article source is Arlan Stehney, Executive Director of the IDB Forum in Pittsburgh, PA.

20 "Plug 'n' Play May Drive Trucks," Amy Zuckerman, *Journal of Commerce*, December 1, 1999. Article source is Arlan Stehney, executive director of the IDB Forum in Pittsburgh, PA.

21 "Personal Services," Amy Zuckerman, *Traffic Technology International*, June/July 2000, pp. 51–56. Joe Marsh, a Spring, Texas consultant to Equiva, the Shell/Texaco/ARAMCO alliance.

22 "Going Beyond 'Online' While En Route," Amy Zuckerman, *Journal of Commerce* online archives, May 10, 1999.

23 "Going Beyond 'Online' While En Route," Amy Zuckerman, *Journal of Commerce*, May 10, 1999. Source is Stephen Buytaert, president and CEO of Acunia, Inc.; and "Personal Services," Amy Zuckerman, *Traffic Technology International*, June/July 2000, pp. 51–56.

24 "Remote Programming Helping Transit Lines, Truck Fleets and the World Compete," Amy Zuckerman, *Supply Chain Technology News*, Fall 2000.
25 "In-vehicle Computing Helping Transit Lines, Truck Fleets and the World Compete," Amy Zuckerman, *Supply Chain Technology News*, Fall 2000. Source of information is Michael Dennis, telematics director at ITS America in Washington, DC. Rosalind McLymont conducted research.
26 List compiled by Rosalind McLymont.
27 "Belly Up to the Barcode," Amy Zuckerman, *Supply Chain Technology News*, September 2000.
28 "Belly Up to the Barcode," Amy Zuckerman, *Supply Chain Technology News*, September 2000.

4 Tracking Change: Tools the Experts Use to Monitor and Affect Technology Trends

Taking charge of your technology future means constantly monitoring technology trends that will affect your organization. There are a number of tools and resources available to tech trenders who want to keep up with the experts, be able to assess the analysts and stay ahead of the competition.

This chapter provides you with an insider's look at the analysts' trade. Tech trenders will learn about the tools they employ and the places where the experts go to get a heads up on technology developments. Those places range from corporations and institutions, to journals, technology user groups and conferences, and the lesser-known world of standards organizations and consortia.

Some tech trenders aren't content with keeping tabs on the trends alone. You want to have a say on future technology direction in your field, or actively participate in organizations that are developing technology. The standards and consortia section of this chapter is your guide to becoming a technology player rather than being a technology bystander.

What tech trenders should know about evaluating analysts

The global business community is hooked on analysts and

trends forecasters, but do they really offer valuable information you can use to make the decisions that will prepare you and your organization for the networked, B2B world? Can they help you track technology change? And what tricks of the trade can you borrow from the world of analysts?

Surveys conducted with chief information officers (CIOs), analysts and CEOs indicated a wide range of opinions on analysts. Some CIOs don't trust the major firms and consider them six months behind – no different from journalists, and only useful as the "storytellers" of the high-tech world. Other CIOs find the major companies useful for providing information on trends and in-depth knowledge of their importance. They listed the following analyst groups to be "pretty good," have a "good grasp," and to be "knowledgeable":

- The Gartner Group and the Meta Group, both in Stamford, Connecticut;
- Forrester Research, Cambridge, Massachusetts;
- Jupiter Research, New York City; and
- Hoover Online of Austin, Texas. Hoover Online has a financial focus.

It's important to note that some analysts only conduct research for wide dissemination, compared with those who work with clients to help them sort their technology needs. Their clients can range from end users to vendors. Some analysts really double as technology consultants, though few if any conduct hands-on work in the field, building solutions or providing networking services. Here's the low-down on what analysts do and how they do it.

What analysts do

Primarily, analysts bring an outside view of technology or business problems, look at the market as a whole and provide assessments about how technologies compare with each other. They work hard at figuring out how to make the value proposition of technology clear to lay people. Tech trenders can turn to analysts to help learn technology's direction, what is on the horizon, what you should be looking at or thinking about one or two years down the road.

Various analysts and analyst firms provide different offerings, areas of expertise and ranges of service. Some may focus on industry niches, others on vendors, and yet others help in implementing systems, though that work is usually relegated to technology consultants (see below). Most analysts sign on with clients for a relatively short period of time – say one to two years. They're then on call to the client to answer questions about technology trends and issues.

Their work depends in part on the client's role in an organization. Analysts will help CIOs sort out contract negotiations with vendors, for example, and help them determine whether the technology they want to purchase will solve the problem at hand. Or they might advise a CIO on developing an e-business strategy. Analysts talk to end users about spin-off strategy and acquisitions, or how to handle mergers and acquisitions from an IT perspective. On the vendors' side, they talk to them about sales and promotion, whom to partner with or how to locate funding.

APPLICATIONS

The journals, magazines and newspapers that analysts tout

Although analysts will tell you they read the trade's and mainstream media "with a grain of salt," read they do. Of late, the Web is becoming a prime source of information for the experts.

Besides the fat glossy mags like *Fast Company* and *Business 2.0*, analysts point to lesser-known journals such as the *Industry Standards*, which is all about Internet development, and appears both in print and on the Web. *Transportation & Distribution* won't be known to many of you outside the transport industry, but some analysts prefer its high-tech coverage to just about anything else. And they say the same for *Supply Chain Technology News*, and *Technology Review: MIT's Magazine of Innovation.*

Here are the general news and business publications that the analysts are reading:

- *Success*
- *Forbes*
- *Fortune*
- *Business Week*
- *Red Herring*
- *The Economist*
- *Wall Street Journal*
- *New York Times*
- *USA Today*
- *Washington Post*
- *Harvard Business Review*
- *Time*
- *Newsweek.*

The high-tech industry publications most touted are:

- *InformationWeek*
- *Computerworld*
- *InfoWorld*
- *Network World*
- *Business 2.0*
- *Fast Company*
- *Wired*
- *IndustryStandard*
- *PC Magazine*
- *eWeek* (formerly *PC Week*)
- *Interactive Week*
- *CIO magazine*
- *Knowledge Management Review* (KM)
- *Complexity Journal.*

And on the Web they say check out:

- msnbc.com (technology)
- Yahoo.com
- CNET.com
- ZDNET.com
- LocalBusiness.com
- Upside.com.[1]

What analysts offer clients

Analysts like to say they offer clients "hindsight ahead of time." Besides the advanced perspective and trend awareness, they're also in the business of saving you time and will hopefully shield you from bad decisions. Here are the sorts of service that analysts can offer tech trenders:

- *Aggregate and filter vendor announcements and claims.* The idea is to get clients to step back and consider why they want to implant technology, whether the cost is appropriate for the organization and the vendor can actually fulfill their marketing promises.
- *Act as a sounding board for the vendor and the end user.* Analysts help vendors formulate strategy, help with product-marketing decisions, some product-development decisions deliver product intelligence, and generally act as a "human portal." In terms of end users, they listen to client complaints and help bring them up to speed. Some analysts have systemized awareness-building programs to help end-user clients get things done. Others actively coach end-user clients on technology trends and change.
- *Time savings.* As tech trenders you can learn about technology yourselves, which this book advises. But if you're tight for time, an analyst will act as your eyes and ears to the high-tech world and be a validator.
- *Act as an honest broker.* Analysts should provide objective analysis and perspective based on an aggregation of industry opinion from the end user and the vendor community.
- *Provide backup analytical skills.* Tech-trending organizations have to have managers and employees, alike, who have honed their analytical skills. A high-tech analyst will have the knowledge base many of you lack, plus be able to bring additional analytical skills to the table.

PLATFORMS

A typical analyst/client exchange

An analyst gets a call asking, "What kind of PCs should we buy?" The first question, obviously, that an analyst ought to ask is, "What do you want to use it for?" If it turns out that it's going to be using a Web browser to connect to a server, "Are you going to need remote access, or are you going to be connected? Are you going to need high-speed graphics or are you not? Are you going to need sound?" All those issues. Then suddenly, it becomes, "What's the business purpose?" and "Do you realize that if you're going to do that, you probably should have a removable storage device, because ... "

So what happens is you start getting into multiple areas of technology that may not have been obvious from the first question – and are likely not even going to be touched by an analyst who's a specialist, and whose product they represent is so highly specific, that you can't step outside of it. What happens then is that because of the breadth of offerings, you don't necessarily cover the problem that the client has in a holistic way.

Other sorts of questions would involve things like, "What are these e-marketplaces being created? How do I do one? Where do I start? What do I buy? Should it be from Ariba or Commerce One? What do I have to do? How do I organize? How much should I spend?" So a typical day is a lot of questions like that.

We try to filter from all the sources I've mentioned and come back to the client and say "OK, mister pharmaceutical company, in your situation, given what I know about you, your business, your architecture, this is the right thing to do. And here is what has worked, here's what we think will work, here's what we think is going to happen, etc ... "[2]

What makes a good analyst

There are good analysts and lousy analysts. But all concerned agree that really super analysts have to be articulate, knowledgeable, offer industry experience, be clear thinkers and are really fast learners. Here are some factors to consider when selecting an analyst that will help tech trenders sort out the so-so from the superstars:

- *Provide problem-solving methodologies.* Analysts should be able to delineate what they can do to solve a client's problems – whether end user or vendor – and offer a clear approach to issues. And they should be able to communicate this fact-based approach and be able to build logical arguments.
- *Have good listening skills and solid values.* Being able to listen and be empathetic is considered very important in this trade. So is integrity and honesty. Good analysts will admit to areas of ignorance and not claim to know it all.
- *Have an analytical mind.* This sounds obvious, but it isn't. You want someone who can cut through the clutter, identify the key issues and put them into perspective. Don't confuse analysis with research. Research is about collecting information and categorizing it to some degree. Analysis is about comparing things with one another, having a perspective – perhaps historical, perhaps experiential – to determine where things stand and what they really mean.
- *Defend positions in a flexible fashion.* In the hyperpaced technology world no one calls it right every time. Make sure your analyst can roll with the times and put away wrong calls. You don't want an egotist who insists he or she is right against all the evidence. On the other hand, you want someone who will stand up for their positions and defend them articulately. Sometimes conventional wisdom is wrong and your person has it right, at least for your organization. For example, some analysts have been touting SGML (Standard Generalized Mark-up Language) for the Web, but others believe this is too expensive an approach. Make your analyst defend that sort of argument.
- *Bridge business and technology worlds.* Whether an analyst comes from the user community or business side, or from the technology side, he or she has to be able to bridge all worlds. They have to bring their particular experience to bear and then move beyond it to define alternatives and decision variables. Look for an analyst who's also a pragmatist.
- *Be aware of company politics and cultures.* Analysts can't function as an island unto themselves. They have to be aware of

organizational politics and cultures and be able to function in a number of different environments.

APPLICATIONS

Tools CIOs use to assess analysts

1 Sort out whether an individual is acting on his or her own, or represents one of the major firms.
2 Locate an analyst you like and believe you can trust, and then build a personal relationship with that individual.
3 Be wary of one-stop shops that claim to do it all. No one can have true depth of knowledge or expertise in all aspects of technology.
4 Assess an analyst based on their values and integrity. If they turn down business because of lack of knowledge that's a good sign.

The tricks of the analyst's trade

Most tech-trending managers have the sorts of skills that make a good analyst. You may not have the time to keep up on technology trends to the extent your analyst can, or the inclination. But for those tech trenders who want to be able to apply analyst's tools to your operation, here are some of the tricks of the trade:

- *Filtering information.* The first and foremost practice analysts provide is filtering information, sorting out the significant from the insignificant. They also keep an eye on emerging trends that may not appear important at the time, but could be the next big buzz. Analysts, themselves, say beware of their bias towards the Fortune 1000 companies, and technology with some track record. Yes, track records and experience are important in selecting technology (see chapter 7), but tech trenders should at least have antennae out for what's new or untried.
- *Good note-taking, research and classification skills.* If you want to play the analyst's game be sure to hone those listening

skills so you can take good notes. You have to want to conduct sometimes mind-numbing amounts of research and be able to classify – or break out – information to create the categories that will indicate trends or other information worth analyzing.

- *Be able to make relativistic comparisons.* Oftentimes there are no statistics or absolute benchmarks to serve as the basis for analysis. Analysts make what they call "relativistic comparisons" to offer perspective for clients. One way to make those sorts of comparisons is to learn from your clients and recognize that every interview offers a two-way exchange and educational opportunity.
- *Develop effective vendor relationships.* Getting along with vendors and communicating with them to provide give and take is what analysts mean by being effective. Vendors are certainly out to sell product, but they also are valuable information sources. As tech trenders, you can develop similar relationships with vendors. But that means taking some time to cultivate relationships with them and to really learn and listen to what they have to say.
- *Turn experiences into case studies.* People always learn more easily when you present either a visual or tell a story. Analysts learn quickly to turn their experience into easily digestible case studies. Case studies also turn them into instant experts and allow them to infer vast knowledge from shallow samples. You can do the same when making a case to your organization for the purchase of a solution, for example.
- *Be able to map old problems onto new trends.* Grasping where yesterday's problems match today's world, or yesterday's solutions fit today's market is a big analyst trick. Sometimes this involves being able to benchmark – or compare best practices company with company – and sometimes it means simply swapping names. So a service bureau now becomes an ASP because this is a hot market.
- *Create new industry terms.* Analysts with the gift of the gab, or a sense of marketing lingo, often gain recognition by creating

new industry terms – what's called buzz words. If you can come up with something more compelling than B2B you might be able to rise to the top of the e-commerce, e-marketplace, e-hub world.

- *Get out and see people in person.* Grab those frequent-flier miles and use them. Top analysts say there's no substitute for face-to-face encounters.

Backup tools that analysts use

For all they talk about high technology, most analysts are apparently not utilizing much more than telephones, cell phones, print-based date books, and the Internet in their own practices. One analyst switched over to the Palm Pilot and then switched back to a date book because he found the technology botched up his calendar. If there's any high-tech tool they all use its the Web. Some are taking advantage of audio and video Web-based conferencing events. But, once again, they say face-to-face encounters still matter. And one of the best places to get out and be seen is at conferences.[3]

SOLUTIONS

A few thoughts on evaluating consultants

There is some crossover between those who call themselves consultants and analysts.

But as noted earlier in this section, technology consultants mainly work hands-on with organizations designing, customizing and implementing technology solutions. Consultants often maintain long-term relationships with clients and act as advisors and adjuncts to IT departments. Here are some tips for evaluating consultants:

1 Make sure they ask searching questions that get to the true nature of your problem, are illuminating and provide insight. This should take place very early on to determine a direction, and continue throughout the process of implementing technology.

2 Ensure consultant questions are useful by insisting they stay focused on the business side, the project's mission and the beneficiaries.
3 Check references as much as is feasible. Also check into the results they've had in previous projects.
4 Make sure they talk to your IT staff to test their technology knowledge, awareness of technology trends and willingness to be flexible.
5 Interest in the overall business, rather than the IT side alone, is a good sign that you are hiring a well-rounded person who will help you move into the networked/B2B world.

The world of standards and high-tech consortia

Tech-trending decision-makers have long known that standards bodies and high-tech consortia are the places to turn for first-hand information on technology trends that will affect their organizations. If you want to beat the analysts, or be able to assess them, the best bet for tech trenders is to learn to track standards and consortia activities on your own. The real insiders actually join a standards organization or consortium, at least as an observer. They know the standards world is where they can find the inside track on technology change and even influence product design and marketshare.

SOLUTIONS

User groups provide information on open standards

One of the best ways to avoid those dead-end choices is to insist on buying products based on open standards rather than proprietary standards. Open standards provide for more flexibility, more competition among manufacturers, better pricing and services. One of the ways to ensure you are buying products that have been based on open standards is to attend user groups. Almost all major technology sectors have user groups. You can ask the manufacturer of your products, trade associations or consultants for the user group most clued into your particular technology concerns.

BizTalk (www.biztalk.org) is one example of a user group. An industry initiative started by Microsoft and supported by a wide range of organizations, from technology vendors like SAP and CommerceOne to technology users like Boeing and BP/Amoco, BizTalk bills itself as a community of standards users.

Its goal is driving the rapid, consistent adoption of the Web language XML to enable electronic commerce and application integration. Much of its business centers on defining the trademarked BizTalk Framework, a set of guidelines for publishing schemas in XML and using XML messages to easily integrate software programs in order to build rich new solutions. Design emphasis is to leverage existing data models, solutions, and application infrastructure and adapt them for electronic commerce through the use of XML.[4]

Manufacturers approach traditional standards bodies when they want to make their product the designated norm. That may be on a regional or international basis. Following developments in this arena, as well as among the myriad of high-tech consortia, gives you an idea of what technology trends are solidifying. No one standardizes pie-in-the-sky ideas. Standardization usually takes place when a particular product – the cell phone, for example – is in wide use. There are exceptions, of course. The evolving world of high-tech consortia – those organizations with funny acronyms like OMG, TOG, W3C and RosettaNet – are also in the game of developing technology (see Solutions section on consortia, p.163).

The standards and consortia world can seem arcane and unwieldy. There are over 600 standards developers in the US, alone. Plus there's an entire international standards arena that operates with its own sets of rules and regulations. Fortunately, this section provides tech trenders with the insider's information you need to bypass these huge numbers of players, and cut through the layers of bureaucracy, so that you can hone into the organizations, their working groups and technical committees that most concern your operation.

Identifying technology sectors heavily involved in standardization

The technology industry is highly dependent on standardization to protect both regional and global market interests, and almost all sectors are represented by standards organizations and/or high-tech consortia. The following are examples of four, prime technology sectors that are heavily involved in standardization, and the organizations where standards work is taking place:

1 *The Internet.* The Internet Engineering Task Force (IETF) is a key player in developing standards that are influencing the design and maintenance of the Internet, which has become a major supply-chain transmission tool. A subset of the Internet Society (ISOC) based on Reston, Virginia, IETF is a loosely organized group of technology experts concerned with maintaining an open Internet. IETF encompasses about 115 working groups that cover a number of broad Internet concerns, including the protocol for carrying telephone calls, Internet maintenance and security and e-mail standards
2 *Standardized document transmission.* The National Institute of Standards and Technology (NIST) and automotive experts have been experimenting with a standardized form of data transmission called STEP (Standard for the Exchange of Product Model Data), which government officials believe is a key to competitiveness not only in the auto industry, but throughout the industrial sector.

   NIST has determined that problems arise for companies when data generated for one purpose is shared elsewhere. Companies run into incompatible software both within one company and throughout the supply chain, which makes electronic communication difficult. Just as important are the huge number of data-entry errors that can bog down information flow.

STEP has been developed to address these sorts of issues, and allow the transmission of a wide variety of data between supply-chain partners. At its most basic, STEP is a translator. Rather than translating data from one software system into another, STEP provides a complete computer-interoperable-product-data format. This means that STEP allows users to integrate business and technical systems data and covers all aspects of the business cycle, from design to analysis, manufacturing, sales and services.[5]

3 *Intelligent transportation systems.* Intelligent transportation systems, commonly known as ITS, are holding out wide promise for improving transportation safety, and speeding transportation through both toll plazas and international border crossings. The Department of Transportation (DOT) has been financing development of over 100 standards to create a national interoperable ITS system where one transponder can function in all toll and commercial situations. Transponders are the devices that can send and receive messages from moving vehicles.

Some of the organizations involved in ITS standards development include the America Society for Testing Materials (ASTM), which is working on a national standard that will work to the 5.9 GHz band. The Institute of Electrical and Electronic Engineers (IEEE) produces general communication standards and is working on developing a national, interoperable ITS standard. The Society for Automotive Engineers (SAE) is responsible for developing in-vehicle standards. SAE is reportedly discussing developing standards that would tie in ITS functions with other electronic capabilities such as improved navigation systems. And ITS America helps coordinate ITS standards development and promotes ITS technology.

4 *Bar codes.* As bar codes evolve from printed labels to three-dimensional chips embedded in products, the standards world is working hard to provide harmonized, bar code functions that could very well revolutionize the supply network. New bar code technology is allowing for larger

amounts of data to be stored in ever smaller labels, or even in computer chips. When coupled with transmission technologies, bar code information can be relayed and captured from a distance rather than in the hand-held fashion of a warehouse or retail checkout line.

The International Organization for Standardization (ISO) is playing a major role in standardizing bar code technology. The committee responsible for this work is subcommittee 31 (SC 31) of Joint Technical Committee 1 (JTC 1). SC31 is working on many aspects of bar code technology, from coupling linear and two-dimensional bar codes, to working on the new three-dimensional codes.[6]

SOLUTIONS

Connecting the dots between technologies, standards organizations and consortia

Locating the key organizations standardizing – or even producing – technologies that affect your organization is half the battle. Once you've got the names, check their Web sites for contact information and start infiltrating. The following is a list of standards bodies and consortia that relate to major technology sectors:

Cellular phones

- Alliance for Telecommunication Industry Solutions (ATIS)
- Committee T1 – Telecommunications (ASC T1)
- Telecommunications Industry Association (TIA)
- Electronic Industries Association (EIA)
- International Telecommunications Union (ITU)

Semiconductors

- Joint Electronic Device Engineering Council (JEDEC)
- Electronic Industries Alliance (EIA)
- Semiconductor Equipment and Materials International (SEMI)
- Institute for Electrical and Electronics Engineers (IEEE)
- American Society for Testing Materials (ASTM)

Internet/Web
- Internet Society (ISOC)
- Internet Engineering Task Force (IETF)
- W3C
- ISO/IEC JTC 1 on Information Technology
- ASTM (related to healthcare transactions only)
- Alliance for Telecommunication Industry Solutions (ATIS)
- Committee T1 – Telecommunications (ASC T1)
- Institute for Electrical and Electronics Engineers (IEEE)
- International Telecommunications Union (ITU)
- Organization for the Advancement of Structured Information Standards

Business to business processing
- RosettaNet

Bar codes
- ISO/IEC JTC 1/SC 31
- AIM USA (AIM is the global trade association of providers and users of components, networks, systems, and services that manage the collection and integration of data with information management systems)
- Uniform Code Council (UCC)
- Graphic Communications Association (GCA)
- HIBCC (Health Industry Business Communications Council)

Intelligent transportation systems (ITS)
- ITS America
- IDB Forum (For Inter Data Bus)[7]

How to identify and utilize pertinent standards organizations

Tech-trending organizations can take the following four steps to identify the standards organizations and consortia that are most important to their operations, plus ways you can utilize the information they provide:

1. Contact your industry trade association or professional organization to determine whether they are involved in any standards-setting activity.
2. Most countries have national standards-setting organizations that can guide you to the appropriate organizations carrying on work in your field. In the US, the American National Standards Institution (ANSI) acts as the coordinator for most US standards developing organizations.
3. Ask standards setters for information on the working groups or technical committees standardizing or developing technologies that concern your organization. Most will provide lists of chairmen – sometimes called secretariats – and help you contact them.
4. Committee chairs or those actively involved in standards setting usually welcome interest in their work and will provide information on committee meetings, deadlines and anything else tech trenders may want to know about the progress of a given standard or standards (see boxes below). Secretariats, on the other hand, are the organizations that provide administrative services to standards writing committees.

APPLICATIONS

How Acunia benefits from standards participation

Playing the standards game has paid off for many companies. Acunia, a Belgian-based telematics company, is highly involved in developing standards in the US. Company officials say standards efforts have paid off with solid public relations. Through its involvement in a number of standards organizations, the fledgling company has gained a growing reputation as knowledgeable and cutting edge. Clients in the US and the EU are signing up for Acunia technology consulting and design.

Acunia works with several US standards developers, including the Automotive Multimedia Interface Collaborative (AMIC), which is a unified forum for standardization of automotive multimedia technology. They've also donated time to the Open Services Gateway Initiative whose concern is standardizing the transfer of data over wiring for home use for applications such as remote programming of washing machines, heat or VCRs.[8]

Seeking out those key organizations you need is a good beginning. Tech trenders who decide to participate directly in the standards-setting process shouldn't attend standards meetings, or send a representative, without structuring information gathering or direct participation to your organization's business needs. This means setting up a standards strategy – what's called practicing strategic standardization management (SSM) – so that your business goals are clearly tied in with standards work. Here are some questions that will guide you in this process:

- Are there currently standards in place which affect the product or service we care about?
- What is gained or lost by participating in the activities of the standards developer?
- If we decide not to participate, what are the possible consequences?

Further, the "standards staff" of your organization shouldn't be held solely responsible for the organization's success in standardization work. They will need the help of technical professionals from outside the normal standards group (i.e. Subject Matter Experts (SMEs). SMEs are often the people best qualified to represent an organization because they can understand how committee requirements will impact your group's product requirements.

Top management on down should be involved in developing this strategy so it clearly ties in with company or organizational goals (see Chapter 5). Sitting in long-winded meetings that range over a variety of highly technical subjects won't serve much purpose unless you have your eyes and ears open for information that might benefit your company or organization, whether that be on the next generation of wireless phones, new modems or B2B processes.[9]

PLATFORMS

An overview of US standards-setting organizations

The following are the types of organizations, agencies and groups that promote standards setting and development in the US:

- Scientific and professional societies like the American Society of Mechanical Engineers (ASME), the Acoustical Society of America, and the American Society of Safety Engineers are often involved in standards development activities that further the work of their organization.
- Trade associations, on the other hand, deal with a particular industry and promote its products or services. Some associations, such as the Information Technology Industry Council and the Aerospace Industries Association, develop standards for the products manufactured by their members, while others might focus on developing standards for products used by their industries.
- Organizations such as the Institute for Electrical and Electronics Engineers (IEEE) and the Electronic Industries Association (EIA) develop technical standards that cut across many industries. Other large umbrella groups, such as ASTM and Underwriters Laboratories (UL), recognize their standardization activities as a primary focus.
- *De facto* (also known as *ad hoc*) standards are normally developed outside the traditional framework and usually appeal to a more narrow market than standards developed by voluntary standards-focused organizations. These "marketplace" standards, though often developed more quickly than standards developed in a more formal process, do not always ensure a level playing field.
- Consortium standards are developed by companies who agree to work together to solve a specific market need. Consortium documents may offer a solution to the problem, but participation on the "problem-solving team" is limited to members of the consortium. Membership often requires a substantial financial contribution.
- Finally, the US federal government is involved, too. Regulatory standards are usually written by government agencies, though voluntary standards frequently become regulatory standards when they are cited in government, industry, or corporate codes or enforceable regulations. Regulatory stan-

dards are enforceable by law; violations can result in civil or criminal action.[10]

Major standards players in the US

The US government does little to promote the development of voluntary standards while retaining the right to assume a greater role in this area, when necessary. The government has focused most of its attention on ensuring that the standards development process is carried out in a fair and effective fashion. The Defense Department has been the largest government standards developer and may very well produce the most standards, in general. Also prolific is the General Services Administration (GSA), which produces federal specifications and standards for federal and state agencies to procure many common products. GSA test methods are used in many industries. However, there is a trend at both DoD and GSA away from standards creation.

Other government agencies known for standards creation include the Occupational Safety and Health Administration (OSHA), the Environmental Protection Agency (EPA), the Food and Drug Administration (FDA) and the Postal Service. In many of these cases a gray area exists between standards and regulations, making quantification difficult.

The Commerce Department is the main government body involved in standards activities both here and abroad. Within Commerce, standards activities are largely divided between the National Institute of Standards and Technology NIST and the International Trade Administration (ITA). NIST handles much of the technical and educational side of standards, as well as technical assistance to developing countries. ITA staffers offer standards-related help to US exporters. The United States Trade Representative's (USTR) office also becomes a player when there are concerns that foreign governments are manipulating standards and conformity assessment practices to their competitive advantage.

When it comes to tracking technology change, the majority of tech trenders will find NIST officials most relevant. That's

because NIST focuses to a large degree on education and has numerous educational programs and publication of standards directories and reports for public sale.

PLATFORMS

NIST e-commerce information sources

The following NIST departments focus on e-commerce and can help tech trenders get started with useful information and even advice:

1 *ATP Information Technology and Applications Office.* The ATP fosters partnerships among government, industry and academia. It co-funds high-risk, industry-proposed research to develop enabling technologies that promise significant commercial payoffs and broad economic benefits for the nation. The ATP provides a mechanism for industry to extend its technological reach and push out the envelope of what can be attempted. Its Web page is: http://www.atp.nist.gov/itao/.

2 *Systems Integration for Manufacturing Applications (SIMA).* The SIMA program seeks to improve the overall integration of manufacturing systems by facilitating the development and testing of information exchange protocol standards, and to foster industry awareness of advances in integration technology. SIMA works with manufacturers, software vendors, standards organizations, other government agencies, and researchers to achieve these objectives. Its Web page is: http://www.mel.nist.gov/msid/sima/sima.htm.

3 *eBusiness Product Lines.* The manager of this small department is responsible for the product line strategy and the development and deployment of the electronic business and electronic commerce products and services through a nationwide system of manufacturing consulting offices. The Web page is: http://www.mep.nist.gov/.

4 *NIST Computer Security Division.* The aim of this division is to improve information systems security by:
   - raising awareness of IT risks, vulnerabilities and protection requirements, particularly for new and emerging technologies;
   - researching, studying, and advising agencies of IT vulnerabilities and devising techniques for the cost-effective security and privacy of sensitive Federal systems;

- developing standards, metrics, tests and validation programs:
  - to promote, measure, and validate security in systems and services,
  - to educate consumers, and
  - to establish minimum security requirements for Federal systems; and
- developing guidance to increase secure IT planning, implementation, management and operation.

You can locate the Computer Security Resource Center at: http://csrc.nist.gov/.

NIST offers a wide variety of services and programs to help US industry improve its international competitiveness through proper use of new technology and an emphasis on quality processes. The following are some of the sectors where NIST provides services and programming that relate to tracking technology change:

- Office of Research and Technology Application;
- Technology Development and Small Business Program; and
- Technology Evaluation and Assessment.

In terms of the private sector, the most efficient way of tracking the activities of the 600-plus standards developers in this country is via the American National Standards Institute (ANSI.) Based in Washington, DC, ANSI is a private, non-profit federation of some 240 technical, professional and trade standards organizations whose main purpose is to act as a clearing house for industry-related product and quality assurance standards. While functioning independently, many major US standards bodies coordinate their activities through ANSI.

ANSI does not develop standards and it does not act as judge or overseer on the standards its member organizations create. These bodies develop standards on a decentralized, committee basis while ANSI helps coordinate those efforts. ANSI certifies that these voluntary standards bodies have arrived at standards through one of three ANSI accredited procedures.

In the summer of 1995, ANSI and NIST signed a memorandum of understanding that grants ANSI government recognition and support as the leading US standards organization and official representative of US interests abroad. The decision to grant ANSI government backing – which was many years in the making – revolved around awareness that US competitiveness abroad was weakened because of fragmented representation in foreign standards activities.

The organization is the US representative to the Geneva-based International Organization for Standardization (ISO) and the International Electrotechnical Commission (IEC).[11]

How tech trenders can use ANSI to track technology change

Although ANSI members don't include every major high-tech company in this country, the *crème de la crème* of the industry participate in ANSI. Even individuals can join for as little as $1000 a year. If you run a tech-trending company – no matter how small – that gives you the right to join the Company Member Council Executive Committee (CMCEC). Meetings take place four times a year. At any given session companies like IBM, Motorola, Hewlett-Packard, Sun Microsystems, Microsoft, Lucent Technologies and many other high-tech giants will be represented discussing their standards concerns. Associations like the Information Technology Industry Council (ITI) and many others often send representatives. CMCEC subcommittees on electronics and telecommunications are superb places to learn about technology change first-hand.

Through ANSI membership you can also connect to about 200 trade associations and standards developing organizations, many of which are involved in IT. These organizations are as varied as ITI, AIIM (the Association for Information and Image Management International), NISO (National Information Standards Organization), GIMA (Graphic and Imaging Manufacturers), and IEEE (Institute of Electrical and Electronic Engineers).

For those who don't have the time to travel the country to speak to standards officials from major companies or associations, ANSI membership offers access to a number of online services that will help you follow the progress of standards being developed in JTC 1. ANSI is the US representative to this joint committee of ISO/IEC, which covers about 50 percent of IT standards developed worldwide.

The National Standards System Network (NSSN) contains a database on more than 12,000 standards – everything from information imaging to storage and Web development – and acts as a national resource for global standards. You can use it to track changes, either existing or upcoming, in any technology you may want to implement. For example, NSSN will be able to provide information on changes being made in the Java standard, which is the basic language for your Web browser. Want to know what is taking place in the area of high-definition TV? JTC 1 has taken over standardization in that area from a consortium and the NSSN will be able to provide you with updates on the work taking place.

SOLUTIONS

Other ANSI online services

Here are two other ANSI online services culled from www.ansi.org that will help tech trenders keep tabs on technology change:

1 *Deposit accounts.* The ANSI Online Electronic Standards Store (ESS) has added a new Deposit Account feature enabling customers to purchase individual copies of electronic documents at any time, but will not require use of a credit card to complete the transaction. The ESS is an Internet-based e-commerce site that allows customers to:
   - search for standards using keywords;
   - select documents for delivery in Adobe Acrobat .pdf format;
   - purchase selected documents online via a secure server; and
   - download the documents directly to their desktop.

   For more information on the deposit account function, please visit ANSI online at http://webstore.ansi.org/ansidocstore/dep_acc.asp.

2 *Free single-user subscriptions to the NSSN's star service* (offer valid for all ANSI members in good standing). ANSI's membership services department reminds all ANSI members in good standing that a free single-user subscription to the Standards Tracking and Automated Reporting (STAR) Service of the NSSN: A National Resource for Global Standards (www.nssn.org) is included as a benefit of ANSI membership. Members were first notified of the free subscription in June 1999.

STAR, the fee-based component of the NSSN, provides an integrated network of databases containing up-to-date information on more than 280,000 approved standards published by the world's leading standards developers.

Further, STAR is the only e-mail-based information service known to notify its users when standards are revised or when new development projects are initiated.

For more information on the NSSN, please visit www.nssn.org. For more on the STAR subscription, please contact ANSI's membership services staff at (212) 642 4900 or via e-mail at membership@ansi.org.

APPLICATIONS

How standards committees and trade associations interact

In the pluralistic and sometimes confusing US standards system, standards development may take place under the auspices of a trade association, a professional organization or an organization entirely devoted to standards development. Standards Committee T1, for example, operates under the auspices of the Alliance for Telecommunications Industry Solutions (ATIS), a member company organization that defines standards and operating procedures for the telecomm industry.

Standards Committee T1 develops American National Standards, technical reports, and technical requirements for telecommunications services, network interconnection, interoperability, and performance. Committee T1 provides technical input to the United States Department of State supporting US participation in international standards bodies. More than 1200 telecommunications engineers and technologists bring their expertise to Committee T1's six technical subcommittees. Committee T1 is a founding member of the Global Standards Collaboration (GSC) group of regional standards development organizations and works closely with the Federal Communication Commission on network reliability issues.

ATIS involves nearly 2500 experts from 500 telecomm companies. Their work focus includes network interconnection standards, number portability, improved data transmission, wireless communications, Internet telephony, toll-free access, and order and billing issues. The FCC frequently refers operations issues to ATIS committees for recommended solutions. Members of ATIS and committee participants include, but are not limited to, telecommunications service providers, manufacturers, software developers, resellers, enhanced service providers, and providers of operations support.

Information on ATIS and T1 is available on the World Wide Web at www.atis.org; by contacting the ATIS headquarters at 202–628–6380; or by writing to: ATIS, 1200 G Street, NW, Suite 500, Washington, DC 20005.[12]

As noted above, ANSI also connects you to European and international standards organizations (see below). For those of you who want to play the standards game, you can actively join in the technical work of international standards committees via ANSI technical advisory groups or TAGs. Access to some TAGs is also available through other private standards developing organizations, so check with SDOs in your industry sector for the best route to joining.[13]

Europe becoming a big source of technology standards

Since the mid-1990s, the European Union (EU) has been reorganizing to develop technology standards that will not only serve to harmonize the European market – as has been the case with GSM for cell phones – but to offer European companies a competitive advantage in the global market. Because the Europeans have a centralized standards-developing system (see major players below), that is often closed to outsiders, the Americans and Japanese in particular have accused Europe of manipulating standards to gain unfair market advantage in the technology arena. European officials are pretty nonplussed by these sorts of accusations, charging the US with dominating technology development through its proliferation of standards developers and high-tech consortia. In fact, European standards officials have been contemplating setting up consortia of their own to compete with the US and others.

Despite all these charges and cross-charges, some US companies have been able to use the European system to their advantage. For example, when Sun Microsystems wanted to turn the Java platform specifications into an international standard and felt the ISO route was not feasible, they turned to the European Computer Manufacturers Association (ECMA) to develop an international standard. This effort eventually failed because of copyright concerns, not because ECMA wasn't open to working with Sun. In other cases, US-based global telecommunications companies like Lucent Technologies are voting members of both Standards Committee T1 in the US and ETSI in Europe.

In recent years, the Europeans have been gearing up efforts to standardize everything from B2B languages and processes to intelligent transportation systems and cell phones. So it should be helpful to tech trenders concerned with tracking technology development to know some of the key European players in the event you want to access information on European standards.

There are several major European non-profit standards organizations the EU has charged with development of European-wide standards. Most prominent are the European Committee for Standardization (CEN), European Committee for Electrotechnical Standardization (CENELEC), and ETSI, which is an outgrowth of the European Conference of Postal and Telecommunications Administrations (CEPT).

The CEN, CENELEC and ETSI central secretariats are the guardians of the authoritative versions of the European standards, and as such are responsible for keeping master texts for distribution to all relevant government and private sector bodies. CEN, CENELEC and ETSI work cooperatively through a system called the "5 mode approach," which allows for joint work ranging from acting as observer to creation of joint committees or working groups. CEN and CENELEC are based in Brussels. ETSI headquarters are in Sophia Antipolis, France.[15]

Accessing the international standards system

Three of the most prominent international standards bodies and policy makers are headquartered on the same tree-lined street in Geneva, Switzerland. The International Organization for Standardization (ISO), International Electrotechnical Commission (IEC) and International Telecommunication Union (ITU) form a triumvirate that, between them, handles standardization of just about every product sector in the world.

In general, IEC focuses on anything electrical, which amounts to all sorts of technology. However, in the 1980s, IEC and ISO formed Joint Technical Committee 1 (JTC 1) to work together on information technology standards. Through this committee and many others (see box), IEC's work ranges from nuclear reactor control rooms to CDs, from refrigerators to transformers, to TV to power generation units, ultrasound, medical equipment, fast trains, fuel cells for energy sources for cars and wind turbines. Wherever there is electricity in modern life, the IEC is involved in developing standards that affect product design, with a main concern being safety. Developing global interoperability is also now a key goal.

SOUND BYTES

European e-commerce standardization efforts

The European Commission (EC) – the bureaucratic arm of the EU, has been funding two major standards initiatives to promote electronic commerce throughout Europe. The aim is to provide the interfaces required for business-to-business Web purchasing.

The first project called ProcatGen (Product Catalogues Global Engineering Networking) is creating standards, guidelines and demonstrator systems that will support information exchange across supply chains. ProcatGen is currently under development. EC officials believe that the ProcatGen standards, specifications and prototype software tools will help in the creation and exchange of product data – and product catalogs – that will ease access to this product information by end-users.

The EC is also sponsoring a "follow project" called B2B-Ecom, which "aims to innovate and improve the delivery of personalized content for intelligent catalogs, and to demonstrate and enhance the integration of emerging e-commerce standards with the content delivery."

B2B-Ecom will be rolled out first in the electrical equipment supply market. The program will focus on the promoting e-commerce for the following functions:

- rules based product relationships;
- change management across the supply chain;
- integration of e-commerce and e-purchasing standards; and
- links to ERP systems.[14]

At this writing, IEC has 190 technical and subcommittees that work with 750 working groups and task forces to maintain the current book of approximately 4500 standards, and develop the new requirements as they come along. The organization has 50-odd member countries representing all major economies in the world and their electrical-related standardization bureaus.

SOLUTIONS

IEC committees point the way to tagging technology change

To help companies track IEC work that will affect their business, the IEC has identified four areas of IEC concentration that will matter most to the future evolution of technology. These are electronic components, multimedia, electronic pollution and renewable energy.

In the area of electronic components key work is taking place in TC 47, which is dealing with integrated circuits; TC 86 is dealing with fiber optics for communication, and TC 91 is working on automatic assembly of all electronic components.

TC 100 specializes in multimedia, including telecommunications, information technology and consumer products. TC 74 deals with the safety of information technology equipment and TC 92 deals with the safety of electronic equipment and devices, including electronic toys and photographic devices.

Electronic pollution involves the disturbances created by electronic equipment of the sort identified in aircraft, Brotons-Dias explained. TC 77 focuses on this issue; CISPR handles radio disturbances, and a new committee – TC 106 – deals with electromagnetic fields and the impact on humans. In this area there is study going on relating to the affect of electromagnetic fields thrown off by cell phones and power lines.

In the realm of renewable energy, there is TC 82 for photovoltaic cells; TC 88 for wind turbines and TC 105 for fuel cells, which is a modern approach to creating energy. Besides these sorts of committees, IEC maintains three sector boards in charge of developing strategies for future technology use. These are not standards developers but executives from companies or those in charge of marketing and discuss and give advice to the IEC technical management boards in order to prepare market relevant standards for the future.[16]

PLATFORMS

An actual IEC standard

Here is an example of the sort of standard that IEC develops on its own, or sometimes in tandem with ISO:

Information technology. IEC 61131–7 (2000–08) Ed. 1.0 – Programmable controllers – Part 7: Fuzzy control programming. This part of IEC 61131 defines a language for the programming of Fuzzy Control applications used by programmable controllers. The object of this part of IEC 61131 is to offer the manufacturers and the users a well-defined common understanding of the basic means to integrate fuzzy control applications in the Programmable Controller languages according to IEC 61131–3, as well as the possibility to exchange portable fuzzy control programs among different programming systems.

ICS codes: 35.240.50, 25.040.40 – SC 65B – 113 pp. – CHF 156,00.

ISO is a worldwide federation of 137 national standards bodies at this writing, each representing a country. Its purpose is to promote the development of standardization and related activities worldwide. In its preparation of international standards, ISO brings together the interests of producers, users, consumers, governments and the scientific community. This work is carried out through almost 3000 technical bodies. More than 30,000 experts from all parts of the world participate each year in the ISO technical work which, to date, has resulted in the publication of over 10,000 1SO standards. As noted above, JCT1 – a joint committee of ISO and IEC – covers about 50 percent of IT standards developed worldwide. For more information on ISO IT projects check the ISO Web site at: http://www.iso.ch/projects/tcinfoframe.html.

ITU is a United Nations agency that prepares "recommendations" that cover the "information highway" industries, from telephones, to radio, cable TV and other areas. It creates both standards and policy for global telecommunication systems and services. Services cover the realm of operator companies providing everything from basic phone service to Internet connection, and can involve everyone from traditional phone companies to cable TV companies. Systems involve the actual technology required to promote global communications.

For the near future ITU is focusing much energy on developing worldwide interoperability and compatibility for telecomm technology (See Chapter 1). With IT, telecomm and broadcasting, ITU officials agree the solution will lie in producing standards for compatible software systems. Global mobility, or having the same terminals, the same level of service worldwide and portability of telephone numbers worldwide is another ITU goal.

APPLICATIONS

Tracking hot telecomm technologies through ITU committees

From electronic commerce to the next bi-directional modem, ITU is working on standards to promote global interoperability. Here are some examples:

1 *E-commerce.* Study Group 16 on multimedia is leading work in this arena and is promoting a project, M3, dedicated to e-commerce. (See www.ITU.int under "new initiatives" for detail on this work.)
2 *DSL technology.* Study group 5 is moving forward with ADSL and X-DSL technology and standards to allow the telephone to be exploited at a higher rate. Cable access is also being explored for Internet use.
3 *Bi-directional modems.* The enhanced V.90 modem, will allow the stream of information in two directions at the same rate (56 vs. 48 bit/s).
4 *Long-distance calls on the Web.* ITU is working in close cooperation with the Internet Engineering Task Force (IETF) on the H.248 standard, which will be a key standard for Web phones. These will allow long-distance calls to be made through the Internet rather than going through traditional telephone sets.[17]

For tech-trending information try the consortia

Myth may have it that new technologies emerge from the basements of struggling entrepreneurs. And there indeed are technology breakthroughs, like the development of the operating system Linux, that can be attributed to individuals. But in reality, for the last 15 years or so, many standardized approaches to technology – and many of the new technologies that are promoting a Web-based world – are being developed in consortia such as RosettaNet, the World Wide Web Consortium (W3C), the WAP Forum and many others.

These consortia allow members to lay their technology cards on the table in the form of intellectual property rights. Through sharing their intellectual property – a sort of high-tech copyright for computer code – they evolve new, more compatible technologies that are then applied to product design. Consortia also play a secondary role. Whether it's what cell phones the world will be buying next year, innovations in Internet security, how trading partners will communicate and how cars will be networked for Internet access, consortia work can also give you a heads up on technology's future course.

Most consortia are born and operate in the same way. Companies, sometimes with government assistance, choose a specific type of technology they want to make standard so it can be applied over and over without new research and development. The programming codes for computer clocks, for instance, was hammered out in the Object Management Group (OMG) consortia. These groups have ranged from 2500 active members, like the Internet Engineering Task Force (IETF), which supervises Internet maintenance, to as few as five.

A small group of committed companies and individuals can create compatible technologies that lead to a new generation of products. This is how the new international specifications for 56K modems were developed in 1998. Larger groups usually develop standards for existing, but conflicting, technologies. The Open Group (TOG) has helped standardize Sun Microsystems' Unified Unix Operating system that drives most of the Web.

PLATFORMS

A closer look at key consortia

The Web is an easy way to locate consortia and gather contact information, as well as detailed information on their work. In most cases, take the consortium acronym and add the prefix www. and the suffix .com and you'll be there in a flick of your mouse. Here's a closer look at some key consortia, the way they are organized, and their accomplishments in promoting a Web-based economy.

- *OMG – the Object Management Group.* Based in Needham, Massachusetts, the OMG was founded in April 1989 by eleven companies, including 3Com Corporation, American Airlines, Canon, Inc., Data General, Hewlett-Packard, Philips Telecommunications N.V., Sun Microsystems and Unisys Corporation. With a membership that now sits around 800, its stated aim is to develop "technically excellent, commercially viable and vendor-independent specifications for the software industry." International marketing offices are located in Bahrain, Brazil, Germany, India, Italy, Japan and the UK, along with a government representative in Washington, DC.

  Objects in this case are the common codes that appear in many programs and thus can be standardized – everything from spreadsheets to computer clocks. OMG spokesmen report that implementations of OMG specifications can be found on many operating systems across the world today. OMG's series of specifications detail the necessary standard interfaces for Distributed Object Computing. Its Internet protocol IIOP (Internet Inter-ORB Protocol) is being used as the infrastructure for technology companies like Netscape, Oracle, Sun, IBM and hundreds of others. These specifications are used worldwide to develop and deploy distributed applications for vertical markets, including manufacturing, finance, telecomms, electronic commerce, real-time systems and health care.
- *WAP Forum – the Wireless Application Protocol (WAP).* This is an open global specification that empowers mobile users with wireless devices to easily access and interact with information and services instantly. Not surprisingly, the WAP Forum, with over 200 members, is the organization that works on WAP standards. It has developed the *de facto* world standard for wireless information and telephony services on digital mobile

phones and other wireless terminals. Its primary stated goal is to bring together companies from all segments of the wireless industry value chain "to ensure product interoperability and growth of wireless market."

WAP Forum members represent over 90 percent of the global handset market, carriers with more than 100 million subscribers, leading infrastructure providers, software developers and other organizations providing solutions to the wireless industry.

These include SBC Communications, Phone.com, Ericsson, INOVATEL, IBM, Matsushita Communication, Alcatel, DDI Corp, Telstra Corp., Nokia, Motorola, Sprint and many others.

- *W3C – the World Wide Web Consortia.* W3C's mission is to lead the evolution of the Web – the universe of information accessible through networked computers. Active work is taking place in Web accessibility, XML activity, operating systems, multimedia collaboration systems for education and programming languages, television and the Web, user interface, technology and social activities. W3C boasts the inventors of the Web as acting president and chairman.

  W3C's stated goals are the following:

  1 Universal access. To make the Web accessible to all by promoting technologies that take into account the vast differences in culture, education, ability, material resources, and physical limitations of users on all continents.

  2 Semantic Web. To develop a software environment that permits each user to make the best use of the resources available on the Web.

  3 Web of trust. To guide the Web's development with careful consideration for the novel legal, commercial, and social issues raised by this technology.

- *ebXML*. ebXML's mission is to provide an open XML-based infrastructure enabling the global use of electronic business information in an interoperable, secure and consistent manner by all parties. ebXML is backed by the United Nations body for Trade Facilitation and Electronic Business (UN/CEFACT) and the Organization for the Advancement of Structured Information Standards (OASIS). Industry groups currently working on XML specifications have been invited to participate in the 18-month project. A primary objective of ebXML is to lower the barrier of entry to electronic business in order to facilitate trade, particularly with respect to small- and medium-sized enterprises (SMEs) and developing nations.

- *OBI – Open Buying on the Internet.* Formed in October 1996 by several Fortune 500 buying and selling organizations to create an open, supplier-neutral, scalable and secure interoperable standard for B2B, first OBI members included American Express, BASF, Ford, GE, Hoffmann-La Roche, Lexmark International, National Semiconductor, Office Depot, Pratt & Whitney, United Technologies Research Center, VWR Scientific Products and W.W. Grainger.

  OBI's vision is to facilitate rapid implementation of Internet-based e-commerce solutions using interoperable, standards-based Internet purchasing systems that are characterized by: universal, high-speed access; inexpensive, paperless information and transactions; and platform-independent software and services. In June 1998, CommerceNet assumed management of the OBI Consortium to facilitate this goal. [18]

Some consortia, such as RosettaNet, are even more ambitious. RosettaNet's 200 active individual and corporate members are developing over 100 specifications to develop integrated business-to-business communication. As part of this larger process, RosettaNet has developed what it calls Partner Interface Processes (PIPs, which will allow the computers of trading partners to communicate directly with each other (see Chapter 2).

Retail giant L.L. Bean is conducting a pilot program utilizing PIPs. If this test is successful, the company has announced it will cease working in a paper-based system, or drop as much paper use as is feasible today. Other companies exploring the use of PIPs are Arrow Electronics, CompUSA, Hewlett-Packard, Ingram Micro, Intel, SAP, and 3Com, all of which have come out in RosettaNet press releases claiming at least some improvement in productivity based on early trial runs in the winter of 2000.

Another large consortium, the Organization for the Advancement of Structured Information Standards (OASIS), is working on developing common Web languages like SGML, SML, and XML that are crucial to the widespread use of e-commerce.

Its major role is coordinating global standardization efforts for these languages to ensure worldwide compatibility between computer systems and Web browsers. The consortium is also updating and making globally compatible the commonly used HTML, which is the basic language used to create Web sites.

Sometimes consortia work in tandem with governments to develop technology that will promote a networked economy. The National Industrial Information Infrastructure Protocols (NIIIP) Consortium has entered into a cooperative development agreement with the US government to create open industry software protocols through the government-backed Advanced Research Project Agency (ARPA). These will allow manufacturers and their suppliers to effectively become, data-wise, the same enterprise, even though many of these intra-company interactions occur between both sophisticated and relatively unsophisticated users and operating environments. These protocols are precursors to "virtual enterprises."

NIIIP defines a "virtual enterprise," of which none yet exists, as a temporary consortium of independent member companies formed to quickly exploit fast-changing worldwide product manufacturing opportunities, usually centered around an individual product. Virtual enterprises will assemble themselves based on cost effectiveness and product uniqueness without regard for organization size, geographic location, computing environments, technologies deployed, or processes implemented. Virtual enterprise companies share costs, skills, and core competencies which collectively enable them to access global markets.

Finding NIIIP representatives even for phone interviews is as tough as locating a secretary in today's corporations. But the NIIIP Web site says that most of their work will be "consolidating and harmonizing the many sets of exist-

SOUND BYTES

Consortia have their critics

Consortia have their critics. Those from the traditional standards-developing arena, view consortia as interesting models for getting work done in a fast-pace, global economy. But they also view some consortia as closed systems that – with the wrong leadership – could end up being competition-busting cartels.

Traditional standards organizations also believe that consortia offer an inferior way of standardizing technology that doesn't involve the openness and accountability they can provide on a global basis. They believe that consortia duplicate work already taking place in the traditional standards world, which means expense for manufacturers and added costs for consumers. There are also fears that consortia can easily lead to creation of cartels.

However, traditional standards setters also admire the ease and speed at which consortia function to standardize technology and meet market demands. They acknowledge that the traditional standards world would do well to learn from consortia if it wants to remain relevant to the high-tech industry.[20]

ing protocols, and then doing pilot projects and demonstration work" to make sure what seems dandy in principle actually functions.[19]

APPLICATIONS

Consortia of choice for Unisys

Like any company, Unisys selects groups and consortia to join that are relevant to business goals. Sometimes there are very detailed objectives to meet, so Unisys works with the I20 Special Interest Group to meet those technical objectives Other consortia it finds strategically important are W3C and OMG.

Notes

1 Sources are Merv Adrian, VP & Research Manager, Giga Information Group, Cambridge, MA, and David Yokelson, the META Group, Stamford, CT. Research conducted by Eddy Goldberg and Randy Bernard.
2 Sources are Merv Adrian, Vice President and Research Manager for the Giga Information Group, Cambridge, MA, and David Yokelson, the META Group, Stamford, CT.
3 Sources are Krimo Salem, CEO of If & Then Inc., San Jose, CA; Jeanmarie Gelinas, Vice President and CIO of Rodale, Inc., Emmaus, PA; Eric Fliegel, CIO, eTour, Inc., Atlanta, GA; Pam Kleier, CEO of constructionzone.com, Louisville, KY; Laurence Smith, a specialist in e-commerce management, Boston, MA; Merv Adrian, VP & Research Manager, Giga Information Group, Cambridge, MA; David Yokelson, the META Group, Stamford, CT, and David Washburn, Principal Consultant at Amherst Information Architects, Amherst, MA.
4 "The Hunt for Interoperability," Anne Millen Porter, *Purchasing* magazine, June 15, 2000.
5 Jim Turner, Chief Democratic Counsel for the US House Committee on Science.

6 "Standards, Technology and the Supply Chain," Amy Zuckerman, *Transportation and Distribution*, May 2000, pp. 43–46. Source on bar codes is Alan Haberman, chairman of ISO SC 31.
7 Stacy Leistner, Director of Communications and Public Relations, ANSI.
8 Stephen Buytaert, CEO of Acunia and Bart Stevens, US marketing director for Acunia.
9 Sergio Mazza, former president of the American National Standards Institute (ANSI), and Stacy Leistner, Director of Communications and Public Relations, ANSI.
10 Stacy Leistner, Director of Communication and Public Relations, ANSI.
11 *International Standards Desk Reference* by Amy Zuckerman, AMACOM Books, New York, 1997, pp. 27–65.
12 ATIS press department.
13 Bob Feghali, VP of business development and chief information officer, ANSI.
14 Peter Howgate, a manager at the UK company, Pindar Ltd, and project coordinator for EU e-commerce work.
15 *International Standards Desk Reference*, Amy Zuckerman, AMACOM Books, New York, 1997, pp. 160–164.
16 Adapted from *Standards, Technology and Global Trends* by Amy Zuckerman, 2000. Source is IEC Technical Director Jean-Pierre Brotons-Dias.
17 Adapted from *Standards, Technology and Global Trends*, by Amy Zuckerman, 2000. The following information is drawn from: a joint interview with Fabio Bigi, Deputy Director of the telecommunications unit of the International Telecommunication Union (ITU); Franklin Cohen, an ITU Study Group Counselor; Francisco Cantero, ITU-T Head of Promotion; and Masamichi Niiya, an engineer in the ITU Standardization Bureau.
18 "The Consortia Boom: Creating the Underpinnings of a Networked World," Amy Zuckerman, *Business 2.0*, October 2000; and from a work in progress *The Consortia Boom*, Amy

Zuckerman. "The Hunt for Interoperability," Anne Millen Porter, *Purchasing* magazine, June 15, 2000.

19 "The Consortia Boom: Creating the Underpinnings of a Networked World," Amy Zuckerman, *Business 2.0*, October 2000; and from a work in progress *The Consortia Connection*, Amy Zuckerman.

20 "The Consortia Boom: Creating the Underpinnings of a Networked World" by Amy Zuckerman, *Business 2.0*, October 2000; and *Standards, Technology and Global Trends* by Amy Zuckerman, 2000. Sources for both are Mike Smith, head of standards at ISO and Ronnie Amit, General Secretary and CEO of IEC.

21 Steve Oksala, former head of Standards, Unisys.

Part II

How to Manage and Organize Your Company or Institution to Reap Technology's Benefits

5 Managing Your Organization in a Networked, B2B World

Technology will make change. That's the most important factor tech-trending managers and strategic decision-makers, professionals and entrepreneurs have to know and accept to stay competitive while designing networked, B2B-oriented organizations. Change is confusing, difficult and often painful. But, as all of you know, there's no way to avoid technology change. Accepting the change technology brings rather than resisting it will help ease you into a world in which technology serves you and your organization, rather than you serving it.

Consider this statistic presented by a prominent high-tech analyst and quality manager. By 2005, something in the order of 65 percent of all organizational initiatives will be technology-driven, not customer-driven. That means that technology is changing so fast, the changes you're implementing in your companies and organizations aren't being driven by customer need, but by the requirement of keeping up with technology change just to be able to communicate with suppliers and trading partners.[1]

With this basic message you've entered a new phase of this book. Up until now, the entire focus has been on how to track technology change to stay abreast of the trends and be able to make informed decisions. The human aspects of your company or organizations have been mentioned in passing, at best. In the remaining chapters, though, the issue of how humans cope with technology will be as much a focus as the technology itself. That's because what's key to controlling your technology future is to consider technology in the light of human needs, business direction and long-term organizational goals, not in terms of whether you implant a Unix operating system, ERP software or design a knock-out Web site.

Sounds simple, but it isn't. Study after study shows that managers in both the profit and non-profit sectors ignore the human issues and grasp at technology as a band-aid solution for what really amounts to human management issues. Yes, technology that's well implemented with human and cultural concerns in mind will make your operation more efficient. But technology that's tossed out to solve what are inherently human problems – without any attempts to address human issues – inevitably falters.

Many believe that the failures of so many ERP implants are based on just this issue. Management did not grasp the level of organizational change these systems brought with them, and did not address the human issues – from computer phobia to job security – that can develop when an ERP system is installed. Experts working in the human aspect of technology implementation say that the point of implementing an information system in your organization is not to increase business value alone, but to change your environment.

A prominent consultant to major corporations opens all client sessions with the question: "What do you want to change?" He finds these clients, among the Fortune 500, shocked by this sort of question. They want things to be better, but they haven't thought about what they need to change in terms of human management within their organizations to make it better. In fact, there are only three basic things technology can do to improve an organization. It can

- make people more efficient, meaning they do a job faster;
- make people more effective, meaning they do a job better; or
- allow innovation, something that was previously impossible or unimaginable.

Learning to use technology in an innovative way should be the goal of all tech-trending companies and organizations. But to get to that stage means not only accepting change, but actively pursuing new ways of managing your organization. This chapter focuses on the changes managers need to make personally, and then within their organization, to create an environment to support the networked, B2B workplace you are creating. Some basic changes in management principles are included, but the emphasis is mainly on how technology will affect your organization and how you should alter your management structure and style to move into the New Economy. Consider the following crucial steps you need to take to manage a tech-trending organization:

- Break down hierarchical structures to allow for information sharing and true collaboration among employees and then throughout a supply network.
- Create new management positions to ensure proper use of technology throughout your organization.
- Improve communication skills so that management clearly expresses priorities.
- Build customer relationships rather than only providing customer service.
- Establish new rules of communication so that the vast amount of information that technology makes available can be used for maximum purpose, and not overwhelm an organization.[2]

APPLICATIONS

A university gains efficiency and effectiveness by embracing technology change

There are companies and institutions that recognize that planning for technology change makes an enormous difference. Take the example of an east coast Ivy League university that was in the process of designing a new building for international studies and chose to consider technology as part of the design process. The aim was to use technology to unite the members of these autonomous units to provide for shared use of documents, conference space and other facilities.

Work flow was redesigned, e-mail accounts with form submissions were developed for certain kinds of business processes, a scheduling system was designed for use of conference rooms and systems were installed to allow for shared documents. Technology was included as part of the operating manual of the building. At last check, all systems were go and the advanced planning appears to have paid off in satisfied academic customers.[3]

The yin-yang of technology change

Like any change, the introduction of new technology can prove as destabilizing to your companies and institutions as it is beneficial – the yin-yang of technology change. Unless handled properly, change can be discomforting and disquieting. When translated into large organizational systems, the impact of change can be what organizational experts call geometric. That means the effects of change compound as each part of the organization deals with its own dynamics, which in turn cause changes in the dynamics of other parts of the organization, and the organization as a whole.

So the promise of technology – speed, efficiency and added innovative tools – won't amount to zilch if you haven't adequately prepped the people in your organization for change and aren't attuned to their ongoing needs. Technology may grossly alter how people communicate in your organization and how they interact. It may break down barriers between departments in companies and institutions in ways that threaten job security. So it is essential for tech trenders to recognize these factors before introducing new technologies. You need to establish processes for both monitoring the impact of technology on your organization, as well as helping people cope with ongoing change.

A cultural tourism director in the Mid-Atlantic states, dates his first awareness of how technology was altering his operation to the introduction of the fax machine. The fax, now almost an obsolete tool in the days of the Internet, allowed for cheaper transmission of paper-based materials on a near real-time level.

That was a big advancement compared with having to mail out every form, and a big cost-cutting tool. Fax machines were also pretty easy to absorb into an organization. They didn't require more than 15 minutes' training for most employees and it didn't take long to set up some internal distribution process that, hopefully, ensured the right faxes reached the right desks.[4]

The major change faxes produced in organizations was speed – speed of delivery, speed of pickup and the need to respond more quickly than in the days when snail mail ruled and overnight deliveries were considered luxuries. This speed proved welcome and unwelcome – the yin-yang of technology implants. Suddenly, that information was available in almost real time and that meant some response was required. No, you didn't have to answer instantaneously, but you didn't have the luxury of waiting a week for turnaround that many professionals built into their projects when they were relying on the postal service to transmit information.

Think about the changes that fax machines impose on organizations and then multiply them exponentially as you consider the introduction of advanced computing tools, e-mail, real-time tracking tools for shipping, business-to-business processing software – the whole array of technology that has invaded companies and institutions in the last 20 years. A lot of what this technology change amounts to is increased speed of information processing and speed of delivery.

Like change itself, speed can be good and bad, advantageous and disadvantageous. Being able to relay information quickly means that the information you're sending had better be accurate. Accuracy becomes even more crucial as networking takes over and information can be relayed and accessed far and wide by huge numbers of people. Mistakes get transmitted along with accurate data and there's less opportunity for catching errors in a networked system. Moreover, having the ability to relay information rapidly doesn't ensure that it's well thought out or worthy of transmission. We still need time to think, sort and analyze.

APPLICATIONS

Major changes technology promotes within organizations

Technology, particularly the Internet is very chameleon-like. It's not just a distribution channel, or a new way to communicate. Connect the Internet to the Web and you have a marketplace, an information system, and a tool for producing goods and services. The Internet affects many things managers do every day from locating a new supplier to managing customer data. Here are some additional ways technology, particularly Web-based technology, will alter your organization:

- *Shrinks human time requirements.* The new technologies can handle redundant tasks and free employees to handle more meaningful work. They can also eliminate the need for entire departments within an organization, which has far-reaching ramifications for employees.
- *Opens internal communication.* More and more organizations are learning to cope with the fact that e-mail opens up communication in-house. Employees, as noted in the text, now can reach to the highest levels of management with their concerns. Organizations need to adjust to the ways technology is democratizing the work place.
- *Shifts the focus to the external.* Internet-based software applications are allowing a new focus on external parties, and the Web offers new ways to collaborate with everyone from customers to suppliers and vendors.
- *Provides direct customer communication.* The Internet/Web allows for direct communication with customers, or their suppliers. Customers can click a mouse and, through their purchase, start a production process rolling far along the supply network.
- *Allows you to operate on the fly.* As noted in Chapter 1, the combination of wireless technologies and the Web mean you can operate on the fly. Thanks to the Internet/Web, training tools can be downloaded into laptops so you can learn while on the road.
- *Creates privacy issues.* The networked, B2B organization means that information is far more accessible to anyone smart enough to access it, not to mention hackers. Managers at companies like Novell talk about working in the fishbowl.

> They expect any piece of information communicated electronically may be broadcast throughout an organization and beyond.[5]

So having the ability to transmit information in real time requires exerting more control over what is transmitted than might have been necessary in the good old days of phones and snail mail. And, unless handled properly, the new technologies can breed misunderstandings and impede communication. Take e-mail. Because it lacks voice intonation, e-mail communications can easily be misconstrued. Once again, misinformation is just as easily relayed throughout an organization as accurate information. Imagine the impact on organizations as a whole, let alone supply networks, when the collective misunderstandings are shared and in real time.

The new technologies have not only sped up our lives, but they've allowed for a huge increase of information that can be transmitted in real time. Many professionals talk about feeling bombarded with information in this day of e-mail. This sort of bombardment leaves everyone feeling sapped and drained. Many executives complain that they never have enough time to accomplish goals because of information overload.

Then there's the fact that change of any kind is destabilizing. In order for people to function in an organization they need to feel technically competent, be clear about power relationships and feel there is a social support system in place. Change often tips the equilibrium balance, disturbing past alliances and support networks and can make people feel incompetent, as any of you, grappling with a new computer program, know only too well.

And technology can easily tip power relationships within organizations in unsettling ways for managers, not to mention creating whole new work processes. For example, it took time for European managers to accept word-processing tools. They just weren't accustomed to typing their own material. In Europe, secretaries were major status symbols and typing was considered their job. In the US, newspapers in the 1970s won a major court battle to allow reporters to type in their own stories instead of passing along copy to compositors who did that work.[6]

How technology affects tech-trending organizational structures

Information has always amounted to power, and that's true for any organization whether profit or non-profit. Because the new technologies – particularly the Internet and Web – allow anyone to access vast amounts of information, this balance of power is being tipped in many organizations where information and knowledge were closely guarded by senior executives. Add to this fact that anyone can access information, the fact that e-mail has allowed employees to reach beyond formal hierarchies, skirt mid-managers and "go to the top" with their concerns. And the new technologies allow for unparalleled networking and the formation of alliances to challenge upper management. That means that technology is forcing traditional, hierarchical organizations to face unimagined challenges to authority.

Some companies are fighting back by imposing firewalls, and other restrictions to information flow and information sharing. Basically, they are trying to reimpose the former order they feel technology tools like e-mail and the Web have challenged. Organizational experts consider the return to hierarchical organizations a losing proposition for institutions that want to thrive. To evolve into networked, B2B organizations, tech-trending businesses and institutions have to break down the walls between old-fashioned departments and be able to communicate fluidly throughout the organization. You will have to pull together project teams very rapidly to complete a specific assignment, and that means promoting collaboration between departments.

PLATFORMS

Technology breeds management problems

Older managers – say age 50 and up – have more problems with technology change than the younger generation that has been evolving with technology. Basically, many of those now managing Fortune 1000 companies were educated and moving up the corporate ladder when companies were paper-focused. As a result, they feel more comfortable with paper on their desks than

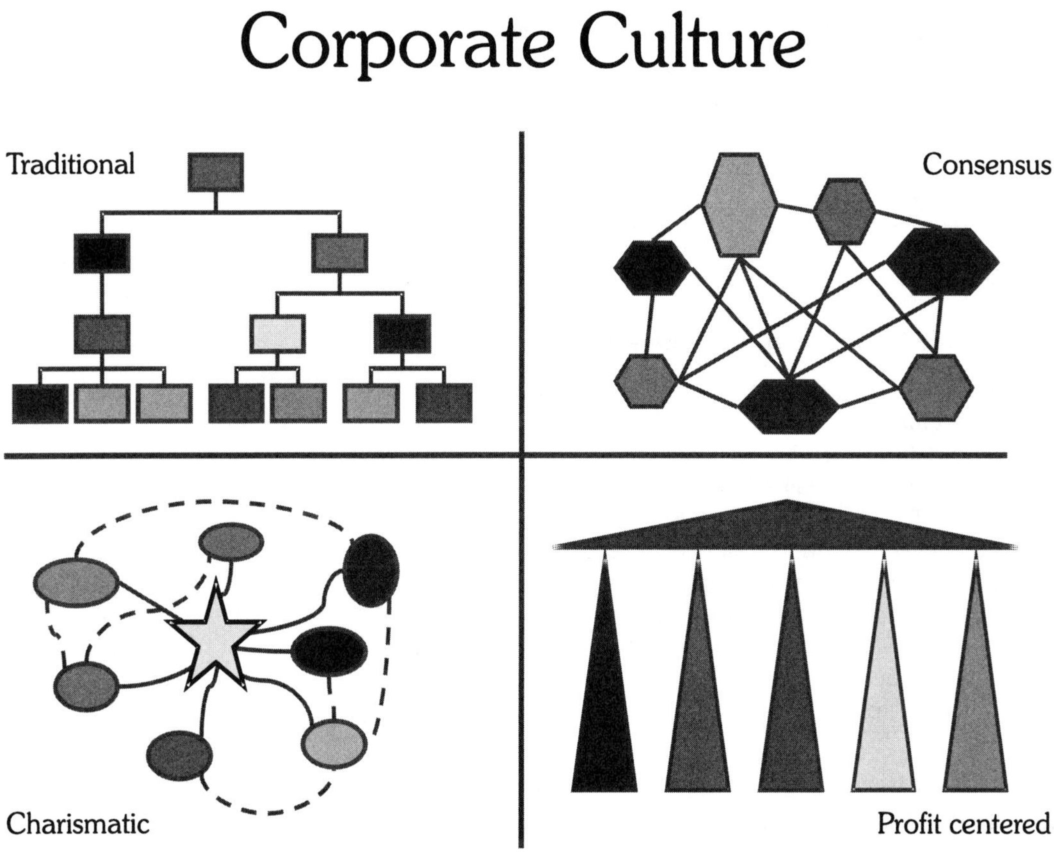

Different corporate cultures require different technology solutions. This graphics shows how four types of corporate cultures are organized, which directly affects human communication, work flow and technology implant. © David Washburn, principal consultant, Amherst Information Architects, Inc., Amherst, MA.

with computer screens. Having to share information with underlings presents one form of discomfort for this generation of management. Even more threatening on a basic level is using the technology at all.

Even if they want to use technology, many top managers simply lack the time – or haven't made the time – to absorb technology basics. They face so many demands that they don't have the amount of time that middle managers, mid-line and employees have to learn the technology. And they don't have the time to understand the details that technology presents; moreover they don't use technology enough to master the details.

Top managers are also more accustomed to talking than to typing. Some believe that voice recognition technology will offer a breakthrough for computer-phobic top management. Others believe that top managers who want to be tech trenders had better put some projects on temporary hold and at least learn some computer basics. Those who think typing is beneath them had better start thinking retirement.[7]

SOLUTIONS

A networked, consensus environment

Digital Equipment Corp. has gone through many ups and downs, but for those who worked at Digital in its heyday – say the 70s and 80s – it represents the model of what a consensus organization should be like. The management was highly decentralized. To sell an idea to senior management you had to get the buy-in of people in your department. Knowing how to communicate well was a prerequisite for success. To hold this all together, Digital was one of the first international companies to institute e-mail across the company to support consensus-making. The operation was hard to understand from the outside, but many insiders thought this was a great way to work.[8]

In other words, you can't afford to retain hierarchical organizations that manage assignments based on power relationships and status rather than expediency. The speed of technology and the demands for quick response throughout a supply network make that sort of management obsolete. Assignments will have to be made electronically and based on optimizing critical resources rather than controlling resources.

For many organizations, these sorts of changes in attitude and management are far more monumental than deploying a new operating system. They mean changing your basic thinking about internal and external competition. To create a cooperative mode of communication not only within the organization, but among all trading partners, means abandoning the notion that the employee in the next cubicle is competition, or that other brand name company in the field is someone to beat. The

New Economy is focusing more and more on alliances and collaboration. To survive, you will have to develop management tools that promote these attitudes.

SOLUTIONS

Big three promote communication among competitors

When the Big Three automakers decided it was time to explore creating a global communication system among suppliers, they didn't stop at implanting e-mail and Electronic Data Interchange (EDI) within their pilot group. They also addressed the human communication flow that underlies any technology-based system.

There was a general recognition that technology couldn't solve all problems. Technology helps you move information from one point to another, but it's what you do with the information that matters. And that hinges on communication issues and processes. That was the general consensus that led the Automotive Industry Action Group (AIAG) – which standardizes processes for Ford, General Motors and Chrysler – to design a pilot program called Manufacturing Assembly Pilot Program (MAPP).

Originally MAPP was set up to address communication between 16 Big Three suppliers of different sizes. Besides implanting e-mail and EDI in all supplier locations, a team from AIAG and outside consultants brought suppliers together to talk out their differences. Communication wasn't flowing much more quickly with technology than without because these suppliers – all competitors – were concerned about releasing information to each other.

To right this situation, common lexicons were created – or what the industry called integrated definition language – and forced all participants to speak the same language. Information processes and information flow were analyzed throughout these companies. Finalized in 1996, the MAPP pilot has since been expanded throughout the industry.

As a result of this project the Big Three have come together with a common set of EDI requirements that extend through the third tier of suppliers. Work continues today extending MAPP principles to lower-tier suppliers. This program is called Voice of the Lower Tier and involves graduate students working with loaned auto executives from AIAG to assess why smaller suppliers are still resisting technology use.[9]

Tech-trending companies and institutions in transition won't change these sorts of long-held attitudes about power, information sharing and competition without recognizing the enormous threat they represent to job security. Some employees on the mid-line level still want to compete because they feel an identity to the organization, but others are intent on holding their turf. Sharing information is just as threatening to employees as to managers because it eliminates special ways they can help the organization. For members of IT departments who have banked their careers on supporting one type of technology, introducing new technologies can seem tantamount to eliminating their jobs.

Add to these concerns the fact that technology change is taking place against a backdrop of massive lay-offs and downsizings, mergers and acquisitions. Employees know that automation, in many cases, means elimination of jobs. They can't be certain that management will replace their former jobs with more meaningful work. The overall effect has been the creation of a suspicious, me-oriented workforce that's more concerned with the work they do than loyalty to any one company or institution.

Tech-trending managers need to evolve a whole new strategy for offering employees rewards and recognition. Behaviors that will benefit a networked company – like openness, being willing to listen, not being concerned with appearing foolish, and the willingness to share information – must be reinforced. And that may mean developing new job descriptions for managers, which reflect their new concern for promoting trust within an organization and empowering employees to think.

APPLICATIONS

The IT turf wars

Ask consultants, from the Ernst & Youngs on down, what it's like to try to implant new systems in corporations or institutions and they'll talk endlessly about the turf wars they experience. It's only human nature to back the technology you know best, particularly if running that technology equals your job and the new technology either eliminates what you're doing or means learning a whole new game.

Here's a story from one technology consultant along these lines. The managing information systems (MIS) division of a major aerospace manufacturer hired him to resolve issues they had with their environmental engineering department. Both departments were at loggerheads because the MIS division wanted to peddle to environmental engineering the systems that they had developed rather than meet engineering's specific demands. Sizing up the situation, the consultant convinced environmental engineering to hire him as their advocate. Eventually, they chose to buy a software package rather than continue disputes with MIS. That proved to be not entirely satisfactory and the consultant eventually produced something customized for them, but without the help of the MIS division.[10]

You also have to re-examine the notion of "goofing off." People used to be fired when they didn't look busy. But in a thinking, knowledge-based company giving people down time to process information – even if it may appear to be goofing-off time by a water cooler – may be key to your competitive success. In this hyped up, high-technology world you have to start defining the new risks to an organization – things like inaccurate information – and develop risk-management processes. Employees should be rewarded or penalized for their adherence to risk management.

And it's important to consider how many of you, or the people you now hire as consultants or in telecommuting arrangements, work from their homes. Besides cutting back on face-to-face interaction, it means that many of you are working more independently without traditional office support systems. There are no water coolers in cyberspace to provide that easy interaction that's often found in offices. No place outside of e-mail, which may be shunted aside or deleted, to share casual thoughts, observations and feelings. It's especially important to note that these new arrangements shut out feelings because they may be the very sorts of things people don't want to put in writing and to share with the world.

Allowing employees flextime or to work at home puts a new strain on managers to be able to trust that a job is being accomplished in the physical absence of the worker. It means a redefinition of value in terms of what employees are providing. Once again, you have to abandon that old notion that looking busy means someone is being productive. They can't look busy if they're not present. What they produce, and on a timely basis, is what counts today. To summarize, you can expect technology to affect your organization in the following ways. It:

- alters the power structure/may create turf wars;
- changes communication flow;
- creates the need for openness, information sharing and collaboration;
- requires a new set of employee incentives;
- alters the idea of competition and competitors;
- breaks down office walls and allows for work on the fly, or from a home office; and
- changes the notion of a "proper" work day.[11]

Ways that tech trenders can learn to manage change

We've been outlining ways that technology affects employees, managers and organizations as a whole. Now it's time to look at how to manage that change and harness it to evolve into networked, B2B companies and institutions. There are some age-old principals of managing change, in general, that are well worth understanding and utilizing before moving on to some specifics of how to manage technology change.

As noted earlier, to function well in an organization people have to feel technically competent, feel secure in their power relationships and feel that there's an adequate support system in place to handle the personal and technical needs that are part of effective work. Change of any sort can upturn these three factors and cause destabilization and a loss of equilibrium. Anyone dealing with change needs to deal with all of these factors. Managers have the tricky task of dealing with the disequilibrium that change invokes in them while helping employees cope as well. This can create additional tensions. With any kind of change it's necessary to re-establish a feeling of technical competence, security in power relationships and a support system to bring back the equilibrium the change has shattered. And that generally means creating the time and space this sort of rebuilding requires.

It's also important to recognize that change creates an emotional cycle very much akin to the stages of grieving, as anyone who has suffered computer crashes mid-project knows all too well. Emotions may range on one end of a spectrum from innocent optimism and hopefulness to rage and disillusion. Sometimes it's hard to differentiate between because change is creating a bad work environment – things like computer malfunctions – and someone feeling bad because they are still coping with the change and haven't assimilated it emotionally.

Unfortunately, many of today's organizations do not invest the time and energy that change requires – particularly technology change which involves both mental and mechanical change and learning. Instead, they focus on the content of the change, the advisability and the efficiency of the implementation of the change, but not the cost of the change and the support that's necessary to recoup the cost. A lot of organizational data suggests that the cost of not paying attention to re-establishing this equilibrium is far greater than the cost of time and energy required to reassure employees. Whether the changes stems from a takeover or a major technology implant, the results of ignoring human needs can be disastrous.

Here are four steps that tech-trending managers can take to restore equilibrium within an organization:

1 Be aware, and help others be aware of the implications of the change for different people in the organization.
2 Communicate clearly the purposes and rationale behind the change.

UNPLUGGING TECHNOSTRESS

Learning to recognize technostress

Ever since Mary Shelley created the Frankenstein monster as a warning against the encroachment of 19th century technology, the character has stood as an emblem of a world run amok, a world that would destroy its creators. By today's technology standards – compared with streaming video, for example – the Frankenstein character is a bit player. He could even be considered cuddly; someone to invite home for tea.

Today's Frankenstein-equivalent is far more subtle and far more complicated. This monster doesn't kill by hands-on means. It's more like dying of a gas leak in a palatial estate – you don't even know you're dead until you read about it in the papers. Its weapons range from mind-numbing boredom to exhaustion, loss, pain and anguish. Its symptoms range from galloping hemorrhoids, raging pimples, boils, and severe halitosis to psychological disorders such as multiple browser syndrome, performance anxiety and chronic platform fatigue. (The runaway phone bills and potential for porno addiction are another story ...)

This Frankenstein lurking just behind your computer screen is simply known as technostress. Technostress is the by-product of a very peculiar kind of human misery – the misery of being trapped in the bizzaro world of high technology where nothing is as it seems. Enter a computer store, call tech support or pick up a computer magazine and you're reminded of the old Monty Python sketch where someone goes to a cheese store to buy – what else? – cheese, but none exists.

Go to a computer store to buy a PC or a Mac and they've got equipment out on the floor, but the display models pretty much all look alike, feel alike and appear to run alike. Differentiation doesn't exist, at least to the naked eye, which is really exhausting to the average computer user – the technozombie – who doesn't even want to think about technology, let alone have to suffer over buying the stuff. (At least the iMac comes in different colors, but that doesn't entirely solve the problem ...) The only escape is to turn back the clock 30 years or more. And who wants to do that? Give up Weather.com? E-Bay? No way.

But how to live with the present? How to live in a world of malfunctioning software, computer crashes and major equipment incompatibilities? How to recognize technostress, and conquer technostress before technostress conquers you? The first step on the pathway to dealing with technostress is to realize that it stems from two factors:

1 the loss of identity that technology can induce; and
2 the loss of equipment, work and cash that technology ultimately provokes.

Then there's the accepting pain factor – otherwise known as the resignation factor. There's no way to entirely avoid technostress, but at least you can prepare yourself to weather this storm by resigning yourself to a modicum of pain. Think of this loss and pain combination (LPC) as plywood for the soul. For example, some computer users report that computer crashes bring to mind a death in the family. Other computer users have pointed out that the computer crashes usually lead to loss of work, and that loss provokes post-crash stress syndrome, which renders its victims too shocked to plug back in. But most of all, remember that technostress is generated from a feeling of loss and of being out of control.[12]

3 Listen and obtain feedback and input on all aspects of the change and their implications, and especially those that are adaptable to particular circumstances.
4 Wherever possible, get significant participation from members of the organization affected by your decisions for technology implementation.[13]

Helping tech trenders harness technology change to benefit your organization

So far you've heard this basic message: accept change and provide human support to make the change in the most positive fashion possible. This section focuses on how to help people, from senior management on down, embrace technology change. That's not as easy as it sounds. Not every manager is won over by New Economy promises of profits, increased productivity and general prosperity. There are as many in the upper echelons of management resisting technology change as much anyone else in your organization (see Chapter 9).

Senior management, and all employees, must truly believe that technology is crucial to the organization's survival before they will buy into painful technology change that alters their job descriptions, work habits, requires learning and costs dearly on the financial side. If you're the tech-trending manager, consultant or vendor trying to make this case you have to insist that this is a matter of survival. No company or institution will thrive without using technology to advance business or institutional goals. You will literally be left out of the electronic communication loop.

And, as noted in the last section on change-management principles, you have to recognize the emotional aspects of change and take them into consideration if you are to successfully alter your organizational structure, employee work habits, or job descriptions to accommodate the demands of the New Economy. The following are seven steps designed to give tech-trending managers the insights – both practical and psychological – you need to harness the technology changes that will benefit your organizations.

1 *Relocate people, if necessary.* You need about 25 percent of the organization embracing the change and about 65 percent of employees to be neutral for it to fly. There will always be hold-outs, but eventually they come around through peer pressure. If they can't adapt, they may need to be relocated into other positions where they won't affect the change you are trying to institute.
2 *Use positive reinforcement.* Although it may be possible to increase pain to make change, it's always better to start with positive reinforcement. Using trendy buzzwords like knowledge management and benchmarking lures some people, especially when tied into a vision for the future that offers improvements. Executives can be won over by focusing on the value technology offers their companies and institutions. Statistics are helpful along with actually stating financial gains and losses recorded that have been published in the media or in analyst reports.
3 *Harness pain.* One truism about change is that everyone is for it unless it affects them. At best, change is bearable when you can anticipate a better outcome than the state you're in today. At worst, it can mean loss, which leads to shock, upset and confusion. That loss can be as trivial seeming as coming into your cubicle on a Monday morning and discovering that your desk is missing or that they've removed your hard drive for servicing without notice. Basically, you've lost control of your environment.

   Technology change is particularly hard to bear because it's not always obvious – even to top management – that there will be improvement. What's certain is that there may very well be disruption, followed by confusion and no one knows whether the outcome will be as desired. Certainly, after following the steps in Chapter 7, technology purchases and implementations should not be so fraught with uncertainty and tension. But even informed choices don't guarantee a perfect outcome in the world of technology.

For all these reasons, many people in organizations face technology change with the sort of thrill reserved for having their teeth drilled without Novocain. It's something to be avoided or even subverted. Experts in change management say the only way around this issue is to up the pain level in the current state – threaten firings for non-compliance, for example – so that any change feels more bearable. Another trick is to convince all concerned that the price they pay for stasis is increased pain in the future. See the Solutions section below for some of the stages involved in harnessing pain to make technology change.

SOLUTIONS

Technology doesn't have to be **that** *painful*

OK, you've heard more than you want about harnessing pain to make change. Here are some tips to help you stop grousing and move into a tech-trending mode:

- *Stop playing ostrich.* The first thing that management has to do is cease playing ostrich and actually recognize that technology change equals legitimate pain. It's your job as tech-trending managers to comprehend the toll that technology change is taking on your organization. This means focusing on issues like the jobs that technology may eliminate, or e-mail overload.
- *Devise a vision for the organization.* Tech trenders from the president on down should devise a vision for the organization that encompasses technology change. This vision should be presented in the most positive light possible, but with a sense of urgency that will inspire employees to endorse the plan.
- *Put IT attitudes into perspective.* Recognize that people in the IT department, as well meaning as they may be, usually don't have the slightest idea how technology affects mere mortals who lack their sort of mind-sets. All members of the organization have to be tapped to both drive, and later help gain endorsement, for technology change.

- *Understand the pain cycle.* Change, as mentioned earlier, creates emotional cycles that range from the most overblown positive to the most grossly negative. "SAP will solve all my problems" is an example of the overblown positive. "This new software will mean I will lose my job" fits into the grossly negative side of the spectrum. Neither is a good place for people to be. The overblown positive position leads to disillusion. People sitting in the grossly negative state will simply bail out, or subvert the project at hand. Some employees have been known to input wrong information in time cards to sabotage a new system, or claim physical injury to avoid using e-mail.
- *Getting people to be realistic means facing emotions.* To get to the place where members of your organization can embrace a realistic sense of what will happen when technology is implanted in your company or institution may mean allowing employees to blow off steam for a while. There are three bail-out cycles that take place on that negative side of the spectrum, and it's crucial to know how to manage people when they hit those points. Anger is one of the critical stages in this cycle. "I'm a long-term employee and you can't do this to me," is the sort of response you can anticipate. You have to let this sort of person ventilate or they could very well bail out. Eventually, if they feel heard, a reasonable person will get to the negotiating phase. It's this phase that leads to realistic acceptance of change, and allows for the compromises and sometimes concessions that will win people over to change.

4 *Let your business plan be your guide.* Successful tech-trending organizations insist that your business strategies guide technology acquisition, which goes a long way to helping you feel in control of your technology decisions and promotes sound management practices. That means focusing, first, on your long-term business or institutional goals in the context of knowing what sort of organization you are today and what you intend to be, as well as gaining an accurate sense of employee skills. Not everyone wants to be an e-commerce leader or a technology leader. The trick is finding out what kind of organization you are and adopting the technologies that are strategically important to your business goals. Buying every new bell and whistle the vendors offer won't make

SOLUTIONS

Managing employee anger and negativity

The British Standards Institution (BSI) has decided to institutionalize the process of managing employee anger and negativity through creation of its guide BS 8600 for complaints handling. It may seem sort of silly to codify a process that amounts to allowing employees to mouth off, but smart managers have long understood that giving employees a voice in a company boosts morale and opens communication channels that can lead to important improvements.

BSI officials report that their new guide is about how an organization might put in place a system for handling complaints. It's for anyone, large or small and for all divisions, not just manufacturing. BS 8600 leaves it up to the organization to decide what sort of system they want for handling complaints. As for how many companies will want to be this systematic about allowing their employees to ventilate, no one knows quite yet. It will take a year or so to see if this approach works any better than threatening to fire employees if they don't endorse that new ERP system.[14]

you successful. Purchasing technology to meet a strategic end and with their customer's needs in mind will.

5 *Don't rush to be a technology leader.* Organizations that have been successful don't want to allow technology to alter the way you present yourself to the world, your customers or vendors. That means you have to select what technology you implement with care. Rushing to become the first in B2B retail will only garner positive publicity if you succeed, but could ruin a going concern with a brand name if the effort fails.

Jumping in too quickly may mean making bad purchases or buying glitch-ridden software that's been tossed on the market in its beta-test phase. For that reason, it's sometimes advantageous to hold back on technology purchases until you're certain the products actually work. It may also make sense to wait for products based on open standards. On the other hand, it's not feasible to hold back too long. The trick, as will be explored in Chapter 7, is counter-balancing business and institutional needs with technology purchases that make sense and have as much built-in transitional flexibility as possible.

6 *Work on improving human processes.* Technology will only reinforce poor management practices and work processes. It will magnify existing problems rather than eradicating them, as anyone with a failed ERP system knows only too well. The key is recognizing that technology is only a tool. It won't fix your organization. Smart tech trenders won't remove humans from business or institutional transactions. Those organizations that try to eliminate people entirely will lose out as much as those that rely entirely on people and paper-based systems.

Think about the frustrations of locating information on a voicemail tree that goes on and on – this can be common in government agencies. Remember how frustrating it was to attempt that Web purchase when you couldn't locate the box that moved you to the order form, and there wasn't anyone listed to call. Those sort of annoyances make customers hang up and look elsewhere for products and services (see Chapter 8).

7 *Be willing to educate employees/customers.* It's particularly important when contemplating a major change – like moving retail sales online – to be willing to educate users and consumers. Teaching customers what to do is a major challenge of the B2B world, and that's whether you are operating a company or institution. Be willing to let customers know you have a new technology, which means a new approach to reaching you. Let them try it, but don't dismantle your old system until you can be certain the bulk of your customers are making the switch and are satisfied with the change (see Chapter 9).[15]

APPLICATIONS

Using technology to promote customer relations

Technology experts are convinced the Internet will drastically alter customer relations and for the better. Not only can commodities be presented at a customer's desktop, but the Internet/ Web allows organizations new ways to reach and monitor their customers. Online customer support is starting to come into its own. And the Internet/Web allows for new ways to learn about your customers, which means a higher retention rate if you can apply what you know effectively.

"By exploring the Internet, companies not only gain opportunities for cost-cutting; they can also create new business opportunities by learning more about their customers. At present, such information tends to be strewn among many different databases, each attached to a particular product line or sales channel. By integrating the data, companies can present a single, coherent face to customers. That task is easier when customers shop online."[16]

Networking, collaboration and geographically displaced teams

You've heard a lot of about pain and suffering. Now it's time to look at the positive side of technology change – the opportunities technology provides tech trenders for managing and carrying out your work lives in a more satisfying fashion. These range from being able to telecommute, to working flexible hours, manage companies and institutions while traveling, and to develop more open, mentally challenging work environments.

- *Networking and collaboration.* Interestingly, when you network your company and institution in the literal sense of connecting computer hardware and software, you are also connecting humans and offering them improved communication. Humans are allowed to network on networks. The lexicon for technology and human interaction has become the same.

  Collaboration is another human organizational term that is creeping into technology parlance and practice. We hear about collaborating trade communities, for example. That's because the Internet is offering opportunities for electronic collaboration that would never have been possible in the days of snail mail and phones, or even fax machines. You can attend Web chat rooms with individuals from all over the world. Organizations are taking advantage of the Web to conduct business this way. For example, standards organizations post work under development on their Web sites and open them to comment from interested parties. Information on change is relayed to participants electronically, rather than waiting for mail delivery.

APPLICATIONS

Collaboration tools evolving

All sorts of new technology tools are evolving to aid in collaboration. The most obvious is use of a company Web site to share information and help tech trenders keep tabs on projects. The shared Web site means you don't have to e-mail numerous members of a project team. And it's especially helpful if team members are globally displaced, or happen to be traveling. All can access information from their laptop while in airports or in hotel rooms.

Companies like Ford and General Electric have evolved their own collaboration tools for sharing information. Ford, for instance, has instituted instant messaging and "e-rooms," to allow employees involved in acquisitions to handle due diligence from remote locations. And Firedrop, a California startup, has developed something it calls a "zaplet." The zaplet arrives like an ordinary e-mail, but when opened it becomes a window to a server or central computer. This allows tech trenders access to all sorts of applications, from spreadsheets to customer databases.[17]

As technology "shrinks" the world, and natural resources start to dwindle, the need for collaboration is growing exponentially. Organizational change experts are working more and more to help diverse organizations – including competitors – work towards some common end. They may need to develop common understandings and, sometimes, common actions to achieve a common objective. One example already noted is the Big Three Automakers' push to improve electronic communication between Ford, General Motors and Chrysler, along with the joint base of 10,000-plus suppliers.

Just as the Web creates multiple junctures for linking up, so new management approaches are evolving that don't depend on a linear approach to getting from point A to point B. This is especially true when more and more outcomes are the results of multiple organizations, as is the case with high-tech consortia. Or, when as noted in Chapter 2, trading partners will be able to grab inventory from a pool of collaborating warehouses to benefit joint projects. The Web becomes a literal model for collaborative work, just as the needs that collaboration spawn affect Web development.

- *Geographically displaced teams.* As companies become more and more global they have to learn to manage from remote locations. And more and more they are managing teams, not just individuals or offices. A whole sub-section of team building – a major management buzz – is now being devoted to managing geographically displaced teams. Even though technology is making it possible to manage across oceans and continents, the basic principles of team management should not vary. If anything, they become more important because the distance doesn't allow for much face-to-face contact.

SOLUTIONS

The Internet/Web bridges the distance

As tech-trending managers know, geographically displaced employees don't have the option of an after-work drink or game of racquet ball. For many organizations, the Internet/Web is the best way to keep communication channels open. It allows all employees access to corporate "views, news and vision."

Some companies are using the Internet, or their intranet, to offer online training. Boeing has gone so far to promote ethics to employees, suppliers and customers, through its online "ethics challenge." Not only is desirable behavior explored – at least as defined by Boeing – but the aerospace giant is using the Internet/Web to spread a common cultural and management approach throughout the company.

Other institutions maintain actual news departments and use their intranet to present ongoing information (see Chapter 8).

And the Internet allows managers to track employee interests and concerns, plus determine if they're paying attention or following up on training. At Cisco Systems the Internet allows top management to learn if employees are tuning into the monthly video explaining where the company is heading. Managers can track who's clicked on and who's thrown it away.[18]

Team success depends on things like articulating clear, common goals; being aware of overlapping competencies and skills; acknowledging each other's contributions and needs; developing clear procedures and ground rules for working together, and establishing common bases for information and data, among others. In general, if you are managing teams remotely, you have to consider the following:

1 How important it is for these groups to be together at various times?
2 What are the most important things for team members to do when they are together?
3 What are the most effective means of accomplishing human and technical tasks when not together?

Picking the right technology to promote long-distance communication depends a lot on your organization's culture. Perhaps you're dealing with global operations that may include foreign cultures and practices – not just organizational styles – and foreign languages. Communication may have significant cultural implications, signaling levels of urgency and importance in one country that would appear insignificant in the US, for example.

Even in the US, different technologies can indicate different levels of urgency. And that sense of urgency can differ from organization to organization. For example, in some companies and institutions e-mails may signal that a quick response is required, but don't expect serious documents unless attachments are enclosed. There are organizations where serious material is still faxed. And the most serious documents are still mailed so the recipient can see a signature – though this may change as electronic signatures become legal tender.

Make sure you are aware of these organizational differences, and cultural nuances, before ascribing technology as communication tools to manage teams. Some companies like Texas Instruments and Nortel Networks have decided that technology is no replacement for human contact. They budget for travel to allow face-to-face contact for their global managers, and in-person training.[19]

New Economy management positions

New management positions are constantly evolving to handle the ever-changing demands of new technologies. For example, ten years ago whoever heard of a chief information officer (CIO), chief technology officer (CTO), chief privacy officer (CPO) or chief knowledge officer (CKO)? It's likely that in the next few years these roles will continue to evolve and new positions will be developed. Already, some companies are exploring setting up e-commerce teams or even divisions, so tech trenders can expect to be adding the title chief e-commerce officer (CECO), or something similar to your organizational chart, in the near future. Let's look briefly at some of these new tech-trending management positions:

- *The MIS (Manager of Information Systems or Services).* This individual usually heads up what was once called the computer department, but now is referred to more regularly as the IT or information technology department or technical services group in many institutions. Responsibilities are to maintain equipment, help staff with hardware/software problems and develop solutions for business problems. Some organizations have an IS manager, which stands for information systems or information services, depending on the organization. This role is pretty much the same as the IT or MIS manager's.
- *The CTO.* Many organizations, particularly large ones, have a CTO acting as a senior technologist, or as one manager said "almost an evangelist on the technology side of the house."

This is the individual who is really entrenched in the technology and works exclusively evaluating solutions and ensuring the technology is functioning properly. In some New Economy companies the CTO actually develops products. It's critical that a CTO have a strong technology background.

- *The CIO.* In general, the CIO is the most senior technology position in the organization and generally reports directly to a president or CEO. Nowadays, particularly if there is a CTO or strong MIS person in-house, a CIO is more concerned with leveraging technology for strategic business ends than working with the actual technology. As will be discussed in the remainder of this section, CIOs must have both a strong technology and business background if they are to serve your tech-trending organizations properly.

How CIOs can help tech trenders better manage technology change

Although the titles and duties may shift from company to company and institution to institution, you will need someone who can weave your technology concerns into your business strategy. As will be detailed in the chapters ahead, the only clear way to take charge of technology rather than having it run your organization is to directly tie it into business goals. For this reason a number of CIOs and analysts have been surveyed to offer you insight into this relatively new position and to outline ways CIOs can help you better manage technology change.

In this section tech trenders will learn more about the qualities that you should be seeking in a CIO, what capabilities this individual should bring to your organization, what tasks he or she should be able to perform and how this job is evolving in this new networked, B2B world. The concern is to provide you the criteria for selecting a CIO who will be able to drive constructive change in your organization.

PLATFORMS

Qualities a tech-trending CIO should have

It's not enough to be smart and well-educated. CIOs today better be able to multitask. Here are the qualities that CIOs must have to be tech trenders in their own right:

- know the business side;
- be a good communicator;
- be a strategic thinker;
- be a good human resource person;
- be able to motivate employees;
- keep staff working for you, rather than moving on;
- be able to negotiate;
- be able to build partnerships;
- be able to facilitate change;
- be a shrewd politician;
- be a good listener;
- be able to paint a picture and be visionary;
- build trust; and
- facilitate change and manage risk.

One of the most important aspects of the CIO job is to be a facilitator of change in your company or institution. It's often up to the CIO to identify that change is necessary, and walk both senior management and employees through the emotional stages that lead to acceptance. CIOs find they have to develop a roadmap to guide an organization through change and ensure that everyone has a common goal and is moving in the same direction.

CIOs know that the key to charting that course is business awareness. The days of tossing technology at problems without concern for business goals is heading to a quick close. The CIO in most organizations acts as the technology advisor to the president, CEO or both. He or she must be tuned into business goals and be aware of business issues. To function in this role, the CIO must also have good strategic/analytic skills, be politically shrewd and aware of your organization's culture.

In this tight job market the CIO has to create opportunities for employees, build trust among the staff, and work to keep talented people from moving on to more lucrative stock options. He or she must be able to forge alliances and partnerships both within the organization and with outside vendors and trading partners. The CIO is a facilitator of change in your organization. And some argue that the CIO must be a visionary, or at least be able to paint a picture so as to bring technology alive to other managers who lack a technology background.

There's no doubt that a CIO can't get by without having an up-to-date knowledge of technology. Some analysts and CIOs argue that a CIO has to be exposed to many technologies before taking this sort of post. Only a few years ago, knowing applications was key. Now a CIO should have a strong awareness of what it takes to network an organization and be aware of the role the Web is playing as a future information pipeline and understand Internet connectivity. There are some organizations that have two CIOs – one in charge of applications and the other in charge of network services and operations. But a strong CIO should understand both fields and be able to function in them today.

Here's the typical sort of issue a CIO is asked to handle: members of the IT department come into the office and ask for half a million dollars for three new servers. The CIO has to be able to ask the whys. Why do you want to do this? Why do you need this amount of power? And he or she has to be able to assess the answers and make a decision that makes both technology and business sense.

In another example, a CIO is confronted with a decision of whether to install a costly data warehouse so the overall organization can better handle information, or install a data mart that is less expensive, can be implanted far more quickly, but concentrates on a specific business unit. Price is one factor he or she must consider. At $1 million the data warehouse is fairly steep. Implanting an organization-wide data warehouse that involves virtually all departments in the enterprise also requires human resource and management skills. But will the data warehouse be able to accommodate the organization's long-term business and technology needs? The CIO has to be able to assess those factors and make a decision. He or she has to be able to provide the organization with a critical path, to walk it through the technology maze, and paint a picture for lay people of what technology choices mean to them.

Being a CIO today means maintaining a balance between technology, business goals and human needs at all times, as well as knowing how to delegate, manage change and manage risk. Those with a technology background might be tempted to jump in and do hands-on work. But that's not the role. So a CIO has to recognize that the value-add to an organization rests in their strategic and management abilities, not in the technological. The message from the field is those who want to work with code but not people, need not apply to this position.

As one CIO puts it: "You've just got to be flexible. You've got to understand you're living with stress. You've got to be looking backwards and forwards at the same time. I mean backwards because you can't forget where you come from. In other words, you can drive yourself crazy because you're never going to reach your goal. Remember to see how far you've come."

PLATFORMS

A CIO's job description

So you want to be a CIO. Here's what comes along with the job description and what you have to be able to perform:

- identify vendors and identify critical paths to apply their solutions;
- know technology and technology trends;
- help lay people cope with technology;
- be able to build a virtual team;
- help an organization recreate itself to take advantage of technology opportunities;
- know multifunctional applications and networks;
- recruit qualified help;
- create growth opportunities for employees; and
- be able to communicate and negotiate with all departments in the organization.

Functioning as a tech-trending CIO in the New Economy

So far, we've talked about the CIO's job in fairly general terms. But there's no doubt that the emergence of the Web is altering that job and its requirements in some very specific ways. CIOs, and CTOs as well, have to be be familiar with the new Web-based and even P2B approach. They have to be able to function both inside and outside the organization and evaluate technology requirements that will affect not only a supply chain but supply network. And they have to be able to evaluate new Web-based markets, develop e-commerce teams and work in a collaborative fashion with many new players.

The experts say the first thing a CIO has to do is focus on integrating all business processes instead of just developing individual automated systems. This means developing complete business solutions and being able to deliver them rapidly throughout an organization. Part of this process involves developing a window on the Web that integrates with company or institutional goals, particularly the financial side of the enterprise.

The New Economy demands that the tech-trending CIO be able to deal with many external parties. These may include vendors, customers and even alliance partners who are former competitors. For example, a CIO involved in the credit card aspect of the banking industry has 8000 employees in his division that used to be his main concern alone. Now, with some business functions taking place on the Web, he has to be concerned with 13 million customers. That's a pretty major expansion of concerns, which is made all the more alarming by the speed of technology. In the pre-Web world an application error might have put 1000 customer service representatives out of business for a day. A similar error can affect 300,000 customers.

CIOs are also finding that expectations are changing in this evolving networked, B2B world. Everyone thinks it's possible to do things faster and faster. CIOs say they used to worry about IT and now they have to know how to build an information highway. They have to make quick studies of the new technologies and move from the tactical to the strategic. And they're dealing with challenging employees who may have picked up some superficial information on a Web site and now believe they're technology experts. No wonder so many CIOs talk about feeling stressed out.

Tech-trending CIOs and CTOs aren't trying to make the B2B leap all on their own. They know the most expedient way to move their organization into the Web world is to hire someone with prior experience in e-commerce who can at least act as a subject matter expert. Hiring consultants is another valid approach. But the tech trenders always keep up with the new technologies and new approaches whether through networking, attending conferences or reading.[20]

APPLICATIONS

New Economy demands on CIOs

With the advent of the World Wide Web, CIOs have to be able to tackle new problems in cyberspace. To handle these new requirements CIOs have to be able to:

- tackle and utilize the new Web-based technologies;
- provide rapid delivery of solutions and transfer of best practices across an enterprise;
- function outside the enterprise;
- evaluate technology requirements throughout a supply network, as well as in cyberspace;
- evaluate new Web-based markets;
- develop B2B strategies in conjunction with ongoing business strategies, tie them in;
- develop e-commerce teams or even divisions;
- realize the impact of e-commerce on the entire organization;
- work with many more people in a collaborative fashion;
- promote accuracy throughout a supply network; and
- cope with an expanded, more visible role.

Tech-trending managers shouldn't forget your sense of humor

You just spent the entire night devising a report replete with tables, charts and columns. Saving your work for the night the computer crashes and you lose most of what you've accomplished into the ether of computer land. Here's another equally sickening scenario. You're halfway through deployment of a new software program and nothing appears to be functioning. Deadlines are creeping along and you're tempted to return to Word Star, or some other safe program of your youth. Sometimes, when facing situations like these, the only thing you can do is laugh. It's just as important to help employees laugh, because laughter is one of the best stress reducers nature has devised. And sometimes it's the only recourse you have when facing malfunctioning equipment and systems.

Believe it or not, there are people who specialize in managing your workplace with a good dollop of humor. Here's what one humor management consultant has to say on the subject:

> "Humor in the workplace works like a thermostat, controlling the climate within the environment. It is a key component of the ambience that greets and surrounds everyone who enters the workplace. Simply put, positive humor fosters a warm and inviting feeling. Negative, divisive humor makes a place seem extremely cold and aloof.
>
> "Humor provides a common language and a common universe in organizations. It's often said that humor works to remove emotionalism and defensiveness that interferes with candid and honest communication. And in this way humor is a coping mechanism. When truth is too scary or difficult to face, humor enables people to detach themselves from potentially emotionally threatening situations.
>
> "The quickest and most effective way to become more proficient at the skill of humor is to lighten-up yourself.

> This will positively affect both the climate at work and the flow of honest communication, another direct and helpful result of humor in the workplace. It is important to be able to laugh about yourself in a self-effacing, not self-derogatory way. And it's also important to pay attention to what makes others laugh and smile. The more you feed co-workers humor, the more positive the work climate becomes.
>
> "Finally, for both selfish and altruistic reasons, it is important to know what makes other people happy so you can bring them joy while making them feel appreciated and respected. Pay attention to what makes your colleagues, family members or co-workers laugh or smile. The more you feed them humor they like, the more positive the climate becomes. And since humor is a skill, the more you practice these techniques the more proficient you become."[21]

If you can face technology change with a smile on your face you'll know that you may well be on the way to developing that networked, B2B organization that you've outlined as key to your business and institutional success. And if you can't quite manage a smile, try writing about your technology frustrations to friends and colleagues. E-mail is a good technology tool for downloading your frustrations. At the very least this approach keeps you from firing the IT department, smashing your terminal or shredding that report. Consider the you-can't-live-with-it-you-can't-live-without-it factor (see box below) before turning to Chapter 6 where you will learn more about organizing that networked, B2B environment.

UNPLUGGING TECHNOSTRESS

The you-can't-live-with-it-you-can't-live-without-it factor

Technology may drive us nuts, but we can't live without it. Without computers there would be no modem hookup. And without a modem hookup there would be no connection to the ready supply of jokes that circulate throughout the Web. Employees would not get their jobs done without a dose of morning humor. Managers would stop strategizing and the world economy would slowly collapse.

Tell you that you need advanced technology while you're in the throes of a computer crisis, though, and you'll toss your laptop in our faces. You feel traumatized – yes, even abused – by your equipment. Your lack of knowledge and control over technology means you experience a one-up, one-down relationship with your computer with the human being the one down. The result is a feeling of powerlessness and anguish that, left unrecognized and untreated, can turn into a monumental case of technostress, or even worse technonihilism. Consider this plea for clemency from a political scientist and professor based in Connecticut, as he begs university tech support to release him from the misery of being trapped in the netherworld of computer mis-repairs:

> "The following is a request for clemency. I am filing it on behalf of my computer, which was assigned to the Gulag Cue two weeks ago. Two weeks ago tomorrow, my NT machine (digital celebris) reported its incapacity to find some fragment of code. This violation – although a first offense – resulted in a sentence of undisclosed duration to the Gulag Cue. Initially, all the data on Prisoner Celebris (or Hal, as I used to call him) was similarly imprisoned. Fortunately, Henk heroically broke into Gulag Cue and liberated my data, sneaking it out on a freshly burned CD-ROM. Such acts of bravery are the subjects of songs sung by stout-hearted men around fires at night … Perhaps they are singing his praises as we sit in our offices and live far less heroic lives."

The professor continues in this vein for at least three more paragraphs, which gives you some indication of the desperation that computer mishaps can provoke, especially when on tight publishing deadlines. It's the lack of definiteness – the "perhaps the machine will be released in a week" – that the poor man finds particularly agonizing. Despairing enough to urge a special friend in tech support to intervene on his behalf: "Mike, if you have the power to break down the walls of Gulag Cue and force the release of Prisoner Celebris … I am certain the discharge would require but an hour. It is, after all, the Cue that imprisons my Celebris, not the offense."[22]

Notes

1 H. James Harrington, chief executive officer, Systemcorp., Quebec, Canada, and former consulting principal for quality at Ernst & Young.

2 David Washburn, principal consultant at Amherst Information Architects, Amherst, MA.

3 David Washburn, principal consultant at Amherst Information Architects, Amherst, MA.

4 B. Michael Zuckerman, director, the Mid-Atlantic Center for the Arts, Cape May, NJ.

5 Adapted from *The Economist* E-Management Survey, November 11, 2000, pp. 1, 9, 15.

6 Alan Hurwitz, principal of Alan Hurwitz Associates, Amherst, MA, and Hal Buell, former manager of the Associated Press global photography department.

7 H. James Harrington, chief executive officer, Systemcorp, Quebec, Canada, and former consulting principal for quality at Ernst & Young.

8 David Washburn, principal consultant at Amherst Information Architects, Amherst, MA.

9 Ken Godzina, executive director, AIAG, Southfield, MI.

10 David Washburn, principal consultant at Amherst Information Architects, Amherst, MA.

11 H. James Harrington, chief executive officer, Systemcorp, Quebec, Canada, and former consulting principal for quality at Ernst & Young, and Alan Hurwitz, principal, Alan Hurwitz Associates.

12 *When Bad Computer Things Happen to Good People,* a work in progress, Amy Zuckerman and Izzy Gesell, 2000. Also, Linda Wine, a New York City-based sociolinguist.

13 Alan Hurwitz, principal, Alan Hurwitz Associates.

14 John Hele, BSI Business Manager for Quality Systems.

15 H. James Harrington, chief executive officer, Systemcorp, Quebec, Canada, and former consulting principal for quality at Ernst & Young, and Bob Rosenbaum, editor, *Supply Chain Technology News.*

16 Adapted from "The Personal Touch," *The Economist* E-Management Survey, November 11, 2000, pp. 32–33.

17 Adapted from "A Little Knowledge," *The Economist* E-Management Survey, November 11, 2000, pp. 19–20.

18 Adapted from "Talking to Each Other," *The Economist* E-Management Survey, November 11, 2000, p. 14.

19 Alan Hurwitz, principal, Alan Hurwitz Associates, Amherst, MA. *Global Tool Kit: Supply Chain,* Amy Zuckerman, A–Z International Associates, Amherst, MA, 1999.

20 Krimo Salem, CEO of If & Then Inc., San Jose, CA; Jeanmarie Gelinas, vice president and CIO of Rodale, Inc., Emmaus, PA; Eric Fliegel, CIO, eTour, Inc., Atlanta, GA; Pam Kleier, CEO of constructionzone.com, Louisville, KY; Laurence Smith, a specialist in e-commerce management, Boston, MA; Merv Adrian, VP and Research Manager, Giga Information Group, Cambridge, MA; and David Yokelson, the META Group, Stamford, CT.

21 *Humor: The Universal Human Resource,* Izzy Gesell.

22 *When Bad Computer Things Happen to Good People,* a work in progress, Amy Zuckerman and Izzy Gesell, 2000; and Marc Eisner, professor of government at Wesleyan University, Middletown, CT.

6 Setting Up a New Economy Organization

There are many companies and institutions today – particularly those catering to the New Economy – that are already in a networked mode and working on developing their B2B strategies and skills. Take the example of two Canadian companies – Systemcorp in Montreal, Quebec and Descartes Systems of Waterloo, Ontario – which are both in the business of selling software solutions.

Systemcorp has a project management software package that aims to bring together human capital needs, financial data, procurement data and knowledge management. Descartes Systems provides online logistics services. Both companies will sell software in the traditional licensed way, but also sell software services online. For Descartes Systems, online sales is the primary focus.

Not surprisingly, to be in the business of selling software online requires tech-trending businesses like these to utilize the most advanced technology for their own operations. In these specific cases this means being fully networked, outsourcing back-office functions to stay nimble, and working with whatever array of software solutions is required to be both fast and efficient.

Because both companies rely, at the very least partially, on the Web to peddle their products, they are deeply concerned about maintaining backup equipment and server capacities that keep them online and in contact with customers at all times. And because they are small companies – Systemcorp has about 110 employees, for example – they are using technology to stretch resources. Anything that provides mobility and allows for operating the business from remote locations is high on Systemcorp's list for potential procurement and utilization.[1]

If there was such a thing as a scale for advanced technology use, these companies would register off the high end of the chart, along with the new dot.com businesses that are banking their whole existence on providing B2B services. But we all know that many companies and institutions are still grappling with issues like networking all departments, controlling e-mail, determining whether or not to implant an ERP system and whether to buy or create software packages to automate various business functions. You may be considering outsourcing back-office functions and many of you are in the throes of designing Web sites. Practicing mobile commerce when you can barely communicate electronically from department to department is hardly high on the list for some companies and institutions, even if they aspire to be tech trenders.

This chapter will offer you an organizational pathway and advice on set-up that will allow you to move to the networked, B2B world of the near future. Right now, tech trenders have to function in two worlds: the three-dimensional world of your office and water cooler, and the cyberspace world where your transactions are taking place. Until technology develops enough to allow for image and voice on the Web there won't be integration of these two worlds. Tech trenders have to bridge the gap between the so-called real world and virtual world of the Web. And that means that your real-world functions have to be in tip-top shape to match the speed and performance demands of the Web.

And, as noted in Chapter 5, changing management styles, work habits and attitudes about information sharing, competition and collaboration are prerequisites to organizing your company or institution to thrive in the New Economy. It can't be stressed more forcefully that old-fashioned hierarchical organizations won't cut it in the networked, B2B world.

Part I of this chapter will help you prepare your companies and institutions for a high-speed, B2B environment. As always, business strategy should be top of the list when dictating a technology course. You will want to explore how information flows in your company, and the sorts of skills your employees have – or lack – to handle the tasks of working in an networked, Web-based fashion (see Chapter 8). Ensuring that employee schedules are flexible to meet the demands of this new world is also crucial.

After management issues are addressed, tech trenders should start assessing what methodologies and technologies you can use to build a bridge into the B2B world. For example, it may be that enterprise resource planning (ERP) will help you integrate back-office functions and help you and your employees practice operating in an integrated, networked environment. You may want to consider other supply-chain methodologies like SCOR (the supply chain operations reference model) to implement improved information and work flow processes.

Part II takes you into the burgeoning B2B arena. You will learn more about various buying/selling models that lend themselves to the networked, B2B world you want to inhabit. Information is presented on building a Web presence and what goes into e-procurement, or purchasing via the Web. Tech trending companies are featured to offer real-life experience and suggestions about how to organize for the New Economy. They offer realistic assessments of the resources – both human and financial – required to set up a dot.com operation.

PART I: PREPARING YOUR ORGANIZATION FOR ONLINE ACTION

Consider this scenario: Joe Tire Manufacturer of Akron, Ohio manufactures tire stems and caps. He's a successful fourth-tier supplier to major automakers, with 150 employees and a good track record in his industry. Like many, many organizations around the world, his company is technologically 20 years behind the times. He's implanted some back-office computing, e-mail and EDI. Almost no one, including Joe, uses the e-mail account. What does Joe have to do to enter the networked, B2B world?

Presume, for the sake of argument, that Joe is convinced he has to become a tech trender and is avidly boning up on new technologies and is promoting change throughout his company. The next thing he has to do is be prepared to spend money – at least $500,000 – in this case to network his operation, build a Web presence, plus provide the backup staff support required for this work (see Chapter 7 for specific technology purchases Joe can make).

To move into B2B, Joe and his top staff need to know about information flow as it relates to the supply chain and procurement – the dual foundations of B2B. He has to start developing partnerships to help with marketing, strategy, industrial development, sales and distribution. He may as well ditch his old marketing and development plans and be prepared to build his own, making his new business plan multi-dimensional so his company can function in an array of B2B exchanges and marketplaces. By leveraging existing business relationships and building on a pre-existing customer base, he can create new business ideas, plus save resources.[2]

This section starts at the beginning of Joe's journey to the networked, B2B world and explores ways that organizations like Joe's can start the process of working in cyberspace. The main focus is on helping tech trenders move into a networked environment.

Tech trenders need to understand information flow

Imagine the supply network as strands of information flowing throughout a company, connecting to suppliers, transportation/ logistics companies, customers, and trading partners, and then looping back into the organization. Today, information is carried electronically, whether through older systems like EDI or via the Internet/Web. Satellite, cellular, radio frequency or microwave technology may all be employed for messaging, and tracking and tracing of goods.

Information is the life force of the supply network and the building block of the new, knowledge-based economy. Without accurate information relayed at the right time and the right place, there are no purchase orders, no shipment messages and no payment. The supply network shuts down and so do your companies and institutions.

Technology may carry the information, but humans are both the source of the information and the drivers of the technology. However, as *Fortune* magazine has pointed out, "human" supply networks are complex and not always efficient:

> "Purchase orders get lost between incompatible computer systems, checks go astray, procurement officers 'guess' how much material to order because information they have to work with is unreliable. Warehouses pile high with unused inventory while other units scramble to find parts. Someone, somewhere in the value chain doesn't get the word."[3]

If these sorts of communication problems are taking place in one organization, imagine what's happening globally with the increase in outsourcing, the growth of multinational operations, and the emergence of global alliances between corporations and institutions. Without human skills – the ability to communicate both orally and in writing, manage information and maintain strict quality levels – the whole B2B revolution will fail.[4]

The Bridgestone/Firestone tire scandal that broke out in public consciousness in the summer of 2000 is a perfect example of communication snafus – whether purposeful or accidental – that threaten any operation. If news accounts prove accurate, then Firestone and Ford Motor Co. both suffered massive communication gaps that meant that information about tire deficiencies was never relayed to those who could fix the problem – the safety engineers. Both companies face enormous losses in product recalls, potential litigation and customer dissatisfaction that could swamp them for years to come, or even lead to bankruptcy. No amount of technology mattered in this case. It was lack of human communication that was at the base of the problem.

And so how communication flows in your operation, how to manage communication flow and distill the information you gather is vastly important to the success of tech-trending companies. It's so crucial, in fact, that Chapter 8 is devoted entirely to the human skills that will allow you to mine the knowledge – practice knowledge management – as you move into a networked, B2B world. Chapter 9 explores some of the ways you can train yourself and employees to better manage information, as well as determine what sort of technology training matters in this New Economy.

SOUND BYTES

Dell and Cisco know the importance of information sharing

Dell Computer and Cisco Systems are two of the world's largest technology companies, but they have a secret they'll share with you. The key to supply chain management – not to mention selling their products is information sharing. In fact, both companies hold management seminars on this topic to pound home this point.

The whole idea behind the supply chain is to allow manufacturers, retailers and shippers to manage as little inventory as possible. But that doesn't work if information isn't shared. Consider the positive benefits when communication channels are open. Suppliers are able to see customers' production schedules and sales data. That allows them to plan ahead for volume and timing of orders.

The Internet is moving information sharing into real time. When a customer places an order by clicking on a company's Web site, the software immediately feeds the order into the production schedule. Manufacturers kick into gear and retailers can tell customers when their order will be placed. Suppliers receive the same information and can ensure that parts are available. All information is transparent and available to all parties any time they want it.[5]

SOLUTIONS

Blockbuster: focus on labor issues, first

There are many ways to improve supply chain performance *en route* to developing a supply network. Blockbuster, Inc. decided to address human issues – particularly labor issues – before moving to technology solutions. According to Blockbuster executives, implementing pay-for-performance incentives and best practices in their distribution center helped boost worker productivity by 50 percent. Labor costs declined by a third.

Blockbuster incentive programs reportedly reward excellent performance and offer employees input into the operation, if not outright control. They receive daily feedback and weekly bonuses worth 15 percent of their average pay. The company also instituted a flex-time program that allows employees to spend more time with families or on outside concerns. They converted from a five-day work week to three, 12-hour work days. That means that management and associates enjoy 200 days off a year. As a result, employees gain a sense of responsibility and ownership, which leads to increased productivity.[6]

Organizing your company or institution so that information flows accurately and smoothly throughout your evolving supply network is key to being able to operate in a networked, B2B world. But many companies and institutions are still bound up in the old hierarchical system that allots communication rights based on an employee's stature in the company, rather than on an employee's effectiveness. Resources are lost because the right employee can't be heard, or is stifled.

And many organizations don't take the time to perform information-flow analyses that will show whether communication and work-flow are meshed in a way that's productive. Ensuring that communication is fluid and flexible and not bound by hierarchical rules is enormously important to pulling together those work teams, and developing the creative solutions the New Economy demands.

Moreover, many Web sites don't function well because companies and institutions don't have the slightest idea how to format information in a way that's readable and accessible. They don't realize they have to keep Web sites fresh and updated and don't know how to edit in a way that makes the task easier. A little journalism, editing and graphic design would go a long way to improving most Web sites' look and performance, which is so crucial to entering the B2B world.

In fact, the media offers a superb organizational model for any tech-trending company or institution concerned with quick, accurate relay of information that's conducted in a democratic fashion so that employees can be heard and their information incorporated into products and solutions. That's because the demands of the networked, B2B, knowledge-based world are very similar to the demands media organizations have faced for years. Like the media, tech trenders have to be able to gather, sort, analyze and disseminate information and knowledge accurately and at high speed. More and more of your company or institutional activities are taking place on Web sites that need to be maintained, and that means having writing, editing and formatting experience (see Chapter 8).

PLATFORMS

The Associated Press: a model for global information dissemination

When it comes to a model for global information dissemination and collaboration between competitors, one of the best is the Associated Press (AP), with its more than 100 offices worldwide that relay thousands of articles and photographs each week through a worldwide information network.

In terms of news management styles, AP is generally a bottom-up system. Most of the news materials come from individual satellite offices scattered throughout the world, all of which are responsible for coverage of their areas. Member newspapers, in turn, provide information to AP. AP, in turn, provides member newspapers with information packages and photographs on a daily basis that they can use in their products.

Here's an example of how information flows through the AP system. A plane crashes in Milwaukee. The closest bureau gathers the information on the crash and instantly transmits it to the state bureau, which then relays the story to the central New York office for final editing and dissemination. Dissemination takes place on a regional, national or global basis depending on the interest level the information generates.

All information generated globally moves through AP's New York office. There are sub-nerve centers in London and Tokyo where information from the various hemispheres is processed. London and Tokyo transmit information to the New York international desk, which then chooses how and where to relay the news.

In some cases, technology has altered the work and information flows. For example, digital technology has eliminated the need for chemical processing of photographs. In the 1970s, AP won a Supreme Court battle that allowed reporters to write their stories directly into computers. This change effectively short-circuited the old union-based typography system whereby journalists hand wrote or typed their articles and typographers set them into print. But, in general, news is still gathered and information processed in much the same way it was 100 years ago. It's the mode of transmission that has changed, or the mode of processing for print, not the method of gathering and analyzing information.

Tech trenders can also think of AP as a model for global collaboration. AP membership includes hundreds of regional newspapers, broadcast stations and television stations throughout the US and subscribers in virtually every country in the world. On the local community level some news companies are competitors and some are not. AP has provided a set of working rules that prevents papers from getting a free ride on news coverage from their competitors.

For example, newspapers in the AP system can deny their stories to those few papers that compete head to head while at the same time providing their news to the thousands of other papers served by the cooperative. Thus, benefits of cooperation are achieved while at the same time maintaining competitive operations in local areas. It is this sort of rule-making and mutual respect that competing trading partners may have to establish if they want to share information for the common good.[7]

It would be a good idea for any tech-trending company or institution intent on improving information flow in a networked world to take a short tour of a local newspaper or television station. The idea isn't to turn you into news organizations, but to borrow some of the "tricks of the trade" media outlets employ for gathering, culling, editing, formatting, disseminating and storing information in vast amounts – and in a generally accurate fashion – utilizing a team approach. This team approach, which is so essential to news gathering and dissemination, may also serve as a good collaboration model, whether that's departments sharing information in-house or with vendors, suppliers and trading partners. Take a look at how wire services are organized for another example of how competitors have devised ways of sharing information in a collaborative fashion (see Platforms, p. 236).

SOLUTIONS

ISO 9000 as a network communication tool

The ISO 9000 international quality management series is known for developing a quality management system in an organization. What lies at the heart of quality improvement is communication. So those who know how to organize a company for ISO 9000 registration, will also be doing a great deal to help tech trenders organize teams to promote improved communication in-house and then throughout a supply network.

Follow these six basic steps and watch how the environment of your company changes as employees and managers become practiced at gathering, sorting, culling, sharing and relaying information pertinent to business and institutional success:

1 *ISO 9000 as an interpersonal communication tool.* ISO 9000, which encourages information sharing as a key to internal auditing, works inadvertently to loosen the communication barriers that exist in many companies. It encourages employees to communicate their concerns about work processes and to promote changes in a way that management can hear.
2 *ISO 9000 as a team-building tool for information flow.* Companies that pursue ISO 9000 in the right way – meaning they involve all employees – create teams for the purpose of documenting work procedures and continued auditing of the quality system they are creating. Information sharing takes place within this small unit, and then the consensus is relayed throughout the company. This same team-based organizational tool can be applied to great effect to manage information flow throughout a company and a supply base.
3 *ISO 9000 as an information-sharing tool.* Sharing information within a team, a department and a full company is at the heart of the ISO 9000 internal auditing process. It's through information sharing that a company gains the full benefit of the ISO 9000 process, because it gains the knowledge needed to enhance quality and performance.
4 *ISO 9000 as a basis for monitoring information flow.* It's one thing to document work procedures and quite another to

maintain a long-term, free-flowing documentation system that will act as an internal auditor without creating more bureaucracy. The key to developing a flexible documentation system is in the setup, and that's both in terms of design and company politics.

The best-running documentation systems are organized very much like newspapers. Employees relay information on work procedures or make recommendations for change to their team leader – or directly, if the company is small – who then relays information to a central quality documentation office. Employees in that office sort, cull and assemble a quality manual for company-wide review. Later in the ISO 9000 process, once the manual is complete, they handle the requests for change that should be filtering to them on a regular basis.

5 *ISO 9000 as a training tool for knowledge management skills.* Because ISO 9000 is a written-based process, it inadvertently promotes reading and writing skills. As companies soon learn, it's quite a task to delineate a work procedure in clear language that can be understood by all.

Companies that involve all employees in writing procedures and change orders are well braced for handling networked systems, e-mail, managing supply chains and then, in time, moving on to creating knowledge products.

6 *ISO 9000 as a basis for continued knowledge management.* Information overload is a problem many companies face while putting in place an ISO 9000 documentation system. Companies that effectively utilize ISO 9000 have developed a documentation system that allows for sorting and culling information. Management and employees, alike, have tied in ISO 9000 practices with general company goals so that information can be prioritized very much in the same way that the news world prioritizes information. They are practicing call information or knowledge judgment.[8]

Tech trenders must integrate business processes and set up networked systems

Tech trenders won't succeed in a highly competitive B2B environment, or function on the Web, if they haven't networked their organization and, as part of that effort, integrated business functions in an electronic fashion. Even if you choose to outsource back-office functions, you still need your operation to run flexibly and efficiently and to create databases to store information. Before you start plunking down cash for servers and database applications and solutions, consider integrating the technologies you already have using the nicheware and middleware described in Chapter 2. There are four options you can choose.

1 *Adopt ERP principles*

Analysts believe one of the best strategies for evolving into a networked, B2B organization is to adopt the principles of ERP without necessarily buying into a full ERP software solution. Or, alternatively, you can purchase those portions of ERP solutions that help you integrate whatever functions you don't choose to outsource. Why bother with ERP? Let's face it, the Internet has not developed to that all-encompassing tool that will eliminate the need for translators, middleware and the like. ERP can be the quickest and easiest way for small and mid-size companies to find a way to integrate a host of applications.

APPLICATIONS

A membership organization goes electronic

Automating member services has had a tremendous impact on the operation of the American National Standards Institute (ANSI) in terms of operational costs and member satisfaction. In recent years, technology has been reshaping the face of this service-oriented membership organization by allowing staff, customers and members to interact globally, as well as providing far more information to members than a paper-based system allowed.

When determining what technology to utilize, the key element has been understanding what the membership – in this case the customer – was seeking from the organization. Members wanted more strategic information on standards and policies, for that information to be disseminated quickly and to be able to respond to policy matters online. Technology has provided those services and more. Standards can now be downloaded immediately. In a couple of cases, major customers like Caterpillar have arranged for immediate, desktop access to standards. This service is reportedly cutting out weeks form the manufacturing process.[9]

There are many reasons that ERP solutions failed in many companies. Over-hype of product lines has been a problem with software companies promising solutions they couldn't provide. But other ERP experts cite the fact that many companies seized on ERP as a means to make themselves Y2K compliant, which didn't work. And ERP presents management issues that many managers fail to address. The following are the two main reasons experts believe many ERP implementations fail:

- the company has not made the strategic choices needed to configure the systems and processes; and
- the implementation process spins out of business control naturally. This is inherent in the ERP implementation process, but can be addressed through development and adoption of new management practices and information flow systems that ERP promotes.

SOLUTIONS

Motorola: removing the weak links

Identifying the weak links in a supply chain is essential if tech trenders are to develop supply networks and other collaborative cyberspace arrangements. As simple as it sounds, soliciting supplier feedback is a major key to analyzing what is and is not working. But many companies and institutions don't bother.

That's not the case at Motorola where ensuring a two-way flow of information has been formalized in a one-page checklist with about 20 traits, including early supplier involvement, response to cost reduction ideas, purchasing professionalism, forecast accuracy and others. The supplier rates Motorola on a six-point scale against each trait. The supplier is asked to rate its best customer, whose identity is not revealed.

Motorola also uses activity-based costing to assess its supply chain. The challenge is to identify cost drivers that affect the supply chain. Some of the criteria to establish the overall ratings include lead time, cost, current supplier, sole versus single source, and custom versus standard component. Another Motorola trick is establishing a supply chain ombudsman to "arbitrate" between the customer and supplier. Finding ways of sorting out disputes, assessing the "truth" and getting both parties to cooperate is part of this job. And, an astute ombudsman will find opportunities to expose weak links in the supply chain and means of strengthening them.

When the semiconductor giant outsources work, it ensures that the service provider is viewed as an extension of the internal factor. That means sharing planning, inventory, human resources, information technology systems, and keeping different corporate cultures in mind.[10]

ERP experts believe that making ERP work means concentrating as much, if not more, on human processes as technology. Consultants specializing in this arena have outlined the following steps as necessary to successfully utilize ERP solutions:

- involve the CEO directly in the process;
- outline strategic priorities and tie them into the implementation process;
- involve the entire organization;
- link management controls with the ERP system; and
- provide employee incentives to ensure the project's success.

Multiply the number of players exponentially when you extend ERP integration into a supply network – which the Internet now allows you to do – and that means you must be able to track information flow and be able to set up default systems to avoid costly errors and failures. And always remember that developing a human process to back up the ERP solutions is just as important as the actual technology.

2 *Alternate ways to manage integration*

For many companies, the world has become an electronic hodgepodge of incompatible systems. As you tech trenders know, that's because software applications have been designed to address specific functions, not the entire supply chain cycle. Customers and

SOUND BYTES

An ERP vendor transitions to e-commerce

Some ERP vendors are staying alive by selling supply chain management applications. Others are moving beyond the supply chain to the Web. Enterprise software giant SAP made recent headlines signing food giant Nestlé SA to its largest software deal ever: $200 million for mySAP.com Web-based applications that will be accessible to all of Nestlé's 230,000 employees in 500 factory sites worldwide.

Nestlé plans to overhaul its entire core business on the Web-based software platform, which will function as role-based and personalized enterprise portals for the Swiss candy maker's entire staff. Nestlé employees will have access to internal and external applications in such areas as supply chain management, product manufacturing, customer relationships, knowledge management, e-commerce, product lifecycles, financial and cost management, and marketing. SAP will customize the portals so that only those employees whose jobs are defined by a specific role can gain access to information required by their jobs.

In other attempts to keep pace with competitor Oracle Corp., SAP also purchased a $250 million stake in e-procurement solution provider Commerce One (www.commerceone.com). Not only does this pact give SAP a sizable share in one of the leading e-marketplace makers, but it also provided SAP with an entrée into the Chauvinist auto exchange being formed by the Big Three. Commerce One and Oracle are both providing the technology that will power this online exchange. SAP has announced plans to bring Covisint beyond the US and link it to global markets.[11]

suppliers usually have their own set of computer systems and software applications that are more often than not incompatible.

What you need to be considering is integration – or the act of taking data from one software application (output), and without human intervention, using it as input into a separate application.

As noted, data integration has been tricky because software programs describe information differently. There's hope that the new Web languages described in Chapter 1 will help, but for now tech trenders must find ways to work in integration without Web assistance.

Besides ERP tools, there are also supply chain planning and execution tools available on the market. Supply chain planning and execution tools promote collaboration beyond your company or institution. They will allow for your systems to communicate, which is the basis of the networked, B2B world that you are working to build.[12]

3 *The SCOR method*

The Supply Chain Council's SCOR (for Supply Chain Operations

TECH VISIONS

New standard efforts could promote B2B

More and more international standardization efforts are taking place to harmonize Web languages and promote business-to-business electronic commerce, all of which will help promote more efficient purchasing and management. In recent months, the United Nations and the Organization for the Advancement of Structured Information Standards (OASIS), have kicked off a worldwide project to standardize electronic contracts and trading partnerships using XML. XML is the Web language being developed to promote B2B practices. It allows for the transmission of business processes, not simply codes for words and graphics.

The partnership, called the ebXML Trading Partners Team, plans to develop specifications to deal with XML requirements and to define a conceptual architecture, a message structure, partner identification, communications protocol and header and core components. Its aim is to standardize a number of different XML specifications and complement other ebXML project teams working to provide the exchange of global business information based on XML.

In a second, unrelated development, a new standard was recently issued that allows companies to electronically "publish" information to help potential suppliers and customers access one another's computers. The standard, known as Universal Description, Discovery and Integration, or UDDI, essentially describes a kind of decentralized electronic directory for businesses that want to locate customers and suppliers through the Internet. UDDI allows companies to store details such as contact information, products and services in one of several central registry databases on the Web. These databases will all be designed to "mirror" one another, so that each is always up to date.

UDDI creators are Ariba Inc., IBM and Microsoft. They say the standard should greatly simplify the process of establishing online marketplaces and other business-to-business e-commerce transactions. They've modeled the standard on traditional phone directories so companies can register simple contact information – including their phone numbers and addresses – on what UDDI creators call "white pages." UDDI "yellow pages" will store a variety of specialized business information, such as industries and geographic locations where a company does business.

Expanding on the phone directory model, UDDI also contains "green pages," which essentially describe how to connect directly to a given company's computer system in order to start or process a transaction. These instructions are specifically designed to let companies with very different information systems communicate with each other. For instance, companies can locate all suppliers for a given product line, review detailed specifications and pricing information and even conduct auctions and online ordering without picking up a phone.[13]

Reference model) could prove a useful tool to help you organize your company and institution to function in a supply network. In fact, experts argue that SCOR's basics, which include a focus on information flow design, are perfectly suited to a B2B world. SCOR has 22 work steps that unite supply chain processes and can easily be applied to conducting business on the Web. For example, SCOR work steps address issues like scheduling product deliveries, reducing both direct and indirect costs in materials purchasing, and learning how to establish a new flow for materials between suppliers in a variety of physical locations. The key, in most cases, is integrating your ERP system with an Internet link to bring many former supply chain practices online.[14]

SOLUTIONS

How to obtain a SCOR overview

To learn more about SCOR, and obtain a SCOR overview, all you have to do is type:
http://www.supply-chain.org/html/scor_overview.cfm.

This will bring you to a PowerPoint presentation that includes the following table of contents:

Slide text

1 Supply Chain Operations Reference-model (SCOR) Introduction
2 SCM Improvement – Companies Continue to Invest
3 Strategic Objectives of SCM
4 Perceived Benefit of SCM-related Investments
5 SCM IT Expenditures – percentage of sales
6 SCM Project Success is Uncertain
7 Who is the SCC9.Supply Chain Council Growth
8 Who is the SCC9.Supply Chain Council Growth
9 Supply Chain Council Directions
10 Supply Chain Council Directions
11 SCOR is founded on four distinct management processes
12 What is a process reference model? process type
13 SCOR Contains 3 Levels Detail SCOR process and a process type
14 Supply Chain Operations Reference Model (SCOR) – Process Definition each Level 2 process category
15 Scope of SCOR processes associated with standard performance metrics
16 Scope of SCOR processes decomposition models mapped to each Level 3 process element
17 Scope of SCOR processes
18 Scope of SCOR processes
19 SCOR Methodology: Applied in Four Steps
20 Level 1 Performance Metrics by process type Deliver Execution processes

21 Analyze Basis of Competition (Level 2) to describe a specific supply chain
22 Configure Supply Chain information for each Level 2 process category illustrate trade-offs in order fulfillment
23 Configure Supply Chain
24 Integrated Level 2 Metrics element definition and standard performance metrics the underlying logic
25 SCOR Implementations features, and vendors supply-chain execution processes
26 SCOR Projects – Major occurs at Level 4 (and below)
27 SCOR Projects – Modest supply-chain thread
28 Superior Performers spend less on Supply Chain Management
29 Supply Chain Improvement Benefits and Deliver Execution processes planning, execution, and infrastructure process types
30 Order fulfillment lead times were reduced 25–35 percent horizontal process integration[15]

4 *Consider hosted solutions.*

The good news is that there is a whole world of hosted solutions that you can now rent from one place, which will make it easier for tech trenders to move into a networked environment. Application service providers (ASPs) are emerging who will provide a vertically-oriented, meaning industry-specific, applications to meet your needs. There will also be business service providers who offer not only the technology, but the services to back it up.

For example, UPS e-logistics applications are starting to provide Oracle and EXE warehouse management solutions as hosted applications. Along with hosting the applications – meaning they store and download them – UPS will provide distribution centers for companies who lack facilities, as well as transportation services. PriceWaterhouse Cooper is partnering with them to provide solutions integration and project management. These services will spare tech-trending companies and institutions the bother of licensing expensive applications and putting them together. Take note, however, that companies like UPS are still experimenting with hosting applications for others and there may be a maturity, learning curve involved in working with them.

But being able to download software applications doesn't mean you should short cut the organizational process. IT consultants warn that process – meaning how work flows and information is transmitted throughout a supply network – becomes more and more important in a B2B environment. Be careful when picking pre-packaged solutions of any kind – let alone software you can download – to study how its implementation will affect your internal and external processes. Too many times, as will be evident from examples in Chapter 7, organizations purchase solutions that don't solve the business problem at hand.[16]

PART II: SETTING UP A B2B ORGANIZATION

Tech trenders have fully automated and integrated whatever business functions make sense for your overall strategy, and some of you have a fully networked operation. You now face that looming world of e-commerce. (Remember, B2B is still a vision for all but the most advanced companies). Before you buy any new equipment, software applications or even design a Web site, it's imperative to decide if e-commerce is right for your organization at this juncture, or if its five to ten years away.

Remember, it's one thing to purchase a book at Amazon.com and quite another to move your operation into cyberspace. Consider e-procurement for starters. On the buy side you will need Web access and the ability to utilize search engines, at the very least. On the sell side, tech trenders will need Web presence, e-catalogs and electronic order fulfillment. Most companies and institutions have long ago computerized the buy side and sell side functions, or at least significant parts of these processes. For this sort of tech trender, the challenge is to further speed up and streamline the entire procurement cycle by more closely linking buyers and sellers.

At its best, e-procurement provides organizations with the ability to automate routine practices and tighten supplier involvement and integration. Tech-trending purchasing organizations are moving beyond this stage and working on developing buy/sell collaboration between suppliers and vendors, creative risk sharing, online auctions, complexity reduction, and management of complex channel relationships. For example, General Electric has created a "trading process network," an electronic system that sends out requests for quotations – along with required drawings – digitally to global vendors. GE managers cite 50 percent cycle-time reductions and lower material acquisition costs among the benefits. Cisco Systems claims its e-procurement processes have reduced acquisition costs by $105 per transaction.

What's good for GE and Cisco may not be what's good for smaller tech trenders. Experts say e-procurement works only when buyers and suppliers have the right management systems and technology in place. Your organization has to be able to support a switch to electronic buying and selling, suppliers must be able to handle new information processing requirements and all systems must be compatible. And, you had better be able to manage content. As will be noted in sections that follow, managing data in a Web environment is far more complicated and detailed than working in print.

And starting a dot.com, let alone making it profitable, is still a dream for most of the world. For example, Purchasingcenter.com of Burlington, MA, launched in the fall of 1999, has been merged into a form beyond recognition. A fledgling Philadelphia-based dot.com named BioSupplies.com has moved from creating a transaction-based e-commerce product for life science researchers in academia to creating software – under the new name Tangerine Technologies – that's extensible and accessible to other verticals. Founders estimated they needed gross sales of $200–400 million annually to make a go of it and the pathway wasn't there on the $4.5 million they raised in venture capital.

Some of the original BioSupplies.com team has cooked up a new dot.com – Varro Technologies – that involves sharing information on the genome with academics and research institutes. This would involve sale of a software product that allows people to access new content. Subscription fees would be charged. To move this concept out of startup would require an estimated $40 million. Founders say it's possible to create a prototype dot.com that's scalable for a few million dollars. But the minute you put the model on servers, which requires specialized hardware to support data loads and have the appropriate software, then you're kicking the costs into the millions.[17]

PLATFORMS

What it takes to float a dot.com

Having a good idea helps. Cash is even more helpful and so is flexibility. Take the case of ScreamingMedia.com, a content aggregator trying to hustle content from big providers like the *New*

York Times and *Business 2.0* to sell to thousands of Web sites. The providers get a cut of the action.

SreamingMedia, which is housed in a renovated wharf building in New York City not far from Hudson River docks, started its life in 1994 as Interactive Connections. That was a scaled down model of today's company. The technology was far more primitive, and content to sell was almost nil, but somehow the owners were able to gather enough resources to keep things afloat. They renamed the business ScreamingMedia in 1998, and benefiting from more advanced filtering capabilities on the Web, have been able to keep on growing. There were five employees in 1997 and 200 by the end of 2000.

Technological improvements really kicked ScreamingMedia into high gear in 1999. By developing more sophisticated filtering software they were able to work with a variety of providers and Web sites, more easily guiding specific content to clients. This allowed sales people to court many more Web site customers, content providers and attract strong sales people. And the company has stayed in its niche rather than trying to be too many things to too many people.[18]

The pathway to B2B

OK, so you're hooked, have the resources and believe the time is ripe for your organization to take the plunge into e-commerce. Here are three major organizational steps crucial to moving into the B2B arena.

1 *The c-commerce vision*

Tech trenders need to think about working collaboratively with trading partners, vendors and the like. This is what The Gartner Group calls c-commerce. Their vision goes beyond e-business, or conducting a broad set of sales, marketing and service activities over the Internet and connecting a company or institution with existing and new suppliers and customers. The c-commerce vision enables multiple organizations to work interactively online to find ways to resolve business problems, save and make money through dynamically restructuring their relationships.

As noted in the last chapter, the world of increased collaborative ventures presents as much a management issue as a technology problem. Companies that are focused on going it alone and haven't been exploring collaborative efforts better start moving in this direction if you want to be successful tech trenders. You will require both a management and technological infrastructure to support c-commerce, which may include the sort of communication work the auto industry has been conducting with suppliers since the 1990s (see Chapter 5).

Analysts predict that c-commerce will become the norm in less than five years. They believe you should start preparing your companies and institutions now by extending, opening and securing your applications architecture to be able to integrate with a wider universe of potential business partners. That means working with vendors focused on your industry, who can ensure that there is a match between your primary needs and their core expertise. And they believe that software and other technology vendors will develop products to support this vision that are related to specific market niches. The game for tech trenders is to align with vendors that can demonstrate a specific focus in your industry.

So-called EC Service Bureaus are also growing up, which offer translation and document exchange messages between business partners over the Internet. Also called global supply web, document exchange services, Internet commerce, and others, the EC Service Bureau model amounts to a new and improved version of the EDI VAN (Value Added Network), adding the capability to translate to and from a wide range of formats including XML, flat files, excel spreadsheets and electronic forms. DynamicWeb, ICC, and AMO are examples of EC Service Bureaus.[19]

2 *Reach out to suppliers/collaboration partners*

If you're a manufacturer, it's time to start talking to your suppliers and bring them into your c-commerce vision. Institutions might start talking to other organizations that offer collaborative advantage. You need to study how to integrate your activities – and what activities you want to integrate – using the Internet as a communication tool.

Tech trenders should know what technology is required besides Internet access. To accomplish this goal, consider all participants as one system. An assessment needs to be made of current equipment and software, where you are compatible and where you are not. This may take some up-front time (see Chapter 7), but it will pay off down the line in less costly technology decisions and easier setup.

Even though you may be conducting negotiations with suppliers and collaboration partners for months to come, it's not too soon to get members of your organization prepared to operate in a c-commerce fashion. This will involve a great deal of the management work described in Chapter 5, particularly developing an open work culture where information is shared, and striving for collaboration not competition.[21]

PLATFORMS

Two c-commerce examples

Here are two examples of c-commerce in action:

- *Product development.* An auto manufacturer designing a suspension system. The manufacturer is seeking solutions to solve dampening problems over rough-terrain use. Its traditional trading partners have little domain expertise in this area, so:
  - the Web is polled to find organizations that could potentially solve this problem;
  - a potential vendor is found; and
  - a real-time, 3-D digital mock-up design session is invoked across a project Web site between the auto manufacturer and the potential vendor to explore possible design solutions and alternatives.
- *Production.* A paper mill installing a new roll-press line runs into a quality problem due to improper heat dissipation in the work cell. To overcome this:
  - an online bid containing the details of the work cell is sent out over the Web to install a new ventilation system;
  - the winning bidder and the roll-press manufacturer remotely supervise the installation of the ventilation system by a local construction group using a Web-based video and data link; and

- data from a temperature sensor is monitored by the winning bidder and the roll-press manufacturer during the break-in period to ensure efficient operation.[20]

SOLUTIONS

Advice from analysts and CIOs about organizing a B2B company or institution

Start transitioning now. If you're not in the game, you're going to be out. That's the message from a number of top analysts and CIOs. Everyone, including these folks who are experts, are struggling to maneuver in the constantly changing e-commerce environment. They say there's no choice, so best to start learning about the subject and training yourself and employees about B2B technologies and methodologies (see Chapter 9). Here are some tips both groups have to offer tech trenders:

- *Know your market.* Having a deep appreciation for your business, the market, the industry and your competition is a first step. You don't want to dump practices and processes that have made you competitive in the past. And, as will become your mantra, you want to link your e-commerce strategy to your business strategy.
- *Align business and IT objectives.* You don't want IT moving in one direction and the business in another. Make sure, particularly as you start building a Web presence, that they are aligned. Your institution's financial applications must be integrated into the planning process, as well.
- *Involve the whole supply network.* Your entire organization, as well as supply network, should be included in the planning stage and implementation of any e-commerce initiatives. You will find all aspects of your business processes affected – from how you go to market, to purchasing goods and working with customers. Outside channel partners, suppliers and vendors are also affected.
- *Establish new positions.* Some experts recommend establishing a position in the organization dedicated solely to e-commerce. This individual would report directly to the CIO. But the CIO, in most cases, has too much to handle to be able to focus on developing e-commerce while supervising the wider IT picture.
- *Be prepared to spend money.* The experts agree that transitioning to a networked, B2B costs money. You can't do this on a

shoestring budget. They say if you want to play, you've got to pay.

- *Know when to outsource.* The real tech trenders know when to outsource or do it themselves. It can be risky, counterproductive and costly to go it alone. Top CIOs say they assess their organization's limitations. They look at the things they can do and the things they can't and, if the balance tilts in the direction of "we can't," they outsource.
- *Select the right technology.* You need to build an IT infrastructure or architecture that's flexible enough – scalable in industry parlance – to adapt to near constant technological change. As will be discussed in Chapter 7, this depends in part on seeking out technology based on open standards. Tech trenders should be seeking out the new technology available via the Web, but also keeping an eye out for stability.
- *Information sharing and accuracy.* More and more humans are being removed from business transactions and from interaction within the supply chain. That makes it imperative for tech trenders to train employees in information flow and set up accuracy checks. Humans have to interact with technology at some juncture, and have to be trained to be accurate or upturn your whole B2B operation. Your back end had better start talking to your billing people. Information sharing is crucial to e-commerce success.
- *Protect your information.* Start creating some sort of security architecture. Information is gold today. You need to understand the risk of the wrong people getting your information and the cost of protecting it. You also have to assign a value to the cost of protection. That's along with deciding what form protection should take, meaning encryption, firewalls, etc.
- *Customer service is paramount.* It's not enough to have a "wow" Web site. If you can't deliver your goods on time, if your billing is sloppy, you're going to lose your customers. Too many organizations are focusing on hot technologies and leaving their customers hanging with sloppy delivery, inability to reach humans to get help, and badly designed Web sites where it's hard to locate pertinent information that would seal a transaction. The speed of the Web makes it imperative that customers can get help when they need it, and fast.
- *Train, train, train.* The experts concur that training for the networked, B2B world is one of the most important things tech trenders can do right now (see Chapter 9). Ask yourself, what sets of skills you need. What level of training is required?

3 *Select e-commerce models that work for you*

A number of different e-commerce models were outlined in Chapter 2. You can expect these models to continue to shift and change as B2B evolves and comes into its own. To review briefly, here are the types of e-commerce models tech trenders can choose from right now:

(a) *Online marketplaces.* Companies like Ariba, SAP, Oracle and Ford have announced online marketplaces that offer a collection of catalogs that allow buyers to source and purchase. The more sophisticated sites have provisions for customer-specific pricing or total site volume pricing. They also offer content to attract users, such as vertical industry news, articles, and even entertainment. And they support some degree of integration so that orders and related documents generated on the site can be automatically downloaded into users' financial systems. That's one reason that ERP vendors like SAP and Oracle are setting up their own marketplaces.

(b) *Trading communities.* In the e-commerce sense, companies use the term "trading community" to describe a group of buyers and sellers that work in the same market-space, sharing common needs, information and business partners. For example, companies that buy and sell on the chemical supplies site, Chemdex, would be considered a trading community.

(c) *Buy-side procurement systems.* Still pretty limited to Fortune 100 companies with lots of money to invest in end-to-end systems, this model allows a purchasing department to direct their end users to preferred suppliers. Companies like Commerce One, Ariba, Intelisys are providing these sorts of applications. The major drawback is cost, which can range from $250,000 to $5 million.

(d) *Service bureaus.* Also known as application service providers or infomediaries, service bureaus basically provide an aggregation of suppliers and distributors of indirect supplies. This allows buyers to access indirect supplies from one location. Service bureaus represent the most common form of B2B sites.

(e) *The sell-side model.* This is the least sophisticated form of B2B and usually involves a supplier setting up shop on the Web with his own products or products available for purchase. This model replaces phone sales, but doesn't add much other value. An example is Staples putting up a Web site and selling its products.

(f) *Exchanges.* These host many-to-many buyer-seller relationships for more commodity-type items. A common type of exchange involves transaction fees to the sellers. In other words someone brings buyers and sellers to a Web site, facilitates one-on-one purchasing and takes a piece of the transaction.

- Public exchanges. Not long ago public exchanges were all the rage. These are places where all sorts of buyers and sellers can meet. Volume and having the right commodity to sell is crucial to making a public exchange work.
- Private exchanges. Another growing option is the private exchange. Mainly being embraced by large companies with certified suppliers, private exchanges offer the benefits of added security and anonymity. They help maintain business relationships and mean that companies can retain electronic formats like EDI rather than standardizing to XML.

(g) *ASP models.* These are software-rental arrangements where the vendor hosts and maintains a piece of software and simply sells the right to access the software. Many see ASP models taking over from the days of buying a piece of software for local installation, and ongoing upgrades are limited. When ASP takes over, so the conventional wisdom goes, it will be much cheaper and more scalable to rely on a service provider for upgrades and maintenance. ASP is also supposed to promote the growth of various types of intermediaries facilitating communications/transactions between buyers and sellers. Product data preparation, maintenance, and dissemination are emerging as basic needs in the marketplace. These solutions are often based on ASP models.

(h) *Sell-side auctions.* This is where multiple buyers compete for products and services with upward price pressure.

(i) *Buy-side auctions, or reverse auctions.* Buyers of indirect materials and services turn to buy-side auctions or reverse auctions because sell-side doesn't work for them. In this model, you, the buyer, get to auction off your requirements. Sellers get the chance to "bid" on fulfilling your need, and at a predetermined point in time, the bid is "over" and the cheapest supplier is given the chance to earn your business.[22]

How tech trenders can build a Web presence

Tech Trenders have your c-commerce vision lined up with suppliers, trading partners and collaborators. You've prepped your staff to work in a shared, collaborative mode and have selected the technology that will provide compatibility among all parties (see Chapter 7). A good, hard look at e-commerce models has followed, coupled with determining that your back-office and logistics operations can handle whatever business you drum up on the Web. Now you're ready to set up Web sites, product catalogs, and whatever tools you need for online action.

Don't get down on yourself if you haven't yet established a Web presence. It's better to move into the e-commerce world slowly and determinedly than to toss up a quickie home page with no purpose behind it. Networks Solutions, a major storage company for Web site domains, says 63 percent of its 840,000 domain names involve companies with a Web address, some rudimentary home page posted and nothing beyond that.

SOUND BYTES

Autos, coal and diamonds are bought/sold online

Given its thousands of suppliers, it's not surprising that the auto industry is embracing e-procurement methods. For example, automaker DaimlerChrysler South Africa (DCSA), a manufacturer of Mercedes-Benz vehicles for the South African market, is moving its dealers online. In recent months, DaimlerChrysler launched DC Online, a B2B automobile ordering and distribution system for its employees and dealerships. The Web-based solution allows dealers to order a vehicle that matches specific customer requirements, have orders electronically submitted and tracked, and deliver finished vehicles to the appropriate dealership.

DC Online combines software from Lotus Development Corp. and IBM Corp., including Lotus Domino, IBM's DB2 Universal Database and Lotus Learning Space distributed learning software. The new system allows more than 100 dealers to order vehicles directly from DCSA that meet specific customer requirements, helping to reduce automobile stockpiles at dealerships, as well as distribution costs and inefficiencies. And the system manages stock and customer information, providing easier access to large amounts of data for controlling the distribution and delivery of vehicles to DCSA dealerships.

The aim, of course, is cost savings. The company estimates DC Online will save it "millions of dollars," while providing dealers unprecedented access to the information they need to be more productive and improve customer service.

The auto industry isn't the only one going online. There are new dot.coms being developed for coal and diamonds. Globalcoal.com is the baby of four international mining giants who are hoping to create the largest, single online marketplace for thermal coal and then move to iron ore and metal. And diamond heavyweight BHP has created an alliance to sell rough, uncut diamonds over the Internet. This will allow wholesalers to cut out intermediaries.[23]

About 31 percent of the sites registered with Network Solutions are established as billboard, advertising or promotional sites. They offer general company or product information, but do not allow visitors to order online.

When it comes to practicing any real form of e-commerce, the percentages dwindle to almost nothing. Only four percent of Network Solution sites actually allow visitors to order products directly on the Web. About one percent of their customers use their sites to develop and maintain a relationship with their customers. Sites in this stage have Web-enabled key business processes on an intranet or extranet – for instance, allowing distributors to check product inventory online. And only one percent use the most advanced Internet technologies to offer real-time business processing for functions like financial management and human resources.

Tech trenders want to push those percentages up and be part of the B2B revolution. That means deciding what sort of Web site you need. Web site designers involved in prepping companies and institutions involved in e-commerce site construction, say your Web site should consist of the sort of product information that will sell you and your organization, and that it should be formatted in ways that work electronically. There are six steps that will get you on your way.

1 *Building an effective billboard Web site*

For many tech trenders it will be best to focus your energies right now on building that effective billboard site while keeping your eyes open for e-commerce opportunities that will suit your company or institution. And that means, once again, looking at your business or institutional goals. Don't bring in writers or designers before you have a very clear sense of what you want your Web site to accomplish and what information you want to present on the site.

In general, many billboard Web sites are plain lousy because they lack clarity of purpose. And if your billboard site is muddled and can't convey a message, that means you'll face more trouble when trying to lure buyers or sellers to your site. Top management often gets in the way because people are nervous about projecting information and are always second-guessing future ramifications of doing so.

Once you have determined the purpose for your site the next issue becomes what sort of content to present and how to maintain it. Companies and institutions are being asked to operate as news organizations, but usually lack the skills to do so. They don't know how to gather, sort, cull, edit and disseminate information and how to set up guidelines for what information is pertinent and what is not (see Chapter 8). For example, a cultural tourism organization was struggling with how to post tour dates on its Web site and how to keep then updated. They turned to a database company for help when they really needed to establish an editing schedule that corresponded with tour dates. For example, on March 1 we edit for March tours; April 1 for April tours, etc. Instead they got caught in the reinventing-the-wheel syndrome.

Companies and institutions also lack skills in achieving, or storing detailed information you want to make available to your customers or trading partners. Because of its ability to provide electronic links and store unlimited information in databases, the Web is a superb archiving tool. But to do it right – to archive the best information and present only what matters and is most urgent, and develop a strong search engine – not only involves information judgment, but the ability to handle sometimes tedious and detailed annotating. Tech trenders should consider outsourcing the development of your archives and development of search engines to those more expert.[25]

APPLICATIONS

Know thy e-self

Smart tech trenders won't simply toss Web sites up in cyberspace without doing some long, hard thinking and analysis of what a Web site can do for your company or institution. Here's a quick checklist to help you with that process:

- *Know why you want a Web site.* If it is not part of an overall marketing strategy, budgeted like any other line item and maintained regularly, you will be wasting time and money.
- *Know what you want a Web site to do.* Is it an online business card or brochure (static, purely informational, fixed), or is it an active contributor to your bottom line (dynamic, transactional, evolving)? Is it for e-commerce, marketing, sales, ordering, tracking, an added benefit to customers, informational, or just to have a Web presence and validate your presence because your competitors are online?
- *Know what features you want.* Visit other Web sites in your industry or arena and see what they offer. Try them out as a customer might. Keep lists of likes and dislikes. Balance features against cost as you would in any decision. You can always add later.
- *Offer more.* Attracting customers to a Web site means providing some value or benefit beyond the retail store, even it's only convenience.

- *Require a visit.* Demand that your designer/consultant spend some time at your facility. The more they understand about your business, the more you'll get from your Web site.
- *Have a single contact.* Find a developer who can understand your business needs and what the technology can (and cannot) do. If they also are your host and ISP (Internet Service Provider), you can solve most problems with one phone call.
- *Meet frequently.* Stay on top of the project. Voice concerns as you think of them. It will cost more to make changes later. While this is software, not a machine tool, redesign takes time and costs money.
- *Take it slow.* Building a site in phases makes sense if you are unsure about your Internet strategy. Technologies and markets change, so require any site to be flexible and adaptable.
- *Budget realistically.* One of the most common misperceptions about Web sites is underestimating their cost. If you want more than an online pretty face, be prepared to spend from $2000 to $50,000 for a functional e-commerce site that ties into your in-house ordering system and can accept credit card payments. Remember that a Web site is a recurring monthly expense.
- *Plan for maintenance.* Learn how to update your Web site yourself. Budget time into your plans for regular maintenance. Your Web site is an evolving, dynamic, sales, marketing and advertising tool. Seek customer feedback and make changes regularly.[24]

SOLUTIONS

What tech trenders need to work with images

It may seem a long way off before you will be handling images on your Web site or in your e-catalog, but it doesn't hurt to understand now what sort of equipment you need to handle images that can be used both on the Web and for release to the media or another dot.com. If a company or institution is interested in distributing pictures in a meaningful way, you need the following equipment:

1 A photo scanner to scan anything from 35 mm film to an 11×14-inch print. That may require two scanners.
2 A computer equipped with Adobe Photoshop, latest release.
3 A modem for transmission of digital pictures – at least 56K – but the faster the better.
4 A good archivist who will handle transmission and requests for photo information. Either PR Newswire or BusinessWire can guide you to top-notch archivists.[26]

2 *Product information*

This involves information your prospects need to know in order to buy from you – the product information a serious potential buyer is likely to seek. A common technique is to post product brochures on the site, but this can be tricky using current HTML technology. Consult a designer about making the photos more legible. Industrial companies can consider posting product brochures as PDF files that, when printed, look remarkably similar to a printed brochure. However, PDF files are not designed for interactivity, just for show (see below).

3 *Targeted marketing information*

You want to present information that will impress prospects and make them concerned to buy from you. When moving onto the Web, don't forget the rules of good advertising and marketing that exist in the print, TV and video world. If you don't have a brand name, the only way to differentiate yourself from competitors will be establishing credibility and expertise.

The advantage of the Web over other forms of communication is that it allows users to "drill down" to the level of detail they desire. You can post just about any information on your site that establishes credibility for you and your product line without swamping others with unnecessary detail. Some chemical companies have been known to post test results that potential customers can access, for example. Many sites include awards or citation sections to impress potential customers.

> "Posting content on your Web site – useful information, such as white papers or how-to articles – is another, more subtle way of convincing potential customers that you are the qualified source. After all, if they read and are impressed with your article on how to select a hydraulic pump, they're more likely to buy the pump from you than another seller.
>
> "Another technique you might consider is designing a button on your home page for 'Recommended Vendors.' It opens to an html file or database of resources, in fields allied

with yours, that your visitors might find useful. When you post a regularly updated recommended vendors section, visitors come to view your site as a useful resource. Knowing that they can find, on your site, the other products and services they need to complete their project, increases the likelihood of them buying your product as well."[28]

SOLUTIONS

What information belongs on your e-commerce Web site?

When deciding what sort of information to include on a buy/sell Web site, the experts say consider the following:

- an overview of your products or services – usually found on your home page or an "About Us" page;
- pages on individual products and services – one per product;
- additional product information – specs, features, options, accessories, models, ratings, upgrades;
- customers – who buys from you?
- projects – what are some of the major projects your firm has handled?
- applications – what applications is your product used for? What industries do you serve? and
- testimonials – are customers satisfied? What do they say about you?[27]

PLATFORMS

Building that effective Web site isn't easy

A small manufacturing company in Deerfield, MA, wanted to grow its basic business: making and distributing a complete line of products for delivering meals on wheels. The partners hoped a Web site would provide outreach to global customers 24 hours a day, and help provide information to potential customers – basically act as a business card and brochure. After a great deal of labor, which took the better part of a year, they found their site allowed them to attract other, larger vendors, to sell their goods into alternate niches. But the getting there was time-consuming. Here are some of the steps they took:

- *Setting goals.* They wanted a site they could maintain themselves, a designer who could act as host and ISP, and the ability to install tracking software on their in-house system that was compatible with the host.
- *Locating a consultant to help.* They insisted a consultant visit their site before making a bid, and that they spoke the same language in terms of goals and strategies.
- *Design and information flow.* Once they had an idea of design, functionality, and content, the partners began by sketching out flow charts, beginning with their future home page and "clicking" through to the rest of the site. They cut up their printed sales literature and taped it together to simulate the path a visitor might travel, filling up several long tables with hand-made scrolls.
- *Site maintenance.* They wanted the ability to add and eliminate products, track visitor utilization data, easily post links, add banner ads, and take and fulfill orders, as well as calculate shipping charges. The consultant/designer they chose specialized in software-generated sites that allow for system integration that's customized and that include databases clients and operate and change.[29]

4 *Putting data in an electronic format*

On the technical side, product data must be formatted electronically so that it is structured to be fully searchable, flexible, extensible and consistent in look. By *searchable* this means robust with attributes and descriptions that can be located in a search; flexible enough to allow for real-time updates and successful customer searches; and extensible enough to allow for back-office integration and syndication to selling partners so information can be distributed to all online channels.

Most of the product – stock unit (SKU) – data used in printed catalogs is not set up in a format that can be utilized online. You can't simply type in your paper catalog or publish the catalog as a PDF file. Printed catalogs are designed to operate in a world where there are sales or customer service representative available to answer users' questions and to fill in any gaps in the information. That means they lack a great deal of information you will want to provide in electronic format. And paper catalogs often present information inconsistently – "black" vs "blk" in the same catalog – which you can't afford to do on the Web.

Tech trenders always have to keep in mind that electronic catalogs don't allow for intuition or human intervention. You have to build the intuition into the catalog, basically considering all parameters that an individual will need to know to locate the product information they want online. This means an electronic product catalog needs to be structured in such a way to generate successful searches. For this reason a really top-notch e-commerce-ready catalog should capture and integrate elements from three main sources:

- The paper catalog as a source of product information;
- Electronic information repositories (ERP, PDF, etc.) where the most current pricing, order history, and SKU data often reside; and
- people, such as product managers, marketing and sales managers, and engineering managers, who have application knowledge, case histories, diagnostics results, and other product knowledge that informs the selling process.

PLATFORMS

The attributes of an e-commerce product catalog

An e-commerce-ready SKU should have the following characteristics:

- complete set of attributes, including such granularities as color, inner diameter, horsepower, material, grit, etc.;
- short, long and paragraph descriptions of the item;
- associated structure or hierarchy that defines to which "family" or product category the SKU belongs;
- image mapped to it;
- can be searched by description and/or attribute;
- can be updated without manipulation or massaging;
- associated keywords and synonyms;
- associated application information, like usage guides, safety and regulatory codes, etc.; and
- uses consistent vocabulary.[30]

SOLUTIONS

Seek these e-commerce data qualities

Manufacturers who do not have robust SKU data will be passed over by today's skilled buyers who are becoming less and less tolerant of waste in the supply chain. Forward-looking manufacturing firms have already made significant inroads into electronic catalog creation by ensuring their data exhibits the following qualities:

- *Searchable.* Eliminating erroneous searches, providing more intuitive searches.
- *Informative.* The buyer has all of the information necessary to distinguish the products, validate their application, and purchase.
- *Extensible.* Can be distributed to "all" channel types – marketplaces, distributors, etc.[31]

5 *Designing effective search engines*

The ability to search and locate a product will make or break your e-commerce site. Too often, crucial information like an easy indicator of where to pay, is missing on many e-tail sites or is placed in such a way as to be hard to locate. What a pity to lure a customer to a product and then lose them because your ordering forms are buried under too much verbiage or graphics. Other sites fail earlier on in the process because products can't be located easily.

You can certainly avoid humorous design flaws such as burying key information. But part of the problem is that the technology isn't up to the task of providing the search ability that B2B requires. Next-generation searching tools like intelligent agents, which allow for customer preferences, are not yet commercially viable. As you design your site, you have to take these technology deficiencies into consideration and work out the best search tool technology can provide.[32]

6 *Moving beyond PDF*

There is a myth that PDF is the pathway to e-commerce because PDF documents simulate the printed page. In essence, they are proprietary electronic files that render information exactly as it appears on a printed page. A PDF version of a manufacturer's catalog is a sequence of "snapshots" of every printed page of the catalog. While PDF documents can be linked to each other to facilitate navigation, the end-user's or distributor's experience is only slightly more effective than thumbing through a paper catalog.

E-commerce, on the other hand, is based upon an electronic exchange of commerce-enabling information (product information, pricing, terms, etc.) among business partners, buyers and sellers, and also within organizations. The diversity of business relationships dictates that this information exchange uses open standards and extensible information. Being able to exchange information among all these parties is the foundation of e-commerce.

The experts say PDF files may be a logical first step towards promoting your full product line. But until tech trenders develop a database for product information management, the power of the Internet will be left untapped. A pure PDF strategy will quickly be eclipsed as distributors and end-users demand more sophisticated, robust, and flexible product information. Some experts believe PDF has these major flaws:

- PDF product data cannot be consumed and transmitted;
- PDF product data cannot be integrated with back-office systems; and
- PDF product data cannot be efficiently maintained and updated.

However, there are PDF proponents who believe this format is useful because of its high fidelity. New versions of PDF now on the market are capable of being interactive and serving as forms and front-ends on Web sites.[32]

Helping tech trenders get e-commerce initiatives off the ground

Old-time industrial product catalog companies like W.W. Grainger Inc. have been spending millions on the bet that they can turn a major profit in the e-commerce world. Located just outside Chicago, the company sells 210,000 types of industrial products to 1.5 million customers. In the past, all of these products were listed in a 4000-page catalog, or more recently via CD-ROM.

In recent years, W.W. Grainger has invested more than $35 million in a range of Internet initiatives, according to new reports. The first initiative was a "digital storefront" called www.grainger.com that was set up in 1995. Online sales jumped from $3–9 million a month as of this summer, which indicates the rapid acceptance of e-commerce.

Bolstered by this sort of success, in 1999 the company set up Orderzone.com, a marketplace that allows customers to move beyond the Grainger product line and order from leading distributors in other business sectors. Orderzone represented a fairly unsophisticated "sell side" site. It offered one-stop shopping, but at its inception it did not track deliveries, retain records of past orders or make it simple for buyers to compare competing products. Unsophisticated or no, sites like Orderzone represent the beginning of efforts to move to a B2B world.

For the average organization, even a "sell side" initiative like Orderzone may be beyond your reach. Service bureau sites represent massive investment of technology and funds with little pay-off as of this writing. To put up a service bureau, alone, means building a Web site, providing Internet access with interactive capability, back-end functions have to be installed for finances and catalogs have to be digitized.[33]

Purchasing specialists advise organizations to identify viable options for buying and selling online and sort them into the following three categories ranging from easy to challenging, costly and financially manageable. Cost will play a major factor in how and when you can move into the B2B world. If money is tight, you may have to set up a long-term budget to manage the hardware, software and consulting and long-term maintenance and support costs that will come with this leap to cyberspace buying and selling. For the time being, small tech trenders may have to settle for some interim options such as partial automation of procurement functions. E-faxes are inexpensive tools to help you move in this direction. E-faxes can be sent directly to a desktop, viewed online and attached to electronic purchase orders for backup.

Installing scanners would involve moderate cost and time expenditures. Scanners allow you to convert hard-copy bids, sales literature and even policy and procedure documents into files

APPLICATIONS

Steps to procuring goods online

It's one thing to talk about e-procurement and quite another thing to carry out purchasing functions in cyberspace. Here's an example of how a maintenance technician, who needs an additional part to complete a repair, can practice e-procurement.

1 The technician accesses the corporate intranet and goes to an electronic catalog that contains information on parts from multiple vendors.
2 The technician searches for the required item (perhaps using a keyword search) and checks specification, price, stock availability, and delivery lead-time. With a few clicks of the mouse, a purchase requisition is completed.
3 The purchase requisition is automatically captured in the company's ERP system, and, if required, routed directly to the appropriate person for approval.
4 A purchase order is sent electronically to the supplier's system. The supplier's system confirms price and availability, and immediately sends a delivery confirmation back to the technician's mailbox.
5 The supplier ships the part according to the instructions on the purchase order and it arrives the same or next day.
6 The invoice, when received from the supplier, is automatically matched with the purchase order and paid without any further approvals.[34]

that can be electronically transmitted. They require little installation and training effort, and can be implemented in a relatively short period of time (6–12 months). Another moderate option would be to become involved in a Web-based price comparison site. Even if you do not intend to purchase directly from the merchants that are linked to these services, they will provide you with a feeling for what you should be paying for a given product.

To actually consider setting up your own site, or become actively involved in trading communities, falls into the challenging option category because it requires upwards of a year setup, and equipment, installation and training costs. Software, hardware and implementation are considered the biggest costs to starting an e-procurement initiative. There will also be ongoing software/hardware maintenance costs and ongoing support costs – things like consulting, catalog maintenance, internal system maintenance – to factor into the financial equation. Software maintenance costs include all updates and enhancements, as well as error corrections.

The experts say make sure the priority definitions, response times and resolution time service levels are included with an escalation procedure, as well as remedies for failure to meet agreed-upon service levels. And don't forget miscellaneous costs, which would include training, customization, development of additional facilities, telecommunication costs and others (see Chapter 7).[35]

Buying online services

There are companies that provide almost all services online. In the logistics arena, for example, customers can turn to companies to manage their fulfillment process and to meet other buyers and sellers of transport/logistics services over the Web. Some service providers offer everything from tracking and tracing of goods in real time to a build-to-order model that allows you to make adjustments to a shipment in real time if problems arise. To

TECH VISIONS

Internet service companies growing

In the 1990s, Descartes Systems in Waterloo, Ontario, Canada had about 800 customers licensing their enterprise software products designed for logistics management. Around 1998 they emerged as an online service provider. By 2000, they had 300 customers to their Internet-based service. The aim is to keep hooking people on downloading software from the Web that covers your needs rather than licensing software.[36]

interact with this sort of company as a customer you need:

- a high-speed Internet connection;
- a reasonably current PC.

Using these services may amount to nothing more complicated than dialing up, connecting to the service provider and downloading information for analysis and return. But some companies also offer the ability for customers to connect to trading partners' systems and manage information in real time within your trading community. To move into the interactive, collaborative mode is more complicated than an e-mail exchange. You may need to hire a consultant, a systems integrator or a boutique consulting firm to make the right connections, and also participate in a short training course the company offers. With the right help, tech trenders should be operating collaboratively within a week or so.

It's hard to put a price tag on these sorts of online services because they vary from company to company and user to user. One company quotes general service at about $20,000 a year. The companies in question say compare that with a software program, which can be obsolete in a matter of a year or so, but may cost a large company $100,000 to license. You would get five years of online service for the same price as the software package.

Of course, the disadvantage to operating online is that you face the risk to losing business if the system is down. Service providers say they implement the sort of disaster recovery plans that are common among telephone service providers. Even so, they recommend customers maintain a database and server in their location to keep their own data on their side of the firewall.[37]

Using intermediaries or aggregators to move online

One way for small tech trenders to move into cyberspace is by using intermediaries and aggregators to get online. In general, intermediaries are already in business on their own and may offer a product, but allow outsiders to use their site for a percentage of the transaction fee.

EBay is a prime example of an intermediary. Linking up with eBay can provide a startup e-business with a low-cost way to sell online – without dedicating the resources to setting up and maintaining a Web site, or paying a third party to build it for you. Another example of an intermediary is Amazon's zShops. For $9.99 a month, a startup can list up to 3000 products for sale. This service also allows small businesses to accept credit card payments without opening their own merchant accounts. Amazon, of course, gets a percentage of every sale, plus a small transaction fee for each credit card sale.

Aggregators create a Web presence for a variety of companies and entice buyers or sellers to their sites. They come in all shapes and sizes, sell or move things, but usually don't own them. For this effort they take a piece of the action, plus banner and ad revenue and usually a registration fee. ScreamingMedia.com pulls together content, which it sells via subscription to thousands of Web sites.

There are many types of aggregators out there whose enticements range from service to novelty. If you want to sell steel, but don't want the hassle of setting up your own Web portal you can contact eSteel.com. SiteStuff.com provides a Web presence for multi-billion real estate management companies. Then there's PeoplePC.com, which acts as a Web front for companies that include Compaq, Toshiba, MCI and WorldCom. The company set up a fancy Web site and has put out splashy advertising that touts highly discounted products. The aim is to deliver qualified buyers on a regular basis and a steady revenue stream.[38]

SOLUTIONS

Tips to improve online performance

Even the most ardent tech trender won't find doing business in cyberspace perfection. After all, you're a pioneer in a burgeoning industry. Here's what the experts say you can do to improve online performance:

- Management is more important than technology, product, service, or vision.
- Aggregators are hot; think convenience.
- Value-add is hot; use the Web to provide more than just sales or service.
- Identify a niche and focus 100 percent on market penetration.
- Keep in touch with the needs of your customers; they pay the rent.
- First to market is a great advantage; so is doing it better than the first movers.
- Allies and partners are where it's at. Find some.
- Delivery must be consistent and fast.
- Have a great search function that is quick and simple.
- Hits do not equal sales. Don't count your chickens ...
- If you can't measure your eyeballs, you can't manage them.
- Don't cannibalize your own channels by going online.
- Sales and deals online keep people coming back; promos work.[39]

Notes

1 H. James Harrington, CEO, Systemcorp., Quebec, Canada, and former consulting principal for quality at Ernst & Young, and Peter Schwartz, chairman and CEO of Descartes Systems, Waterloo, Ontario.

2 Material is adapted from *B2B: How to Build a Profitable E-commerce Strategy,* Michael Cunningham, Perseus Publishing, 2000, pp. 52–54.

3 *Fortune* magazine, July 7, 1997.

4 "The Human Side of Information Technology," Amy Zuckerman, *Supply Chain Management Review,* Spring 1998, p. 80.
5 "Enter the Eco System," *The Economist* E-Management Survey, November 11, 2000, p. 30.
6 "Logistics Conquers a Brave New World," Mary Aichlmayr, *Transportation and Distribution*, August 2000, pp. 28–38. Sources include William J. Wissing, Vice President of Distribution at Blockbuster, Inc., and Kurt Salmon & Associates consultants Chris Dowd and Randy Moore.
7 *Global Tool Kit: Supply Chain,* Amy Zuckerman, Human Skills section, A–Z International Associates, Amherst, MA, 1999. Source is Hal Buell, Director of Photo Services, PR Newswire former Assistant General Manager for the Associated Press News Photos, and a former member of the AP Senior Management Group.
8 This material is adapted from *ISO 9000 Made Easy,* Amy Zuckerman, AMACOM Books, New York, 1995.
9 Bob Feghali, Vice President of Business Development and CIO of ANSI.
10 "Remove Supply Chain's Weak Links No Matter Whose Fault They Are," Joseph Mazel, *Supplier Selection & Management Report,* July 1, 2000. Source is Jim Limperis, Senior Contracts Manager, Supply Management, Motorola, Inc.
11 "SAP's Sweet Deal," Dave Blanchard, *Supply Chain Technology News,* August 14, 2000, p. 1.
12 Sources are Henry Bruce, vice president of marketing, Optum Software, White Plains, NY; and "Navigating the E-Commerce Maze," Deborah Wilson, Deborah Wilson Consulting, December 15, 1999.
13 "New Web-Publishing Standard Aims to Simplify E-Commerce," David Hamilton, *Wall Street Journal,* online edition, September 5, 2000; and "UDDI Rollout a United Front," Stephanie Bruzzese, Line 56.
14 "Putting the 'e' in enterprise," Peter Bolstorff, *Supply Chain Technology News,* August 2000, pp. 60–62.

15 Source is the Supply Chain Council Inc. 303 Freeport Road Pittsburgh, PA 15215, USA. Phone: +1.412.781.4101; Fax: +1.412.781.2871; Email: info@supply-chain.org.

16 Sources are Stewart Cheifet, principal of Stewart Cheifet Productions and producer of "Internet Cafe" and "Computer Chronicles" (PBS and other networks); Karen Peterson, Research Director, the Gartner Group, and "Making ERP Succeed: Turning Fear into Promise," Scott Buckhout, Edward Frey and Joseph Nemec Jr., and Michael Cunningham, CEO the Harvard Computing Group, Westford, MA.

17 "Is an E-Procurement Solution Right for You?" Craig DeLano and Rex Tibbens, Mercer Management Consulting, June 1, 1999, appeared on PurchasingCenter.com in the summer of 2000, and Jay Venkatesan, co-founder of BioSupplies.com and CEO of Varro Technologies, Philadelphia, PA.

18 Source is Colin Mulcahy, ScreamingMedia Director of Technical Implementation and Support, and a company founder.

19 Sources are GartnerGroup RAS Services, Copyright © 1999, SPA-08–5311, August 3, 1999, and, "Navigating the E-Commerce Maze: An E-Commerce Primer," Deborah Wilson, Deborah Wilson Consulting, December 15, 1999.

20 GartnerGroup RAS Services, Copyright © 1999, SPA-08–5311, August 3, 1999.

21 Kevin Fitzgerald, publisher and editor of *GlobaleSupply* magazine.

22 "Navigating the E-Commerce Maze: An E-Commerce Primer," Deborah Wilson, Deborah Wilson Consulting, December 15, 1999; Mark Vigoroso, executive producer, NewMediary.com, and Kevin Fitzgerald, publisher and editor of *GlobaleSupply* Magazine.

23 "DaimlerChrysler Puts Its Dealers Online," *Supply Chain Technology News*, August, 14, 2000, p. 12; and "The Internet Economy Goes Underground," Jeffrey Davis, *Business 2.0* online edition, November 1, 2000.

24 "A Good Web site is Hard to Build," Eddy Goldberg, appeared on http://www.entrenetwork.com, summer 2000.

25 Hal Buell, Director of Photo Services, PR Newswire former Assistant General Manager for the Associated Press News Photos, and a former member of the AP Senior Management Group.

26 Hal Buell, Director of Photo Services, PR Newswire former Assistant General Manager for the Associated Press News Photos, and a former member of the AP Senior Management Group.

27 "Does Your 'Second Generation' Site Get A Passing Grade?" Robert W. Bly, *Network Solutions*, Friday, September 8, 2000; and *Guide to Web Content and Design*, Roger C. Parker, MIS Press, online edition, 2000.

28 "Does Your 'Second Generation' Site Get A Passing Grade?" by Robert W. Bly, *Network Solutions*, Friday, September 8, 2000; and *Guide to Web Content and Design*, Roger C. Parker, MIS Press, online edition, 2000.

29 "A Good Web Site Is Hard To Build," Eddy Goldberg, appeared on http://www.entrenetwork.com, summer 2000.

30 "What is an 'E-Commerce-ready' SKU?" Mark Vigoroso, executive producer, NewMediary.com.

31 "What is an 'E-Commerce-ready' SKU?" Mark Vigoroso, executive producer, NewMediary.com.

32 "What is an 'E-Commerce-ready' SKU?" Mark Vigoroso, executive producer, NewMediary.com.

32 "PDF Not Up to E-Commerce Challenge," by Mark Vigoroso, executive producer, NewMediary.com., and David Washburn, Principal Consultant at Amherst Information Architects, Amherst, MA.

33 "E-comm How To's" from *Global Tool Kit: Supply Chain,* Amy Zuckerman, A–Z International Associates, Amherst, MA, 1999.

34 "Is an E-Procurement Solution Right for You?" by Craig Delano and Rex Tibbens, Mercer Management Consultants, June 1, 1999, appeared on PurchasingCenter.Com, August 2000.

35 "How to Start an e-Procurement Initiative: Three Experts' Advice," Joseph Mazel, *Supplier Selection & Management Report*, July 1, 2000. Sources include Richard G. Weissman, former Director of Purchasing, PurchasingCenter.com; Kevin J. Williams, Purchasing Specialist, ESPN, Inc., and Russ Boyd, Supply Contracts Manager, Perot Systems Corporation.

36 Source is Peter Schwartz, chairman and CEO of Descartes Systems, Waterloo, Ontario, Canada.

37 Source is Peter Schwartz, chairman and CEO of Descartes Systems, Waterloo, Ontario, Canada.

38 "The Digital Economy: Taking it to the Web," Eddy Goldberg, info@entrenetwork, April 21, 2000.

39 "The Digital Economy: Taking it to the Web," Eddy Goldberg, info@entrenetwork.com, April 21, 2000. Information source is Les Ball of the University of Massachusetts School of Management.

7 Making Practical, Flexible, Cost-Effective Technology Choices

Ah, the crux of the matter ... How do tech trenders know what technology to select today that will be worth anything in say, six months time? How to build towards the B2B world without bankrupting your company or institution?

These are questions affecting – and even afflicting – just about all of us. Surveys show that only ten percent of the working population are capable of using technology. But the technology available today is designed for those ten percent who are really competent, rather than the 90 percent who want to utilize it and don't have the foggiest idea of what RAM or a server is (see pp. 83–5 for common definitions). Our technology is driven by complexity, not simplicity. And we continue to segregate computer specialists from the rest of the organization, which accounts for so many IT failures.[1]

What makes this all the more arduous and onerous is the fact that IT spending accounts for one half of all investments tech trenders like you are likely to be making today, whether you are a company or institution. That's for software and hardware combined.[2] Facing this sort of enormous expenditure at a time when technology is changing so fast is enormously perplexing to almost all technology consumers. Consider these technology-related issues that a museum organization has been discussing, and see how many of them sound familiar to you.

- Some of our problems and issues involve getting accurate and up-to-date information on systems and their needs. Everyone tells you they can provide a system to serve your needs, but once they begin this is not always true.
- We already need to upgrade the memory on our machines because we can't run anything but the computer software at one time.
- We're concerned about the latest technology on both the hardware and the software side. Museums tend to get outdated software that can address immediate needs, but for how long?
- It would be helpful to have someone to offer technical advice in setting up specifications and reviewing proposals; someone independent of the outcome. They would also have to be extremely knowledgeable of updated issues and future trends. We just don't know who to believe out there.[3]

Prepping tech trenders to make informed technology choices

This chapter will provide you with the tools you need to make those practical, flexible and cost-effective technology decisions that will help you transition to a networked, B2B world. No, you won't necessarily be prepped to choose between an SAP or Oracle ERP software solution or decide how many servers your organization requires. It's impossible to address individual technology questions in this context. But you will be able to work more effectively with your IT department, vendors, consultants and online technology service providers. For a good percentage of what will help tech trenders take charge of technology choices is mindset – a willingness to take the time to learn enough about technology options to pose intelligent questions to technology experts, coupled with a willingness to make change.

There are other factors, many of which you can control, that will help you make informed technology choices. Tying IT directly to your business goals is a key way of making technology

UNPLUGGING TECHNOSTRESS

Coping with chronic platform fatigue

You're exhausted, tired, depleted of strength, full of lassitude, just plain fatigued. The mere contemplation of purchasing a PC versus a Mac produces such severe exhaustion that you're bedridden for months. The technoshrinks say you're suffering from CPF, short for Chronic Platform Fatigue.

In extreme cases, CPF can be close to life-threatening. Glancing at computer magazine advertisement – let alone an article outlining the properties of each platform – has been known to induce shock in those most susceptible to CPF. Some people suffer actual brain seizures, or crave tubs of Ben and Jerry's "Cherry Garcia" ice cream. The fat intake only exacerbates the problem. Lesser sufferers may simply experience momentary fatigue when confronted with the actual choice of a computer platform. This is understandable to all but technonerds. All those "rams" and "rems" ... Consider this list of four options out of a list of 22 for an ancient PC circa 1998:

Item 1	MSI, MS-5154, 430Tx, 512K, Baby/at CPU, AMD, K6-233
Item 2	Heat sink w/fan p6/6x86
Item 3	SDRAM 4.64 163pin, 32MB-10, 3.3v
Item 4	QWANT, BIGFOOT WM5433CY 4.3GB

Technozombies, anyway, want to buy a computer the way they buy a car – look, feel, drive. Where are all the colors? The upholstery? All those computer drives not only look alike, but to a technozombie they drive alike. Apple Computer founder, Steve Jobs, recognized this fact when he designed the space-age blue iMac and reportedly his plug 'n' play boxes are selling like hotcakes.

The fact that Jobs now works for the Microsoft empire only adds to the confusion, and to the general exhaustion around this subject. In fact, writing this stuff is so tiring it's time to take a nap ...[4]

serve your tech-trending organization rather than you serving it. However, learning to articulate business goals in the context of selecting technology isn't as easy as it sounds. This is particularly true in large organizations where communication between departments – particularly IT and general business – is either non-existent or strained. Corporate culture has to be considered. You also have to ensure that your employees or staff have the skills and wherewithal to handle new technologies. And you will want to be able to respond to internal and external demands for technology improvement.

Here's a quick look at five major factors tech trenders should address before embarking on the technology selection process. Once again, the good news is that many of these issues are things you can control and that, when addressed, will make it easier to decide what new technologies are right for your organization. Moreover, they'll ensure success once a choice is made.

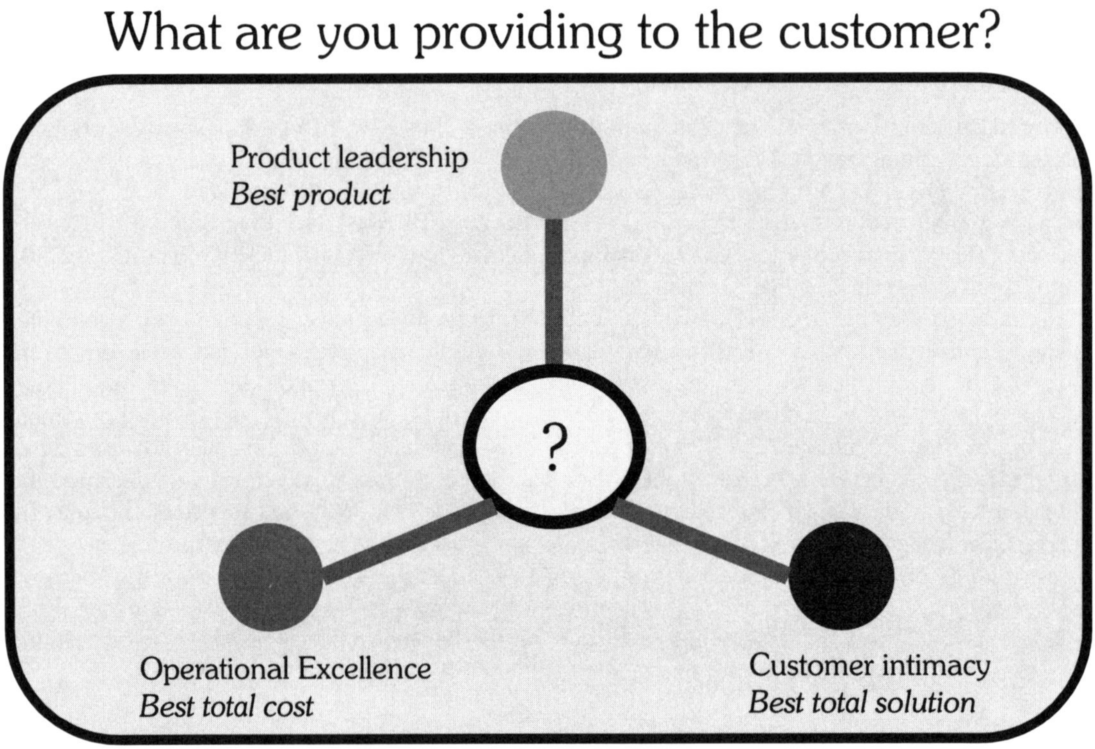

One has to make choices about what sort of company to be and what sort of product creation, services, etc. to emphasize. These choices have a major effect on technology and how to use it.
© David Washburn, principal consultant, Amherst Information Architects, Inc., Amherst, MA. Concept from *The Discipline of Market Leaders: Choose Your Customers, Narrow Your Focus, Dominate Your Market,* Michael Treacy and Fred Wiersema, Addison-Wesley, Reading, MA, 1997.

(These issues will be examined more fully in the context of preparing and carrying out an IT assessment and strategy.)

1 *Adopting a technology mindset.* Technology consultants are learning that the degree to which managers are willing to change, directly affects what technology solutions they're willing to choose – what they call a technology mindset. Being a tech trender means being open to explore new options, new terminology and adopt new business procedures that match technology's capabilities. It also requires that

management at all levels be united in one approach and back projects with proper staff and resources.

SOLUTIONS

A technology mindset means being flexible

Staying flexible is key to having a technology mindset that will benefit you and your organization. The engineering department of a major US aerospace manufacturer had a fixed idea of how their organization handled a set business process involving federal regulations. They had a set means of meeting those regulations and purchased a software package that offered a different approach for doing so. Management of the department refused to change their business process to fit the off-the-shelf package and the vendor couldn't accommodate their style. It ended up being a wasted purchase.

If this same department had adopted a tech-trending mindset their technology outcome may have been far different. They would have assessed their business needs and sought a solution that met their needs without undue work or expense. In this case, developing a proprietary solution that fitted their business process would have been less time-consuming and costly than trying to customize an off-the-shelf solution and failing. Another approach would have been to try, at least for a limited time, to process the software solution provided to see whether it produced the desired results. In other words, they could have worked on being flexible and open to exploring new processes.

2 *Tying technology choices to organizational goals.* New technology releases are taking place daily, or so it seems. Accept that there is no way you can implant new technology as fast as it's being developed and placed on the market. The technology experts say don't change technology without a cost justification that directly ties into your organizational goals (see section below on conducting an IT assessment).

3 *Determining a staff comfort level.* A key question to ask is whether you and your employees or staff are comfortable with your current technology levels. Microsoft, for example, has been pushing new releases of Windows just about every other year or even annually. Some organizations find

employees haven't adjusted to Windows 95 when they're being asked to work in Windows 2000. This leads to feelings of incompetence and discomfort within an organization. Rolling out the latest and greatest technology may destabilize your organization. So assessing employee comfort levels will be one indication of when to make change.

4 *Addressing the technology/culture gap.* Selecting the technology that will work for you often means bridging the technology/culture gap – or the gap between the changes technology imposes on your organization and where your corporate culture sits today. Once again, technology will change work habits and procedures. You want to introduce technology that fits your organizational culture as much as possible rather than bucking the culture.

   Although it's important for an organization to be flexible and keep an open mindset, you can't expect people to change 100 percent to adapt to a technology. It's best to find some middle ground with a technology that's either custom-made for the culture, can be adapted to the culture, or doesn't require the culture to make monumental changes to adapt to it.

SOLUTIONS

Ways to avoid the technology/culture gap

There are many things tech trenders can do to avoid promoting a technology/culture gap. For example, companies intent on maintaining strict hierarchical control shouldn't implant company-wide e-mail systems that provide employee access to all management channels. Impose some rules about e-mail use, or even firewalls if you must. On the other hand, if you're intent on breaking down communication barriers within your organization, then e-mail will provide a tool for everyone to communicate directly.

A second example of how you can avoid the technology/culture gap involves PCs and information sharing. If you want to encourage information sharing, PCs may not be the answer. They create islands of information that may disrupt the efficiency of a department and make information inaccessible to others in the event of a crisis. Networking all PCs is one way around this problem, but cultural issues have to be addressed in a networked environment. Employees have to be encouraged to share information. Providing data security tools may help those squeamish about sharing. More likely, this is a management issue better addressed through incentives.

5 *Know what's driving your decisions.* Sometimes you won't have any choice but to implant technology to meet external demands from customers and trading partners. General Motors, for example, requires suppliers to transmit data via EDI (electronic data interchange). They don't have to own the equipment, but they have to be EDI capable.

Besides customer demand, most organizations purchase new technologies because what they have in-house is either inadequate to meet business goals or failing. In either case, you're already in a potential crisis mode when the purchase is made. Ideally, tech trenders will make purchases in alignment with business strategies rather than because of emergencies.[6]

Walking tech trenders through the IT assessment process

The IT assessment process will help tech trenders organize themselves to make practical, cost-effective technology choices. This process may seem time consuming, but its aim is to offer your company or institution the organizational and decision-making tools that will keep you from selecting useless, malfunctioning or obsolete technology, or technology that won't fit your corporate culture. Technology consultants who practice this sort of assessment find that clients who are strategic enjoy this methodical approach to sorting out business goals, taking technology inventories and eventually creating a strategy for moving ahead. They find making this sort of assessment helps prevent wasteful technology purchases, and ultimately leads to technology success.

IT assessment process

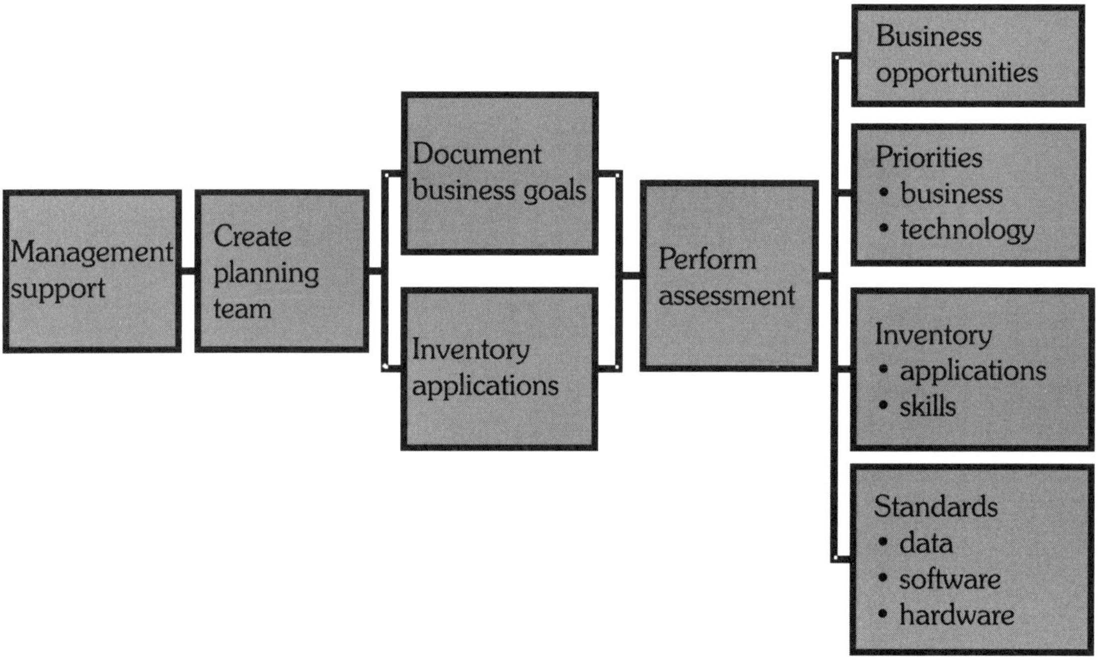

This illustrates the IT Assessment Process outlined in full in this chapter.
© David Washburn, principal consultant, Amherst Information Architects, Inc., Amherst, MA, 1993–2001.

Tech trenders take note that top management must be brought in at least two times during this process: in the beginning to approve time and resources for staffers to make this sort of assessment, and before purchases are made to offer final approval. Basically, it's smart to keep senior management in the loop. Here are five things tech trenders can do to conduct an IT assessment:

PLATFORMS

IT assessment lingo

This is the sort of lingo your technology consultant or IT department will use when conducting an IT assessment:

1. *Business opportunities.* These are sort of the high level opportunities for the business to either improve current operations, or to do innovative things.
2. *Priorities, both business and technology.* This is setting the order in which the various opportunities will be exploited or developed.
3. *Inventory of applications and skills.* These refer to software applications or human skills a company should be utilizing.
4. *Standards for data, software, hardware.* In the context of technology purchases, standards refer to data, software and hardware that are compatible or harmonized with other tools so they can be reusable or integrable.

1. *Develop a planning team.* The planning team for any technology selection should include an operational leader, business people and technology people. By operational leader, you want someone at a high enough level to be able to take charge and make things happen, and who's also available enough to drive the process, stay involved and is invested in the outcome. This person should be able to bridge communication gaps between the business and technology people.
2. *Document business goals.* It's not enough to talk about business goals. In light of the ever-changing technology landscape, it's important to document those goals and key objectives. Although critical success analysis isn't the only tool for taking stock, it can be useful in the context of sorting out what technology choices will match business goals. This sort of analysis focuses on identifying the five or six things an organization must do to be successful, or conversely those things that will lead to failure if ignored.

   They may range from improving sales and marketing to developing a better order system. Whatever areas you identify as key to the success of your organization will be the areas you should consider automating or upgrading, as the case may be. If this is a department making this sort of analysis, make certain your views mesh with upper management. Even conduct interviews with senior managers to synchronize goals and strategies.

The interview process will allow you to very quickly bring to the surface the important issues affecting your organization and help you develop a consensus around goals. None of you want to relive the story of many a mid-manager who wasted tremendous time and money on software implants because their department goals weren't in sync with top management. And, remember, the only IT projects worth pursuing will be the ones that support those critical areas. Technology should be selected that will build business opportunities.

PLATFORMS

What the experts consider "basic" technology requirements

There are some basic technology requirements that apply to all tech-trending organizations – things like basic communication tools including Internet connectivity. Analysts and CIOs offer their views of the basics you need depending on whether you're a small, mid-size or large organization:

- *Small organizations.* Network your company or institution. Consider setting up an intranet, which is a great way of promoting internal communication and a common information base. If you want to have a Web presence seek out freeware to ease financial strain. Be aware that you will probably use packaged solutions and hire consultants to help with IT expertise.
- *Mid-sized organizations.* You need to network, set up an intranet, databases that provide e-mail access to all employees, some form of knowledge management, data modeling and planning. A mid-sized company may have most of the elements of a large company, but just fewer numbers involved. You should be building a Web presence. You will have some internal IT support, but may hire consultants as needed.

- *Large organizations.* It's a given that large organizations should be networked internally and be working on developing a supply network. Besides your intranet, you should have an internal e-mail system. You should be able to extend communication to your key customers and suppliers.

Data security is a major issue to address as IT support. You may outsource support, training and maintenance, but providing those services will be very important.[7]

3 *Inventory your applications.* It's important to capture basic information about the sort of technology you are currently using, how it affects your organization and at what cost. Once you have gathered the sort of information outlined below, you will be able to chart it to see whether the technology you currently own is providing high value at the lowest cost possible. After all, your goal is to gain the most out of the technology you purchase for the least amount of expenditure. Obviously, you want to avoid purchasing technology that is expensive and provides low value, but too often that's just what companies and institutions do. Your inventory should include the following data:
   - A description of the applications from spreadsheets to full-blown interdepartmental information systems.
   - Notes on where the data is coming from. Is it being generated internally (other departments), or externally (suppliers, vendors, customers, government agencies, etc.)?
   - A list of those dependent on the data and how they use it.
   - Summaries of how the organization benefits from the various applications in use, including what part of the organization is the beneficiary. Does the application only benefit one individual, a department, the entire organization?
   - A list of applications based on operational cost, or price tag. Many companies or institutions never tally up what they're spending on technology.

Application – evaluate value versus cost

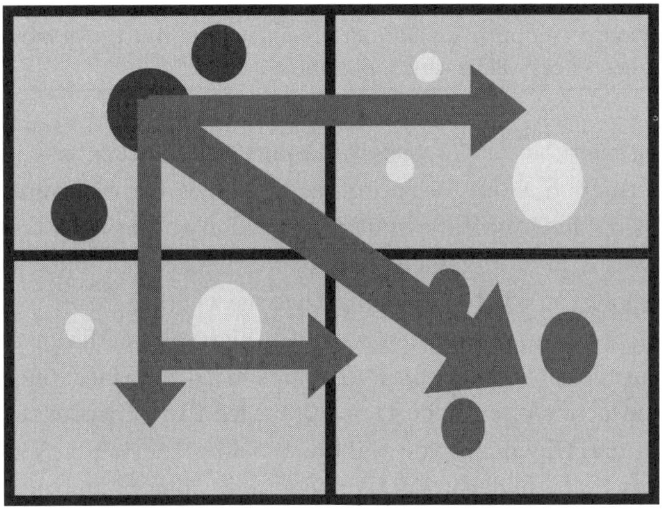

Helps set priorities

This matrix offers an illustration of the direction companies want to shoot for when purchasing and enhancing technology. Obviously, they want high value and as low costs as possible.

APPLICATIONS

Making technology choices at a membership organization

At the American National Standards Institute (ANSI), a membership organization, financial resources are often tight. That means that cost is always a main factor in technology selection. That's not only the cost of the software and hardware, but the resources required to provide backup support, training and maintenance of the technology systems.

Besides cost, the second driver affecting technology selection is function. Given financial restraints and staffing limitations, technology must satisfy the needs and demands of ANSI's staff and members while reducing ongoing maintenance and support. Technology is viewed as a tool for solving business problems. The business problems are addressed, first, and then the chief information officer (CIO) and his IT staff analyze what technology will be the most appropriate.

With the increase in IT development and the enormous pace of technology growth, selecting the best technology for the job has become more and more difficult. It's a "damned if you do, damned if you don't" situation. One way ANSI is coping is to move from five operating systems to one, which helps them implement changes that go across the entire operation for a lot less cost and time.

They're also very concerned with vendors. They only pick those with strong indicators that they will survive for the next five years. Hiring competent people to apply the technology is another major challenge for ANSI, and many non-profits that can't compete with the salaries IT staff can earn in the corporate world. They cope by hiring recent college graduates and tapping the resources of members, many of whom have huge IT departments.[8]

APPLICATIONS

Types of technology in use in a New Economy company

There are about 110 employees at Systemcorp, a Canadian software manufacturer, a New Economy business involved in selling a management-related software package both via licensing or on the Web. The following is the sort of technology Systemcorp maintains to operate its business.

The Web is their primary driver and their Web site is housed outside Systemcorp in a domain server. Web access is crucial and maintained for both Netscape and Internet Explorer. With an effective Web site at the cornerstone of the business, the Web site has to be extremely user friendly and has to be designed to attract leads.

E-mail is a prime internal and external communication tool. All employees are networked and work from PCs. The company maintains a number of servers primarily for its software development work. A mainframe computer allows them to do software development for IBM.

In terms of computer programs most everything is done through a Seagate Crystal report generator that allows you to take data and manipulate it. There are Zip programs to compact large files and Norton anti-virus programs to combat computer viruses. They use Microsoft Project, Microsoft PowerPoint and all Microsoft Office Tools, as well as a Web-demo program that allows potential clients to walk through a demonstration via the Web.[9]

Once all this information is gathered, you can chart it based on expense and effectiveness. This exercise will give you a clear view of where to place your time and energy. Any technology that is both expensive and is producing no value should be chucked. The last thing you want is to be working with technology that provides negative value. Ideally, all technology should be providing high value at the lowest cost possible.

Take a good hard look at what technology you aren't using. That will clue you into whether the technology doesn't fit your culture, whether your people lack the skills to use it, or whether it just doesn't match business goals. Sometimes it takes time for technology to pay off, so don't make hasty decisions about removing applications before giving them a chance to work. This inventory checklist will also show you where you are lacking technology and offer some direction for what you might want to select.

4 *Determining staff skills.* You can see the need for several applications to automate various business functions, or to improve on the technology you now own. It's important at this stage to take stock of the skills your staff bring to the picture. If they lack the skills to operate some new technology, that will mean wasted time and money, plus a demoralized staff (see Chapters 9 and 10).

5 *Gain senior management support.* Why spin wheels? You're going to need the backing of senior management in terms of financial and staff support for any new technology to work,

UNPLUGGING TECHNOSTRESS

The computer user checklist (CUC)

You want to know what sort of computer user you are, right? If you don't own up to your lack of knowledge you may end up with the task of installing Linux. Answer yes or no to the following questions. In general, answering yes to most questions means that you're not a Luddite, could be a technozombie and may even be a technocompetent. Technonerds will find these questions beneath them and will be able to identify themselves that way.

1 Do you read computer magazines of any sort?
2 Does iMac turn you on?
3 Do you know your serial port from your parallel port?
4 If a hazardous waste spill emptied your office, would you spend the rest of the day (pick five):
   - Reconfiguring your hard drive?
   - Bungee jumping?
   - Baking cookies?
   - Gardening?
   - Cleaning house gutters?
   - Watching reruns of 1950s, '60s, '70s, '80s and '90s TV shows?
   - Catching up on e-mail?
   - Christmas shopping at the mall?
   - Reading Hobbes' *Leviathan* from cover to cover?
   - Attending wine tastings?
   - Collecting dinosaur bones?
   - Drag racing?
   - Going out in drag?
   - Catching up on the latest offerings on Amazon.com?
   - Other?
5 You feel exhausted at the mere thought of calling tech support or visiting a computer store?
6 Do you suffer anxiety when cocktail party talk centers around computer upgrades?
7 Do you know what Java is?
8 If you can't open e-mail attachments do you:
   - Call a friend?
   - Try figuring it out on your own?
   - Shut off the computer?
   - End the relationship with the sender?
9 Can you tell a computer virus from a medical virus?[10]

so you might as well start during the selection process. The best way to gain senior management support is to start with the outcome – how you want technology to affect your organization. You need to tell management what they will get for their money, and how much time, energy and staff this change will require. Show them results, as in "when we're done with this process this is what you'll have." Once again, tie your technology presentation in with business goals. Prove to them that the technology in question will further those goals, and better yet, build profits.[11]

APPLICATIONS

Case study: a bank makes an informed technology purchase

A multi-state bank wanted to give their staff access to corporate data. At the time they hired a technology consultant to help with this process they had already outlined their business requirements fairly effectively and determined what capabilities they wanted. They were in the process of making strategic technology choices.

As part of the IT assessment process, the consultant worked with the bank staff to map their business requirements onto alternative software products. They were concerned with purchasing products with standards for hardware and data that would allow the purchases to transition and evolve, and to ensure that all selections matched business goals.

The consultant helped the bank staff to develop a script to present to all potential vendors. Each was given a week to address the issue outlined in the script and present a solution. Vendors had to demonstrate how their products would solve these problems, not simply say so. End users were brought in to evaluate the tools during the demonstration process.

It became clear to them during the assessment and vendor interviewing processes that no product was perfect. All of the vendors in question had strong attributes. In the end, it came down to selecting the product that met most of their needs. The decision was an informed one. Product limitations were recognized upfront and plans were made to address them in the implementation phase.[12]

How size and finances affects technology selection

The size of your operation and resources will play a major factor in your technology selections. Tech trenders don't need to be told that small companies and non-profits often operate on far tighter budgets than major corporations. Making the wrong technology choices for small organizations can be devastating. But even large companies don't want to waste time and money on technology that will become obsolete or that doesn't fit the need.

Application – evaluate benefit/beneficiary

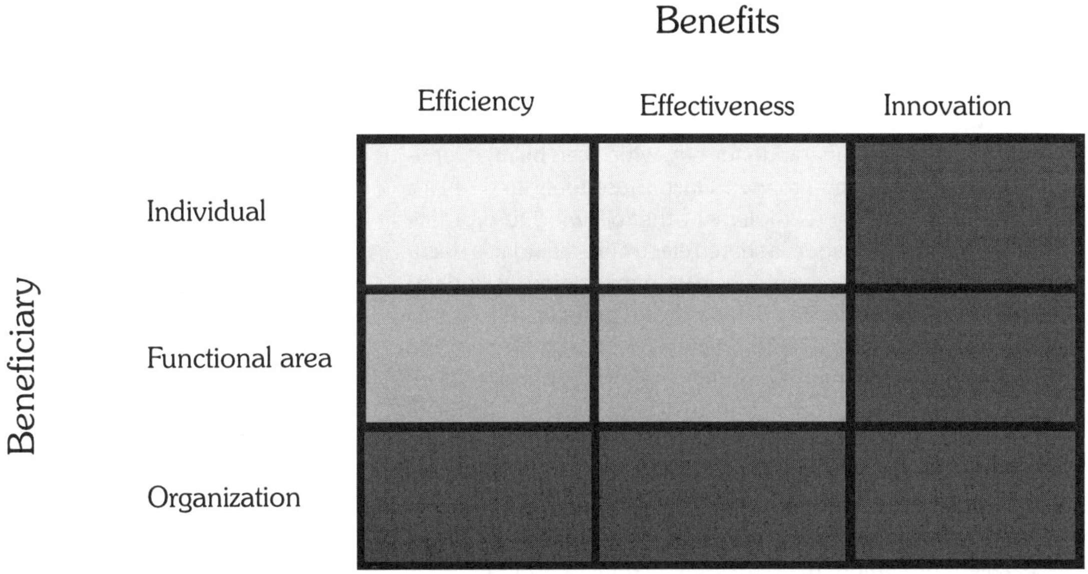

This chart illustrates the benefits that technology can provide an organization, an individual or a group.

One thing that should help companies in the startup phase – or those contemplating upgrades or automating new processes – is having some sense of what technology matches the functions you want to automate. For example, you can choose between Internet or EDI to transmit back-office data to manufacturing customers or trading partners, or choose some combination of both. A small company may opt to outsource the work to a service center that offers EDI translation and transmission services. A large company may find purchasing equipment more cost-effective.

SOLUTIONS

What technology matches your automating needs

A good part of placing tech trenders in the technology driver's seat, involves understanding what technologies correspond to your business and institutional functions. The following provides you with a list of the sorts of technologies that correspond with everything from internal communication to computing.

- *Internal communication within an organization.* To utilize the following collaborative tools you must be networked and establish a standard operating format, which can be an operating system or a Web browser. Once those tools are in place it would be optimal to implement the following to promote internal communication: a shared electronic calendar, a document data base, search engine, instant messaging, skills database, resource availability database, and groupware ERP.
- *External communication with suppliers, vendors, customers.* You can use the same internal communication tools, but that requires you have a connection to the Internet or a private network. When you reach outside your organization, then security becomes a significant concern. Tools for external communication will also include EDI and supply chain management solutions. There's also the evolving B2B world that is detailed throughout this book (see Chapters 2 and 6).
- *Computing.* Some jobs, like large transaction processing, still require mainframes. More and more computing is taking place on networked servers that run on operating systems like Windows, Linux or Unix. Web servers are now available so you can start conducting transactions in cyberspace.
- *Business applications.* Whether you want to automate your invoicing, inventory or human resources, you have the hardware infrastructure in place. What you will need are specific software applications to cover these sorts of functions. In IT lingo, these are called business applications.

Let's return to Joe Tire Manufacturer and his dilemma: what technology should he pick for his 150-employee company to start transitioning to a networked, B2B world? IT experts were asked to help Joe make some decisions based on one-time allotments of $100,000, $250,000 and $500,000. Not surprisingly, if the half a million dollars were spent wisely, Joe's operation could be state-of-the-art. But there are still many things he can do to start the transition with even a quarter of that amount. Here's how the dollars translate into technology:

- Expenditure of $100,000. At this level of spending, Joe can make his operation more efficient. He doesn't have enough budgeted to be truly innovative, but he can start networking his operation. One way to spend the money would be to buy 30 PCs, some laptops, a really top-notch printer, and a server so all equipment can be networked and operate a database. There might be enough left over to purchase an e-mail server. A good chunk of this money will be spent on training and ongoing support.
  Accomplishments. This sort of setup would allow employees to do computerized spreadsheets or improve a specific business function like waste management. If there's money for the e-mail server, all employees would be able work off Joe's e-mail account.
- Expenditure of $250,000. An infusion of $150,000 (besides the $100,000 already spent) means that Joe can start thinking of reorganizing his operation and become more effective. He can initiate integration efforts across department lines and start developing a Web presence. He would have essentially the same hardware setup as described above, but be able to purchase a beefier server and a wider variety of software solutions. The server, alone, would cost at least $20,000. Joe might also consider purchasing some groupware software (now often Web-browser based) that usually includes shared documents, shared calendars, online discussion groups and basic workflow automation and task assignments.

  To accomplish these changes it's recommended he hire 1.5 employees to develop, manage and run his far more complicated IT operation. He has a place to store so-called knowledge, so he may want a document management function to back up quality, testing and procedures to help him meet federal regulations. This would have to be an off-the-shelf product, but without legacy systems to accommodate and with prices dropping, that shouldn't prove too costly.

Accomplishments. This is a big technology leap for Joe's organization. This setup means that all managers can store and retrieve critical business documents. Workflow automation allows Joe's company to develop online forms and to electronically track the flow of business information throughout the company. This means his staff can search for information anywhere in the groupware database. If all is carried out properly, Joe will be able to increase quality and approach just-in-time management of business and manufacturing functions.

- Expenditure of $500,000. Now Joe has the opportunity to be innovative and start moving into the B2B world, but a good chunk of his costs will go into hiring additional IT support, upgrading existing equipment and maintenance. He can explore outsourcing his shipping department, for example, and start developing a supply network by investing in the software interfaces he needs to work with his suppliers.

  At this level, Joe can start to consider custom software development that reflects his company's unique business strengths, and allow him to differentiate himself from his competitors. This may be software that allows him to operate much more efficiently and therefore at higher profit margins, or to provide different products and services. Also, he has the finances to invest in a Web server and join a Web exchange. His main expenditures outside of employee time are for high-speed Internet access, increasingly sophisticated software and training for business managers.

  Accomplishments. Joe may not be operating on the Web entirely, but he has the capacity to share technical information databases, allow customers access to technical expertise, Internet-accessible order tracking, and can develop a "proposal wizard" that aids customers in developing more accurate proposals and specifications. He is evolving a supply network of customers, suppliers and third-party logistics operators that allow him to both manufacture and ship just-in-time. And he's able to do e-procurement through his Web interface.[13]

Tips for small tech-trending organizations

Now that you've seen how dollar amounts can translate into technology change, there are a number of general things small tech-trending organizations can do to maximize efficiency, effectiveness and start moving into becoming technology innovators. The following are four tips for small organizations facing technology choices:

1 *Focus on automating what you do best.* Technology experts say the biggest problem small and mid-size organizations have is trying to automate all of their business functions when they lack the staff and financial resources to do it right. They advise them to concentrate on automating those functions that they do best and where advanced technology will provide efficiency and added income. And that's whether you're in the business of providing financial consulting services, manufacturing automotive components, or organizing tours.

   An automotive part manufacturer, for example, should be exploring technology that will improve your manufacturing process, and then farm out billing and receivables to a business that has the technology to handle those functions most efficiently and effectively. Don't try to implant the hardware and software to do this sort of work. That could prove time-consuming, costly and may lead to a business failure without the requisite staff and financial support.

2 *Outsource sales, marketing and advertising.* Small organizations should also consider outsourcing their sales, marketing and advertising rather than purchase technology to do this work. These are functions where human skills matter.

The technology available will be expensive and often obsolete by the time you master it.

3 *Locate a technology troubleshooter.* You will be more and more dependent on your technology for business or institutional survival. If you can't afford an IT department, or a full-time IT employee, you must locate a company or individual who can help you maintain your hardware and software, and who can troubleshoot in the event of crises. This person should also be able to advise you about how to best use the technology you have purchased, about outsourcing and future technology selections.

4 *Buy equipment geared to individual functions.* You may be tempted to buy equipment that's loaded with a variety of functions. The cost may be right and a machine that includes phone, fax and color printing, for example, will take up less space. Avoid this temptation. When one function breaks you'll be out of luck and out of equipment.

PLATFORMS

Selecting technology for a university language center

How to keep up with technology change without sinking a fairly slim budget is always a juggling act for the staff at the Foreign Language Resource Center at the University of Massachusetts. The center, which aims to simulate foreign language experiences through use of whatever advanced technologies it can afford, has three full-time employees servicing about 2,000 students and faculty weekly.

Because of budget and staff limitations, there's an effort to maintain a balance between cutting edge and older technologies. For example, the newest computers the center owns can handle functions like video editing and have digitized sound. More and more services are being placed online, including audio lessons. And there is a new push to purchase software online.

The advantage of keeping some legacy equipment is that it allows for purchase of really cutting-edge hardware and software so that the center stays abreast of technology change and can learn and evaluate the newest and fastest, plus Web access. The downside of keeping mismatched technology is the added cost of operating and maintaining older equipment.

Because they can't afford to be on the "bleeding edge of technology change," these are the criteria staffers try to keep in mind when making technology selections:

- Will this be a cheaper, more reliable product in the future?
- What's the purpose of the equipment? Will we be buying the equivalent of an SST for the purpose of merely crossing the street? If so, it's too complicated and will increase labor costs for training staff as well as the initial costs of installation. This applies both to hardware and to software applications.
- How much new equipment is necessary? Should we stagger purchases?[14]

SOLUTIONS

A small company's technology strategy

Once again, we're turning to Systemcorp for some examples, because this is a small company with forward-thinking ideas and goals. Farming out whatever back-office work they can has been a main goal of this Canadian company, along with expanding security systems related to their servers and improving the reliability of their operation. There's also a big concern about being able to transfer the database from server to server to avoid crashes.

Management is exploring voice-recognition systems to make their system easier for employees and customers to use. And they're focusing more and more on wireless communication with equipment like Palm Pilots to allow employees to be mobile. In fact, mobility and compactness are key concerns. Locating a communication system that will allow them to work globally while offering a sense of intimacy – of sitting around the table – is also part of the Systemcorp technology strategy.

And more and more, they're relying on centralized computer centers storing an increasing amount of data on other people's servers instead of their own. Rather than pay $50,000 for a site license to maintain a database, they pay $200 a month to have someone else run a project for them.[15]

Tips for large tech-trending organizations

The issues of what to automate and how to make smart technology choices are just as serious for large organizations as they are for small ones. The difference is that large companies and institutions have more resources to throw at the problem and more margin for error. Here are four ways that large organizations can avoid bad technology choices and solve some of their technology problems:

1 *Practice simulation modeling.* It used to be that major companies had the leeway to make some bad decisions and to ride on decisions that produced OK results, but not the best. Nowadays, there is very little leeway for decision-making that falls in the OK category. You need to be performing at the top of your league almost all the time.

One way to ensure you are making best-in-class technology decisions is to practice simulation modeling. The great thing about technology is that there are programs available that will allow you to conduct a causal model for the entire business and assess the change that technology will make on the organization. You can run a three-year projection in a matter of minutes. This approach can be used to test out the impact of both software and hardware on your company.

Computer simulations can also be used to test product design without having to actually build anything. In 1985, it used to cost a company like Ford $60,000 each time it purposely crashed a car to study the effect of accidents on the vehicle. The same test can be simulated on a computer for about $100.[16]

2 *Seek customer-focused technology products.* There will be more and more demand on corporations and even institutions to produce products specifically for one major customer. Companies like Nortel Networks are already working in this fashion, and institutions such as museums and universities are also customer driven.

You should be looking at software packages that meet customer-focused needs, or technology that will meet those needs. If you consider off-the-shelf versus developing proprietary solutions, they have to be easily customizable. Prepare to see more and more demand from customers who want software to do a specific job, rather than purchase mass-market products. Already, software vendors are responding by designing basic systems that consultants or technology specialists in-house can customize for specific customer concerns.

3 *Purchase information-screening programs.* In this day of e-mail overload it's good news that vendors are producing software to help you screen information. You can program your e-mail to be sorted automatically, tossing out whatever information you don't desire. That may be jokes, advertising, promotionals, etc. And some programs can reroute e-mail to other departments automatically. These sorts of products are still immature, but they're being improved all the time.

4 *Consider "in-sourcing" IT development.* Rather than outsource various technology functions you might consider "in-sourcing" them. In-sourcing means creating alliances with major service providers to customize functions for you. For example, Sprint recently teamed with Ernst & Young to have E & Y develop IT solutions for them. They formed a completely separate company whose sole purpose is to develop IT solutions for Sprint. Although E & Y staffs this company, the employees are housed at Sprint.[17]

Working with vendors, consultants and online technology service providers

As will be discussed more fully in Chapter 9, controlling your technology future is very dependent on having enough technology knowledge to work effectively with vendors and IT service providers. Vendors can be a useful source of information if you're prepped to talk intelligently with them. And you may need IT service providers to help with technology selections, maintenance and troubleshooting. You want to guide them as least as much as they guide you. Here are five factors to consider that will help tech-trenders improve relationships with these sorts of IT professionals:

1 *Learn about your vendor's culture.* Vendors often make technology that reflects their own cultural mindset. One technology expert divides vendor cultures into traditional or hierarchical, consensus or Web-networked and charismatic or guru-led, and profit-centered. For example, IBM was once a hierarchical company and the technology it produced represented that approach – little computers talked to middle computers and those talked to big computers. Then Apple, a guru-led company, came along with its user-friendly PC that allowed networking between groups. Digital's networked computing (DECNET) also promoted consensus building. Everything was built around DECNET and could be networked from day one. This expert considers Microsoft to be a bunch of smokestacks – small groups that don't talk to each other.

  Before developing a relationship with a vendor, check out their organizational culture. Determine if it matches your own, or if the fit would be a stretch.

2 *Be willing to adopt new terminology.* Sometimes adopting a tech-trending mindset means being willing to use new terminology. Packaged software often comes with its own terms and lexicon. You can't expect an off-the-shelf product to match the terminology that's common in your company or institution, but may need to use what's provided. Bringing in a consultant, as one company did, to attempt to alter the software package's terminology proved time-consuming, costly and fruitless. It would have been easier, in the long run, if the people in the department changed their language to meet the product they had selected, or simply developed their own proprietary product based on their in-department terminology.

3 *Stay open minded.* People often bring a mental image of what they want accomplished to developing a software solution. Although it's good to do some visualizing, getting locked into a vision before talking to vendors or technicians can lead to costly system failures. In one case, a company had a mental model of how to account for waste removal and kept feeling a software solution came up short because it didn't meet their mental image of how it should perform. In the opinion of the consultant brought in to solve the problem, it was the human thinking not the software package that came up short.

4 *Encourage a uniform organizational mindset.* Technology may provide tech-trending organizations options you have not envisioned. To take advantage of those opportunities means having an open mind, being willing to re-examine goals and ensuring management buy-in at all levels. In the same aerospace company top management wanted to improve waste management. A technology consultant recommended purchase of waste management software that required data input for immediate tracking of waste generation.

Although more time consuming in the short run, the cost savings from being able to keep more immediate tabs on waste generated were estimated to be $2.8 million over five years. Problems evolved with a mid-manager who resisted assigning the additional work to employees that the software required. She was intent on promoting efficiency and reducing employee work time and wasn't hearing top management concerns. The software was eventually implemented, but the job took years longer than planned because this mid-manager constantly presented obstacles, which led to delay after delay. There was no uniform organizational mindset around technology.

5 *Closely monitor staff levels.* Many companies are running lean today, depending on technology to handle a myriad of simple tasks. Technology can't entirely supplant humans. You need proper staffing to provide coverage and pick up the added burdens that technology change creates.

> Remember that technology takes time; time during the selection process, time for training, time to implement and time for adjustment. Often that's time taken away from regular work. If you don't have adequate staffing, you won't be able to free yourself and others to make technology change.[18]

APPLICATIONS

A case study in technology selection confusion

Examining how companies and institutions "do it wrong" can be just as informative for tech trenders as learning about best practices. Back at our major aerospace company the environmental engineering department has purchased an Oracle system to integrate a variety of functions, but no one in-house understands how to work with it. The Management Information Systems (MIS) department hires an outside consultant to sort things out.

Sitting down with the environmental engineers, the consultant soon learned they had no idea why they needed Oracle. The recommendation had come from another firm, which had lost out on the bid to implement it and taken its knowledge with them. He found the MIS department not terribly concerned with engineering's needs – they hadn't recommended Oracle, after all – and the engineers not able to articulate exactly what they needed.

Eventually, he was able to get the engineers to clarify their requirements and recommended a database be set up that could store a million pieces of information. Oracle ended up being something they could use which, given the $185,000 price tag, was a good thing. But, like many large companies, they had made the purchase blind and without any real understanding of what the solution had to offer them.[19]

How tech trenders can evaluate vendors and consultants

It's often very trying for even the most advanced tech trender to evaluate vendors, their products and offerings. Any of you who run a business or institution are being bombarded with vendor advertising and promotionals. The IT assessment and many tips in this chapter will help you winnow out this onslaught based on your business needs and goals, which then determine what functions you want to automate and/or upgrade. It doesn't hurt to have someone in-house store this sort of advertising and categorize it for future consideration.

Let's say you have identified the need to integrate back-office functions and have literature from five software vendors. You don't only want to evaluate them, but to use the evaluation process to garner information about how to most effectively address your issues. The experts suggest you look for domain expertise and maturity rather than market position, alone. You should purchase only software modules – when dealing with a supply chain planning system, for example – where there are proven business benefits. Get references from other organizations with similar business problems, as well as similar functional and technical environments. And demand demonstrations that support your business goals and that utilize your own data. The following are more details on three key recommendations:

1 *Develop scripts and demand proof.* Develop a script to present all five vendors or consultants that starts with: "This is my business. This is what I need the software, hardware, online system, etc. to do." Next bring the vendor or consultant in-house and have them prove that their product or services can solve your technology problems. Here are questions to present them:
   - Do you offer collaboration capabilities? Because of the pending move we will all make to a B2B world, selecting a system that enables collaboration is a definite must. Organizations have to be able to provide trading partners with timely, accurate information. That means the applications you seek should provide browser-based demand, and supply your organization with the ability to tie in collaboration with workflow. You also need a sys-

tem with built-in alerts to provide notification of problems and inconsistencies, and that allows for automatic process execution.

- How mature are your applications? Application maturity can be measured based on functionality maturity and vertical maturity. Looking at functional maturity first, it's important that you avoid the purchase of software modules that don't cover current and anticipated functions. As vendors expand their offerings, and add modules onto existing products, many modules vary in maturity and integrity. Tech trenders must make vendors prove that they will provide functionality that is available (not just promised on back order), mature and deployable when you want it.

SOLUTIONS

Analysts and CIOs advise tech trenders on technology picks

From conducting formal research to knowing how to assess vendors, this is what top analysts and CIOs have to say about making informed technology choices:

1 *Do research and request formal responses.* The top analyst groups like the Gartner Group, Forrester and Jupiter (see Chapter 4) are considered good sources of information on hardware/software. But to get the precise information you need on a product, tech trenders are advised to send out formal requests for information (RFQs in the trade). Conducting in-depth due diligence is also in order, meaning talking to clients, looking into the health of the manufacturer and evaluating proposals based on cost and appropriateness to the business or institutional requirements at hand.

2 *Assessing vendors.* Staying objective is key. Too often people come in with preconceived notions of vendors. If you keep your objectivity high, you stand a much better chance of making the right decision. You can have a formal process, but be objective. Tech trenders should also look for a reputation for delivering ongoing results, good references and evidence of ongoing support. Make sure the vendor is assigning experi-

enced people, not kids just out of college and that you feel you can build a relationship with this company. If it's a big project, insist the vendor work on a pilot version with your organization. If the risks are high, stick to a tried and true vendor. And make sure they offer reasonable timetables and payment schedules.

3 *High end versus low end.* You don't always need a Cadillac or Mercedes. The rule of thumb many analysts and CIOs apply to selecting technology is that if you see a great deal of fluctuation in this sector go for the low-end product. Most likely you'll be making a change soon. If you see stability, then you can go for the high end and make a long-term investment.

4 *Reputation matters.* If you're in a low-risk situation you may want to try out something new. But for many tech trenders on tight budgets, analysts and CIOs say stick with known technology that has a long (relative in this industry) track record. One CIO touts Compaq servers and NT or Windows environments saying they've provided "rock solid" performance over the couse of the last decade.

5 *Quality of support.* The product may be great and the price is affordable, but if the ongoing technical support isn't there, you should go elsewhere. Some analysts and CIOs say the quality of support is the most important criterion tech trenders must consider when making a purchase.

6 *Standards matter.* Seek out technology that's standardized, meaning based on open standards. That allows for flexibility or scalability. And make sure you purchase technology throughout your organization where the standards are compatible. Major corporations have saved hundreds of millions of dollars by making standardization a key factor, which then ensures some level of compatibility across an organization and supply network.[20]

- How mature are you as a business or institution? Vertical maturity refers to the vendor's experience level. If you select vendors without specific industry experience, you put yourself at risk. Many vendors, particularly in the supply chain planning arena, are trying to satisfy the needs of targeted vertical industries, but few can do so. As vendors expand their offerings to enter new industry verticals, their initial solutions may still be immature.

Vertical maturity is not just a matter of the length of time the product has been released. It also hinges on the vendor's commitment to the industry vertical, meaning its track record in development, deployment and success in the field. Knowing a vendor's position on the vertical maturity scale is critical to determining risk and implementation time. And make sure they are assigning you seasoned staff to work with your organization, not someone right out of school with no practical experience.

- What sort of demos do you offer? Avoid generic demos. Be aware that a generic software demo won't reveal immaturity, or always enable users to visualize day-to-day performances. Be sure to make vendors address these issues during a demo presentation. That's a good first step to implementation.

2 *Evaluate references.* References should come from an organization with the same demographics – global reach, business problems and industry or institutional needs – as you. It is important to check references provided by the vendor. Those not provided can also act as indicators and highlight possible problems. You can seek out information about a specific vendor by networking at conferences, or following up on contacts.

SOLUTIONS

Reference checking

Tech trenders may not have the luxury of implementing mature software that has already been deployed many times. You may have to work with a startup company or asked to be joint-development partners with existing software vendors. How you check references will depend on which of these circumstances you encounter.

If working with a startup vendor, look for individual capabilities, meaning whether the development team has delivered on a similar project before. Check what's called viability, or the amount of funding they have, executive pedigree and support. Joint-development partners can check references from others in similar situations, or who had similar functionality requirements. Checks should center on the ability to deliver in the time allotted, as well as the completeness of the delivery.[21]

3 *Single suite versus incremental purchases.* Vendors are going to push large software suites for obvious reasons – they're expensive and lock you in with that particular vendor for a longer time period than if you bought a single solution. Naturally, there's an appeal to buying a sweeping solution that promises to solve all of your technology problems, but that approach is strewn with potential pitfalls as any organization that has bought into large-scale ERP solutions has learned.

As noted above, the maturity of modules may vary within a large-scale package and may offer only a slice of supply chain and other functions while advertising "full solutions." And your corporate culture may not be prepared either emotionally, or in terms of skills, to handle the enormous change a large-scale suite requires.

On the positive side, the large suite will require less integration than melding solutions from a variety of vendors. Don't shy away from long-term, overarching solutions, altogether. Study them with the assessment tools provided in this book, always keeping business goals in mind. If the large-scale sweep offers collaboration capability and vertical maturity, if your organization is ready for major change, and if vendor interviews and references indicate that their solutions are solid and well tried by others, the large-scale suite may be right for you.[22]

Moving onto the Web and selecting online services

One day, tech trenders will be able to download all software and related services from the Web. The technology will be rented with a service contract provided rather than having you purchase licensing rights. It's a lovely dream and one that isn't entirely out there in cyberspace. Even if Web-based services are still limited, this is a direction that tech trenders need to know more about. Technology consultants are already starting to look at what companies can do with a browser, first, before choosing technology solutions.

But they warn that much of what's available via the Web today are interactive brochures. It's much more challenging to utilize the Web when you want to work interactively between customers or trading partners. Although Java word processors and other Web languages are maturing, they haven't reached the level of being able to provide a prescribed function in the way that a program like Word allows users to move an arrow throughout a file and get you the results you expect – whether it's closing a file, cutting and pasting text or formatting. Once people have experienced the responsiveness that today's computer programs offer – as flawed as they can be – they sometimes balk at conducting centralized computing via the Internet because it's not yet that responsive.

APPLICATIONS

Picking e-procurement software

Many companies, including the majors like SAP, are starting to offer software to promote e-procurement functions. To cut through the advertising hype, treat the purchase of a packaged e-procurement solution as a strategic sourcing decision. Besides examining your sourcing needs and matching a product to fit them, you have to focus on vendor stability and research and development capabilities. Ask them questions like: "What proportion of revenues do you put back into development?" "Are you retaining good people?" "What is the strategy for each industry?"[23]

Purveyors of online services compare the evolving Web-based service market to the emergence of the modern telecommunications industry. When telephones first appeared, the caller played a major role in cranking the phone to reach an operator who then placed it. People were involved in manipulation of the actual technology on a level far beyond what takes place today, where we can call anywhere in the world by pushing a few buttons.

With the Web-based world still in its infancy, tech trenders have to be far more involved with the actual technology – the networking of legacy systems, the application for middleware, etc. – than you will be in the future. For example, when voice-activated computers come into their own, you won't need to know anything about actually running your equipment anymore than you know about the operation of a telephone or television. You'll be concerned with negotiating a good service contract.

Today, only a handful of you contract online services or even know they exist. The experts say that this will change as the technology improves and awareness grows. One vision of this new world of Web-based software and technology solutions amounts to a cyberspace Main Street where all sorts of functions are available in Web site storefronts. So tech trenders will rent software at the PowerPoint or Excel cyberstores rather than purchasing licensing rights from Microsoft. And in a w-commerce world (for wireless e-commerce) you will be connected 24 hours a day to the Web and be able to download functions from any location in the world. Companies like Systemcorp are already evolving their w-commerce strategies.[24]

SOLUTIONS

An aerospace company turns to the Web to resolve IT problems

For example, a major aerospace company in the early 1990s needed a waste manifesting and shipping database that produces documentation on hazardous waste shipments for state and federal agencies. At that time, a technology consultant developed a database and application that all resided on the mainframe. This included the data storage, the business logic and the human interface. Information was accessed using dumb terminals, which were predecessors to today's PCs.

In the late 1990s, the application was rewritten and the business logic and the human intervention were moved down to smart PCs, meaning they are no longer simply monitors and keyboards, but have computing power. The data continued to be stored on the mainframe. This was beneficial because the tool on the PC was more flexible, dynamic and allowed the user to interact more effectively with their data.

The third generation of this application is being developed at this writing. The PC solution satisfied the user, but it's proven to be very difficult to maintain and expand to other participants in the company. So a new strategy has emerged to deploy the application through Web browsers, which would make it accessible to all 4000 PCs in the company without any special setup or software. This addresses the company's desire to put more data and control in the hands of business managers, so they can look up their own data for reports, and maintain their own business structure data. This is an instance of technology reinforcing business objectives to make business managers responsible for the environmental impact of their operations.[25]

Notes

1 H. James Harrington, chief executive officer, Systemcorp, Quebec, Canada, and former consulting principal for quality at Ernst & Young.

2 "Solving the Paradox," *The Economist* New Economy survey, September 23, 2000, p. 11.

3 Mary Case, Director, QM2: Quality Management to a Higher Power, Washington, DC.

4 *When Bad Computer Things Happen To Good People,* a work in progress, Amy Zuckerman and Izzy Gesell.

5 David Washburn, principal consultant at Amherst Information Architects, Amherst, MA.

6 David Washburn, principal consultant at Amherst Information Architects, Amherst, MA.

7 Krimo Salem, CEO of If & Then Inc., San Jose, CA; Jeanmarie Gelinas, vice president and CIO of Rodale, Inc., Emmaus, PA; Eric Fliegel, CIO, eTour, Inc., Atlanta, GA; Pam

Kleier, CEO of constructionzone.com, Louisville, KY; Laurence Smith, a specialist in e-commerce management, Boston, MA; Merv Adrian, VP and research manager, Giga Information Group, Cambridge, MA; and David Yokelson, the META Group, Stamford, CT.

8 Bob Feghali, vice president of Business Development and CIO at ANSI.

9 H. James Harrington, chief executive officer, Systemcorp, Quebec, Canada, and former consulting principal for quality at Ernst & Young.

10 *When Bad Computer Things Happen To Good People,* a work in progress, Amy Zuckerman and Izzy Gesell.

11 The IT assessment is based on a process designed by David Washburn, principal consultant at Amherst Information Architects, Amherst, MA.

12 David Washburn, principal consultant at Amherst Information Architects, Amherst, MA.

13 IT information from David Washburn, principal consultant at Amherst Information Architects, Amherst, MA.

14 Irene Starr, director, the Foreign Language Resource Center at the University of Massachusetts, Amherst, MA.

15 H. James Harrington, chief executive officer, Systemcorp, Quebec, Canada, and former consulting principal for quality at Ernst & Young.

16 "Untangling e-conomics," The New Economy Survey, *The Economist*, September 23, 2000, p. 6.

17 H. James Harrington, chief executive officer, Systemcorp, Quebec, Canada, and former consulting principal for quality at Ernst & Young.

18 David Washburn, principal consultant at Amherst Information Architects, Amherst, MA; and H. James Harrington, CEO, Systemcorp, Quebec, Canada, and former consulting principal for quality at Ernst & Young.

19 David Washburn, principal consultant at Amherst Information Architects, Amherst, MA.

20 Krimo Salem, CEO of If & Then Inc., San Jose, CA; Jeanmarie Gelinas, Vice President and CIO of Rodale, Inc., Emmaus, PA.; Eric Fliegel, CIO, eTour, Inc., Atlanta, GA; Pam Kleier, CEO of constructionzone.com, Louisville, KY; Laurence Smith, a specialist in e-commerce management, Boston, MA; Merv Adrian, VP and research manager, Giga Information Group, Cambridge, MA; and David Yokelson, the META Group, Stamford, CT.

21 "Guidelines for Selecting an SCP System," Karen Peterson, Research Director, the Gartner Group, Tactical Guidelines, TG-10–9365, June 9, 2000.

22 "Guidelines for Selecting an SCP System," Karen Peterson, Research Director, the Gartner Group, Tactical Guidelines, TG-10–9365, June 9, 2000.

23 "Is an E-Procurement Solution Right for You?" Craig DeLano and Rex Tibbens, Mercer Management Consulting, June 1, 1999, appeared on PurchasingCenter.com in the summer of 2000.

24 David Washburn, principal consultant at Amherst Information Architects, Amherst, MA; Peter Schwartz, chairman and CEO, Descartes Systems, Waterloo, Ontario, Canada; and H. James Harrington, chief executive officer, Systemcorp, Quebec, Canada, and former consulting principal for quality at Ernst & Young.

25 David Washburn, principal consultant at Amherst Information Architects, Amherst, MA.

Part III

Training to Meet Tomorrow's Technology Challenges

8 Human Skills to Increase Technology Benefits in a Networked, B2B World

We've talked about networks and servers, browsers and RAM, ERP and the Internet, but what about all that data and information tech trenders are generating and storing in such vast quantities? Downloading information into databases is a fairly worthless task if you don't have the resources to analyze information and utilize it for strategic purposes – what's called practicing knowledge management. Technology provides the tools to sort and disseminate information, and some software programs can even prod the thinking process. But in the end it's the human brain that is the tool you need to hone for maximum utilization of data, information and even knowledge.

Being able to manage vast amounts of data and information accurately, let alone relay that information throughout a global supply network or post it on a B2B site, requires an entirely different set of skills than implementing a software solution. Establishing a Web site and then maintaining it on an ongoing basis is an editorial job, not something one practices in computer engineering. Making sure that the information you transmit to trading partners, or what you promote in your e-catalog is accurate, is an editing task that has nothing to do with comprehending the technology that underlies the electronic aspect of this process.

Yet, many companies and institutions will put IT managers in charge of developing Web sites without the slightest recognition that operating technology has nothing to do with managing information. They ask their employees to create "knowledge" products from the information they gather without assessing whether their staff can read for comprehension, let alone be able to practice the advanced analysis that sort of job requires.

To best manage a supply network, set up a B2B operation, begin to practice knowledge management, or simply get the greatest bang from your technology investments, tech-trending organizations must set up information/communication chains to match workflow. That means knowing how information truly runs through an organization – from department to department, company to supplier, to trading partners and customers and back again – rather than following preconceived notions based on a corporate chart.

Employees need to be able to gather, sort, store, analyze and disseminate data and information. That may mean something as seemingly simple as gathering data for a shipping notice, sorting out which elements go where, and ensuring that the notices are sent at the proper juncture. When these data elements are collected *en masse* they become information to process. The end result – a report on shipping trends culled from this information – could result in what's called a knowledge product.

Smart tech trenders are realizing that they must treat information as a commodity – a must-have item. They're realizing that missing data elements on a freight bill or EDI transmission, or inaccurate information on an e-catalog listing, means lost revenue. Having the right information, or being able to mine it for strategic advantage, is the pathway to a profitable networked, B2B existence.

And really innovative tech trenders recognize that technology isn't always fun for managers and employees, alike. Rather than ignore problems like computer phobia or the IT Knowledge Gap, they are providing behavior modification and training programs to address these issues (see Chapter 9).

Information is changing the way we work

Standardization	=>	Customization
Centralization	=>	Decentralization
Transportation	=>	Communication
Dependence	=>	Self-help
Autocracy	=>	Participation
Hierarchy	=>	Network
Information scarcity	=>	Information overload

This chart represents the mega trends the business world is experiencing. The left column represents Old Economy practices. The right column represents what technology is allowing the business and non-profit world to do.

PLATFORMS

Skills you need to get the greatest bang from technology investments

To get the greatest bang from your technology investments, you need to be able to:

- gather, sort, store, cull and disseminate data, information and knowledge;
- analyze and break out information into useful units to be applied strategically; and
- set up information/communication chains to match workflow, whether regional or global.

Analyzing means knowing how to ask the right questions. Breaking out information means knowing how to organize information and knowledge. Setting up information chains means knowing something about operating human communication systems.

The good news is that the skills that will help you succeed in the networked, B2B are practiced every day in the media and in the publishing industry. They are taught in journalism and broadcasting schools and are easily transferable to any setting. Some related skills are starting to be taught in relationship to writing, designing and maintaining Web sites. The bad news is that the media can be a closed place that throws a veil of mystery around its practices and is not always accessible to those outside the profession.

The aim isn't to turn you into media experts, but to offer you some tricks of trade that will help you get the maximum benefit from your technology dollars. By focusing a little energy on grappling with computer phobia, mapping information flow, and offering some basic training in reading, writing and analysis skills, you may find that all the hype around this being a knowledge world isn't hype at all. That the information that lies within those databases may actually be spun into the knowledge you can access for competitive success. To gain that sort of success companies and institutions must:

- understand the impact that technology makes in their corporate culture and in workflow;
- create an information/workflow system based on human style that acts as a support or infrastructure to technology;
- train employees in the writing-based and analytical skills they need to maximize technology use; and
- remember that it's humans, not technology, that drive an organization and that speedy, accurate information flow is crucial to success in the networked, B2B world. Issues like computer phobia are real and need to be addressed in a productive fashion.

This chapter will address, first, the issue of the human/technology disconnect, or the distaste and distrust that many people have for technology that is underlying their inability to adopt technology tools, or even handle simple office functions. Subsequent sections provide many tips and thoughts for improving the human skills that will positively affect information flow and allow your organizations to move into a networked, B2B world, and even into the knowledge age.

APPLICATIONS

ERP implants reveal management and human skills issues

Besides the obvious technology issues that implanting an enterprise resource planning (ERP) system can create, there are also human problems that evolve when moving ERP functions into a supply chain or supply network. Some technology consultants argue that most of the problems are human, not technological. They suggest the most common human problems that arise with ERP implementation surround the company's organization, workflow and corporate mentality and question whether they're suited to a specific ERP system.

If the organization isn't running well, and there can be tremendous performance variances, then ERP surfaces problems rather than solving them. This is especially true in a decentralized environment, as many ERP systems are built on a centralized model. Introducing ERP solutions will also highlight problems with human reading and analytical skills and make data and content accuracy tantamount. Too often those implementing the ERP solution are focusing on task achievement and technology issues, and not analyzing a company's skill level in handling data and content that the ERP solution will not only store, but help disseminate at high speeds.

> "If you make a mistake anywhere [along an ERP system] it will cause problems downstream. The challenge is around processing knowledge, or inadequately processing knowledge. This means understanding the upstream/ downstream effect of actions. For example, if customer service is entering a sales order and gets the delivery address wrong then that error will go through the sourcing process, will get shipped to the wrong address and cause supply chain errors."[1]

The human/technology disconnect

A major document-related corporation finds younger employees to be technology whizzes. But ask these same employees to describe the content they're manipulating electronically and they can't answer.

CEOs are expected to guide their corporations down profitable growth paths, but many of the older generation – say those in theirs 50s and beyond – don't even use computers. Yet they are being asked to sign off on millions in technology expenditures.

Managers are drowning in e-mail and some organizations are experiencing e-mail gridlock. In too many cases senior management lacks the editing skills that would help impose some information management rules within the organization and ease the e-mail flow.

These are just a few examples of the human/technology disconnect, or the inability of humans to deal with technology, and the lack of the human skills required to manage information within organizations. The human/technology disconnect is one of the most serious issues you as tech trenders face as you prepare your organizations for a networked, B2B world. All that effort, all those expenditures will go to naught and your technology tools will fail if you don't address human concerns. These range from computer phobia involving top managers, on down to the lack of reading, writing, editing and analytical skills required to manage the information your technology allows you to generate, store and disseminate.

Amazingly, the networked/B2B revolution, which is so dependent on the manipulation of data and information, is emerging at a time when many Americans have all but stopped reading, let alone writing. Managers of Fortune 500 companies concede that some members of their work force are technically illiterate, and yet are being asked to run advanced equipment that is data- and information-based.

PLATFORMS

CIOs raise concerns about misused or ignored data

Many managers forget the back end of their operation, but that's where most of the money – and the data – is flowing. For example, being able to mine invoices for information on marketing trends would give many organizations a leg up, but too often technology is tossed together with no thought for data use. Data is retrieved from "all over the place" and mapped into something undefined with no thought behind the action.

Tech-trending CIOs recognize that data is a must-have commodity and treat it with respect. During the system design phase they explore what data they will want to retrieve, what purposes it will serve and how quickly they will need to access it. They decide how up-to-date they want their data and information to be, and what to do about security.[2]

Problems don't stop with the blue-collar end of the work force. Managers may not be much more skilled in communicating – let alone in writing – than their employees, and yet more and more of their communication is via e-mail, which is strictly written-based. Older employees – meaning over the age of 30 – are often computer phobic. In one prime example each order taker and planner at a major trucking concern was provided with their own computer terminal. But on any given day, less than half of these employees used the equipment. Many still relied on an earlier technology – the ballpoint pen.

Then there's the issue of accuracy. The Internet, for example, speeds transmission of information but it doesn't guarantee that the information being transmitted is accurate. If organizations aren't careful, they will be transmitting inaccurate information more quickly than ever before, and causing problems throughout their supply network and trading community.

Promoting a human/technology partnership

What lies at the heart of the human/technology disconnect is a very basic human ambivalence, and even distrust, of technology. For all the opportunities it creates, technology also creates losses – loss of human contact, loss of identity, potential loss of jobs and even the fear that work will be lost to computer crashes. Moreover, much of today's technology is incomprehensible to the bulk of the population. We're still far from a plug 'n' play world where operating business functions is as simple as plugging in a phone and fax. Being able to really succeed in a high-tech world requires learning that is either beyond the ability of even some tech trenders, or simply may not be among your range of interests (see Chapter 9).

Tech-trending organizations want to address the human/technology disconnect by promoting a human/technology partnership where all sorts of human concerns, as well as skills, are addressed in conjunction with developing technology solutions. But that means accepting that humans are central to technology success. There are management gurus, sociologists and others who are questioning whether technology is already playing too great a role in organizations to the detriment of both humans, and the success of company and institutional goals. The whole premise behind the B2B world, for example, is to promote computers talking to computers. And there is a widespread, popular notion that technology will spare people from

UNPLUGGING TECHNOSTESS

Technology frustrations threaten to swamp the World Wide Web

Let's face it: life can be pretty crappy out there in the land of computer users. It's tiring to choose equipment that all looks alike and feels alike. It's annoying to install programs that are supposed to be simple, but really require degrees in advanced Rubrics Cube programming. It's frustrating to face equipment failures that take time away from more fruitful pursuits, like sending e-mail jokes to colleagues or delivering 100 virtual pizzas to your old high-school principal. And speaking of e-mail, the Internet – for all its wonder – provides yet another set of technology issues for us to master.

We live in a high-tech environment that is still evolving. It's like living inside a Nova episode where you're a cute antelope baby nibbling grass on the savannah, blissfully unaware that the lion is licking his chops thinking of you. Anyone who works on a computer knows that we are far from existing in a "plug 'n' play" and "user friendly" world, as great as those terms sound in advertisements. In fact, we might say this is more of a plug 'n' pray world. (That is, if you can find the right place to implant the plug. That's a compatibility issue, but we'll get into that later. The praying part is easy.)

To the average computer user, aka technozombies, this world can be overwhelming and exhausting. You want your equipment to work – like any appliance, your refrigerator, your iron, your vibrator – so you can get the job done. You want to be able to select your equipment by look, feel and drive – the way you would a car – and not be bothered by having to actually learn how the product functions. What's worse is that these complications are to be expected.

Statements like, "they're beta testing it," or "you shouldn't expect it to work" make us realize what a topsy-turvy world this is – the computer world of the absurd. There used to be a time when manufacturers took pride in releasing quality products – or at least hid built-in obsolescence. But the high-tech world has turned their malfunctions into advertisements. It's like, "Hey people, we're so cool. Our equipment, software, whatever ... won't work in six months." Anyone who can't cope with that really should hang it up and raise sheep in Iceland, or check out the cool site www.irefusetogetsweptalonginthistechnologyhysteria.com.

And they've accomplished this through some pretty tricky mind games that make all of us technozombies feel incompetent; like anyone over 30 is too stupid to get it. They're saying to us, "Better ask the eight-year-old down the street who really knows this stuff." That keeps us in the over-30s crowd from questioning the "powers to be" of the computer world about why their products are so grossly incompatible and "buggy." It's a sad day on the evolutionary calendar when children know more about the way the world works than adults do. Darwin has been reversed ...

And while we're bitching about the computer world of the absurd, let's not forget about system crashes and/or modem failures that keep all of us technozombies from life on the Web as we know it. When your modems don't function you can't access your cyberscopes, set up kayaking lessons in Mozambique, or pick up those double-fudge brownie recipes from Australia. Computer crashes keep you from printing out that Christmas list in July or printing out your kid's report on, of all things, computers. You can't log onto Priceline.com, which is really disastrous. Not to mention missing the porno sites ... (The most fun about easy access to porno is trying to find someone you know in a picture. Sure the odds are long, but the thrill you get when you find that person is indescribable, or so we've been told.)

Tally up the extent that computers crash mid-project, modems don't connect and software proves incompatible. Multiply these issues by millions, even billions of computer users worldwide, and it's obvious that a mountain of frustration is building that could swamp the World Wide Web. If computers came equipped with stress dots for every glitch, bug and irksome crash, there wouldn't be room on the monitor screen for content.[3]

doing redundant, tiresome tasks that technology can handle, and that you will funnel your employees into more fulfilling work – what the *cognoscenti* call knowledge work.

A major problem with this vision is that it presupposes your employees have the desire to work with technology, or the skills to handle knowledge-based work. Moreover, this vision also assumes that technology can handle redundant tasks better than humans, or worse that humans aren't really needed to staff companies and institutions. Already, some organizations are suffering from over-automation. Take the example of eliminating secretaries and receptionists. Managers of all sorts are now swamped with voicemails and e-mails, which slow down their work days and subvert valuable time into answering sometimes worthless communications.

Other organizations, as noted in earlier chapters, try to conduct all business in cyberspace. But as managers at Nortel Networks have learned from unhappy experience, humans require face-to-face contact. "A pivotal error for organizations is substituting technological contact for face-to-face dialog. Although IT is a wonderful facilitator of data and information transmission and distribution, it can never substitute for the rich interactivity, communication and learning that is inherent in dialog."[4]

Tech trenders must address human issues

Addressing human issues such as computer phobia, promoting improved human communication throughout your organization, supply network and trading groups, and improving human/technology interaction are enormously important to the success of tech-trending organizations. Believe it or not, computer phobia – or human aversion to working with technology – is very real and quite rampant. Some innovative companies are dealing with computer phobia head on through a combination of behavior modification and training programs.

Just as there are tech-trending companies working to help employees with computer phobia, so there are organizations studying how to improve the human interface with technology.

The aerospace and automotive industries, which are promoting more and more advanced technologies in planes and cars, are both conducting advanced research in how humans interact – interface in computer lingo – with technology. They recognize that as long as we don't want Andrew the Android flying our planes or driving our cars we have to address how to help humans interact safely with technology, particularly under the potentially dangerous circumstances of being in the air or on a highway.

APPLICATIONS

Aerospace vendors work to improve the human/technology interface

The aerospace and automotive industries are good places to look for research in the human/technology interface. In both cases, particularly with airplanes, humans have to interact with complicated technological equipment. For example, a flight management computer in an aircraft relies heavily on pilot input. The issue for those developing software for these functions is to find ways of presenting information electronically, determine what information to present and learn how individuals will interpret the information on their screen while performing complicated, and sometimes dangerous, functions.

Because these industries have had to contend with the human/technology interface for many years, they have developed good prototyping and test facilities and work on making their technology designs people oriented, rather than function oriented. That makes these industries, particularly aerospace, prime models for the software industry, now looking at developing navigation equipment and Internet access for automobiles.

And with the increased introduction of electronic components in household appliances, vendors agree that addressing the human/technology interface is inevitable. "We're looking at how safely these interfaces are being developed. We don't want anything to detract from safety issues, and it's the same thing in the workplace. Workers are now multitasking, controlling several things at the same time from window to window, which means that information has to be presented in the most usable way possible."[5]

Other tech-trending organizations are recognizing that human communication is crucial to success in our hyper-paced world where so much business is transacted on the run or fly, via e-mail or even through Web sites. Corporate mergers and downsizings also highlight the need for improved communication. For example, when Lockheed Martin, based in Fort Worth, Texas, restructured several years ago, managers there realized that many of their technology experts had been moved, placed on other teams or were no longer working for the company. All of this change resulted in massive human communication problems that directly affected technology use.

To address lagging communication issues, the company organized a team of about 55 people headed by a vice president to evaluate needs and fix problems arising from the reorganization. Included in this team were 30 people identified as opinion leaders in the company plus 25 executives whose focus was on delineating the lines of communication and creating a support structure for supervision. The intervention team conducted face-to-face interviews with 500 randomly selected employees. Interviews lasted approximately an hour and a half and were designed to address open communication, sense of urgency, and personal commitment and engagement. Employees were asked: "Why these things happened and why they didn't? Why things get done and why they don't."[6]

PLATFORMS

The Lockheed Martin company-wide communication survey

Promoting communication is a prime concern at Lockheed Martin's Fort Worth headquarters. In recent years, Lockheed managers have conducted a written company-wide communication survey on a quarterly basis that involves a third of its employees each go around. The survey is done on the company intranet, or with some in-person response. There's a 60 percent participation rate. These are the sorts of questions employees are asked:

- How do we open communication?
- What are behaviors that define communication?
- To what extent do workers get something from the organization?
- To what extent are workers allowed give something to the organization?
- Whose opinion do you respect?[7]

Connecting the human information pathway to your electronic information trail

In the rush to hook up your computers so they can start concocting all sorts of B2B deals, don't forget that humans are part of this scenario. Unless you want Hal the computer running your company or institution, there will always be some human interface with technology. Employees must input information into a system, keep track of its flow throughout a network or trading collaborative, and analyze data and information to assess its worth. Managers must process information for strategic ends.

Humans also cause errors, which is one of the prime motives for automating business or institutional functions. Automate all you want, but you can't entirely remove humans from information flow. On the other hand, with the tips offered in the rest of this chapter you will be to attain a high level of accuracy by working with the people in your operations and training them to more effectively interact with technology (see Chapter 9). This may mean reorganizing your company or institution's information flow between departments, suppliers, trading partners or customers. It certainly means setting up procedures humans can follow – sometimes with technology support – to ensure that the data and information traveling throughout your supply network, or between trading partners, is right on target.

Tech trenders must always keep in mind that human information flow equals the underpinnings of your operation. Remember that those electronic networks you are creating have a human as well as technological pathway. In fact, the human pathway should be the basis for the technology you implant unless you develop a technology solution to improve old practices. Even so, don't consider implanting any new technology that will alter human work habits without studying their interface. As documentation for management system standards like ISO 9000 has indicated in thousands of case studies, work rarely takes place the way senior management envisions it. Company after company have discovered huge discrepancies between how individuals carry out what are supposed to be identical procedures, let alone how these procedures are handled between various shifts, departments and plants.

APPLICATIONS

Exercises for charting information flow and technology use

A tech trending organization wants to learn how information is flowing in its organization and set up some guidelines for who will be on the receiving end of various types of information. It also wants to determine who in the organization gets what technology.

Using a facilitator, gather a wide sample of your organization's management to participate in a day-long session. The facilitator devises a matrix that all participants will fill in. On one side of the matrix are the types of positions represented at the session. On the other side are the categories of information your organization generates. The idea is to then determine, based on this chart, who will get what sort of information. Information management rules emerge from this exercise.

The second exercise will help you determine how to allocate technology and is very similar in nature. Once again, a matrix is key. On one side of the matrix list the sort of job functions represented by individuals in the room. Maybe there's finance, legal, IT, manufacturing, etc. On the other side of the matrix list all the technologies at use in your organization. Focus on one type of technology at a time – say, communication technologies. The outcome will give you a clear picture of who needs to be using e-mail, cell phones, Web-enabled phones, etc.[8]

And that brings us back to the media model because news organizations cannot survive without timely, accurate information flow. In the media, information is a must-have asset that leads directly to producing products on a daily, and even hourly, basis. Humans are integral to the news world, they are trained to operate as teams, and are organized to work with precision. Once again, taking a tour of a local newspaper or TV station will provide you with a very clear example of how information flows throughout a news organization and how it is used.

Many organizations are utilizing news-world methodologies unwittingly. When companies or institutions create teams to gather information, when they develop common languages to promote information flow and train their employees in the skills required to manage data and information, they are borrowing from the communications world model. Some companies are doing this consciously, others not, but the results are the same – improved communication, improved information management and improved bottomline results.

As noted in Chapter 5, organizations like the Associated Press (AP) have outlined a human system for gathering, sorting, culling and disseminating information in an accurate and timely fashion. The AP and its hundreds of affiliate newspapers has been able to automate many practices without missing a deadline because the humans in their operations are organized in such a way as to promote accurate and timely information flow. News employees are also trained in writing and editing skills, are alert to information priorities, and speak in a common lexicon for easier, quicker comprehension.

Not only does the AP offer a model for information management on the micro level, but its global system provides a model for companies attempting to link offices, suppliers or customers electronically on a worldwide basis. For example, on a global basis the AP photo department handles between 8000 and 9000 pictures a week. All photographs have to be processed –

electronically nowadays – and provided with extensive 32-field codes for transmission and archival purposes.

Employee flexibility is key. Those who work with the AP system learn to "roll with it," as they meet the ever-changing demands of covering ongoing events on a daily and even hourly basis. But over the years, a common system of procedures also has evolved for gathering more static information such as stock indexes and other statistics. And the AP maintains a highly evolved archival system that allows editors and writers to access archival stock – both print and photographs – quickly and efficiently.

SOUND BYTES

Ford creates a corporate newsroom

More and more the news-world habits and operations are invading corporations. Some companies are even touting corporate "newsrooms." Ford Motor Co., for example, claims to have the world's largest intranet with 170,000 staff worldwide linked online. The company uses this tool to alert management and employees about company direction. A newsroom has been established to update pertinent information several times a day, and is available to Ford employees worldwide.[9]

SOLUTIONS

What tech trenders and can learn from media model

The methodology and skills required to operate in this information/knowledge age exist in the news media where vast amounts of data and information are processed and packaged each day at high speeds and with relative accuracy. Here are seven ways (tricks of the trade) that companies might consider for getting better use of their advanced technologies:

- News operations are organized around a feeder or flow model for the speedy relay of knowledge and information to those responsible for creating the final document or publication.
- Employees are trained in writing, editing and formatting skills.
- All writing takes place in a prescribed style for easy comprehension and quick editing.
- A common lexicon speeds oral communication and creates a team atmosphere.
- Accuracy checks are built into the workflow.
- Archival data, information and knowledge are stored for easy access.
- Rules are established that prioritize what information matters today, what matters tomorrow and what should be tossed out.

Here are two examples of common issues many companies and institutions face as they implant advanced technologies, and ways that media world "tricks of the trade" can help:

- *Relaying of accurate data.* Someone in the shipping or traffic department of a company must gather information on a shipment, produce documentation and ensure that the shipment goes out on time. This information may be culled electronically or manually. The concern is accuracy and timeliness. To gain accuracy and timeliness the humans involved in this process need to be trained in the basics of gathering information accurately. Someone has to design an information flow system that ensures that accuracy checks are implanted. And someone has to set up a deadline system to ensure timeliness.
- *Addressing e-mail overload.* Managers are always complaining about e-mail overload. This does not have to be a problem if top management practices information control, meaning they set rules for what information in a company should be released via e-mail and what should not. Tying the gathering, sorting and storing of information into business or institutional goals will quickly offer tech trenders a means of setting up information rules based on company or institutional priorities.[10]

Skills tech trenders need to thrive in a networked, B2B, knowledge world

You've heard a lot about creating a human/technology partnership to promote information flow. This section looks at the reading, writing, interviewing (information gathering) and analytical skills your staff need to perform in a networked, B2B world. Included in these seven skill sets are some examples from tech-trending organizations about how they address human skills:

1 *Interviewing or information gathering.* ISO 9000, the international quality management standard, is a documentation-based approach that offers an interesting tool for improving information management and interviewing skills (see Chapter 5). A former quality manager at LMI, a manufacturer of industrial pumps based in Acton, MA, saw a way of promoting company-wide communication and interviewing skills through the ISO 9000 process.

Rather than ask the prescribed questions that ISO 9000 requires for earning registration and passing auditing requirements, he decided to beef up the interviewing process and ask managers and employees additional questions about the company's operation. Through his surveying throughout the operation, he was able to garner useful information about how the company was handling its quality efforts, and came up with recommendations to improve communication and information flow. Plus he learned a lot about how to ask the right questions to elicit the information he needed.[11]

SOLUTIONS

How to: gather data

Companies and institutions don't need to be news organizations to benefit from some of the skills that news world promotes. For example, a major transport company implants computer terminals in its war room for all planners and order-takers. With some training in data gathering, planners and order-takers could gather market/sales information during the order-taking process.

How to gather data is a bit of a mystery for many organizations. Experts who specialize in writing for technology or writing in corporate settings, suggest that one way to hone interviewing and data-gathering skills is to move from "open" to "closed" questioning. Imagine the following steps as a funnel, channeling the flow of your research:

- Ask open-ended questions. Lots of them. Open-ended questions do not imply or prompt their answers. For instance, "How do you feel about the new satellite system?" is open-ended. A closed question asks, "Don't you agree that the new satellite system has been a success?" Naturally, you'll take notes of your interviewee's replies. Forget about grammar, spelling or other details at this point. (Not later, of course. See the section on accuracy checks below.)

- Closed questions are good in the right place – after the open-ended questions are done. Here the funnel narrows, as you begin to zero in on what your interviewee actually feels. "In what ways has the new satellite system worked for you? Can you give some examples?"
- Listening check. When the open/closed session is complete, and you think you've understood your interviewee, provide a series of compact summaries of what he or she has said, and ask if you've got it right. Make any necessary corrections. Repeat until both you and your interviewee are satisfied.[12]

2 *The importance of analysis.* Managers at Coopers & Lybrand's knowledge strategy centers in New York City believe that managing information and knowledge "is about teaching people to zero in on critical insights and how to leverage and apply those insights. There seems to be a belief among information technology (IT) professionals that if they can just get a better search engine ... then those systems will be able to do what a great analyst can do, but what separates great analysts from OK analysts is that great ones have the ability to see what others don't. There's an ability to see patterns and to see what lies outside the patterns."[13]

At Sears Roebuck & Co. – the giant retailer based in Hoffman Estates, IL – top managers are recognizing that retailers need training in information management, including basic analysis. They are finding their business becoming more fact-based and very sophisticated in terms of analytical tools available to merchants and managers. Many employees haven't been trained to do information-based work. For example, they may have just the basic training that's required for understanding statistical methods, and a lot of catch-up is required for them to work in a networked, B2B system.[14]

3 *Oral and written communication tools.* Several years ago, electronics manufacturer Texas Instruments recognized that to

improve cycle time in its silicon wafer production it needed to work on oral and written communication skills. In a special pilot program, employees worldwide were trained for eight weeks in the vocabulary, techniques and tools required for cycle-time reduction in the wafer area.

As a result of this intense communication effort, a best practices manager at TI says this select group of employees "are sent out with a common goal, mission and vocabulary, as well as e-mail addresses. Then they're brought together regularly to share techniques ... In terms of communication, our vision is to raise everyone in our company up to the highest level of performance."

The TI Office of Best Practices promotes this type of sharing across Texas Instruments through a quality program called T-I Best, which is based on generally accepted criteria used in national quality awards, such as the US Malcolm Baldrige Award. Once again, the emphasis is on communication. As one key manager explains, T-I Best "provides vocabulary. We're constantly bringing together our facilitator network to help them do their job better. We work on helping them interview the source."[15]

APPLICATIONS

Bell Helicopter Textron works on reading, writing, listening and communication

Bell Helicopter Textron of Fort Worth, Texas is working on defining the company's informal human communication network to better capture information flow as it really takes place. Managers there recognize that technology functions more effectively when it reflects a human communication system. Effective use of information flow coupled with technology translates into a smooth-running supply chain and bottomline results. As part of these efforts, managers are recognizing the need to train employees and managers, alike, in the writing-based skills technology requires. They offer remedial reading and writing courses all the time, as well as courses in listening and communication.[16]

4 *Accuracy and data quality.* As the intersection between the business and IT side of companies and institutions, CIOs are constantly being confronted with issues of accuracy and data quality. They see myriads of examples where inaccurate information infused into a supply network threatens to swamp organizations. Consider a retailer who put out wrong pricing information. Not too long ago that error might affect a few hundred customers before being rectified. But if the same error was made on the Web, the retailer would be reaching potentially millions of customers and face a massive crisis in its order department.

In another realm, producers of shipping and logistics-related software find that customers most commonly fail to send out complete information. For example, they may only cover 80 percent of the shipment. Only 80–90 percent of the time will they report when a shipment has left port. Or they won't be timely. Maybe a shipment has departed for port, but it isn't reported for 20 hours. They recommend users need to form some sort of editing or accuracy check process that traces back to the source of data collection, or the beginning of the information collection and processing cycle.

At Motorola headquarters in Schaumburg, IL, there's a long-term recognition that quality equals information accuracy, and information accuracy equals bottomline results. To promote this approach, Motorola has created the Six Sigma program, which preaches and teaches accuracy as an "attitude." This is, for example, an attitude about making virtually defect-free products regardless of what you're doing, whether you're making a phone, semiconductor, an invoice for an engineering design or drawing, or a purchase order to a supplier.

To promote Six Sigma throughout Motorola, employees take what amounts to "Six Sigma 101." This is a general course that outlines the communication process underlying Six Sigma, and helps people learn to promote an accurate, defect-free manufacturing process. Employees also take courses in specialist fields such as statistics and design, as appropriate.[17]

SOLUTIONS

How to: create accuracy checks

A US producer of electronic copying equipment networks its global suppliers for electronic processing and tracking of shipment data. Many inaccuracies arise, some based on timeliness issues, some on incorrect inputs and others on missing information or shipping elements. Training to communicate for accuracy – and the actual creation of a system of accuracy checks – is plainly required.

Accuracy checks are crucial and, until the necessary software is developed, will remain a basically mechanical process. It may be necessary to train people in the system to heighten their accuracy awareness. According to experts in writing for technology use, it's crucial that whoever is inputting data, or even scanning it, be aware of the following factors:

- *The content.* Companies will have to devise checks-and-balances systems to ensure accuracy. Possibilities include working with a checklist, appointing an "editor" to proofread, or even commissioning a computerized check with a more advanced system.
- *Timeliness.* Companies need to develop deadline schedules, and adhere to them to ensure that information is filed on time. Checks should be instituted both in-house and at the receiving end.
- *Significant variation.* Expect the unexpected. Sometimes the best ideas come from the unanticipated connection of disparate ideas or information. Here again, appropriate training is vital.

And the following are some tips devised to provide more accurate electronic data interchange (EDI) transmissions, which is a tool for transmitting vast amounts of data between trading partners and is a major factor for many companies moving into a B2B environment:

- Ensure accuracy through extensive editing of both outbound and inbound data sets;

- Enhance control through acknowledgment processes and audit trails;
- Offer timeliness through electronic data communications;
- Provide efficiency through the:
  - compressed nature of EDI formats;
  - conveyance of implied meaning by associating EDI formats with a published public standard; and
  - elimination of the requirement for explicitly transmitting headings and field names to indicate meaning.[18]

5 *Creating common lexicons.* Companies as diverse as the Big Three Automakers and Sears are devising their own lexicons to speed information flow and promote accuracy. As part of its Manufacturers Assembly Pilot (MAP) program to improve communication between major manufacturers and suppliers, promoters developed what they called an "integrated definition language" to speed information flow. This was a modeling language developed by the US Airforce, which has proved effective in many other companies.[19]

Sears has also found that a common vocabulary promotes common work procedures. This is especially crucial to the open, information-sharing environment Sears is trying to promote among its 300,000 employees (whom they call associates). Management policy is that information is shared on a broad-based level rather than being locked up. Sears wants everyone in the company to know what their customers are saying about our service and what their associates are saying about our workplace. Even financial information is shared.[20]

6 *Learning archiving procedures.* Besides learning what information is useful and what is not, young journalists are also trained in procedures for gathering and processing statistical information. It's these sorts of archiving procedures, coupled with technology, that allow communications companies like AP to store and access enormous amounts of information.

Nowadays, archives at news organizations are entirely automated. But that means that human skills, especially the analysis that goes into making an educated guess to conduct an electronic search, are more important than ever.

PLATFORMS

Information judgment skills as a basis for analysis

There are many tricks for breaking out information that will become the basis of statistics or of general analysis. The basis for analysis is categorization. When management sets rules for what information is most important to circulate throughout an organization, what is not relevant at all and what might be stored for future use, they are helping employees categorize. Here's how this process can lead to some basic trend analysis:

- Management sets in place rules for what information is crucial to meet corporate goals and what information is not.
- Employees should then be taught how to categorize information so they can quickly access what they need to get a job accomplished. This can be done in a variety of a ways:
  - by timeliness (useful now, save for the next quarter, store for future use); and
  - by topic.
- The process of categorizing information helps employees focus on what information is useful at what time and in what place.
- Trends often emerge in the process of categorizing. When employees start questioning the trends and larger pictures that emerge from categorizing, they are practicing basic trend analysis.

---

7 *Benchmarking.* In the massive effort to turn supply chains into collaborative supply networks, companies are utilizing a variety of performance-testing tools including benchmarking. Experts consider benchmarking one of the most potent tools in a company's arsenal because it provides the ability to offer specific, process-by-process comparisons and keep quality levels on track. Process benchmarking is a systematic approach or process to drive change in an organization.

Benchmarking experts say that the process arrives at change by doing process-to-process comparisons and developing data about performance output levels for process. In other words, it is the search for those practices that lead to superior performance. Benchmarking is effectively employed to compare specific company functions against the operations of another firm on a process-to-process basis. It can be used, for example, to compare suppliers' designs or to compare performance levels in purchasing.

Entering the knowledge world

When management at Pfizer Inc. talks about tracing patterns in shipment status records for information that can be applied to improving customer service, they are actually practicing rudimentary knowledge management.

When the staff at Johnson & Johnson fine-tune sales forecasts on a weekly basis because they have electronic access to retail inventory counts, they are practicing a form of knowledge management.

When teams at Phillips Lighting recognize that employees in shipping can gather information to be applied to marketing decisions, they are ready to practice knowledge management.

Knowledge management is a major industry buzzword that hit the business mags in the mid-1990s and hasn't entirely receded as a sought-after activity. As hokey as it may sound to talk about mining the corporate or institutional brain, it makes sense to make better use of the data and information that's flooding your organizations today. After all, most organizations practice at least a rudimentary form of knowledge management when they produce reports, white papers or other forms of analysis.

In a paper-based system, information is pooled through memos, meetings and ensuing projects. Information is shared via personal communication, phones and meetings. Knowledge assets, including know-how, are created through these processes. They are linked in the form of reports and memos. New knowledge assets and new know-how are created, and become part of the company's knowledge warehouse.

As more and more organizations are networked, there's the opportunity to link all of the technology and all of the functions into a collaborative knowledge warehouse that anyone can mine through strong search engines and knowledge management applications and solutions. On an individual company basis this process allows for the accessing of inventory records to create sales strategies. In the world of collaborative trading it could mean developing marketing trends for a whole industry based on mining collective data.

By networking your databases, tech-trending organizations can enjoy unparalleled sharing of data and information. New ideas, concepts and know-how can result from the process of sharing. The following list describes the corporate knowledge management process – also known as the knowledge flow – from data and information to the creation of knowledge and improvement of corporate intelligence:

- *share*: data, information, knowledge, wisdom;
- *create*: new intellectual assets;
- *improve*: corporate intellect and wisdom (wise decision-making); and
- *apply*: corporate wisdom for strategic business use.[21]

PLATFORMS

Setting up an international knowledge warehouse

A multinational manufacturer of telecommunications products is undergoing a phenomenal market switch. In the last five years 50 percent of its market has moved overseas with sales outlets in over 30 separate countries. Each country has different customs and shipping requirements.

Although shipments are being made regularly on an international basis, they are happening haphazardly with each department operating as it sees fit. No company-wide operating procedures exist for international shipments. And no company-wide procedures have been established or stored electronically so that new employees can carry on the complicated task of meeting foreign customs and manufacturing requirements. Revenue is being lost because noncompliance issues crop up with individual shipments, and because there is no software implanted in-house that will calculate foreign currencies and exchange rates. Payment, therefore, is being made in ways disadvantageous to the company at large.

The director of global logistics recognizes the need to input both human and electronic processes that will allow better control of the company's approach to international trade. He proposes writing up work procedures and policies and establishing an international database that can be accessed through the company's Web site. What he has done, in essence, is establish an international knowledge warehouse for his operation. He understands that once all company-wide data, information and knowledge are collected, sorted and linked under one system he and his staff will be empowered to make more intelligent and wiser business decisions. Moreover, he anticipates the creation of new knowledge assets through this process that will offer market direction and breed more profits.[22]

Besides having the requisite technology in place, practicing knowledge management requires finely honed analytical skills. Tech trenders have to be able to ask the right questions, categorize large amounts of information and discern trends. And they need to be at ease working with the computer programs that will aid them in this work. You can have a facility for analysis, but even the best analysts require training and practice. The following are six steps tech-trending organizations can follow to promote the practice of knowledge management:

1 Appoint a chief knowledge officer (CKO) to manage the process.
2 The CKO will train a management team to help him or her determine what knowledge assets are crucial to business success and help the business and IT team apply them strategically.
3 Part of this process involves charting what knowledge exists in the organization.

4 The CKO works with the IT team to ensure that the right IT solutions are in place to perform knowledge management.
5 The knowledge team designs, develops and implements a chart for sharing knowledge assets with the key players in the organization.
6 They conduct frequent surveys to assess how much knowledge is being shared and its impact on the organization.[23]

Human skills for the B2B world

All the skills required to promote the accurate flow of data and information within an organization or a supply chain, not to mention strategic use of that material, become that much more important when moving into a B2B world. As noted in Chapter 6, the sort of errors or inconsistencies of world usage that can fly in a print catalog will raise havoc in a B2B operation. Yes, spell-checkers can help. But computerized spellcheckers and grammar devices are no substitute for human editing and proofing. Here's a quick review of the six principles that will guide in development of an efficient supply network or B2B venture:

- conduct a communication flow study to determine how information is moving between operations *before* technology is implanted;
- create a custom communication/workflow system based on these findings;
- train employees in the written skills required to operate on an electronic basis;
- create a common lexicon among suppliers that builds team consciousness and improves communication flow;
- establish common operating procedures; and
- build in human and electronic accuracy checks.

Maintaining Web sites, B2B catalogs and other electronic formats

In many ways there's very little difference between developing products – or what's called content – for electronic publication or for print publication. The writing is basically the same, except for learning to work in 500–1000-word segments and break out material frequently, which is increasingly common in print, as well. No one wants to read pages and pages of information while sitting online.

What is different is the amount of coding that the Web requires, which has a major impact on design and ongoing maintenance of a Web site. For information to appear on the Web it must be coded in HTML. Anyone familiar with computerization in the news world of the late 1970s will be familiar with the extensive sort of coding that is required for words to appear in bold or italics on the Web, for colors to emerge, headings to be sized and just about any other element that appears under the name "style." Those maintaining Web sites need to know everything a graphics person knows about working in print style and layout, plus be able to work with extensive HTML coding.

APPLICATIONS

How nyt.com keeps that news current 7×24

No, tech trenders won't have to staff their Web sites with the vigilance of nytimes.com or any major dot.com news outlet. But it doesn't hurt to learn how the pros keep their sites updated in near real-time.

- *Staffing.* Employees are maintained around-the-clock (7×24 in high-tech parlance), which allows for continually updating breaking news.
- *Judgment.* The *New York Times* editorial judgment pervades its dot.com, that means that all and every employee has rules to follow about what is most important and on down.
- *Placement.* The most important stories go on the home page and links are established for sidebars or stories with less news import.

- *Do not make arbitrary changes.* Change isn't made for the sake of change. Upgrades only take place when something significant has happened and is worth reporting.
- *Don't forget analysis.* Being the provider of the news-behind-the-news – otherwise considered analysis – can make you a winner in terms of grabbing reader attention.
- *Kill dated material.* No one expects General Motors to be the *New York Times, Washington Post* or any one other major daily. But there's nothing worse on the Internet than dated material. Even if what you've posted is evergreen – meaning long-standing – make sure you spruce it up every few weeks so that it looks a bit more current.[24]

HTML coding will make it far more laborious to change content on the Web than it is in print. And this will be the same whether you're developing Web sites, e-catalogs or any other electronic format. The following are eight tips for coding your sites to make ongoing maintenance quicker and easier:

- *Select the right individuals.* Make sure you have both an IT person and someone trained in news writing and editing working together on your site. Always remember that Web sites are basically media efforts and require the sort of expertise practiced in the news world, including writing, editing and the ability to practice information or news judgment about what content matters on any given day. IT people are still required to help the editorial person work with Web languages and coding.
- *Centralize control of templates.* If you want the same look and feel to permeate your Web site then you need to develop reusable templates that will be applied to most pages – or centralized control of templates. Templates equal the stock material that you want to see on all pages, whether headers, footers, borders, content or art elements.
- *Try not to mix graphics and content.* Graphics and content interfere with each other when graphics are used to display content. If a Web designer decides that all her headlines must be exactly 48 points in Arial Narrow and that nothing else will do, then she is stuck making a little graphic

for every headline on her site. When headlines change she'll have to load her image program and make a new graphic.

- *Pick the right management platform.* You need to select a management platform that will separate out content from design. The best bet is to locate a platform that operates on XML rather than HTML because XML automatically separates out the way you store content from its display, which makes editing quick and simple.
- *Style sheets will vary.* You can work with style sheets, which are essentially standardized Web templates, beware that the content look will vary from browser to browser. That's because there is no one standard that governs style sheets and there are at least two browsers – Netscape and Internet Explorer – that are commonly used. So a box that fills up a page in Netscape may appear to fill half a page when viewed through a Internet Explorer browser. The content won't vary, but the look will. If you separate your replaceable content from your stock templates the variation won't be as troublesome.
- *HTML strong points.* HTML is very good for hierarchical content such as table of contents and outlines – anything that's stacked vertically on a page. Work with this strength rather than working against it.
- *Don't forget aesthetics.* There are rules of good taste and rules of bad taste. Just because the Web is a new medium doesn't mean you have to abandon the basic rules of graphic arts – whether that involves color choice, use of art, layout and amount of content piled on a page. The Web is awash with knockout sites and e-catalogs and equally awash in graphic monstrosities. Some of the major search engines are the worst offenders, with front pages that are so packed they're barely legible.
- *Off-the-shelf solutions.* The new dot.com content aggregators tout good content-management systems as means of helping fledgling webmasters keep things straight. There are some fairly sophisticated off-the-shelf solutions that let pros and amateurs alike do sophisticated Web sites and that go

a long way towards making site updates easy. Front Page is the prime example. Once you've made a selection, bring all aspects of your operation into the selection process to ensure that what comes out of the box fits the intent of your webzine or portal business.[25]

Notes

1 "Stretching ERP Beyond the Enterprise," Amy Zuckerman, chief logistics officer, March 2000. Information source is Neil McGee, Former Manager of ERP Support Services at RWD Technologies in Columbia, MD.

2 Krimo Salem, CEO of If & Then Inc., San Jose, CA; Jeanmarie Gelinas, Vice President and CIO of Rodale, Inc., Emmaus, PA; Eric Fliegel, CIO, eTour, Inc., Atlanta, GA; and Pam Kleier, CEO of constructionzone.com, Louisville, KY;

3 *When Bad Computer Things Happen to Good People*, a work in progress, Amy Zuckerman and Izzy Gesell.

4 Liam Fahey, a professor of management at Babson College and noted knowledge management expert.

5 Phil Cole, European Business Marketing Manager for Virtual Prototype Inc., Montreal, Quebec, Canada.

6 Karie Willyerd, Director of People and Organizational Development, Lockheed Martin, Fort Worth, TX.

7 Karie Willyerd, Director of People and Organizational Development, Lockheed Martin, Fort Worth, TX.

8 Alan Hurwitz of Alan Hurwitz Associates, Amherst, MA.

9 "Talking to Each Other," *The Economist* E-Management Survey, November 11, 2000, p. 15.

10 Lydia Long, Director of Operations for Verité, Amherst, MA, who provided research for this section; and Hal Buell, former manager of the Associated Press global photography department.

11 Jay Bigler, former LMI Quality Manager, Acton, MA.
12 Source is Michael Egan, a team-building expert and English professor at the University of Massachusetts, Amherst, MA.
13 Mik Chwalek, a former partner in Coopers & Lybrand's knowledge strategies group.
14 Joe Smialowski, CIO for Sears, Roebuck and Co.
15 *Global Tool Kit: Supply Chain,* Amy Zuckerman, A–Z International Associates, Amherst, MA, 1999.
16 Robert Lang, chief of Bell Helicopter's ISO 9000 effort.
17 George Koons, manager of quality systems at Motorola Lighting.
18 Michael Egan, a team-building expert and English professor at the University of Massachusetts, Amherst, MA; and *Global Tool Kit: Supply Chain,* Amy Zuckerman, A–Z International Associates, Amherst, MA, 1999.
19 Tom Hoy, former associate director of the Auto Industry Action Group (AIAG) in Southfield, MI.
20 Joe Smialowski, chief information officer for Sears.
21 Adapted from a white paper on Corporate Intellect Processing by Amy Zuckerman and Gary Dienes, President, Management Systems International (MIS), Inc., Stoneham, MA.
22 Adapted from a white paper on Corporate Intellect Processing by Amy Zuckerman and Gary Dienes, President, Management Systems International (MIS), Inc., Stoneham, MA.
23 Adapted from a white paper on Corporate Intellect Processing by Amy Zuckerman and Gary Dienes, President, Management Systems International (MIS), Inc., Stoneham, MA.
24 Bernie Gwertzman, editor, nyt.com
25 Seth Rothberg, principal, /home/industries, Amherst, MA; and Colin Mulcahy, Director of Technical Implementation,

Support and a founder of Screaming Media in New York City.

Additional credits for this chapter: this information is based on the author's original work. Some is adapted from the Human Skills section of *Global Tool Kit: Supply Chain,* Amy Zuckerman, A–Z International Associates, Amherst, MA, 1999. Other material is adapted from articles that have appeared since the mid-1990s in a wide variety of publications including *Fortune* magazine, *Quality Progress, Journal for Quality and Participation, Supply Chain Management Review,* and many others.

Sources include Lydia Long, operations director for Verité, Amherst, MA; Michael Egan, a team-building expert and English professor based at the University of Massachusetts, Amherst, MA; Hal Buell, former manager of the Associated Press global photography operation; the staff of Management Systems International (MSI), Inc., Stoneham, MA; Paul White, Vice President of Marketing at Strategic Technologies Inc., Iselin, NJ; Neil McGee, former manager of ERP Support Services at RWD Technologies in Columbia, MD.

9 Training to be a Tech Trender

An outpatient surgical center in urban New Haven, CT, needed to upgrade its management software. The office manager, who was a low-level computer user with almost no computer awareness, was put in charge of the job. This was a major IT project that required "surgically" removing an old system and implanting a new one. The individual involved didn't have a clue how to proceed.

Neither did anyone else in the surgical center. No one knew how the core system had been laid out and how users were trained to work on it. Purchases were made willy-nilly based on whatever previous consultants and vendors had recommended. The manager in charge of the project took the attitude of better-the-evil-we-know-than-the-evil-we-don't, which meant the long-standing vendor was in control of the situation, and other product offerings received only cursory evaluation.

The result of this lack of knowledge, skills and awareness was a much higher-cost product for the center and one that never really functioned well. A great deal of expensive customized work was required to integrate the new system into existing systems both at the center and the sponsoring hospital. Certain core architectural issues came to play after the new system was implemented that had a profound effect on performance, causing serious system issues for the user and the vendor.[1]

The president of an IT training center for high-level corporate clients complains that senior managers have no idea where things reside electronically throughout the enterprise. They don't know what a server is, or they'll tell you that you can get that information off the E drive, as if that's the universal resource shared by the world. They don't know where things reside within their system, how things are hosted, and whether they're onsite or offsite. True, you don't need to know how your CPU works to type a letter in Word, and you shouldn't have to understand the principles of telephony to make a phone call. But this training-center president argues that, in this less than ideal world where plug 'n' play is far from reality, some basic awareness of technology is a necessary management skill.[2]

> "Some managers don't understand the difference between an Internet and intranet. That may sound trivial, but it's serious when you talk about data security. We've actually encountered managers in the defense industry who don't understand the distinction," reports the European marketing manager for a software manufacturer.[3]

PLATFORMS

What managers of all types don't know about technology

The IT/knowledge gap is a very real threat to technology's future. Here are some real basics that managers of all types don't seem to know:

- *Computing essentials.* Many managers don't know or have a really good grasp of their computing essentials – what's hardware, what's software. A lot of people will say the hard drive or disk is making funny noises when they're really referring to the system box.
- *Computer speed.* Managers will ask IT trainers whether having a lot of programs loaded on their computer will slow it down. Computers aren't like trucks that slow down when filled with 2000 pounds of material. You have so much storage capacity – called memory – but that doesn't relate to speed. However,

having a number of programs open and running *will* affect the speed.

- *Windows versus applications.* Often managers don't know the difference between Windows and the applications such as word-processing programs. They'll say they're using Windows to write a letter. In reality, Windows is a PC operating system and they're writing a letter on a word-processing program like Word, WordPerfect, etc.[4]

Identifying the IT/knowledge gap

These are all examples of the IT/Knowledge Gap, or the lack of the most basic knowledge of technologies that are employed on a daily basis in the work world. Prevalent throughout the global business and institutional worlds, the IT/Knowledge Gap affects all levels of manager and strategic decision makers. As noted in the introduction, techno-illiteracy threatens to upturn technology's progress and even the huge spurt in global productivity that technology has spawned.

IT consultants, CIOs and analysts can offer case study after case study as evidence of the IT/Knowledge Gap. A consultant in New Haven, CT, finds that a lot of managers, a lot of supervisors and strategic decision-makers are essentially techno-illiterate, meaning they are ignorant of core IT concepts. Sadly, it's common to find people who lack tech awareness and tech savvy in charge of an IT project.[5]

Chief executives in the media, publishing and in universities often aren't much more capable of dealing with technology than their corporate or institutional peers. A New York City consultant who works with major media corporations and universities finds tremendous variability when dealing with senior managers. Many don't know enough about the technology they're signing for to determine whether it's a good investment or not. They put technology people in charge of the content side of Web sites without recognizing – even though content may be their own business – that IT individuals rarely make good content people. And, often, they're so insecure about their technology knowledge that they forget that technology is simply another facet of their business.

Moreover, these same senior managers are not familiar with technology terms, yet toss them around in major contracts without the slightest clue of what they signify. Whether they know it or not, they've left themselves tremendously vulnerable in a world where one entity may own the content and another entity may own the code and it's not always easy to determine which is which. If the contract language isn't correct, the contract won't stand for much.[6]

Many companies and institutions appear to be operating in some sort of technology quagmire, always putting out brush fires and never using technology strategically. As noted in a number of earlier chapters, managers don't relate work processes to technology. For example, they end up with a corporate initiative that says there are too many customer databases in the organization, but that initiative doesn't relate to how business is conducted with customers on a unit basis. It's the old game of technology looking for a problem to solve, rather than it being applied to corporate goals and processes.[7]

IT trainers see the IT/knowledge gap all the time and struggle to help people overcome it. They find some types of managers have more difficulty assimilating technology awareness than others. Here are the types of computer users who present the most demands on trainers:

- *Middle-aged-to-senior men.* Down the line, everyone interviewed for this book identified male managers over the age of 50 as the toughest to train. The older and more senior in an organization the more problems they pose, particularly as many still don't use computers.
- *Middle-aged-to-senior women.* Women in their 50s and older who haven't used computers can be tricky to teach. Many of them are scared of the equipment and equally scared to make mistakes. They were brought up to be good girls, not to make mistakes and leave mechanical items like cars and computers to men.

- *The slightly knowledgeable.* Those managers who come to training sessions with a little bit of knowledge can be difficult because they hold a small piece of the puzzle, but don't get the big picture. Many are smart people, successful in other aspects of their job, who don't expect to have to take time on technology training. There are others who address their managerial zeal to a computing task and get angry at the equipment when it doesn't respond.

  The older members of this set will latch onto a process that feels secure to them, but will not be willing to move into an easier operational mode. So, for example, the only way a lawyer was willing to save a document was by shutting down the machine, saving the program when prompted, and then canceling the shutdown. Hitting the save button would have been a lot easier and less damaging to the equipment.[8]

Age and attitude aren't altogether to blame for the IT/Knowledge Gap. Time constraints can be very real for many managers today who are forced into constant adherence to the bottom line, coping with a near constant influx and out-flux of employees in some sectors, and bombarded with new information. It's no wonder that many senior executives relegate technology knowledge to the IT department. They can barely keep above water.

There are experts who believe the IT industry is partially at fault for the IT/knowledge gap. In general, the IT industry presents their products and services in a problem-solving fashion that is incomprehensible to an estimated 90 percent of business or institutional managers. Their message doesn't emphasize enough what the technology in question can do for a business, but focuses more on technology properties like memory, drive, etc … And it can be quite difficult to get high-tech manufacturers to link their technology to business goals in any comprehensible way.

But complaining about the IT industry won't help tech trenders make a decision on purchasing that additional server or whether to buy and off-the-shelf software solution rather than developing something proprietary. It won't help you master the

UNPLUGGING TECHNOSTRESS

Identifying yourself on the computer user social spectrum (CUSS)

Hey, you can't conquer technostress and become an effective tech-trending decision maker without coming clean on what sort of computer user you are. Identifying yourself on the Computer User Social Spectrum (CUSS) chart will help you start sorting out your technology woes. Here's a sampling of computers users. See where you fit.

- *Luddite or ostrich.* At one end of the spectrum there's the computer Luddite, otherwise known as the "ostrich." This is the sort of person who's convinced technology will simply go away and the world will return to its normal focus on television and baseball.
- *Technozombie.* The technozombie suffers glaucoma of the mind when confronted with ads from computer magazines. They're not anti-technology, but they fuzz over at the thought of upgrades or when confronted with reading a computer manual. You are the sort of person who longs to see the rise of some benevolent computer software monopoly so you have one choice of Internet server.
- *Technocompetent.* Although a minor percentage of the population, there are actually computer users who are quite competent in their approach to equipment and software. They may not be computer geniuses or even entirely computer literate, but they do not fall apart at the sight of a terminal or suffer convulsions at the mention of the word browser. They approach computers as useful tools to apply in their work and handle the ups and downs of computer use with ease. *Tech Trending* should help you move into this category, at least with the help of good tech support.
- *Obsessive/compulsives.* Obsessive/compulsives can't stop memorizing the latest bytes and bites, and actually read computer manuals and computer magazines rather than strewing them on coffee tables to look impressive. This doesn't mean they understand what they're reading, but they actually find the topic of computer science interesting and even captivating. These are the sort of people who have to learn how a car runs before they can take driving lessons.
- *Technobatterers.* This is quite a wide-ranging group, in part because there are many as many disagreements in the literature about the connotation of the word batterer as there are arguments about the proper use of technology. Some sufferers are related to keyboard pounders, only in a more extreme form. There are others who literally punch or hammer their equipment until its smashed beyond recognition. Technobattering requires long-term techno-shrinking, or even medication.
- *Data retentives.* The data retentives are those who are concerned with the proper organization of data. These are the sorts of people who insist on coming into another user's office and rearranging their desktop icons, or setting up work files upon work files in a miasma of over-organizing spirit. If you are a data retentive – and most of you know who you are – you probably wear belts and suspenders, backup your zip and disk drives daily and save all old phone bills for 25 years.
- *Technohipsters.* The techno-hipsters are probably the most tiresome of breed of human computer users. These are the people – mostly guys – who fake the slightly nerdy, slightly hip appearance of Silicon Valley teenage billionaires. They always have the latest technology lingo down pat, and are always the first to insist on upgrading to the latest whatever … Underneath, though, they're not much different than the rest of us – utterly confused – right?
- *Technonerds.* You are the only people who really understand your equipment; who can really figure out Windows 98 and strip those glitches down the root (\) of your original DOS base. Although outwardly gentle in appearance, your deep grasp of technology, and the fact that you tend to live for technology, can be very frightening to Luddites and technozombies, who prefer the whole Technology World of the Absurd take a walk.[9]

basic concepts of networking, Gnutella or peer-to-peer. There's nothing wrong with acknowledging that the ever-changing technological world is frustrating, but if you want to be a tech-trending manager it's not OK to get stuck in a complaining mode.

So, once again, we come back full circle to the purpose of this book: to become a tech trender means accepting that technology is crucial to your organization's survival. It means adopting a positive mindset, accepting change, learning technology basics and keeping up with the trends. To become tech aware and tech savvy you're going to have to devote a good deal of your time to the learning process, and may have to alter your work habits to accommodate the need to continue technology learning. Once again, IT trainers suggest that technology learning be considered life-long learning. As they point out, the technology innovators and movers and shakers aren't going to sit on their hands and stop developing new technologies because Joe Tire Manufacturer has finally mastered networking basics.

Many companies and institutions would benefit from regular, ongoing in-house technology awareness and technology understanding programs. IT experts – trainers, consultants, analysts, CIOs and CTOs – encounter few organizations that provide this level of training on a routine basis. What they do find is that information on technology are gathered in an *ad hoc* fashion and distributed in a fragmented way. As a result, the IT department usually drives business goals based on what they believe them to be rather than based on concrete, affirmed knowledge. And there's often no one at the top, or in the middle, who's knowledgeable enough to stop them.

What tech trenders need to know to address the IT/Knowledge Gap

A number of consultants, trainers and tech-trending managers have been asked what they think managers at all levels need to know about technology, as well as the depth of knowledge that's appropriate for various management positions. They all agree that conquering the IT/Knowledge Gap isn't merely about knowing a server from a browser or an intranet from the Internet. Becoming a tech-trending manager usually requires an individual to alter work habits and bone up on the human skills outlined in Chapter 8. This section focuses mainly on what managers need to know about technology to become tech trenders. Subsequent sections will outline actual training approaches and tips for altering work styles and habits. The final section looks at ways tech trenders can train for the demands of the B2B world.

SOLUTIONS

How tech trenders can integrate IT and general business training

Tech trenders don't want to separate their IT training from general business concerns. Here's one trainer's recommendations for integrating the two:

- relate project management to technology issues in your company;
- work on team facilitation because so much IT work is now dependent on cross-functional teams;
- business process re-engineering is a lot of what you'll be doing when you implant technology. Review those skills in the context of an IT project; and
- change-management skills are crucial to all tech-trending managers. Tie them in with the technology change taking place in your organization.[10]

Before you take a tour of the technology already in place at your company or institution – a good beginning way to build tech awareness – tech trenders need to have a working knowledge of seven IT basics. These will give you a better grasp of the technology your organization uses every day:

- *Basic technology terms.* Ranging from the difference between hardware and software, to protocols, tech trenders need to be familiar with the lingo that the consultants and vendors are tossing around. It's not enough to know that some experts define protocol as the organization of bytes that make up network communications. Tech-trending managers need to be able to understand those terms in the context of their operation.

- *Elementary networking.* What is a server? What are operating systems? What do the basic network protocols mean? You need to be able to apply this information to your business or institution.
- *Windows, Word and Excel for dummies.* If you're using a PC, you should know the basics of Windows. Not only the click, drag and double-click, but the Windows directory structure. Some believe knowing the basics of Word, the most common word-processing program, is also necessary. And they think some Excel basics for spreadsheets are also something you should know about.

PLATFORMS

A sample course for non-IT professionals

This is an excerpt of a technology basics course for students majoring in humanities. It should give non-IT professionals a good idea what knowledge you need to become tech trenders.

Part 1 – operating systems

1 Make the computer usable to you. Today, they are so well designed that they make computers accessible to most people. In the olden days, they were still really accessible only to very technical types.
2 Previous versions used to be called DOS – disk operating system – because that's what they did, they made the computer peripherals available.
   (a) You had to type in commands, and the computer printed typed responses.
   (b) The commands scrolled off the top of the screen.
   (c) Not very user-friendly.
3 Of course they still make the computer peripherals available, but in an easier fashion.
4 BIOS – Basic Input/Output system – we talked about this last time from a hardware standpoint.
   (a) This is the firmware that:

    - tells the computer what to do when you turn it on;
    - what peripherals there are; and
    - date and time.
  (b) isolates the hardware from the software.
    - When you put on new hardware, you change the BIOS.
    - Your software doesn't have to change.
5 The operating system lets you tell the computer:
  (a) what the default directory is – or in a software package whether you should go to the most recently used directory – this is easier on the Macintosh – there are still vestiges of DOS in Windows;
  (b) how to start up an application like word processing or Eudora;
  (c) where to send the stuff to print on a printer – and which printer;
  (d) about multitasking – running more than one program at a time; and
  (e) about multiuser – more than one person can use the system at a time.

Part 2 – platforms

1 A platform is the combination of the hardware and the operating system.
2 An IBM PC with Linux operating system is a different platform than a PC with Windows.
3 A Mac is a different platform from a PC.

Part 3 – applications programs

1 These are on top of the operating system and the languages. Probably written in a higher level language and definitely use the operating system.
2 These programs are what make the computer system useful to you.
3 Most applications programs work with documents
4 Some examples of applications:
  (a) word processing; and
  (b) spreadsheets and database managers.[11]

- *Know core concepts of systems.* You need at least an overview of the core concepts of systems available on the market. This means making a distinction between a distributed application, a centralized application, and a desktop application. Tech trenders should be able to know the difference between a PC server and a RISC (reduced instruction set coding) server, for example.

- *Software evaluation.* All managers responsible for systems implementation and system evaluation should have at least a cursory background in software evaluation, and be able to know what it can do for them and how to apply it to their business needs.
- *Know what is platform-independent.* The open standard world is promoting solutions that can run on any operating system, or what's called "platform-independent." You need to know what that means when selecting a solution. If you want flexibility, it would be best if software could run on anything from a laptop to a Unix server without any reconfiguration necessary.
- *Understand mission-critical versus safety-critical.* In some industries safety issues are tantamount. This is particularly true in aerospace and automotives, for example, where technological errors can mean lost lives. Tech trenders in these sorts of fields need to know whether they're aiming for an end result that is mission critical – meaning it gets you from Point A to Point B – or safety critical, meaning that safety is the overriding concern. Which goal you pick will have enormous cost implications. For example, a safety-critical tool make cost $500,000 compared with $5000 for the mission-critical variant.[12]

SOLUTIONS

How vendors can teach you some technology basics

A vendor is going to be biased, but that doesn't mean he or she can't provide useful information. Tech Trenders use sessions with vendors to learn more about technology trends, as well as the specific solution the vendor is peddling. Vendors also use these sessions to educate potential customers.

One vendor finds customers seem unable to comprehend the concept of software that's platform independent, what's also called reusable or portable software. He says customers tend not to believe him and keep insisting that software must be reconfigured to function on different platforms.

The best cure for this kind of confusion is through an actual demonstration. He'll take a piece of software that's running on a laptop, burn a CD and then implant the same software on what appears to be an incompatible operating system. Tech awareness usually follows, but is not guaranteed.

What depth of IT knowledge and training would be beneficial

Becoming a tech-trending manager isn't synonymous with becoming an IT manager or expert. A CEO, for example, doesn't need or want the depth of technology knowledge of a CIO or CTO. But determining what amount of knowledge and training will allow you to make strategic technology decisions isn't as simple as it sounds. Consultants, vendors and other technology experts believe the non-IT professional should aim for having enough working understanding of the technology you have in-house, as well as long-term technology trends, to be able to comprehend choices and recommendations being offered you.

One way for you to go about making this assessment is to ask what technology information is needed to do a job, and how many people will be affected. Obviously, if you're being asked to sign off on a new operating system and you don't know what the term means, it's time to learn enough about networking to make an informed decision. One IT consultant spent three months working with a client on producing a database and struggling with this manager who was trying to decide what language to write it in. The consultant felt the individual was over-working the turf; struggling with a micro-management detail that wasn't worth the effort.

PLATFORMS

What CIOs think is critical training for tech-trending managers

CIOs agree that management must be prepared to reskill both IT staff and non-IT staff, alike. As one CIO puts it, it's a bit like closing a steelworks and setting up a brokerage. The skills required to operate a paper-based organization that operates with a few automated functions are a far cry from what's necessary to operate in the emerging B2B environment.

They'd start with computer literacy, which is defined as at least being able to function in Microsoft Word, knowing that there's an information repository in cyberspace called the Web that's accessed through the Internet, and being comfortable conducting Web searches. Some CIOs believe companies and institutions should make computer literacy a requirement for employment.

Although most of this chapter focuses on training the non-IT manager, CIOs say don't forget about retraining your IT staff. That veteran COBOL programmer may have difficulty learning Java-based e-business organization and have to be entirely re-educated. In fact, they say teaching your IT people Java – a specialized language that's used in many computer platforms today – is one of the most important things you can do.

Other information they consider pertinent to all managers includes the basics of system integration, which is key to achieving results in a networked organization. Tech trenders have to be able to understand the principles behind integrating external solutions into your internal network or internal programs. Your IT staff have to be able to perform these tasks in a way that one CIO describes as "slick and bullet-proof." Locating people with integration skills is a challenge today, but many CIOs believe more and more systems integrators will emerge, as this is the wave of the future.

They also urge all employees to know Internet, Web and Web language basics. Some CIOs say it might be helpful for all employees to learn the basics of HTML, the elementary Web language.

By "all employees" they include sales, marketing, human resources and finance. In fact, some CIOs believe sales and marketing staff must be able to be articulate about the technology their company or institution is utilizing.[13]

As IT trainers point out, there's always a sentence, a paragraph and a book-length answer to just about any question. In most cases the non-IT professional probably needs the one-paragraph answer to most IT issues. So for example, if a consultant says you're using a TCP/IP system versus a NetBEUI – which are common networking choices – a manager needs to ask why should I bother with one rather than the other? Or if someone is trying to persuade you to adopt Linux as their operating system you need to know what the advantage would be. The answer is that Linux is a stable operating system that's typically better for Internet servers, but not for average computer users because it can't handle common programming languages like Word.

As the head of a training company expresses it, you need to know enough to be able to draw a picture of your company or institution's technology infrastructure. If you don't have that good mental map of where things are and their purpose, then you probably don't know what's taking place technologically within your organization. Do not try guessing. Guessing just isn't the same as knowing.[14]

APPLICATIONS

How training demands vary based on management position

What you will need to learn and the amount of training required to become a tech trender will vary very much depending on your role in the organization. The IT Department, CIO and CTOs need to be constantly abreast of technology trends and developments, and be able to either develop proprietary solutions or work directly with vendors, consultants or analysts translating your business strategy into technological functions. Here's what a number of IT experts say non-IT managers need to know about technology depending on their position in the company or institution:

- *Mid-managers.* Anyone acting as a liaison between their department and the IT folks needs a great deal of training. They need to keep up on the trends and have a working knowledge of all technology already implemented. If specific solutions are being discussed, they need to understand the business goals underlying the technology and what impact those solutions will have on the company as a whole, not just their department. IT trainers find mid-managers need more awareness of the entire supply network and how information flows beyond their own department. They will explain integration points within a supply network, focus on accuracy and timeliness.

If your senior management haven't done a decent job of laying out their technology vision, don't take this personally. Think like the tech-trending manager you are and recognize that whatever IT training being offered will enhance your job prospects. One way of gaining this knowledge is to ask for some tutoring from the IT department or outside consultants. Practice tracking change based on the tips provided in Chapter 4, which include reading, working with analysts, attending user groups, conferences and seminars that provide on-the-spot learning about specific technologies. Networking with peers in other companies can also provide much-needed information.

- *Senior managers*. Someone as high up in the organization as a CEO needs to have at least a mental map of how technology is laid out in his or her company or institution. They should know what's being outsourced and what's being handled internally. As noted many times, they need to keep up on technology trends, start working on a computer and be able to conduct their own Web searches. They certainly don't need to be able to run a network, but they need to understand how technology pieces come together to affect their business or institutional goals and the bottom line.
- Other senior managers should have a vision for what your supply network will look like after implementing systems, what processes you will use and how to implement them. Moreoever, you should be able to assess the impact of technology implants on all facets of your organization – including employees and business processes. You should have a clearly defined role in this process and know how to manage the situation.[15]

Tech-trending training for non-IT personnel

It may sound from all this talk about the IT/Knowledge Gap that organizations aren't conducting any training for non-IT professionals at all. Yes, it is difficult to locate packaged training programs for non-IT managers, but it isn't the case that companies and institutions are ignoring the training component. As noted in Chapter 8, there are tech-trending companies and institutions that make communication and human skills training – coupled with technology training – a top priority for their entire organization. And there are consultants offering very solid training programs to sometimes balky clients.

New economy companies are naturally among the first to embrace and promote technology training. A CIO at a San Jose, CA, high-tech business believes that establishing an ongoing training environment is tantamount to staying in business today. As he points out, "The Internet and business are changing so fast, the only way to keep up is to have really strong training programs for your employees. Alternately, you should send them to training programs, seminars and whatever is required to make them understand what is happening out there. New IT solutions are being created every day, and unless your employee is out there and finds out about them you'll be in the dark."[16]

Not only does training keep everyone in the organization posted about ongoing technology change, but it can act as an incentive or perk to employees who might be tempted to move on. CIOs like this one, who struggle to retain their staff, find that top employees consider training the possibility of growing on the job. Some actually consider ongoing training a condition of employment today, which means that companies with a strong training component often use that as a lure to prospective employees.

Businesses aren't the only organizations promoting IT training. At the American National Standards Institute (ANSI), for example, IT training is a big concern. Staff can take off-site training in Excel spreadsheets, word processing, PowerPoint, Adobe Exchange, database management and development, to name a few of the offerings. To keep staff abreast of rapid technology change, the ANSI IT department has a staff member dedicated solely to answering questions about technology trends and generally helping out staff. The main concern is to make technology education a top priority; something all staff must do as part of their day-to-day job.[17]

SOLUTIONS

A non-profit's recommendations for providing IT training support

Short-staffed organizations like non-profits often couple IT support with training, which is a way of multi-tasking and utilizing their IT employees to the best advantage. Organizations concerned about involving all computer users, combating computer phobia, and providing the support and training they require may benefit from these tips from a CIO of a non-profit organization:

1 *IT support information.* Always make sure your organization can reach IT support as easily as possible. This gives employees confidence that they are being backed up and helps combat computer phobia. Have employees post the IT support number right on their desktop computer.
2 *Keep communication lines open.* Keeping the IT department communicating with the rest of the organization in a clear and timely fashion is more of a challenge than it might seem. Some organizations stage at least monthly update sessions and then communicate IT plans throughout the company or institution. For example, the development of a new Web site isn't kept under wraps until launch, but is widely publicized. Keep the information flowing throughout the development of the site so there will be no surprises later, and even some excitement is generated.
3 *Establish a clear service level.* Make sure that internal computer users have a clear path to service. You might let user groups customize their own service agreements with the IT department. Make sure that there is open communication about training options and that external training is available if you can't handle a particular topic.[18]

Many consultants and consulting groups find they have to conduct some training – even if they don't call it that – to bring clients up to the level of being able to communicate about their technology direction. Training may be so informal that the client isn't aware that learning is taking place, or formalized to the extent that seminars are conducted as part of a consulting group's package of offerings. There are groups that won't work with clients without walking them through some basic IT awareness work.

A prominent consulting group offers a series of seminars on topics like B2B that explore the major facets of technology that make up this process, and how an organization can utilize this technology in a strategic fashion. Actual demonstrations are sprinkled into the lecture. A cross-section of the client organization is encouraged to attend to ensure that technology knowledge isn't restricted to the IT department.

Here's an example of the sort of problem this group will present to clients for joint exploration and learning: a client perceives they have a customer relationship problem. To address this problem they are considering removing a number of databases and installing one that can share information. Without examining their organization and ongoing business goals, they decide to make this course of action their primary focus. To compound matters, they haven't explored a host of other options like purchasing customer-relationship or knowledge-management solutions, or putting a frequently-asked-question application on their Web site that can be served from their customer-relations database. Maybe they have the Web site option in mind, but then get no value from it because it's not hooked into the appropriate knowledge database.

Once these sorts of scenarios are laid out and the client can see that learning more about the technology options available to them amounts to a smart business practice, most consultants and IT trainers find them amendable to training. However, managers under pressure are naturally going to want to jump to solutions rather than take the time to train. Consultants and trainers find that they have to speak to them from the business side, and keep maintaining that focus, to get them to listen and participate in training. It's commonly noted that managers will buy into training if the emphasis is on the bottom line.

Some consulting groups will actually turn down clients who refuse training and just want a solution without being willing to learn about the problem at hand, let alone comprehend the solutions being offered. IT consultants find these sort of clients to be more trouble in the long run because they define their requirements by technology terms, not by their business needs.

PLATFORMS

Tech trenders need training in data accuracy for bottom-line results

A vice president for a national IT training company focusing on ERP and business-to-business procurement systems and customer relations is constantly experiencing wariness in the field because people don't have the skills and discipline to work in an accurate, timely fashion. Clients will implement costly ERP systems that remain unused because of fear that inaccurate data will boomerang on billing, time sheets and a whole array of back-end functions.

For example, an oil company implemented SAP to reduce inventory costs. Six months after implementation, though, employees were still managing inventory on Excel spreadsheets rather than using SAP systems for data input and timeliness. The employees were afraid to move onto SAP because they didn't have any skills relating to accuracy. They were afraid to input into an integrated system and make mistakes.

There's nothing difficult about training for accuracy and timeliness. As was noted in Chapter 8, these skills are the basis of Journalism 101. IT trainers like these try to show clients what's going on visually in their organization in terms of work flow and information flow. They try to give them a sense of the entire supply chain – from order to cash, shipping, invoicing and collecting money – and how its integrated into a supply network. They find that once employees grasp that functions are actually integrated, or how they're threaded, they can set up exercises for monitoring data quality and accuracy at each juncture.[19]

As for learning themselves, consultants estimate they spend 30 percent of their time on the technology learning curve just trying to keep ahead of the trends.[20]

A New York City consultant to media companies and universities finds that clients who successfully use technology think about their customers first, then they figure out how technology can achieve their goals. Part of this process involves determining what they need to know about technology to obtain a positive outcome. For example, the female chief executive of one of the world's largest media companies has made technology training a top priority. She's also made technology a way of life, utilizing computers and other equipment in her work, keeping up with the trends and learning whatever new processes she needs to stay current. With her new-found knowledge, she's been able to use technology to transform her print and publishing empire.[21]

SOLUTIONS

Tech-trending training tips for the non-IT manager

Once again, most managers don't have to become computer programmers. Here are some tips from IT experts on how you can easily absorb the knowledge you need to become a tech trender:

- *Learn about change management.* Attending some sessions or workshops in basic change-management skills will help you change your own mindset before trying to alter your entire department or organization. Make sure the session addresses organizational design and the sort of emotional issues outlined in Chapter Five.
- *Draw on your knowledge-base.* Remember that you are skilled, intelligent people who function very well in all business or organizational realms. Draw on your expertise, experience and success when facing technology learning. Work to connect technology to your organizational goals and it won't seem so overwhelming or amorphous.
- *Combat computer jargon.* Just because the MIS director of a vendor tosses around technology jargon doesn't mean you

have to quietly back and accept it. Challenge them to drop the jargon and speak to you in English, or whatever native language is the norm.

- *Turn IT experts into allies.* Don't consider IT experts the enemy. They hold valuable information and can offer you *ad hoc* tutorials. Make contacts with members of your IT staff and seek their help and advice. Think of vendors in the same positive, they-can-teach-me, light.
- *Set up a learning schedule.* Yes, you can learn a lot about technology in a session with a vendor or from walking your company or institution with your CTO. But IT trainers recommend you set up an actual learning schedule and try to stick to it. Senior management, for example, might spend three weeks of active immersion in technology trends and in learning how technology is used in their organization. This would amount to about two or three hours a day during that stretch. Following this crash course you should devote a portion of a day once a month to keep on top of new developments, while ensuring you read about technology developments on a daily basis.
- *Keep practicing.* Applying technology, as in running a computer, is a mechanical as well as a mental skill. That means you need to keep at it and practice regularly. If you take a course in Windows, for example, and don't work in Windows you will forget most of what you've learned. What a waste.
- *Explore higher education.* Nowadays, many MBA programs offer concentrations in information services. Young mid-managers contemplating returning for advanced education might consider taking at least some courses in this subject.[22]

Some self-help approaches tech trenders can apply to technology learning

It must be emphasized that tech trenders can't ignore technology learning any more than they can ignore return-on-investments. This is a discipline; something you must learn about every day and practice every day. Tech-trending executives have provided the following five types of topics you can absorb on your own in the course of a work day:

1. *Information storage.* Start learning about the technology that's related to your desktop and how it affects storing information. This is particularly important for executives who have never filed anything in paper, let alone electronically, and rely on underlings to handle routine office tasks. To avoid losing your material, or filing it away and not being able to locate it, it's recommended you make a paper copy and set up an electronic storage system that mimics your paper filing system.
2. *Formatting information.* Formatting information is part and parcel of developing a filing and storage system. You have to learn to put information into a format that's easy to understand.
3. *Information management rules.* Senior executives need to sort out mentally what information is most pertinent to the organization and what is least, what is useless and can be tossed and what should be stored for possible future use, what belongs in immediate take-action files and what belongs in long-term action files. As noted in Chapter 8, this sort of categorizing of information should then be incorporated into information management rules that are disseminated throughout the organization. Hopefully, you will be able to staunch the flow of tiresome advertising and other useless items that clog your e-mail files.
4. *Reading on the screen.* It takes a certain skill to read on a computer screen. Looking straight forward makes it difficult to read and our eyes are designed to read across the screen. Managers who have never worked on computers might ask more experienced staff for help.
5. *E-mail screening.* If you are really pressed, then employ someone immediately to screen e-mail for you. Applying the sort of information management rules outlined in both Chapter 8 and this section should help eliminate a lot of the garbage mail that no manager needs or wants.[23]

Taking emotions and human concerns into account

To be successful, training has to take into account emotions and other human concerns. As silly as the term "computer phobia" sounds, it's a very real problem that IT trainers and consultants encounter on a daily basis. The pride factor can be equally stifling and affect an executive's ability to learn and succeed in the new economy. And, once again, poor human communication skills will swamp the most sophisticated technology solution. Here are ways tech trenders can address these issues:

For many people, the automatic response to technology is panic. IT trainers quickly learn they have to consider the "fear factor" when training new computer users, just as consultants and other IT professionals need to consider computer phobia when implementing complex new systems. You can't assume that just because someone is intelligent and an eager learner that they will be able to master technology.

How one trainer handles the "fear factor"

Consider this example of a trainer working with inventory clerks on how to use the material management procedures contained in SAP. The trainer expected to encounter fear and a sense of impending humiliation that students – especially older people with minimal formal education – often feel when trying to learn a complex software program. She knew that the biggest barrier to learning was not ability, but attitude. And she knew that the best way to handle an atmosphere of terror was with patience, humor, and constant reiteration of a few simple techniques.

But in ten years of teaching SAP, she found this particular class was the most challenging. Of the twelve participants, one apparently had Parkinson's disease, two were close to hyperventilating the minute they opened the manual, and one – she called him "Matt" – was an enormous and very disruptive half-teddy/half-grizzly bear of a man. Every time she explained when or how to do something using the new system, Matt would stand up, turn around, and proclaim to the class his difficulties with the old system. He always apologized, "No offense to you, ma'am, and I'm sure it's not your fault, miss, but I'm just trying to explain to you that this piece of garbage will never work ..."

She watched in fascination and amusement for the first couple of Matt's dramatic renderings, wondering what to do. It was clear that he was smarter than he appeared at first because he grasped things fairly quickly. Since his self-esteem was nonexistent, he received attention by acting out. And as quickly as she understood the problem, she also knew the solution: she made him teach the class. He sat down at her computer, while she stood behind him with one hand on his shoulder (as a gentle restraining device) and the other pointing out where we were in the manual. He went step-by-step through the procedure, getting all the attention he craved, while she steered him through the written instructions. Everyone clapped when he completed the lesson, and the trainer liked the approach so well that she asked another student to take over for the next section.

Later in the afternoon, "Sam," a very timid man of about 60 or 65, answered a question for the first time. The trainer was so delighted when he decided to join in the discussion that she spontaneously gave him a peck on the cheek. The students loved her unconventional teaching style, and she received a standing ovation at the end of the course. Most importantly, they learned what they needed and felt good about the course – and themselves – even though they were scared out of their wits beforehand. It was the best course she had taught in 10 years of teaching SAP, and their supervisor reported that the actual implementation went without a hitch. This trainer bases her success on the fact that she recognized and honored the fear in the class and helped them work through it during the training.[27]

UNPLUGGING TECHNOSTRESS

The identifying technostress questionnaire (ITQ)

Unless you own a computer repair shop – or are a bonafide saint – all of us who confront the blue screen regularly suffer from some form of technostress. But the degree of stress can vary depending on your age or sex and personality. Your outlook on life can make a big difference in the amount of technostress you will experience, as will your religion, taste in Chinese food and preference in TV shows.

Emotionally speaking, not everyone reacts to computers in the same way or to the problems they can produce. Grown men have been known to cry when their system crashes, while some women remain impassive at the sight of that blue flickering screen that means a blank-out. You may find computers so threatening that you will be tempted to abandon computer land entirely, and spend your leisure time playing croquet rather than tuning into Priceline.com. Or you may be so enamoured of Web chat rooms that you have to attend addiction recovery groups to be severed from your keyboards and actually see the real-life world once in a while.

To help you determine whether you suffer from technostress, we've developed the Identifying Technostress Questionnaire (ITQ). Positive responses to at least five questions means that you are an average computer user who should eat properly, get plenty of rest and seek out medical help when needed. Up to eight yesses means it's time to seek the help of a qualified technoshrink. And ten yesses means you are off the chart and in dire need of psychiatric, medical and spiritual assistance.

Identifying technostress questionnaire (ITQ)

(Answer yes or no. Do this on a sheet of paper. We couldn't figure out how to make columns with this computer program.)

1. Have you ever pulled the plug on your PC because you're sick of coping with frozen screens?
2. Does the sight of *Internet World* magazine make you queasy or give you migraines, rashes or boils?
3. Do you break out in cold sweats or suffer heart palpitations when you hear technology lingo like RAM or portals?
4. Are you frantic when you spill coffee, tea, oatmeal (whatever) into your keyboard?
5. Does reading yet another Bill Gates profile in a national magazine make you feel suicidal? Homicidal?
6. Do you long to return to the world of *I Love Lucy*, *Leave It To Beaver* and *The Flintstones*?
7. Do you get weepy or feel blue when your computer crashes?
8. Does calling tech support induce hot flushes or sweaty palms?
9. Are you afraid that funny little green people live in your monitor?
10. Do you think if you actually embrace your computer that you will become bald, myopic, develop halitosis or all three?

It's our guess that you will answer yes to at least five of the questions on the identifying technostress questionnaire (ITQ), which means you suffer from a low level of technostress. But even low levels can lead to far bigger problems. It's important to catch these problems now, before the next upgrade, which will only compound things.[24]

SOLUTIONS

Bell Helicopter Textron copes with computer phobia

Bell Helicopter Textron, based in Fort Worth, Texas, has encountered a great deal of computer phobia especially with "older" employees over the age of 30. Given the fact that the average age of Bell employees is almost 50, there are many people in this category.

Members of the IT department at Bell first encountered this issue in the course of trying to upgrade their department's technologies. One manager, who was hired to address human communication issues as part of Bell's competitive IT strategy, was particularly concerned with the inability of many employees to cope with the technology at their disposal. It was decided to tackle the computer phobia issue during the roll out of a new e-mail system.

Utilizing an approach that had been successful in the past, IT managers organized a 27-person "swat team" to personally address both e-mail concerns and computer phobia. The idea of the "swat teams" was to gauge technology "frustration levels," and offer humans to answer questions in person about technology and new software. After swat team members visited employees throughout the building, they learned that that pre-existing written instructions for computer use were inadequate. How-to tips were created and communicated, and eventually 4000 people were successfully converted to a new e-mail system.[25]

Veteran trainers say it's imperative to reassure people that they can succeed if you expect people to learn new technologies. It's also crucial to be patient and compassionate. Unfortunately, many companies ignore the fear factor when planning major technology advances and suffer later when employees sabotage implementation of the system.

Tech trenders should seek out trainers who understand the underlying causes of computer phobia and are willing to work with people to eliminate the fear that technology provokes in them. Humor, game and patience are some key skills that trainers need to have, along with the recognition that people are afraid of being humiliated in front of other employees or even managers.

"Make it fun, make your own mistakes, which makes it possible and allowable for them to make mistakes. You can honor them as humans, first. Remember that you will have a mix of people who are technically competent and technically incompetent. Even if they don't have technology knowledge you can bring their other experiences to bear and recognize those."[26]

Curing the pride factor

Over and over again consultants, vendors and IT trainers confront the pride factor among senior managers who are unwilling to admit that technology is going over their heads. Outside professionals can always tell when they're encountering the pride factor from the glazed expressions on the faces of the clients. But older men, and particularly those in senior management positions, are often too proud to stop and ask questions.

There are ways to "cure" this problem without embarrassing those afflicted. Many consultants and trainers open their sessions with the insistence that all attendees ask questions. They will artificially implant question and answer periods if no one responds, or even plant questions if they are there with a cohort just to make it a safe environment for a senior executive to let down his or her guard and join in.

Another trick is getting senior managers off-site so there is no question of them appearing foolish to lower-level managers or support personnel. Some trainers, vendors or consultants pitch their presentations to the lowest common denominator, taking the risk to bore some people for the benefit of the larger group. And they make it clear that it's far better to ask a few questions, and even grapple for understanding, then get saddled with unworkable technology.[28]

PLATFORMS

Tech trenders must keep pushing human skills

You've heard this before and you will hear it again: keep those human communication channels open. Managers at Lockheed Martin have been doing just that, and have even devised a number of training programs to address internal communication. One of them is called the "Path of Dialogue" course. It's a two-and-a-half day, 20-hour session that aims to address interpersonal communication needs.

In one session 300 company "opinion leaders" out of a total of 500 participated. Those attending found the process extraordinarily eye-opening in terms of who in the organization was communicating with whom. Many employees reported feeling good about the fact that senior managers were taking the time to talk to them, and even taking notes.[29]

Training for the Web-based, B2B world

The IT/Knowledge Gap becomes a veritable gulf when you start moving into cyberspace. Technical managers at New Economy companies often meet managers who can't differentiate between a content aggregator and an Internet Service Provider. They expect design companies to host Web sites, which isn't their job.

New Economy companies that either develop Web sites, or sell content to Web sites, encounter widely varying degrees of technical sophistication among their client base. There are entrepreneurs who are highly knowledgeable about Web-related technologies and managers in Fortune 1000 companies who are almost entirely ignorant both of technology and the level of support they need to dedicate to developing a B2B company replete with a Web site, e-catalogs and the like.

In general, many tech trenders would benefit from a crash course in the Web marketplace, the players and the technologies involved in promoting online services. Tech trenders need to understand that the Web industry is becoming fragmented into a number of different types of service providers. For example, you need to be able to differentiate between an Internet Service Provider (ISP) and a Web designer, a content aggregator or a domain provider.

Tech trenders will find that working out on the Web involves mastering some new skills. These may involve learning how to use Web search engines to improving the human skills outlined in Chapter 8. It's doubtful that many of you will be learning the intricacies of HTML or XML, but it doesn't hurt to have some working knowledge of what underlines Web languages. Tech trenders are going to have to learn more about firewalls and encryption to protect their information as it flows more freely among trader partners who may be competitors.[30]

PLATFORMS

Some Web basics

The following are some excerpts from a basic course on the Web and HTML – the common Web language – to give you some idea of the sort of training you and your employees could use:

Where do Web pages come from?
Web pages come from the Web server. Displaying Web pages requires two programs. You're familiar with the Web browser. Netscape Navigator and Internet Explorer are the two most common browsers. The other program is the Web server. The Web server is a computer program like your word processor or spreadsheet. It runs continuously on the computer that stores the Web page you requested. What it does, is sit quietly listening for requests from outlying browsers. When the Web server receives your request for a Web page, it looks for that page and, if it finds it, sends it back to the browser.

Demo
For the most part, the Web server is invisible to you. But you've probably all seen something like this before: Launch a browser and point to a page that doesn't exist. The file not found error message comes from the server. This is a message sent your browser by the server.

Concept
The Web server/browser relationship is called client/server. The

Web server is, of course, the server. The browser is the client. Clients request services from Servers. In this case, the browser requests a Web page from the server. The Internet is pretty much made up of client/server programs. Typically the client resides on the computer you're using; the server, on the remote computer. You've probably heard of, if not used, FTP or Telnet programs. They're also examples of client/server programs. One of the most popular Web servers is called Apache.

What's a URL?

A URL is a TLA (three letter acronym) for Uniform Resource Locator. I've also seen it called Universal Resource Locator. Either is acceptable, I guess. I usually pronounce it like the mountain range in Russia-Urals. But I've heard it pronounced like Ur, the city Abraham came from, url. And some people just say U-R-L. It's the URL that makes it possible for you to click here and go there. It's also what you see in the address window of your browser.

Demo

Type an address in the address window. And that's what an URL is – an address, a way of naming a location. It has several parts.

- The "http:" signals the protocol being used. In this case, it's the Hypertext Transfer Protocol.
- The "//" merely separates the protocol from the remainder of the URL.
- www.widgetdeluxe.com represents the Internet address of the computer on which the requested page lives.
- "/intro/pageone.html" is the path and file name of the requested page on the www.widgetdeluxe.com computer.

Note the forward slash path separators. They mean the same thing as DOS\Windows backslash separators. But the forward slash is used by the Unix operating system and most Web servers and Web pages run on Unix systems.

Concept

The concept I'd like to introduce here is the protocol. The URL we just analyzed represents our first look at the HTTP protocol. HTTP is an acronym for Hypertext Transfer Protocol. So, what's a protocol? Very simply, it's a language. Our protocol here today is English, more or less. But if any of you started speaking to me in Spanish, French, German, Hebrew, Greek, Chinese, etc., etc., I'm sorry to say that I wouldn't understand. We would no longer be using the same protocol. To generalize: a protocol is a set of agreed upon signals that allow for communication.

Remember: when we load a Web page, two programs are required. The browser is the client. The Web server is the server. In order for the browser to make its request to the Web server and for the Web server to honor that request, the programs have to speak the same language, the same protocol, which in this case is HTTP.

The URL is only one part of Hypertext Transfer Protocol. You need to understand it, but the part of the protocol you're going to learn today is HTML, Hypertext Markup Language which uses URLs ...[31]

As simplistic as this sounds, tech trenders have to learn to be comfortable with basic Web tools like e-mail. And, yes, there are managers who still avoid e-mail, which in this day and age is akin to refusing to use a telephone. This is a must-have, must-learn item. It will also help you to spend time with professionals who are involved with Web site development and maintenance. Let them explain the basics and how they cope with challenges, what tools they use and how those tools fit into the Web marketplace.

Learning to maximize Web use

It's become a cliché that the Web is a monumental information dump. Some report there are at least 500 billion documents currently floating around cyberspace. There's a lot of fantastic material available to you at your fingertips and plenty of garbage, not to mention dark holes or Web sites with nothing more than a homepage. As one executive puts it, "large portions of the Web are vaporware." The following are three tips for maximizing your Web use:

1 *Sorting out Web wheat and chaff.* Get up on the Web and start moving around so you can better ascertain when a Web

search makes sense, and when picking up the phone is still your best bet. For example, government sites are usually sure bets and chock full of important and useful information. As noted in Chapter 4, the Department of Commerce is overflowing with useful information on the New Economy. Try the Economics and Statistics Administration – www.esa.doc.gov – for an ongoing series of reports on the Digital Economy. And the 10-K report from the EDGAR database of the Security and Exchange Commission (SEC) – www.sec.gov – is a superb place to locate financial and strategic information on public companies.

Beware that many company sites are mere billboards. But, if you are seeking information on a competitor, you may be able to learn quite a bit about their products, prices, promotions, partners and positioning from their Web site. It's a lot quicker and easier than accessing an annual report through the mail.

More and more publications, companies and institutions are offering free online newsletters that provide a huge amount of targeted information. Besides being "delivered" directly via e-mail, they offer the opportunity for you to lift and cite material directly in reports, white papers and whatever work you may be performing. Once again, note the word "cite." Lifting text without attribution is a violation of copyright laws.

2 *Understand Web search capabilities.* Every tech-trending manager needs to understand current Web search capabilities so that, at the very least, you can guide staff members or researchers who will be digging up information for you. You need an elementary understanding of the prominent search engines and what they can or cannot do for you. That means getting online and starting to surf.

Given the enormity of the Web, no one Internet search engine will cover more than a small percentage of what's really out there. Don't expect uniformity between search engines as they run on different database logic, which means the same keys words may not be indexed in the same way for two different searches. Be aware that search engines also generate money through their listings, so paying customers may get the advantage of your hits.

For maximum success, Web experts suggest trying at least three search engines for every topic you are researching. This sort of trial and error will teach you the strengths and weaknesses of each and will help you tailor your searches for better results. Another alternative is launching a search on a single engine in a variety of ways to see what results you can generate. For example, if you are searching for a specific phrase you might try various key words and see what pops.

3 *Learn about Web security tools.* Knowing the "ins and outs" of firewalling and encryption becomes more and more important as we evolve into a Web-based, B2B environment. Try to take an elementary course on this subject of the sort outlined in the box below. And also consider security concerns that amount to common sense like not bringing sensitive information with you on a laptop that can get stolen in airports. Some big-time executives have suffered that fate and still wonder whether their company secrets will find their way into the wrong hands.[32]

PLATFORMS

A sampling from an e-commerce technology course

Objectives:

- Define various types of firewalls and e-commerce server hosting options
- Discuss privacy, integrity and authentication for e-commerce transactions
- Understand digital signatures and digital certificates
- Describe SSL and SET
- Define digital cash and micropayment systems
- Identify e-commerce storefront software vendors
- Describe the importance of XML for e-commerce
- Identify XML standards and industry activity
- Firewalls and Web Site Hosting

Firewall

A firewall is a software barrier between two networks designed to prevent unauthorized traffic while permitting authorized traffic. A typical firewall has several elements and may consist of:

- additional software running on existing equipment, e.g., a router, a server, even a PC;
- hardware/software combination built specifically for this purpose; or
- combination of the two.

A firewall may include additional elements such as:

- proxy server;
- remote access device; and
- authentication server.

Firewalls and Web site hosting – hosted Web site

A hosted Web site is maintained by an outside service provider so access to your Web site does not involve any machines in your own network.

Advantages

- no security threat to internal network;
- lower administration costs; and
- easy access to Web site from outside world.

Disadvantages

- Access to Web site is no better for internal users than for someone on the outside.
- Site updates, backup, administration are under control of hosting service (may or may not provide same frequency and quality of service that you could provide internally).

Firewalls and Web site hosting – dual-homed gateway

A single computer is connected both to the internal network and to the Internet.

Advantages

- Corporate Web site can be internally or externally managed.
- External Web site can be installed on the gateway machine, though performance can be a problem.

Disadvantages

- Internal network security can be compromised if unauthorized external party gains access to internal network card in gateway machine.
- There can be a bottleneck because all internal-external traffic must pass through gateway.[33]

Notes

1 Mark LaPolt, an IT consultant based in New Haven, CT.

2 Harold Wolfe, President of Helios Custom Training, Inc., Northampton, MA.

3 Phil Cole, European Marketing Manager, Virtual Prototype Inc., Quebec, Canada.

4 Don Lesser, president, Pioneer Training, Inc., Holyoke, MA.

5 Mark LaPolt, an IT consultant based in New Haven, CT.

6 Janet Wikler, President, Wikler and Company, Inc., New York, NY.

7 Michael Cunningham, president and CEO of Harvard Computing Group, Inc., Westford, MA.

8 Don Lesser, president, Pioneer Training, Inc., Holyoke, MA.

9 *When Bad Computer Things Happen To Good People*, a work in progress, Amy Zuckerman and Izzy Gesell.

10 Dana Sohr, vice president for the Enterprise Systems Group, RWD Technologies, Columbia, MD.

11 Adapted from "Introduction to Computer Science," developed by Andrea Goodman, Swamp Drainer, who is also a part-time member of the Assumption College Computer Science Department, Worcester, MA.

12 Don Lesser, president, Pioneer Training, Inc., Holyoke, MA; Phil Cole, European Marketing Manager, Virtual Prototype

Inc., Quebec, Canada; and Mark LaPolt, an IT consultant based in New Haven, CT.

13 Pam Kleier, CEO of constructionzone.com, Louisville, KY; Eric Fliegel, CIO eTour, Inc., Atlanta, GA; and Jeanmarie Gelinas, vice president and CIO, Rodale, Inc., Emmaus, PA.

14 Don Lesser, president, Pioneer Training, Inc., Holyoke, MA; Harold Wolfe, president of Helios Custom Training, Inc., Northampton, MA; and Mark LaPolt, an IT consultant based in New Haven, CT.

15 Michael Cunningham, president and CEO of Harvard Computing Group, Inc., Westford, MA, Harold Wolfe, President of Helios Custom Training, Inc., Northampton, MA; Don Lesser, president, Pioneer Training, Inc., Holyoke, MA; and Dana Sohr, vice president for the Enterprise Systems Group, RWD Technologies, Columbia, MD.

16 Krimo Salem, CEO of If & Then, Inc., San Jose, CA.

17 Bob Feghali, Vice President of Business Development and CIO at ANSI.

18 Bob Feghali, Vice President of Business Development and CIO at ANSI.

19 Dana Sohr, vice president for the Enterprise Systems Group, RWD Technologies, Columbia, MD.

20 Michael Cunningham, president and CEO of Harvard Computing Group, Inc., Westford, MA; and David Washburn, principal consultant at Amherst Information Architects, Amherst, MA.

21 Janet Wikler, president, Wikler and Company, Inc., New York, NY.

22 Source is Bob Feghali, vice president of Business Development and CIO at ANSI; Michael Cunningham, president and CEO of Harvard Computing Group, Inc., Westford, MA; Don Lesser, president, Pioneer Training, Inc., Holyoke, MA; Janet Wikler, president, Wikler and Company, Inc., New York, NY; and Mark LaPolt, an IT consultant based in New Haven, CT.

23 H. James Harrington, CEO, Systemcorp, Quebec, Canada, and former consulting principal for quality at Ernst & Young.

24 Adapted from *When Bad Computer Things Happen To Good People,* a work in progress, Amy Zuckerman and Izzy Gesell.

25 Sandi Walker, Vice President of Information Systems, Bell Helicopter Textron; and Denise McKinight, Bell Manager of Electronic Commerce.

26 Felicity Wright, Team Leader, RWD Technologies, Inc., Columbia, MD.

27 Felicity Wright, Team Leader, RWD Technologies, Inc., Columbia, MD.

28 Phil Cole, European Business Marketing Manager, Virtual Prototype, Inc., Quebec, Canada.

29 Karie Willyerd, Director of People and Organizational Development, Lockheed Martin. Lydia Long, Director of Operations for Verité, Amherst, MA, researched this information.

30 Colin Mulcahy, Director of Technical Implementation and Support, ScreamingMedia, New York, NY.

31 "Intro to HTML" by Seth Rothberg, principal, /home/industries, Amherst, MA.

32 Kevin Fitzgerald, publisher and editor-in-chief of *Global Supply* magazine; H. James Harrington, chief executive officer, Systemcorp, Quebec, Canada, and former consulting principal for quality at Ernst & Young; Colin Mulcahy, director of Technical Implementation and Support, ScreamingMedia, New York, NY; and "Research in the Dot Com Economy: Tips for Success," *Network Solutions,* September 8, 2000.

33 Adapted from "E-Commerce Technology Training," Michael Cunningham, president and CEO of Harvard Computing Group, Inc., Westford, MA.

Index